Narrative Theory

Kent Puckett's *Narrative Theory: A Critical Introduction* provides an account of a methodology increasingly central to literary studies, film studies, history, psychology, and beyond. In addition to introducing readers to some of the field's major figures and their ideas, Puckett situates critical and philosophical approaches toward narrative within a longer intellectual history. The book reveals one of narrative theory's founding claims – that narratives need to be understood in terms of a formal relation between story and discourse, between what they narrate and how they narrate it – both as a necessary methodological distinction and as a problem characteristic of modern thought. Puckett thus shows that narrative theory is not only a powerful descriptive system but also a complex and sometimes ironic form of critique. *Narrative Theory* offers readers an introduction to the field's key figures, methods, and ideas and reveals that field as unexpectedly central to the history of ideas.

Kent Puckett is an associate professor of English at the University of California, Berkeley. He is author of *Bad Form: Social Mistakes and the Nineteenth-Century Novel* (2008) and *War Pictures: Cinema, Violence, and Style in Britain, 1939–1945* (forthcoming).

Narrative Theory
A Critical Introduction

KENT PUCKETT

University of California, Berkeley

CAMBRIDGE
UNIVERSITY PRESS

CAMBRIDGE
UNIVERSITY PRESS

University Printing House, Cambridge CB2 8BS, United Kingdom

Cambridge University Press is part of the University of Cambridge.

It furthers the University's mission by disseminating knowledge in the pursuit of
education, learning and research at the highest international levels of excellence.

www.cambridge.org
Information on this title: www.cambridge.org/9781107684744

First published 2016

Printed in the United States of America by Sheridan Books, Inc.

A catalogue record for this publication is available from the British Library

Library of Congress Cataloging-in-Publication data
Names: Puckett, Kent, author.
Title: Narrative theory / Kent Puckett.
Description: Cambridge ; New York : Cambridge University Press, 2016.
Identifiers: LCCN 2016015462| ISBN 9781107033665 (hardback) |
ISBN 9781107684744 (paperback)
Subjects: LCSH: Narration (Rhetoric) | BISAC: LITERARY CRITICISM / Semiotics & Theory.
Classification: LCC PN212 .P83 2016 | DDC 808/.036–dc23 LC record available at
https://lccn.loc.gov/2016015462

ISBN 978-1-107-03366-5 Hardback
ISBN 978-1-107-68474-4 Paperback

Additional resources for this publication at www.cambridge.org/9781107033665

Contents

Acknowledgments

Writing so much about narrative theory required a lot of thought and even more help. My amazing editor Ray Ryan encouraged me to write the book, hung in there while I was (and was not) writing it, and was there to congratulate me when at last it was done: beginning, middle, end. Sarah Starkey, Jeethu Abraham, Ezhilmaran Sugumaran, and Susan Thornton offered terrific help getting the book into shape. I relied at different points on the skill and intelligence of Sanders Creasy and Luke Terlaak Poot. I could not have done this without them. Many, many thanks go to the anonymous readers of both the proposal and the first draft of the manuscript; their generosity and intelligence made this a much better book. Matthew Garrett offered encouragement and sharply focused criticism when they were most needed; I took all of his advice and the book is better for it. I thought and talked about this book and its arguments for a long time before I wrote a word, a fact that allowed me to benefit from the brilliance of many colleagues at Berkeley; conversations with Charlie Altieri, Dan Blanton, Ian Duncan, Eric Falci, Cathy Gallagher, Dori Hale, Abdul Jan Mohamed, Jos Lavery, Josh Gang, Colleen Lye, Elisa Tamarkin, and Alan Tansman shaped and sharpened arguments I make here. I benefited much from students in a number of classes I taught on narrative and novel theory, in particular participants in the 2003 graduate seminar, "Novel Theory, Narrative Theory, and the Sociology of the Novel." Questions that came up in that class continue to motivate my thinking about the critical possibilities and practical limits of narrative theory. Mitch Breitwieser offered early and excellent advice; one should always take Mitch's advice. I continue and will continue to rely on David Miller as a model for thinking critically and creatively about narrative and its discontents. Eric Bulson read and commented on large sections of the book, helping me to see better what I needed to write and for whom. Adam Boardman gave me what I needed most while writing: time and peace of mind. My parents, Kent and Franceen, and my sister, Nora, were, as usual, beautifully and selflessly supportive. Kara Wittman read or listened to me read almost every word of this book, and more than once. She is my best critic and my best friend. This book is for Harry, my favorite story.

Chapter 1

Introduction

Story/Discourse

We tell ourselves stories in order to live.
Joan Didion, "The White Album"

There are lots of ways to think about narrative theory. We might consider the countless casual interactions people have with books, movies, news stories, stump speeches, comics, conversations, and rumors. Whenever someone (on the phone, in a book club, online, or in line at the store) talks about a story's beginning or end, its pacing, the believability or the likability of its characters, he or she is engaging in a kind of narrative theory, an effort to understand particular narratives in relation to assumptions and expectations that govern either some kinds of narrative or narratives in general. We might also consider more professional efforts to understand or to evaluate narratives, the work and writing of critics and academics who make their livings assessing or analyzing stories either in terms of particular aesthetic, social, or political values or in terms of the expectations and ideas that circulate at a given moment in time. We might think here of the film critic who sees every film in a season and so can say with authority what films work best and why; or of the think-piece blogger who looks at a handful of contemporary novels in order to see how the war on terror or the new ubiquity of social media affects the way we tell stories now; or of the literary critic who reads Renaissance drama or Victorian fiction in order to identify how history's different ideas and practices shape the form and content of narratives (how Elizabethan stage design limits or conditions the beginnings and ends of plays, how serialization affects thinking about suspense, how culturally specific ideas about death and dying affect thinking about the possibility of closure, and so on). These are also theories of narrative, attempts to understand both the role that narratives play in particular cultures at particular times and the shaping effects that a culture's assumptions and beliefs have on the development and evaluation of narrative as such.

A third kind of narrative theory is the subject of this book. Narrative theory in this more limited sense names a more and less coherent intellectual tradition that works explicitly to understand the general rules of narrative alongside the many particular forms that narratives can take. It is often associated with the rise of structuralism in the 1960s and includes but is not limited to what is sometimes referred to as classical or postclassical narratology.[1] It in fact goes back at least to Aristotle and draws on and influences many of the major intellectual movements of the twentieth and twenty-first centuries: phenomenology, psychoanalysis, Marxism, feminism, postcolonial theory, queer theory, cognitive science, evolutionary psychology, and so on. It takes as its subject the question of how different kinds of aesthetic order, arrangement, and inflection can differently manage and thus make meaningful different and sometimes the same events; it considers both the *what* and the *how* (and sometimes the *who* and the *where*) of the stories we tell. Narrative, in this sense, is what results from the effort to make real or imagined events and objects meaningful in relation to one another, whether that effort is fictional, historical, political, financial, psychological, social, or scientific; *narrative theory* is, in that case, what we do when we try in a variety of ways to understand those different efforts to arrange events and make them meaningful. This narrative theory focuses, in other words, on the necessary relation between two aspects of narrative: (1) the events, the actions, the agents, and the objects that make up the stuff of a given narrative and (2) the shape that those events, actions, agents, and objects take when they are selected, arranged, and represented in one or another medium. In what follows, I will try to focus on this sense of narrative theory as *a study of relations* without losing sight of its connection to other efforts to understand and to make stories.

~

The last few decades have seen the publication of a number of important works of narrative theory in this third sense, works that take up one or another aspect of narrative – narrators or ideal readers, the cognitive or ethical aspects of narrative, narrative and new media, narrative and evolutionary biology, and so on – as well as works that offer differently broad accounts of the questions, the methods, the controversies, and the texts that make up the wide field of contemporary narrative theory. A number of these have been indispensable to me as I have tried to think about what belongs in a critical introduction to narrative theory.[2] Where, however, this book differs from some of these others is in how it understands its role as an introduction. That is, where these books are often excellent at addressing the *what* and the *how* of narrative theory, they are – and, I think, properly so – less invested in the *why*. That is, much of the work in narrative theory since the late 1960s has been

dedicated to establishing the discipline, to clarifying its methodological investments, to laying out and demonstrating its tools, and to identifying what does
and does not qualify *as a narrative* in one or another sense. It is because this
work is so good that I feel free to turn my attention to a different but related
set of questions: why is there or why should there be narrative theory in the
first place? What motivates our shared and broadening cultural interest in the
analysis of narrative as well as in narrative itself, a broadening interest that
some critics have cast as a "narrative turn" felt throughout the humanities and
social sciences? As Martin Kreiswirth puts it, "Narrative has become a
significant focus of inquiry in virtually all disciplinary formations, ranging
from the fine arts, the local and natural sciences, to media and communication studies to popular therapy, medicine, and managerial studies."[3] When
did it become self-evident that narrative ought to be treated not only as a fact
of human life but also as an especially pressing problem for these different
fields? What drives individual writers and thinkers to turn when they do to
the theory of narrative?

I hope, in other words, to make a historical and conceptual case for the use,
the force, the apparent necessity, and the real intensity – sometimes even the
pathos – of some theories of narrative. As a result, I will try here both to
construct a loose history of efforts to think about narrative, an account –
another narrative, if you will – of how it was and when it was that narrative
began to take on the disciplinary and cultural centrality that it has today; I will
also try to read some of these works against the grain, to see them as
sometimes talking about narrative in order also to talk about *something else*.
Once again, there are many fine books that do great and essential work
explaining how some of these different texts work; there are books on
narratology or structuralism, Aristotle or Hegel, Henry James or Roland
Barthes. I will refer to these more particular works often; several are listed
in Suggested Further Reading. Instead, though, of once again explaining or
defining narrative theory, I will try rather *to interpret* it, to reveal some of its
motivations, and to understand what other ideas or desires govern a particular writer's particular turn to narrative as an especially important aesthetic,
cultural, or historical problem. In this sense, I will want to think both about
theories *of* narrative and about some of these theories *as* narratives, as
sometimes more and sometimes less linked efforts to think about how
meaning is made at different moments in time.

What will emerge, in that case, is a maybe idiosyncratic prehistory and
history – a *genealogy* – of narrative theory, an account that treats narrative
theory as a powerful way of thinking about the world and our efforts to make
sense of what the world means. In a fine account of the beginnings of

narratology, David Herman, drawing on Nietzsche and Michel Foucault, writes that "genealogy is a mode of investigation that seeks to uncover forgotten interconnections, reestablish obscured or unacknowledged lines of descent; expose relationships between institutions, belief-systems, discourses, or modes of analysis that might otherwise be taken to be wholly distinct or unrelated."[4] While I will often draw on and refer to recent work on and developments in narrative theory, I will also look at works and movements that appeared *before* or *alongside* and that seem to me to have made narrative theory possible. I will thus look at a number of works and fields that seem initially to have little to do with narrative theory proper, at works of philosophy or political theory or history, at works that seem dedicated to particular narrative genres as opposed to narrative in general. My claim is that in order to appreciate why and how writers and thinkers from Aristotle to the present have turned when they did to questions about the representation of events, about plot, about character, about narration and narrative discourse, we have to understand not only what narrative theory is but also why it has, at particular moments in time, seemed capable of answering questions that both include and exceed the nuts and bolts of narrative structure. I hope, in that case, both to situate narrative theory within a wider field of inquiry and to identify some necessary qualities or concerns that have made thinking about narrative so vital.

~

In *The Cambridge Introduction to Narrative Theory*, H. Porter Abbott defines narrative as "the representation of an event or a series of events," as, in other words, a relation between, on the one hand, a real or imagined action or event and, on the other, a *representation* of that real or imagined action or event.[5] Abbott goes on to suggest that, while there is and always will be controversy about how exactly to define narrative, his definition "allows us to look at the full range of the most interesting and vital aspects of the field: the complex transaction that involves events, their manner of representation (whether it be by narrator, actor, paint, or some other means), and the audience. The difference between events and their representation is the difference between *story* (the event or sequence of events) and *discourse* (how the story is conveyed)."[6] I will rely both on this definition and on the *story–discourse relation* it assumes in nearly everything that follows; that said, I am less interested in supporting a particular definition of narrative than I am in understanding how competing definitions work within narrative theory. Indeed, as Abbott says, part of what makes his definition "controversial" is its reliance on the idea of *representation*, a fact that has seemed to some critics too limiting or ideologically loaded.[7] We will see as we look at writers such as Lukács, Bakhtin, Barthes, and Genette how different theorists have made thinking about the ideological character as well as the historical limits of representation into an important part of narrative theory.

So, despite important reservations, most definitions of narrative do tend to assume one or another relation between events and the representation of events: Gérard Genette writes that "if one agrees, following convention, to confine oneself to the domain of literary expression, one will define narrative without difficulty as the representation of an event or sequence of events, real or fictitious by means of language and, more particularly, by means of written language."[8] Marie-Laure Ryan notes that "most narratologists agree that narrative consists of material signs, the *discourse*, which convey a certain meaning (or content), the *story*, and fulfil a certain social function."[9] For Jonathan Culler, "there is considerable variety among these traditions, and of course each theorist has concepts or categories of his own, but if these theorists agree on anything it is this: that the theory of narrative requires a distinction between what I shall call 'story' – a sequence of actions or events, conceived as independent of their manifestation in discourse – and what I shall call 'discourse,' the discursive presentation or narration of events."[10] Monika Fludernik holds that "the story vs. discourse distinction perhaps constitutes the most basic of all narratological axioms."[11] Suzanne Keen refers to it as a "basic and ubiquitous convention of structuralist narrative theory."[12] And Abbott writes that "this analytically powerful distinction between story and its representation is, arguably, the founding insight of the field of narratology."[13] Although it ends up going in many different and sometimes conflicting directions, narrative theory almost always begins with the *story–discourse* relation.

Some of the theories at which we will look do manage to add one or another third term to the basic opposition between story and discourse. These third terms tend to take one or another form: such critics as Barthes and Genette take care to distinguish the narrator or narration from story and discourse – the *who* from the *what* and the *how* – and, as we will see, critics including Ferdinand de Saussure, Claude Lévi-Strauss, A. J. Greimas, and even Nietzsche acknowledge the existence of a deeper structure at work in narrative form, a level of structuration or experience that sits somewhere beneath or beyond the event. That said, although there are these third levels, the analysis of narrative form tends nonetheless to restrict itself to the basic pair: "The supplementary terms or layers," writes David Wittenberg, "are motivated in part by the difficulty of ascertaining how 'discourse' could remain a coherent figuration for representing 'story' without reference to a material or quasi-material substratum in an actually produced text. Yet even this tripartite or multiple usage tends to devolve back into the more basic or convenient binarism" of story and discourse.[14]

What, though, do narrative theorists really mean by story and discourse? As the represented events as opposed to a representation of those events, *story* tends in mimetic or classic or "natural" narratives to follow certain rules of chronological and spatial order: effects follow causes, one day comes before or after another, you cannot be in two places at the same time, some things – birth, death, April 1, 1987, the first moon landing – happen once and only once. Shlomith Rimmon-Kenan writes that "the notion of story-time involves a convention which identifies it with ideal chronological order, or what is sometimes called 'natural chronology.'"[15] As the representation of events as opposed to the represented events themselves, *discourse* follows an entirely different set of rules: where story is limited by certain apparently "natural" laws, discourse is relatively unbound in how it can arrange, attend to, and manage events; unlike story, discourse "can expand and contract, leap backward and forward."[16] A whole *narrative* is in that case the relation and tension that exist between these two different levels; it is the fact that we can read back and forth between them and follow the different rules that organize them.

Because of the difference between story and discourse, the same events can be represented in a more or less unlimited number of ways and can thus lead to an unlimited number of different narratives. For instance, Raymond Queneau's *Exercises in Style* (1947) tells and retells a single, simple story – someone sees a young man in a funny hat and then sees him again two hours later – in ninety-nine different ways: one story and ninety-nine narratives. Another story – a man walks around Dublin – can take up one sentence, ten sentences, or 680 pages (the Gabler edition of James Joyce's *Ulysses* [1922] ships at 2.1 pounds). Similarly, the narrative representation or *discourse* of a failed marriage (we will represent its chronologically fixed *story* as ABC) might begin at the beginning, looking at the hopes and aspirations of a couple, before moving on to the rocky middle and forlorn end (ABC); it might instead begin with the middle, when tensions have begun to rise, and track back to the beginning before moving on past the middle to the end (BAC); or it might begin at the end, flashing back from breakup to beginning and then representing the events that brought about the end (CAB). In each case, the story – a once-happy marriage fails – remains the same while different arrangements of similar or the same events at the level of discourse make for very different narratives, which is to say very different senses of what those same events might mean or how they might make us feel. What defines each narrative is, in that case, how it manages a particular relation between these two levels – story and discourse – and their respective rules.

Many classic narratives work to naturalize or to obscure the artificial or made quality of the *story–discourse* relation (they seem to want us to "lose ourselves" and to become absorbed in the content and not the form); Brian Richardson writes that "mimetic texts" – his term for texts that assume a "natural" relation between events and representations of events – "often try to disguise their artificiality."[17] Other kinds of texts can instead call self-conscious attention to the constructed nature of the narrative relation. Just for instance, *unreliable narratives* depend on an intuited and motivated difference between the appearance of discourse and the imagined truth of a story; when we know that a narrator is unreliable, we look for places where discourse will not or cannot lead to an accurate reconstruction of events at the level of story. When, for instance, the narrator of Dostoevsky's *Notes from Underground* (1864) tells us, "I lied about myself just now when I said I was a wicked official. I lied out of wickedness," he not only offers up a beguiling paradox (does lying wickedly about one's wickedness amount to a kind of truth?) but also drives a wedge between story and discourse.[18] Because he is the narrator and can thus choose what and how to narrate, the possibility that the underground man is a *wicked* narrator willing to "misreport" the facts of the case makes it hard if not impossible to square the rules that govern the two levels of his underground notes. James Phelan has identified six types of unreliable narrators: "They can underreport or misreport; they can underread or misread (underinterpret or misinterpret); and they can underregard or misregard (underevaluate or misevaluate)."[19] In each case, narrators can be unreliable because they "abuse" and thus call attention to the *story–discourse* relation.

Some types of experimental narratives – Alain Robbe-Grillet's *La Jalousie* (1957) is a classic case – go further and sever the connection between story and discourse insofar as the represented events break or ignore or imply the absence of the natural laws of story (characters die more than once, they appear in two places at the same time, the laws of "natural" chronology are disrupted, etc.). Richardson, the major theorist of "unnatural narratives," writes that the *story–discourse* relation does "not work if applied to many late and modernist and postmodern texts, since they are predicated on distinctions that experimental writers are determined to preclude, deny, or confound."[20] We might also look, as David Wittenberg does in *Time Travel: The Popular Philosophy of Narrative*, to cases in which the imagined mechanics of time travel seem to make events at the level of story just as fungible as their representation at the level of discourse: "In a time travel fiction, even a relatively normal one, no such underlying coherence in the *fabula* [or story] may be assumed."[21] That said, in most cases even these extreme and outlying examples nonetheless rely on the *story–discourse* relation as a norm against which to work; as Richardson writes, "They nevertheless bear a dialectical relationship to the concept of mimesis, since it is only through that concept that we can understand its violation."[22] By *mimesis*, Richardson means something like the representation of events and thus something like the *story–discourse* relation (I will return to the concept of *mimesis* in the next chapter). To understand a narrative *as* narrative has thus often been seen as the effort to understand how a given case manages or pointedly refuses to manage a representational or "mimetic" urge implied by the relation between story and discourse.

Indeed, one of the fullest and most influential applications of the story–discourse relation appears in Gérard Genette's *Narrative Discourse: An Essay in Method*. Although I will discuss *Narrative Discourse* at length in Section 6.3, it will be helpful to introduce some of its terms now. In each of Genette's several chapters, he details another aspect of the story–discourse relation, using it to offer an increasingly complex reading of Marcel Proust's *À la recherche du temps perdu*. How, he asks, are the events that make up a story arranged and shuffled, sent forward or pushed back to produce a particular temporal "order" of discourse? In what ways can the same event be stretched, shrunk, accelerated, or stopped cold so as to produce different effects of discursive "duration"? How are events staggered, punctuated, or repeated in order to produce a "tempo" specific to one or another narrative? In the process of describing the different modulations of story and discourse, Genette develops an elaborate taxonomy, one that relies on a whole set of odd-sounding but powerfully analytic terms: "anachrony," "paralepsis," "paralipsis," "metalepsis," "diegetic," "extradiegetic," and "intradiegetic" as well as more homely but no less useful terms including "scene," "summary," "ellipsis," and "pause." As we will see, we can take the act of naming the different things that narrative can do is part of a larger effort to make narrative strange, to reveal what can seem "only natural" as a complicated and intentional human activity; this urge to show narrative's work aligns Genette with the modernist or postmodern writers Richardson described earlier. It also, as we will see, connects him directly to the Russian Formalists, whom I will discuss in Section 5.2. Genette focuses on the variable relation between story and discourse as a source of aesthetic tension particular to narrative, as that which gives narrative an apparently inexhaustible and disturbing power. Put differently, looking at and naming different aspects of the story–discourse relation give us the ability *to see* what is weird about almost any narrative.

As I have already said, although many texts work to disguise or to naturalize the relation between these two levels, to subordinate the particular machinations of discourse to the whole effect of a given novel or film, others call alienating and productive attention to the fragility or artificiality of the story–discourse relation, a fact that Genette's scheme helps to explain. For instance, in the devastating third act of *King Lear*, Lear's Fool addresses the audience directly, offering a "prophecy" that foretells chaos, reversal, and social collapse: "Then shall the realm of Albion / Come to great confusion."[23] He then goes on to comment on both the content and the form of his own prophecy: "This prophecy Merlin shall make; for I live before his time."[24] The joke is a hard one: because *Lear* is set chronologically *before* Merlin's later Arthurian setting, the Fool offers not only a prophecy but also a prophecy of a prophecy, foretelling a time when Merlin will in turn foretell a future that looks a lot like the narrated present of *King Lear*; he imagines a future Merlin looking into his future (the future's future) and seeing something like the past. While it might be impossible or at least unwise to try to tease out the whole temporal logic of the Fool's vision, we can say that it is a moment that pushes story and discourse to the verge of collapse, to a point when the relation between events and the possibility of events meaning something appears to have been shattered or almost shattered; of course, by the third act of *Lear*, the failure of social and filial bonds has led to the edge of civil war. The narrative structure of *Lear* seems thus to reflect the play's painful content, as an otherwise intelligible relation between narrative levels and narrative times seems to short-circuit. Shakespeare uses the Fool's anticipation of Merlin's prophecy, which is also a vision of a past that is the present of *Lear*, in order to register in the fractured space between story and discourse what it feels like when history and violence conspire against narrative and social coherence, when, in other words, our familiar narratives are no longer adequate to our experience.

There are, as Genette points out and as we will see, a number of other questions, paradoxes, and contradictions that can make the apparently straight-forward relationship between story and discourse both complicated and aes-thetically rich. There is, for instance, the basic question of which comes first, story or discourse. On the one hand, it might seem clear that story is a sequence of real events that must precede its appearance in textual, spoken, or cinematic form. We understand that the Second World War and its various events had to have happened before they could be narrated in the form of novels, films, history books, etc. It is impossible to imagine *Saving Private Ryan* (1988) or *Catch-22* (1961) or *The Rise and Fall of the Third Reich* (1960) preceding the Second World War; it might in other words seem obvious that story must occur before discourse and that discourse is simply an aesthetic or conceptual way to organize the raw and abundant data of already available experience into one or another meaningful form. On the other hand, we can also imagine story as happening not *before* but rather *after* discourse; this is to imagine a particular discourse – a novel, a film, and so on – as a script or a blueprint that allows us retroactively to imagine or to create a "natural" order of story events; Luc Herman and Bart Vervaeck write that "just like any deep structure, the story is an abstract construct that the reader has to derive from the concrete text."[25] Emma Kafalenos defines *fabula* (the Russian Formalist equivalent of "story") "as a construct that readers make from a *sjuzhet*" (the Russian Formalist equivalent of "discourse").[26] Monika Fludernik writes that "the story is *always* a construction and an idealized chronological outline."[27] Richard Walsh asserts that "fabula is always relative to and contingent upon both a given sjuzhet and a specific act of interpretation."[28] Writing about the case of postmodern or experimental narrative, Brian Richardson writes, "The representational model of a writer transcribing a preexistent story is here dissolved and supplanted by one that stresses the act of invention and the free play of an author who invents what he claims to recount; or to put it another way, mimesis is here replaced by poiesis."[29] David Wittenberg offers an especially robust philosophical account of what he takes as the narratively necessary but finally false priority of story over discourse: "I will call the ruse of fictional historicity the 'postulate of *fabular* apriority'."[30] And, because she sees story as a conceptual effect rather than an empirical cause of discourse, Rimmon-Kenan write that "far from seeing story as raw, undifferentiated material, [her book, *Narrative Fiction*] stresses its structured character, its being made of separable components, and hence having the potential of forming networks of internal relations."[31] As opposed to standing as the unprocessed occasion for one or another narrative, the stuff of story is in these accounts always already a structured part of a larger narrative process. For these writers, it is only the textual presence of discourse that allows us to imagine and conceptually to construct a series of events that may or may not have happened and that, in any case, cannot exist *as story* (whatever their real status as a series of events) outside our narratively-primed minds.

For some, the chicken–egg question of priority in narrative theory is essentially unanswerable. Jonathan Culler writes that "either the discourse is seen as a representation of events which must be thought of as independent of that particular representation, or else the so-called events are thought of as the postulates or products of a discourse."[32] He goes on to argue that the tension between these two possibilities is essential to narrative theory: "Neither perspective, then, is likely to offer a satisfactory narratology, nor can the two fit together in a harmonious synthesis; they stand in irreconcilable opposition, a conflict between two logics which puts in question the possibility of a coherent, non-contradictory science of narrative."[33] In this reading, narrative theory is based not only on a relation between two levels as opposed to either level taken in isolation but also on a deeper paradox, a question of priority that seems to suggest something essentially strange about narrative theory or narrative itself.

We might think of Nicolas Roeg's film, *Don't Look Now* (1973), where narrative reversals and elisions are imperfectly and thus eerily thematized in a plot that turns on the possibility of clairvoyance. In the film's opening minutes, John Baxter, an architectural scholar, sits looking at a slide of the interior of a Venetian church that he is set to restore. Sitting in one of the church's pews is an obscure figure in a red hooded coat. Meanwhile, his children are playing outside, his son riding his bike, while his daughter wanders beside a pond wearing a red plastic raincoat. At the same moment that she falls into the water and drowns, Baxter seems psychically "to see" the accident and, thus startled, spills something on the slide, causing the red dye of the coat's image to spread across its surface. That red stain points in two directions: to his daughter's simultaneous death by drowning and to his own doomed future. At the film's end, Baxter is violently murdered by a dwarf in a red coat, suggesting that the figure he had seen in the slide was a kind of extrasensory premonition as well as what Genette would call a narrative *prolepsis*, a moment when discourse reaches forward in order to introduce a moment from a story's future into its discursive present. And because the red coat, which appears throughout the film, not only points forward but also back to the opening scene of his daughter's death, it stands as both a *prolepsis* and what Genette would call an *analepsis*, or a flashback to a prior narrative moment. As a result, the splash of red seems to cut across the film's narrative levels, drawing past, present, and future together in a single violent image. On the one hand, this is an aspect of the film's *story*, in which John appears able to see into the future just as he must remember his past; on the other hand, it is an effect of *discourse*, a product of the way in which Roeg has obscurely but powerfully edited his film to create visual echoes that drift suggestively across its surface. Because, in other words, the film entertains the idea that one might be able really to see into the future, it is difficult to say whether leaps forward and back in the film's discourse are meant to represent the supernatural nature of the film's story or whether they are meant as a discursive arrangement and thus an interpretive comment on or critical disruption of those events. This is, perhaps, why the film is called *Don't Look Now*: because it is in some sense about being caught between the backward-looking pull of grief and the forward-looking push of premonition – a push-and-pull that takes the narrative form in differently directed *anachronies* (Genette's term for the temporal displacement of story events at the level of discourse) – the film is, in fact, about the psychic and narrative inability *to look now*. Indeed, it is not until the moment of his death, the moment when the meaning both of his loss and of his visions becomes clear, that John is able to stop *looking then* and thus to inhabit the *now* of both his life and the film that represents that life. Roeg's film seems intentionally to confuse story and discourse in order to call attention to instabilities that might be necessary to narrative as such. This possibility, that narrative theory is founded on a paradox, is one to which I will return. I want, however, to bracket the question of the insolubility of this problem for the moment in order simply to register the fact that, for all of its potential difficulty, the need to think about narrative in terms of an anything-but-simple relation between story and discourse has been taken as more or less given in narrative theory.

~

In these terms and in what follows, I will thus assume the story–discourse relation as narrative theory's methodological common denominator, as, in other words, a way to differentiate between works that simply have one or another thing to say about narrative and works that need to be understood as part of the critical tradition I want to sketch out here. Because, however, I am most interested in works that were written before narrative theory became a discipline of its own, the distinction will be more and less explicit from case to case. I want in other words to argue that versions of story and discourse are at work in modes of thinking that go beyond – sometimes far beyond – what is usually understood as narrative theory. Starting with the distinction, I want to argue for a broader and more capacious sense of narrative theory as a still coherent field, one that overlaps in some unexpected ways with work in historiography, philosophy, and political theory. If we expand our sense of narrative theory to include other attempts to make events meaningful via acts of representation (fables, histories, novels, prayers), it becomes clear that the story–discourse relation might be a motivated version of other conceptual schemes more broadly characteristic of nineteenth- and twentieth-century critical thinking. At the same time that I want to broaden the definition of narrative theory by looking for the story–discourse relation where we might not expect to find it, I also want to think about efforts to see the relation as historically or ideologically specific, as, in other words, a relation more important to some times and places than to some others. This is, once again, to follow recent work by Richardson and others on postmodern, nonnatural, or antimimetic narratives that test the story–discourse relation. Monika Fludernik's "Natural Narratology" similarly depends on understanding the story–discourse relation within specific formal and historical parameters: "Natural Narratology therefore does not entirely reject the story vs. discourse distinction but relegates it to those parameters which depend on a realistic cognization of both the story-world and the narrational act."[34] And David Herman writes that "despite its prevalence throughout the history of narratological research, however, the story/discourse distinction remains an analytic construct whose limits of applicability have yet to be established."[35] A number of narrative theorists have, in other words, asked whether there are historical limits to story and discourse, whether that form of narrative is in fact tied to a particular moment in time or a particular genre such as the novel. (I will address this question directly and at length in my discussion of Roland Barthes, Gérard Genette, and the journal *Tel Quel*.) Does it make sense to see story and discourse and thus narrative theory as a historically specific and thus an impermanent endeavor? To ask what historical conditions have made it self-evident to think about narrative in these terms, to wonder how it is that so many can agree on one and only one model of narrative structure? To anticipate the end of narrative theory or, indeed, of narrative itself?

In his great essay "Reification and the Consciousness of the Proletariat," Georg Lukács – whom I discuss in Section 4.2 – identifies what he calls the "antinomies of bourgeois thought," a series of seemingly essential philosophical oppositions – subject and object, *noumena* and *phenomena*, fact and value – that serve as the limiting conceptual categories of a society that derives its shape and its ideas from the internally divided structure of the commodity form. For Lukács, the conceptual categories of philosophy, sociology, and political theory take their shape from the constitutive difference between use value and exchange value.[36] The idea, simply put, is that very different aspects of a society will reflect that society's fundamental character, which the Marxist Lukács understands as an effect of its economic structure, in this case a capitalism wholly reliant on the split and alienated exchange form of the commodity. This is a complicated argument. For now I will simply ask: could it make sense to think about story and discourse as another of Lukács's antinomies, as an expression of a historically specific logic? Should we see narrative theory as both a powerful analytic tool and a limited expression of a historically specific and ideological worldview? If story and discourse represent another expression of a particular ideology, is it possible to imagine what occurs next or to see what occurred before? What would such a history not only of narrative theory but also of the story–discourse relation look like? What would it mean to imagine an end to narrative? These are, of course, big and possibly unanswerable questions; what is more important to me is that they are questions that arise regularly if tacitly in some of the most important works of narrative theory, works that treat narrative both as a field of possibilities as well as an encounter with an existential limit.

Indeed, this is why I look throughout not only at theories of narrative but also at theories of specific narrative genres. While, in other words, accounts of narrative theory often explicitly distance themselves from theories of the novel or any other genre, I am interested in how particular theories of narrative motivate their analyses of the story–discourse relation by focusing on its appearance in one or another historically conditioned genre: tragedy, comedy, epic, history, the novel, and so on. We can think here of Aristotle's use of tragedy to reveal more general aspects of representation, of Lukács's shifting commitment to the novel as "the epic of a disenchanted age," of the implicit relation between comedy and history in Hegel and Marx, as well as of more radical examples such as Barthes's reliance on a single short story in *S/Z* or Genette's brilliant treatment of the exceptional Proust as paradoxically exemplary in *Narrative Discourse*. This interest in the mobile and speaking relation between narrative in general and particular narrative genres goes back to the opening lines of the *Poetics*: "I propose to speak not only of poetry in general but also of its species and their respective capacities; of the structure of plot required for a good poem; of the number and nature of the constituent parts of a poem; and likewise of any other matters in the same line of inquiry."[37] For Aristotle, tragedy is both his primary object of inquiry and a representative of poetry as such; as is always the case with Aristotle, knowledge is produced in the space between the particular and the general. Looking forward to later figures, this interest in the relation between narrative in general and particular generic expressions of narrative appears as what I will call the *comparative analysis of narrative forms*. In other words, several of the figures I look at make related and layered arguments about the play between narrative theory and the specific forms that narrative takes at different moments in time (this is the case in Erich Auerbach, Bakhtin, Lukács, and others).

This argument is built on two assumptions: the first is that genre is a deeply historical phenomenon, one that both expresses a particular set of historical conditions and helps to shape individual and social beliefs, hopes, ideas, and expectations at a given moment in time; Heta Pyrhönen writes that genres have an "intimate link with society, for they are social institutions that always stand in some relation to dominant ideology. In Todorov's words, genres, like any other institution, 'bring to light the constitutive features of the society to which they belong.'"[38] The most explicit account of the historical nature of genre appears, as we will see in Section 4.3, in the work of Mikhail Bakhtin, where he aligns genre with the idea of the *chronotope*, a particular social configuration of ideas about time and space that shapes and limits what it is possible to say or even to think about the world. So, narrative genres are historical. The second assumption is that narrative *as narrative* is not historical or, at least, not historical in the same way that genre is historical. That is, while particular configurations of story and discourse change over time, the basic structural fact of narrative as the relation between story and discourse remains stable. As far as we can see, there have always been narratives. So, where a narrative genre is historical, narrative as narrative appears to be *more or less* timeless. What, as I will show, makes the comparative analysis of narrative forms powerful is the relation between these two assumptions. In other words, just as we can say specific things about specific genres because the stability of narrative as such provides us with a fixed point of comparison, so can we say more and more precise things about narrative as such when we track its movement through the different historical and ideological demands that specific genres and thus specific cultures make on it. All of this is to say that, while the study of genre has often appeared as separate from narrative theory, the two are in fact deeply linked, a fact that requires, once again, that we expand the terms of what we understand as narrative theory.

~

As I have already suggested, this interest in testing the methodological possibilities and limits of narrative theory has led me to consider some thinkers who do not usually figure or at least do not figure largely in some of the best recent accounts of narrative theory. In addition to some of the more central figures – the Russian Formalists, structural narratologists including Gérard Genette and Roland Barthes, even a novelist such as Henry James – I look at figures from philosophy and literary criticism who might seem eccentric to narrative theory and its primary concerns. This is a result of my interest in speculating about the historical significance of the story-discourse relation. That is, while it can sometimes seem that the terms emerged suddenly in order to deal with a very particular set of methodological problems, I try instead to show that we can trace *the idea* if not the words back to a few related moments in intellectual history and, more particularly if not exclusively, to the philosopher Georg Wilhelm Friedrich Hegel. Although he is not primarily a literary theorist, Hegel nonetheless helped narrative to emerge as an autonomous and especially modern object of study; or, rather, Hegel seems best to embody a moment in intellectual history when, for a variety of reasons, narrative emerged as an all but unavoidable concept.

There are two aspects to this claim for Hegel's place in the history of narrative theory. The first is that Hegel shares and in some sense embodies a novel set of cultural conditions that prepared the ground for narrative as a privileged object of analysis. The most important of these conditions emerged in the wake of the French Revolution, when military, social, and technological developments merged to make the narration of history something other than what it had previously been. The historian Peter Fritzsche writes that

> what made the past seem so remote and the movement of history so meaningful to nineteenth-century observers was the deep rupture in remembered experience that came with the French Revolution. Two intertwined forces were at work in this period: the massive dislocation of revolution and war, and the narration of that dislocation as change or progress, which was seen to extinguish tradition. Without the machinery of narration – the notion of epoch and the sense of new time which structured histories, prefaces, and memoirs – material changes could not have been interpreted as of one piece or identified as an encompassing historical passage that elevated parochial tragedies into more meaningful, legible common fates. And without the restless mobilization of men and women into new economic arrangements, new geographic places, and new political services, the narration would have lost its pertinence, its authority, and its urgency.[39]

An updated version of arguments about narration and ideology that appear in Lukács's *The Historical Novel* (1947) and Karl Mannheim's *Ideology and Utopia* (1929), Fritzsche's case is that narrative emerged both as a necessity and as a new object of study in the wake of the French Revolution, an idea that Hegel shared. The conditions that led to and followed from the French Revolution seemed to show that different people, different classes, and different nations could hold fundamentally different and yet nonetheless coherent ideological accounts of the same events; they had found ways discursively to arrange, to represent, and to mobilize the past, present, and future in the service of specific cultural and national ends. "The concept of ideology," says Terry Eagleton, "arose at the historical point where systems of ideas first became aware of their own partiality; and this came about when those ideas were forced to encounter alien or alternative forms of discourse."[40] To have different ideologies was, in other words, to maintain *different narratives* of the recent and not-so-recent past, a fact that made the ability to interpret those other narratives into a matter of national and strategic significance. As a result, if one was going to live in the modern world, one needed a theory of narrative, which is to say a theory of events and the representation of events not only to understand that world but also to compete and to survive. As we will see in Section 4.2, Lukács came to see the contemporary novels of Sir Walter Scott as a novelistic equivalent to Hegel's narrative response to the revolution, an idea that Ian Duncan echoes in his *Scott's Shadow: The Novel in Romantic Edinburgh*: "Scott's invention of historical fiction involves, dialectically, the specification of history – the new force and density of which is registered in ways that have been well described by twentieth-century criticism – and also of fiction: a specification that brings the abstraction of both history and fiction ... as discursive categories."[41] For Duncan, Scott saw narrative as a way to "contain revolution's apocalyptic potential ... in part by displacing it into the past, and in part by investing it with the tropes of fiction." In Scott as in Hegel, the revolution helped to *activate* narrative as a social problem. One might also consider Margaret Cohen's recent account of the relation between the revolution and the rise of the sentimental novel in France: "The importance of sentimentality in Revolutionary self-representation may help to explain the power of the sentimental novel in the Revolution's wake."[42] Just as Scott's historical novel allowed history to represent itself to itself, so did modes of sympathy and "social acumen" associated with the "feminine" form of sentimental fiction allow a society traumatized by revolutionary Terror to figure itself against or as moving toward other possible outcomes; this is why, for Cohen, the sentimental novel can be read as a form of mourning, an attempt to put the recent experience of revolutionary upheaval into a kind of retrospective or counterfactual order. In these terms, the development of a specifically *literary* narrative theory needs to be seen in relation to the larger emergence of narrative as a term central to historical reckoning, political analysis, and the cultivation of national character.

It is against this backdrop that we need to see Hegel's more or less direct influence on some of the most important theories of narrative. Like others of his generation, Hegel draws on explicitly narrative models in order to confront and to surpass what he took to be the flawed or outdated thinking of an earlier moment in philosophy. In order, in other words, to think not only about the experience of revolution but also past the Kantian divide between ideas and things, Hegel imagined history as a narrative of development from the blissful ignorance of its beginning, through the narratable turmoil of its middle, to the unifying resolution of its ultimate end. This more or less Aristotelian model of history as a plot – a beginning, middle, and projected end – allowed Hegel both to see a way past the bad divisions between form and content that he saw at work in Kant and to understand seemingly senseless or tragic events within the terms of history understood as a whole story; if the French Revolution seemed to be a disappointment and a disaster from within the flow of history, from the perspective of history's ultimate and narrative culmination, it could be imagined as part of a larger and more coherent story that might resolve local tragedies into the larger and synthetic narrative form of comedy. As a result of these several aspects of Hegel's larger project, his work represents a moment when narrative and the necessity of different narratives – both as the historical problem and as a powerful, even undeniable form of philosophy – became visible as an essential aspect of modern life. This is not to claim that Hegel "invented" narrative or the analysis of narrative; it is rather to suggest that Hegel's context, his concerns, and his disposition joined to facilitate a cultural turn toward narrative both as a particular problem and as an autonomous object of study.

This claim, that Hegel helped to make narrative one of the preeminent philosophical problems of the nineteenth century, reveals some other unexpected figures – Marx, Nietzsche, Lukács, Auerbach, and others – as also consequential within and to the story of narrative theory. This is both to establish some of the intellectual contexts out of which structuralist and formalist theories of narrative emerge – Hegelian theories of history, neo-Kantian efforts to update the primary categories of the understanding, models of cultural analysis emerging from the early sociology of Max Weber and Georg Simmel, and so on – and to take seriously the degree to which narrative theory can itself be considered as a more broadly critical and philosophical endeavor. More to the point and as I have already suggested, I want to consider the story–discourse relation in the context of a set of conceptual antinomies that both structure and are the subject of what we might broadly construe as *critical theory*, the large nineteenth- and twentieth-century endeavor to question apparently given relations between facts and values, between our sometimes bewildering experience of events as they seem accidentally to happen and the different, more or less motivated schemes that we impose onto those experiences in order to given them sense, direction, hope, and meaning.

That is, seen in this wider context, narrative theory's broad commitment to understanding the play between the levels of story and discourse appears not simply as a local methodological innovation but rather as an effort to engage in rigorous and self-consciously restricted terms with some of the key problems of modern life. I do not, however, want simply to make analogies between narrative theory and philosophy; rather, when one begins to connect the dots of reading, influence, controversy, and acquaintance, it becomes clear that narrative theory not only shares important family resemblances with phenomenology, psychoanalysis, and critical theory but also existed in an informing and reciprocal relation with these different movements. In one sense, I am interested here in rolling back the specialization of narrative theory; since the synthetic moment of structuralist narratology in the 1960s, the field has become increasingly codified with journals, conferences, sub-fields, etc. While that move toward self-conscious disciplinarity has been strong and enabling and has produced a terrific level of methodological clarity, it has also obscured some of the messier intellectual sources of narrative theory, some of the tacit concerns and, indeed, some of the desires that made figures across the twentieth century turn to the analysis of narrative and to the technical relation between story and discourse. I want, in other words, to think about what might be risky or fraught about narrative theory.

I thus think of what follows both as an introduction to the theory and practice of narrative analysis and as the intellectual history of a self-conscious kind of writing that sometimes needs to disavow its consequences or takes on the character of a merely methodological project in order to obscure its political stakes. This is to see some important works of narrative theory as exercises in what the political philosopher Leo Strauss called *esoteric writing*, "a peculiar manner of writing which would enable [thinkers] to reveal what they regard as the truth to the few, without endangering the unqualified commitment of the many to the opinions on which society rests."[43] More recently, Arthur Melzer has written that esoteric styles of writing emerge in response to the experience of social or political conflict: "the conflict between philosophy and the city ... consists not simply in the opposition of certain specific philosophic theses ('dangerous truths') to certain particular dogmas or laws of the city – although such oppositions do also exist.... Rather, it consists in a conflict between two incompatible ways of life. The city requires authoritative settlement and closure; philosophy demands openness and questioning."[44] As we will see in the following chapters, the idea of just this kind of conflict is at the heart of both Aristotle's and Hegel's theories of tragic narrative; both argue that conflict is necessary to narrative both because it motivates plot and because it helps to structure the relation between narrative levels that I have been calling story and discourse. What is more, the particular conflict that Strauss and Melzer address, the conflict between "two incompatible ways of life," is itself a fundamentally narrative conflict, a conflict over discursive arrangements of the same events that results in large claims about what those events and thus life itself might mean; as we will see, what connects the several figures I discuss is their shared sense that a contest over producing and interpreting the narratives that make life meaningful had emerged as a defining aspect of politics and aesthetics. It makes sense, in that case, that narrative theory would emerge at moments of conflict both as a form and as a theory of esoteric writing, as an effort to talk about crises of meaning from the hidden perspective of a methodological analysis of what makes life meaningful in the first place. As I have said, that is what a narrative theory must be: an account of what makes events mean what they seem together to mean.

~

We might think here of one of the founding figures of narrative theory, the Russian Formalist Viktor Shklovsky. In the "first preface" to his *Knight's Move*, a collection of essays on Soviet art and literature, Shklovsky reproduces an image of a knight making its crooked, meandering way across a chessboard and writes that,

> There are many reasons for the strangeness of the knight's move, the main one being the conventionality of art, about which I am writing.
> The second reason lies in the fact that the knight is not free – it moves in an L-shaped manner because it is forbidden to take the straight road.
> The articles and feuilletons included in this book were all published in Russia from 1919 through 1921.[45]

As we will see in Section 5.2, the passage is characteristic of Shklovsky's method, which is in turn central to the development of narrative theory; it was, indeed, written at roughly the same time as Shklovsky's *Theory of Prose*, one of narrative theory's most important early texts. His brief account of the knight's move uses short, one-sentence paragraphs to create a mixed generic effect, a blend of argument, observation, aphorism, memoir, and joke; this "parallel" technique – the use of parallel grammatical constructions to imply but not to own a relation between distinct ideas or events – is an attempt to apply the possibilities of cinematic montage to prose, a fact that announces the resolute and self-conscious modernity of Shklovsky's broader project. His interest in the "conventionality" of the knight's move is, as we shall see, part of a larger Formalist commitment to "baring the device," to showing how art does or should expose and thus *defamiliarize* the conventions, habits, and rules that structure everyday life, a project that was both aesthetic and tacitly political for Shklovsky and his colleagues. And, his interest in the knight's path as passing over something other than a "straight road" anticipates his influential account of plot as a middle space of Shandean digressions, missteps, and hesitations; as he writes in a related context, "A crooked road, a road in which the foot feels acutely the stones beneath it, a road that turns back on itself – this is the road of art."[46]

Finally, the passage's parallel layering of the knight's productive unfreedom and book's date of composition evokes without naming directly the politically fraught conditions under which Shklovsky wrote and his own understanding of the relation between the art of writing and political persecution. A participant in a failed anti-Bolshevik coup in 1918, Shklovsky wrote the essays in *Knight's Move* while in exile; Svetlana Boym writes that "threatened with arrest and possible execution, Shklovsky crossed the Soviet border on the frozen Gulf of Finland and eventually found himself in Berlin. *Knight's Move* was written in Berlin as the writer reflected on whether he should return from exile, back to Russia, where his wife was being held hostage."[47] As painful as it all undoubtedly was, Shklovsky managed for a time to turn persecution, exile, and the threat of death into a fruitful if mordant aesthetic constraint; as he wrote to Roman Jakobson (another figure and eventual exile central to the story of narrative theory) at about the same time, "I am exploring the unfreedom of the writer. I am studying unfreedom as though it were a set of gymnastic equipment."[48]

What is striking for us is the fact that, when faced with these conditions, when in need of knight's move that could motivate his very real unfreedom, Shklovsky chose to develop an early and influential form of narrative theory, an account of plot, style, narrative technique, story, and discourse that continues to inform all subsequent narrative theories; we need, in that case, to see why and how his need to say something he *could not say* took the form of a narrative theory. This leads to two questions: to what degree should his narrative theory be seen as a specific response to these conditions, as a coded or defamiliarized half-response to an almost impossible life? And to what degree might its origins as a strategic answer to persecution remain an element of narrative theories derived from Shklovsky's work? Does it make sense to look for aspects of a theory's past in its present. These lead to a broader set of questions: what might we get if we returned other narrative theories to their points of origin? What might we learn about what is always quietly political about method, about narrative, about narrative theory? Why, after all, do we *need* narrative theory?

We might consider another, more recent example. At the beginning of Joan Didion's essay "The White Album," she writes, "We tell ourselves stories in order to live."[49] She goes on to gesture briefly and evocatively toward a few minimal but nonetheless eerie plots: "The princess is caged in the consulate. The man with the candy will lead the children into the sea. The naked woman on the ledge outside the window on the sixteenth floor is a victim of accidie, or the naked woman is an exhibitionist, and it would be 'interesting' to know which."[50] In each case, the imposition of narrative forms onto events helps to give sense, meaning, significance to what might otherwise seem absurd or simply horrible: "We live entirely, especially if we are writers, by the impression of narrative line upon disparate images, by the 'ideas' with which we have learned to freeze the shifting phantasmagoria which is our actual experience."[51] Didion in other words sees narrative as the later imposition of significant form – discourse – onto story: the events as they occur.

On the one hand, we could take Didion's observation as a prescient nod to what many take as the almost or in fact biological necessity of narrative; Abbott writes that the "likeliest" explanation for the near-ubiquity of stories "is that narrative is the principal way in which our species organizes its understanding of time."[52] In these terms, narrating is something that we do to live in the most basic of senses; for humans understood as social animals, narrative might indeed be part of what we do to survive. Brian Boyd argues that "narrative arises from the advantages of communication in social species. It benefits audiences, who can choose better what course of action to take on the basis of strategic information, and it benefits tellers, who earn credit in the social information exchange and gain in terms of attention and status. That combination of benefits, for the teller and the told, explain why narrative has become so central to human life."[53] In the hothouse of evolutionary psychology, where we serve society so that society can serve genes that finally serve themselves, narrative emerges as one of our most distinctively human strategies for survival. Or, as an evolutionary psychologist might put it, we tell ourselves stories so that *the species* might live.

That said, the evolutionary explanation does not capture the peculiar anxiety of "The White Album," which Didion wrote in 1970s Los Angeles, at a time when the old stories, maybe when all the stories seemed to have lost their ability to make sense of life, when a sun-bleached mix of violence, paranoia, drugs, and political disappointment had seemed to disrupt both the necessity and the efficacy of narrative as a means of organizing or evaluating life: "I am talking here about a time when I began to doubt the premises of all the stories I had ever told myself, a common condition but one I found troubling."[54] It seems significant that Didion chooses a moment of narrative's historical and cultural *failure* to reflect on our technical and existential reliance on narrative, that she offers so assured and concentrated an account of narrative forms and conventions at a moment when those forms and conventions appeared to have given way to a pervasive and suicidal resistance to meaning as such. But, then again, maybe that is the point; it becomes both possible and necessary to develop a narrative theory at those moments when narrative seems to have been pushed to and past its limits, when one needs a knight's move or a crooked path in order to say something, to say anything about what things are really like. Thomas Carlyle begins his essay "Characteristics" with the observation that "the healthy know not of their health, but only the sick: this is the Physician's Aphorism; and applicable in a far wider sense than he gives it."[55] This is what Didion implies, too: that narrative becomes visible and thus calls out for a theory only when it has already begun to break down; narrative reveals itself as in need of a theory when narrative is "sick."

I will argue that Shklovsky and Didion's mixed sense of the possibilities and real limits of narrative *for life* is characteristic of a certain strain of narrative theory, as is its appearance at a moment of social or political uncertainty. Seen from this perspective, the figures I look at – Mikhail Bakhtin, Erich Auerbach, Roland Barthes, and so on – chose to write about narrative theory in spite of or in response to social worlds that had lost their "normal" capacity for meaning. Like Shklovsky and Didion, I want to see these figures and their efforts to make up theories about stories as part of a long and conflicted history; I want to suggest that we tend to feel that stories need theories precisely at those moments when stories do not work as smoothly or as confidently as they do in times of relative calm. I want, in other words, to see whether there is – as I think there is – a more than coincidental relation between the origins of narrative theory and trouble, a relation that might be worth recovering now when we seem once again to have discovered our need not only for narrative but also for narrative theory.

Chapter 2

Action, Event, Conflict

The Uses of Narrative in Aristotle and Hegel

2.1 Beginning, Middle, and End: Aristotle and Narrative Theory

> I like to take in hand none but clean, virgin, fair-and-square mathematical jobs, something that regularly begins at the beginning, and is at the middle when midway, and comes to an end at the conclusion; not a cobbler's job, that's at an end in the middle, and at the beginning at the end.
> Herman Melville, *Moby-Dick; or, The Whale*

To begin at the beginning: something very like the story–discourse relation appears in Aristotle's *Poetics*, one of the first and still most influential works of systematic literary theory. Reading the *Poetics* can be a strange because all-too-familiar experience: although the text is from so distant and different a time and although it focuses on the particular genre of Athenian tragedy, its concerns and questions about the nature of literary representation and narrative form nonetheless feel very familiar, a fact that would seem indeed to suggest the near-universality of some aspects of narrative. Although Aristotle's *Poetics* covers a wide range of issues – the nature of dramatic spectacle, the emotional effects of a good tragedy on an audience, the theatrical use of song, and the role of the chorus – it is most centrally concerned with the nature and structure of tragic plots: "the first essential, the life and soul, so to speak, of tragedy is the plot."[1] Aristotle understands plots as what Cynthia Freeland refers to as "artifacts constructed by tragic poets within constraints of a kind of realism of intended representation of actions," as, in other words, the aesthetic arrangement of actions that took place in a real or an imagined time into an ordered and organic form – beginning, middle, and end – that either reveals or in fact produces those actions as meaningful.[2] Tragedy is, in other words, a generically specific configuration of the two narrative levels that we have been calling story and discourse, and the *Poetics* is thus an early – maybe the earliest – example of what I am calling narrative theory.

What makes one plot better than another? What are its necessary components? What makes the whole structure of a tragedy meaningful? While the
answers to these questions are, of course, many and complicated, what stands
at the center of Aristotle's thinking is an attention to the right and rightly
proportional relation between appropriate actions and the literary forms that
those actions take when they are represented in the plot of a successful
tragedy. Aristotle's primary concern is, in other words, how actions find
expression in tragic representation: "Tragedy," he writes, "is essentially an
imitation not of persons but of action and of life."[3] Aristotle's word for
representation is *mimesis,* and he sees a successful tragedy (or, rather, a
successful tragic *plot*) as a structured, coherent representation of an event or
a series of events:

> We have laid it down that a tragedy is an imitation of an action that is
> complete in itself, as a whole of some' magnitude; for a whole may be of
> no magnitude to speak of. Now a whole is that which has beginning,
> middle, and end. A beginning is that which is not itself necessarily after
> anything else, and which has naturally something else after it; an end is
> that which is naturally after something itself, either as its necessary or
> usual consequent, and with nothing else after it; and a middle, that
> which is by nature after one thing and has also another after it. A well-
> constructed plot, therefore, cannot either begin or end at any point one
> likes; beginning and end in it must be of the forms just described.[4]

Aristotle's style here is characteristic of the *Poetics*: deceptively simple or
simplifying, his account of the relations among plot, imitation, and aesthetic
effect is in fact enormously complicated. There are at least three aspects of this
compressed passage that we should highlight: for Aristotle a good plot is
made, it is *ordered*, and it is *whole*.

When Aristotle says that "well-constructed plots should ... not begin or
end at any arbitrary point," he is owning, if tacitly, an important difference
between events and the representation of events.[5] Where actions or events
simply happen, their representation, what Aristotle calls a plot, or *muthos*,
occurs when, as Seymour Chatman puts it, those actions or events are
"selected and possibly rearranged."[6] While they are definitely related, a plot
is at last something *other* than what it represents. In part, this is to acknowledge that, where events or actions seem simply to happen (or to have
happened), a representation of those events or actions bears the trace of an
author's shaping intention; unlike the beginning or end of an ordinary life,
which is rarely chosen, the beginning or end of a plot is something that a poet
must choose. Plot is, in other words, the result of a shaping and informing

intention, a considered process of selection and arrangement that gives events a meaning and a structure they would not have on their own.[7] Aristotle points to some specific choices that characterize narrative representations of events and thus some of the essential differences between the internally coherent economy of a representation and the essential messiness of life. Life does not begin at the beginning or end at the end; it is hard to tell where or on whom we should focus our attention; it all often passes by without offering a moral or even making much sense; recognition and reversal – what Aristotle refers to as *anagnorisis* and *peripeteia* – rarely arrive in life with the focus, attention, and clarity of consequence that characterize them in a successful tragedy. Where absolutely *everything* happens in life – the trivial and the nontrivial, the noble and the base, the good, the bad, and the ugly – in a representation a poet or author must filter out nonessential aspects of an event or sequence of events; because, unlike life, plots are about something, they cannot be about everything.

Aristotle points to Homer's judicious selection of events in the *Odyssey*: "He did not make the poem cover all that ever befell his hero."[8] If he had tried to "cover all," the resulting poem would not only be impossibly long but also very boring. Although Odysseus had an unusually exciting life, it nonetheless would have had its long stretches of dull downtime or practically *unnarratable* experience; some parts of a day, a year, or a life are simply more interesting than others. We might think here of E. M. Forster's observation that books almost never bother to represent sleep despite its importance to every life; a literary character is almost "never conceived as a creature a third of whose time is spent in the darkness."[9] We could also think here of D. A. Miller's account of "the field of the narratable" in *Narrative and Its Discontents*: "The anchors of traditional narrative are basically a system of restraints imposed upon the field of the narratable. . . . Order and orientation are thus secured by clear distinctions of relevance: between round characters, full of intriguing possibilities, and flat ones, reduced to a prescribed function or gesture that they aren't allowed to overstep; between the primary notation that constitutes and important sequence and the subsidiary notation that is felt mere to fill it in; between motifs that are bound in a pattern of inescapable coherence and motifs that are free to be deleted or not without substantially altering the story."[10] For Miller, *narratability* marks out the difference between stuff that bears a necessary relation to a particular narrative and its representational norms and stuff that seems, within the terms of those norms, more or less peripheral, more or less dispensable. (We will return to the technical difference between "bound" and "free" narrative materials in Sections 5.2 and 6.2.)

Aristotle's, Forster's, and Miller's respective senses of what makes some events more or less appropriate to a given narrative anticipate recent discussions of *narrativity*, a contested term that some narrative theorists invoke in order both to differentiate between actions or events that lend themselves more and less readily to narrative representation and to account for the degree to which some narratives seem somehow more narrative than others; although it is hard to say why, we seem to know or to feel that a story about a car accident has a greater degree of *narrativity* than one about a good night's sleep despite the fact that both are representations of actions or events (crashing and sleeping). *Narrativity* is thus something like pornography: although it is hard to define, we know it when we see it. For H. Porter Abbott, *narrativity* "is a vexed issue, and as with many issues in the study of narrative there is no definite test that can tell us to what degree narrativity is present."[11] In one way, *narrativity* touches on the very Aristotelian question of what qualifies as an appropriate action in a given narrative; as David Herman points out, narrative can serve as a test of what does and does not rise to the level of representable action within particular social or existential contexts: "Protocols are needed to distinguish a range of discrete, more or less richly profiled acts – acts located in a storyworld – from an undifferentiated mass or agglomeration of behaviors. In this construal, narrative furnishes a heuristic for marking off regions of purposive action within the general field of activity."[12] The contextual difference between higher and lower levels of narrativity becomes for Herman one way to understand what makes one action or event different from another. Narrativity is also seen less as a quality of the actions that make up a narrative than as a quality of whole narratives themselves. Gerald Prince, for instance, defines narrativity as "the set of properties characterizing narratives and distinguishing them from non-narratives."[13] Prince points to a number of qualities (wholeness, conflict, the presence of "discrete, particular, positive, and temporally distinct actions," etc.) that seem to contribute to a given narrative's or narrative event's relative quotient of narrativity.[14] Similarly, Marie-Laure Ryan has argued that *narrativity* is a measure of the degree to which a particular narrative depicts a world of "particular entities and events" and makes "that world coherent and intelligible by evoking a network of relations . . . among the entities and events"; for Ryan, narrativity is less something that a text simply does or does not possess than it is "a fuzzy set allowing variable degrees of membership."[15]

While Herman's, Prince's, and Ryan's different senses of narrativity all depend on some account of the relation between action and representation, in *Towards a "Natural" Narratology*, Monika Fludernik makes the radical move of dissociating narrativity from action almost completely: "Most basic forms of narrative are exclusively built on an action scheme, but acting and thinking are equally part and parcel of the dynamic human predicament of living in a world with which one inevitably interacts."[16] In these terms, a car accident could be thought of as possessing a high degree of narrativity either because of its status as an act that motivates or leads to other acts or because it is what Fludernik calls a "mimetically motivated evocation of human consciousness and of its (sometimes chaotic) experience of being in the world."[17] We might think here of the difference between most cinematic representations of plane crashes – e.g., *Alive* (1993), *Cast Away* (2000), or *World War Z* (2013) – which exploit their status as defined events that lead to and stem from other sharply delineated events, and the representation of the unnamed narrator/protagonist's (Ed Norton) *fantasy* of a plane crash in *Fight Club* (1999): "Every time the plane banked too sharply on take-off or landing, I prayed for a crash, or a mid-air collision – anything." Although a lot happens, the scene attends more to the *experience* or *feeling* of a plane crash than to the event itself; the shot pans deliberately across the plane as wind tears it apart and then cuts back to the narrator's detached and yet curious, maybe titillated gaze. The scene's pace also seems to fall somewhere between fast and slow, giving its presentation of destruction an oddly considered feel. These different aspects – the shot's focus on the narrator's or focalizer's perspective, its neutral treatment of destruction, and its measured pacing all join to create an especially *experiential* kind of narrativity. Although the two effects – plane crash as act or plane crash as experience – are very different, they both *feel* narrative. For Fludernik, accounts that have focused too closely on the action as the minimal unit of plot fail to see what is differently narrative about the experiential example; they fail, in other words, to see the necessary relation between narrative and consciousness, a relation that allows us to imagine narratives without plot, an allowance that becomes all the more important in the face of modernist or postmodernist texts that undermine traditional expectations about plot and plot structure; she writes that "it is only by redefining narrative on the basis of consciousness that its continuing relevance can be maintained."[18]

It is, I think, with something like narrativity in mind that Aristotle acknowledged that one needs to make decisions about what belongs and does not belong in a given narrative, a decision made both on the basis of what an event is and on the basis of how those events ultimately fit together into a plotted whole; and, insofar as those choices both are governed by the demands of interest, form, or genre and ultimately determine what form the narrative discourse will take, they will determine the nature of the narrative itself. To continue with Aristotle's own example: we can imagine how a different selection of the same events could have resulted in a very different *Odyssey*. One could, for instance, imagine an avant-garde, Warholesque *Odyssey* that ignored all action and instead focused entirely on Odysseus's periods of sleep or an absurd, existentialist *Odyssey* where everyone sits around and talks about where Odysseus is and when he is coming home; or we might think of Kafka's retelling of Odysseus's encounter with the Sirens, in which he focuses not on the narratively rich idea of Odysseus's hearing the Sirens while lashed to his ship's mast but rather on the curiously dull idea of Odysseus, his ears plugged with wax, *not* hearing the Sirens, who, in any case, were not singing anyway: "But Odysseus – let us put it like this – did not hear their silence."[19] This is also the kind of experiment that Jean Rhys and Tom Stoppard offered with *Wide Sargasso Sea* and *Rosencrantz and Guildenstern Are Dead*. In both cases, they created plots out of the unrepresented events that were implied by but left out of their respective source texts, *Jane Eyre* and *Hamlet*. Aristotle's emphasis on the selection of events is thus less trivial than it might have seemed; he accentuates the intentional nature of the narrative selection of events in order to differentiate representation from action, to highlight the crucial difference that the selection of events at the level of discourse makes, and to accentuate the degree to which all representations – good or bad – are at last *made*.

In addition to underscoring the made quality of plots and the necessary selection of events, Aristotle calls particular attention to the temporal arrangement of events in discourse; he writes that "plot ... is simply this, the combination of the incidents."[20] Whereas an action needs to follow certain natural laws (causes occur before effects, a past occurs before a present that in turn occurs before a future), an *imitation* of an action can begin at the beginning of the action, can leap into story *in medias res* (as with the *Odyssey* or the *Iliad*), or start at the end before flashing back (as with *Oedipus Rex* where the crime takes place *before* the plot begins and much of the play's necessary action – the murder of the father, the riddle of the Sphinx, etc. – is revealed only in backward-looking exposition). This is why Aristotle takes care to offer a relational and oddly precise definition of the three temporal components of plot: "A beginning is that which is not itself necessarily after anything else, and which has naturally something else after it; an end is that which is naturally after something itself, either as its necessary or usual consequent, and with nothing else after it; and a middle, that which is by nature after one thing and has also another after it."[21] The point here is not only that beginnings, middles, and ends only have value in relation to each other (you cannot, after all, have a middle without a beginning or end), but that actions and events take on different meanings when we put them in the merely structural position of beginning or end. The same event (a birth, a marriage, a death) will mean something very different depending on where it falls in the represented discourse of a narrative. The ordering of events is, in that case, one way in which representation confers significance on life, one way in which discourse not only represents events but also gives value to events it represents.

For instance, the first pages of the *Odyssey*, with their invocation of the Muse and the introduction of Odysseus's son, Telemachus, do not represent the earliest events in the story. Homer instead starts in the middle of things – *in medias res* – and then turns back in order to narrate events that occurred chronologically *before* the poem's beginning; and, because we start with the son instead of the father, the poem encourages us to see the *Odyssey* as a poem about generations, inheritance, and futurity in a way that we might otherwise not. This is something that the poet Tennyson brings out in his abbreviated Victorian retelling of the tale: "This is my son, mine own Telemachus, / To whom I leave the sceptre and the isle."[22] How different the *Odyssey* would seem if, like *Citizen Kane* (1941), it began with the hero's death; or, if like *Tristram Shandy* (1759–1767), it lingered for pages and pages on the obstetric details of Odysseus's birth. In other words, Homer arranges the discrete actions in a particular order with a particular emphasis in order to produce the specific aesthetic representation and thus the specific aesthetic effect that we call the *Odyssey*.

And, if a "good" plot is, for Aristotle, made and ordered, it is also whole; he writes that "the story, as an imitation of action, must represent one action, a complete whole."[23] Where raw events rarely announce their ultimate significance in history or in everyday life, literary form allows us to imagine them as merging to produce a single significant whole; as a result, the brute fact of stuff happening is converted, as if by magic, into something meaningful. Everything fits; everything works. In part, Aristotle's sense of the immanent significance of the whole results from his sense of the innate order and value of living things, an idea that Plato anticipates in the *Phaedrus* when Socrates asks his interlocutor whether he will agree that "every speech must be put together like a living creature, with a body of its own; it must be neither without head nor without legs; and it must have a middle and extremities that are fitting both to one another and to the whole work."[24] Aristotle directly recalls this idea when he remarks in the *Poetics* that "beauty is a matter of size and order, and therefore impossible either in a very minute creature . . . or in a creature of vast size."[25] The point here is that the whole of a narrative is, indeed, more than the sum of its parts and that, like organic life, wholeness is something that both animates and exceeds the material things that would seem to make it up.[26] As a result, when we look for the meaning of a narrative, we should, Aristotle suggests, look less to the parts than to the organizing relation that stands between, over, and above those parts; and, what is more, that relation needs to be understood as an effect of an author's informing mere events – the ordered parts of a plot – with a discursive design that converts them into something whole.

Wayne Booth paraphrases Aristotle's investment in a whole plot in this way: in a successful work of narrative art "the *parts* do their job fittingly, they have been *made* to fit, to fit better than the parts fit in that other comedy or tragedy or meditative sonnet or tragic opera."[27] (As we will see in Section 4.1, Booth's understanding of narrative as a rhetorical act sees its wholeness as the result of the shaping intention of an addresser as he or she attempts to inform or to persuade an addressee, a position that he adapts more or less directly from his reading of Aristotle.) Aristotle's focus on the proportional structure of a work, on its effort to divide itself into an appropriately managed beginning, middle, and end, is an effect of Aristotle's decision to see the whole form of a narrative as something distinct from the content of its parts; Paul Ricœur writes that Aristotelian plot, in this sense, is "an integrating dynamism that draws a unified and complete story from a variety of incidents, in other words, that transforms this variety into a unified and complete story."[28] What in that case makes Aristotle's *Poetics* a recognizably *narrative* theory is the fact that he insists on the difference between actions and the representation of actions; that he recognizes that any representation of events must suggest the possibility of other, differently managed representations; and that he differentiates between good and bad representations on the basis of their ability to fit their different parts into a more or less proportional, coherent, and thus aesthetically and emotionally satisfying whole.

~

Fair enough. Why, though, did Aristotle insist on the importance of the difference between actions and representations of actions? Why put so much emphasis on a distinction between the *what* and the *how* of narrative? For one, it is important to see Aristotle's sense of plot as a representation of actions in relation to his great teacher and rival Plato.[29] Because Aristotle sees the difference between an action and a tragic representation of an action as more or less clear, more or less intuited, he assumes that audiences will also see that difference, that they will not be fooled or confused into thinking that a representation of life could take the place of life itself. Because mimetic representations announce themselves *as* representations; because they bear the visible traces of the intentional activity that went into transforming a sequence of actions into a single, structured representation of those actions; because, once again, they are *made*, there is little chance that a reader could confuse a representation of life with life itself. Aryeh Kosman writes that Aristotle thus "reminds us of the iconicity, the fictionalizing modality of artistic representation," which is to say to its announced difference from and relation to a world.[30] This is why tragedy's potentially horrible mix of pity and fear produces pleasure instead of or at least significantly in addition to pain in Aristotle; he writes that "the tragic pleasure is that of pity and fear, and the poet has to produce it by a work of imitation; it is clear, therefore, that the causes should be included in the incidents of his story."[31] Because narratives alert us to their artifice, to the difference between an action and the representation of an action, we are able to enjoy them with enough critical distance so as not to lose ourselves. This is why we can enter a theater and watch Oedipus's sufferings with a distinctly aesthetic mix of sympathy, pleasure, and dread (what Aristotle calls *catharsis*); to lose sight, even for a moment, of the tragedy's artifice would be intolerable.

Plato, less sanguine about the obvious difference between art and life, worried about the ethical consequences of poetry, about the possibility that representations of life might distort our view of life and thus lead to bad or misguided or antisocial behavior. This is why he famously argues in the *Republic* that poets should be exiled: "All such poetry is likely to distort the thought of anyone who hears it, unless he has the knowledge of what it is really like, as a drug to counteract it."[32] Poets pose a threat to the stability of a society because their representations interfere with a citizen's ability to see things clearly. The question of literature's seductive ability to distort or derange our sense of things derives in part from Plato's theory of forms, his sense that the perceptible world of things reflects a more perfect, ideal realm; Stephen Halliwell writes that "In his account of the creation of the world [Plato] explicitly describes the visible world as being as like as possible to the eternal 'in the mimesis of unchanging nature': the world is a *mimema* of a model, and all the transient shapes and properties which come into being in the stuff of the world are themselves '*mimemata* of eternal objects.'"[33] For Plato, our world is a mere reflection of more universal, more stable truths; our limited, human experience of the world is thus a poor representation, a degraded copy of something prior and pure. As a result, what we might call the second- or third-order mimetic representations of literature offer real and potentially deranging competition with "real" representations of forms and thus have the capacity to distort a citizen's understanding of his or her relation to the world. Although or, rather, *because* they are at best copies of copies and thus removed from the truth of things, literary representations can interfere with a citizen's ability to see the world and the republic clearly. That is why Plato says that poets, the makers of second- or third-order representations, should be exiled: literary representations are too powerful, too seductive to tolerate. It is, of course, no coincidence that Plato's own greatest works are themselves literary representations of real or imagined conversations between Socrates and other eminent Athenians. If you believed that literature can do so much to convince, persuade, and seduce, it would of course be a hard thing to give it up.

Aristotle's response to Plato thus involves a self-conscious reduction of literature's power to affect individuals and the world. G. M. A. Grube writes with some knowing exaggeration: "Indeed, it is a curious paradox of literary history that the author of probably the most famous, and certainly the most influential, critical work on poetry had, quite obviously, very little feeling for poetry, and a much more restricted view of its importance than his predecessor."[34] Because Aristotle does not subscribe to Plato's theory of forms and does not see the phenomenal world as a reflection or representation of something more real and more true, the representational nature of literature and, more specifically, literary narratives does not pose a political or ethical threat to life. Literary representations cannot and do not compete with the real. As Halliwell puts it, Aristotle "reacts against [Plato's] view of mimesis by releasing the artist from the obligation of transcribing or reproducing reality in any straightforward way, by charging mimesis with the power of embodying universals rather than particulars, and by treating the poet not as an affirmer . . . but as a skillful maker of dramatic fictions."[35]

Three aspects of Aristotle's response to Plato are important to highlight here: first, literary representations announce themselves as fictions in a way that both neutralizes their political threat and draws a reader's attention to them as literary fictions, as, in other words, imaginative and artful constructions as opposed to simple reflections of or alternatives to the world; second, because narratives are constructions, they need to be assessed not (or at least not only) in terms of their relation to the world but rather in terms of their structural coherence. What makes a work a good representation of an action is the fact that its parts (beginning, middle, and end) join into an appropriate and coherent whole. The representation demands, in other words, that it be assessed on its own terms. And, third, Aristotle's thinking about the structural nature of tragedy does seem at least to imply a theory of politics and the state. While readers have sometimes seen the *Poetics* as distinct from Aristotle's other philosophical or political concerns, its implicit or at least possible origin in an argument with Plato about the dangers that literature might pose to the hearts and minds of a republic's citizens is important to bear in mind. Read in relation to Plato, the *Poetics* can perhaps be seen as an effort to save a place in the state for art and its undeniably political ability to produce pity and fear, to order discrete events into a larger aesthetic whole, and, indeed, to affect minds and to make life meaningful; and insofar as what saves the aesthetic might be the difference between *story* and *discourse*, this possibility has important consequences for an account of narrative theory.

~

Aristotle's division of tragedy into actions and representations of actions should be seen in relation to tragedy's special role in Athenian culture, where it was one aspect of what Raymond Williams would call a whole "structure of feeling"; according to Williams, the characteristic features of tragedy as an art form and as a shared social experience

> were not systematized by the Greeks themselves: it is a culture marked
> by an extraordinary network of beliefs connected to institutions,
> practices and feelings, but not by the systematic and abstract doctrines
> we would now call a theology or a tragic philosophy. The deepest
> inquiries and modes of understanding run back, continually, into
> particular myths, and this quality is of critical importance in
> understanding the nature of the art.[36]

Although, as Aristotle acknowledges, a few tragedies were written about avowedly fictional characters, the majority were based on widely shared legends, most of them about the lives of a few families from the doomed city of Thebes; Deborah H. Roberts writes that "like much of ancient literature," Greek tragedy "took its plots primarily from a body of stories that were continuous with each other and to some extent known to audience or reader."[37] As a result, audiences seeing most of the many tragedies produced in the fifth century would have already been familiar with the events of a given play; Peter Burian writes that "from the point of view of plot, the history of Greek tragedy is one of continuously recasting tales already known to the audience."[38] Although viewers would have gone to a play knowing more or less *what* was going to happen, they could not have known *how* a given tragedian was going to present those familiar events; that, presumably, is part of why they went. Tragedy in fifth-century Athens thus offered viewers a special opportunity to think about the nature of narrative design and, more to the point, about the difference between familiar actions or events and original or innovative aesthetic representations of those familiar actions or events. Because Athenian tragedy forced poets and audiences to confront the differ-ence between a particular and idiosyncratic literary representation and a shared communal myth, it put them and, later, Aristotle in a position to reflect on the structure of tragic plots in a way that anticipates narrative theory's story–discourse relation. Because almost every viewer of Athenian tragedy would have had a strong sense of the difference between the shared source material and the discursive form that that material took in any given instance, almost every viewer of Athenian tragedy was, as it were, a natural narrative theorist, a more or less self-conscious analyst of the formative difference between events and the aesthetic representation of events.

~

Aristotle's methodological focus on tragedy as a particular literary representation of a shared set of communal myths raises other important if less obvious social consequences. As I have already said, Aristotle manages – against Plato – to tame literature by positing a real and visible difference between actions and representations of actions, between the messy stuff of life and a "fitting" fictive representation of some parts of life as a whole and single thing. Although it does clarify some issues, this difference leaves the reader or audience looking simultaneously at two different kinds of things: the discrete events that take place as a plot unfolds over time and that plot insofar as it is viewed as a separate and whole thing. One needs as a viewer to toggle back and forth between what we might call a local and a global view of a given tragedy: its parts are significant because they fit within a larger structural whole and that structural whole is significant because it is made up of those same parts. The events need the plot, the plot needs the events, and it becomes increasingly difficult the more one thinks about it to determine which of the two takes priority. As I pointed out in the Introduction, the question of priority has bedeviled narrative theory from the beginning: does story make discourse or does discourse make story? Do events precede their representation, or does a representation somehow *produce* events as significant and thus knowable? It makes sense, in that case, that we would find this paradox in Aristotle; it also makes sense, given the resolutely synthetic character of Aristotle's thinking, that its consequences would exceed a merely literary reading of the *Poetics*.

The great classicist Jean-Pierre Vernant argues that something like the paradox of story and discourse is central to Aristotle's view of tragedy; for Vernant, Athenian tragedy is fundamentally about the simultaneous social experience of two different orders of time: "The drama brought to the stage unfolds both at the level of everyday existence, in a human, opaque time made up of successive and limited present moments, and also beyond this earthly life, in a divine, omnipresent time that at every instant encompasses the totality of events, sometimes to conceal them and sometimes to make them plain but always so that nothing escapes or is lost in oblivion."[39] For Vernant, this tension between what he calls "the time of men and the time of the gods" is part of what gives tragedy its celebrated capacity to reflect deeply on questions of fate and free will. What feels and is indeed contingent from any situated human perspective must also and at the same time be fated in the time of the gods, and it is the necessary difference between those two perspectival aspects of one and the same narrative that gives tragedy its emotional and explanatory force. In an essay on the place of this same conflict as it appears in the writing of history, Hannah Arendt notes that, "This paradox, that greatness was understood in terms of permanence while human greatness was seen in precisely the most futile and least lasting activities of men, has haunted Greek poetry and historiography as it has perturbed the quiet of the philosophers."[40] And Barbara Goward, writing about the narrative form of Greek tragedy, casts this same difference in technical terms:

> Greek tragedy, speaking very generally, gives rise to two experiences
> of time: the synchronic time of many of the *stasima* (lyric sections),
> capable of vast shifts of temporal perspective, conspectuses and parallels,
> tangential reflections on age, the power of love, capacity of man and so
> forth, and the more immediate diachronic time of the iambic trimeter
> sections of episodes (non-lyric sections) in which individual characters
> are seen moving through time towards fixed end points.[41]

Tragedy is thus defined by an internal tension – a conflict, if you will – between events as autonomous, discrete, and apparently meaningless in and of themselves and events as they exist in relation to each other and as significant parts of a coherent and meaningful whole.

Vernant goes on to argue that this motivating conflict between two kinds of time – the limited, partial time of human beings and the unlimited, totalizing time of the gods – was the result of social shifts particular to fifth-century Athens, a moment when two powerful but incommensurate systems of belief found themselves at odds: "The drama brings to the stage an ancient heroic legend. For the city this legendary world constitutes a past – a past sufficiently distant for the contrasts, between the mythical traditions that it embodies and the new forms of legal and political thought, to be clearly visible; yet a past still close enough for the clash of values still to be a painful one and for this clash still to be currently taking place."[42] According to Vernant, tragedy emerges in fifth-century Athens as a particular if coded response to the incomplete transition from a city-state grounded in a belief in the direct and mysterious power of the gods to one based in a rationalized set of legal codes that would slowly and incompletely supplant those earlier beliefs. According to Vernant, this felt transition is, for instance, visible in Greek tragedy's tendency to rely awkwardly on a legal language both properly and poorly suited to the events at hand:

> The tragic writers' use of a technical legal vocabulary underlines the affinities between the most favored tragic themes and certain cases that fell within the competence of the courts. The institution of these courts was sufficiently recent for the novelty of the values determining their establishment and governing their activity still to be fully appreciated. The tragic poets make use of this legal vocabulary, deliberately exploiting its ambiguities, its fluctuations, and its incompleteness. We find an imprecision in the terms used, shifts in meaning, incoherences and contradictions, all of which reveal disagreement within legal thought itself and also betray its conflicts with a religious tradition and moral thought from which the law is already distinct but whose domains are still not clearly differentiated from its own.[43]

Tragedy, in Vernant's view, is thus essentially ambiguous because it is a response to a state that was itself the product of what Rebecca Bushnell identifies as "a tension between the past and the present . . . tragic characters are bound by their own histories, but they still live in the present of their performance."[44] Tragedy is, in other words, an embodied "confrontation between the ways of the past and those of the present," which tragedians cast in terms of an equally absolute but maybe more narratable confrontation between persons and gods, fate and free will.[45]

What is more important here is that that confrontation also finds expression in two kinds of narrative time, the discrete, broken, limited, and human time of events as events and the form that that human time takes when it is seen as viewed, formed, and ordered from the suprahistorical position of the gods, a position from which discrete events must add up to something greater. It is a conflict between an obscure and partial human time and time experienced as a larger, more significant, and finished whole; it is the conflict between what Oedipus *thinks* he knows about the world and what the world, as represented by the blind seer Tiresias, in fact knows about him. Tragic conflict is, in other words, an embodied and philosophical conflict between story and discourse, between unprocessed events experienced as one follows the other and what those events look like when organized into a whole and coherent representation. Vernant helps, in other words, to reveal an analogy among three orders of experience: the social tension between the Athenian experience of the time of men and the time of the gods; the tension between free will and fate as it was thematized in Athenian tragedy; and the tension between events and the whole representations of events as it structured those same tragedies and, indeed, as it structures narrative as such.

We can put the large and frankly speculative case this way: Aristotle could more or less "discover" narrative theory in the wake of the rise and fall of Greek tragedy in the fifth century because of the way tragic writers had embedded an awareness of historical crisis in the very form of their tragedies. One can see this in their reliance on a shared set of communal myths and legends, stories familiar to almost everyone, as well as in their use of ambiguously dated legal language, in the tensions that exist within the great tragic characters, and in the very structure of tragic plotting. In each case, one can see an effort to work through the feeling and the consequences of social changes that were taking place in Athens, a shift from one system of practices and beliefs, one based in the felt if bewildering presence of the gods, to another, one based in an increasingly secular and democratic but nonetheless partial codification of the law. Tragic narrative forms were, in other words, one way not only to manage but also to embody the feeling of history as it happened.

This instability was, for instance, apparent in the fifth-century legal principle of *pragmatic innovation*, a term that Melissa Schwartzberg uses to refer to Athens's willingness to change its laws as it went along: "The flexibility of the law in the fifth century had the consequence of unpredictability, because the laws were changed so frequently that it was difficult to anticipate the consequences of actions."[46] In these terms, the experience of Athenian democracy was lived in the space between events as they occurred and what those events might in time come to mean. Indeed, this Athenian tendency to change course midstream, at once exciting and disturbing, appears in Thucydides as one cause of the Peloponnesian War. Faced with Athens's bewildering, charismatic, and characteristic capacity for change and growth, the conservative Spartans felt they had no choice but to go to war: "It is the law, as in the arts so in politics, that improvements ever prevail; and though fixed usages may be best for undisturbed communities, constant necessities of action must be accompanied by the constant improvement of methods."[47] And because the Spartans were waging war not only against the Athenians but also against the Athenians' seemingly innate capacity for innovation, change, and self-reflection, their war as, as it were, a war with narrative itself.

We can thus see Aristotle's *Poetics* as a response to this remarkable moment insofar as it is a narrative theory, which is to say that it is an account of how a particular narrative genre motivated the relation between story and discourse in order not only to represent a prior historical moment – the legendary families of Thebes – but also to register and to try, however incompletely, to account for the experience of historical change in the present. Where a character like Oedipus was always more or less blind because he could not see – as no one can see – what happened before and would happen after his place in the present, an audience's almost certain familiarity with the whole Theban legend combined with the play's self-conscious status as an organic whole made up of a beginning, middle, and end to produce an effect of nearly timeless inevitability. The narrative experience of tragedy was, in that case, a doubled or divided experience of an internal and suspenseful seeing of individual events as they unfolded and an external and certain sense of how individual events would and, in fact, already did hang together. In this sense, the narrative distinction between what Vernant calls the time of men and the time of the gods anticipates a distinction that narrative theory makes between these two aspects of any narrative; Emma Kafalenos writes that "for one to be able to grasp a number of events as a configuration entails being able to grasp individual relationships between event and event, and event and configuration. These individual relationships, when combined, form the network of relationships that seeing-events-together implies. The two perspectives I distinguish are two aspects of the same act, but the distinction is important in defining the act."[48] In other words, the historical conditions of Athenian tragedy both produced a form and demanded a theory that could manage two different aspects of the same historical moment: the experience of event as discrete and autonomous event and the feeling or, rather, the hope that events would come to make sense in relation to one another. This might be one way to read Aristotle's famous claim that literature is philosophically superior to history; because literature deals in probabilities – not only what happened but also what could have happened – it has the potential to represent the *process* of historical change as well as the historical events themselves. We might say, in that case, that where one needs a theory of history to say what has already happened one needs a theory of narrative in order to account for the present fact and feeling of history itself. Athenian tragedy and the historical conflicts that it sought formally to embody demanded a narrative theory; and that is what Aristotle offers in the *Poetics*.

~

This is one reason why *Oedipus Rex* takes on the status of what we might call a *masterplot* in Aristotle, a narrative against which all or many others might be measured or compared; H. Porter Abbott writes that "the greatest *masterplots* are narrativized over and over again because they engage conflicts that seem to be a permanent part of our circumstances as human beings."[49]

Aristotle makes the case in characteristically muted terms, praising Sophocles' play for its ability to use dramatic plot in and of itself to produce a particular set of tragic feelings:

> The tragic fear and pity may be aroused by the spectacle; but they may also be aroused by the very structure and incidents of the play – which is the better way and shows the better poet. The plot in fact should be so framed that, even without seeing the things take place, he who simply hears the account of them shall be filled with horror and pity at the incidents; which is just the effect that the mere recital of the story in *Oedipus* would have on one.[50]

As opposed to a play that would rely on shock or spectacle to produce its effects, *Oedipus* works on its audience as a result of qualities immanent to the play's plot. Fear and pity are *essential* to *Oedipus Rex* because they are necessary effects of its plot, which is to say an effect of the way it manages the representation of events at the level of narrative discourse.

For Vernant, what Aristotle takes as the aesthetic and emotional force of *Oedipus Rex* is once again absolutely particular to a moment in the history of ancient Greece. Like tragedy itself, Oedipus embodies an unfinished tension between two incommensurate but nonetheless powerful ideas, the idea of the divine authority of the gods and the idea of the secular power of human laws. On the one hand, Oedipus is the man who defeated the Sphinx by answering its riddle; he is a man who sees more than other men and thus approaches the status of the divine; on the other hand, he is a very human king, a leader who, at his moment of greatest power, claims not to need the gods in order to live and to rule; Vernant writes that "seen from a human point of view, Oedipus is the leader with second sight, the equal of the gods; considered from the point of view of the gods he is blind, equal to nothing. Both the reversal of action and the ambiguity of the language reflect the duality of the human condition that, just like a riddle lends itself to two opposite interpretations."[51] This duality is both a reflection of a particular moment in the political history of Athens and something more general.

The essential doubleness of Oedipus, the tension between human will and divine fate, between the law of the state and the justice of the gods, is indeed already present in the riddle of the Sphinx, the riddle that Oedipus solves and that puts him on the throne of Thebes and into the incestuous marriage bed of his mother, Jocasta. The Romantic prose writer Thomas de Quincey summarizes this part of the story in this way:

> The riddle proposed by the Sphinx ran in these terms: "What creature is that which moves on four feet in the morning, on two feet at noonday,

and on three towards the going down of the sun?" Oedipus, after some consideration, answered that the creature was MAN, who creeps on the ground with hands and feet when an infant, walks upright in the vigor of manhood, and leans upon a staff in old age. Immediately the dreadful Sphinx confessed the truth of his solution by throwing herself headlong from a point of rock into the sea; her power being overthrown as soon as her secret had been detected. Thus was the Sphinx destroyed; and, according to the promise of the proclamation, for this great service to the state Oedipus was immediately recompensed. He was saluted King of Thebes, and married to the royal widow Jocasta. In this way it happened, but without suspicion either in himself or others, pointing to the truth, that Oedipus had slain his father, had ascended his father's throne, and had married his own mother.[52]

Sophocles does not represent the scene of the riddle and its solution directly; Oedipus and others make frequent reference to it as a founding event, but it itself is left in the background or on the outside of *Oedipus Rex*. This is partly because, as with so much of the Theban cycle, Sophocles could count on the fact that Athenian audiences would have been familiar with the story of Oedipus's intellectual achievement. Archaeological work has in fact shown that the image of Oedipus standing before the Sphinx was one of the most popular motifs in Greek decorative art; Almut-Barbara Renger writes that "of the roughly one hundred images of the hero that are known to us (predominantly painted on vases), over 70 percent feature this scene, and roughly 40 percent come from the fifth century BCE, from the time before *Oedipus the King*."[53] Although the original wording of the Sphinx's riddle has been lost,

> the most reliable reconstruction of the riddle is based on a compilation of relatively late antique texts in Greek. An English translation reads: "There is a creature on earth which has two and four feet, a voice, and three feet; of all the creatures that live on earth, in the air and in the sea, it alone can change its nature. But the strength of its limbs is at its lowest precisely when it supports itself on the greatest number of feet."[54]

Although there is much to say about the Sphinx's enigma, I want to look just for a moment at the ambiguously narrative nature of the riddle and its solution. In its most familiar form, the answer "man" is indeed a deeply narrative answer. It counts on the fact that, although we see men and women at different moments in time, those moments will come to make sense within the larger context of a *whole* life; it is an answer that anticipates Aristotle's sense that the best plot is the plot that sees the significance of the event in relation to a beginning, middle, and end. "Man" indeed names the whole relation among the three necessary parts of this narrative: youth as beginning, maturity as middle, and old age as end. The riddle and its solution are, in other words, a coded and condensed theory of plot. Oedipus's solution to the riddle is thus a minimal instance of the narrative logic that Aristotle sees Sophocles' play as so successfully embodying. As it turns out, the solution to the tragic riddle is the structural fact of the tragic plot itself, the plot that can more or less string together the isolated events of a life into a luminous and significant whole; and, insofar as it shows how events join to form a plot, the solution to the riddle is a condensed form of the story–discourse relation: it is narrative in a pure if attenuated or rather reduced form. It is, in that case, significant that Oedipus's answer leads not to greater sense but rather to catastrophe: plot, it seems, cannot save us.

De Quincey accounts for the ultimate failure of Oedipus's solution with another, related answer to the riddle:

> For, in our opinion, the full and *final* answer to the Sphinx's riddle lay in the word "Oedipus." Oedipus himself it was that fulfilled the conceptions of the enigma. He it was, in the most pathetic sense, that went upon four feet when an infant … that, in a more emphatic sense than usual, asserted the majestic self-sufficientness and independence of all alien aid, which is typified by the act of walking upright at noonday … [and] that by his cruel sons would have been rejected from Thebes, with no auxiliary means of motion or support beyond his own languishing powers: blind and broken-hearted, he must have wandered into snares and ruin; his own feet must have been supplanted immediately: but then came to his aid another foot, the holy Antigone.[55]

De Quincey goes on to praise the riddle precisely for its doubleness, for the fact "that it contains an exoteric sense obvious to all the world, but also an esoteric sense – now suggested conjecturally after thousands of years – possibly unknown to the Sphinx, and certainly unknown to Oedipus; that this second riddle is hid within the first; that the one riddle is the secret commentary upon the other; and that the earliest is the hieroglyphic of the last."[56] What, in other words, de Quincey sees is that the riddle is significant precisely because it calls attention to the tragic ambiguity of Oedipus's situation and, maybe more, to the essential doubleness of the tragic plot. Oedipus the man is a particular thing that instantiates of the general category *man*; he is the part as it is more or less representative of the whole; he is a living representative of the tragic conflict between the time of men and the time of the gods that, as I have suggested, animated tragedy for the Greeks of the fifth century. Alex Woloch writes that "it is precisely in solving the riddle that Oedipus misses his own name; in fact, just as he becomes aware of what man is (the creature with four, two, then three legs), he also offers a new definition of what man is (the creature who is *aware* that he walks on four, two, then three legs)."[57] As "man," he is a narrative; as "Oedipus," he is the bearer or the beginning of a narrative theory, the self-conscious figure who, as one of literature's first detectives, works to reconstruct the events of the past into narrative order for the present.[58]

We should go even further: if "man" and "Oedipus" can stand as two ambiguously nested answers to one and the same riddle, two answers that meet to trace out a relation among the object, the occasion, and the nature of narrative theory, there is yet a third solution, one that points to and beyond the importance of narrative form to the idea and experience of Greek tragedy. Vernant writes of the riddle that

> confusing and mixing them up, it referred to the three successive ages of man that he can only know one after another: He is a child when he crawls on four legs, an adult when he stands firmly on his two feet, and an old man leaning on his stick. By identifying himself [through his incestuous relation with his mother] simultaneously with his young children and his old father, Oedipus, the man standing on his two feet, obliterates the barriers that ought to keep the father strictly separate from the sons and the grandfather so that each human generation occupies its appointed place both in the sequence of time and in the order of the city. Here is the last tragic reversal: It is his victory over the Sphinx that turns Oedipus into, not the solution that he guessed, but the very question posed, not a man like other men but a creature of confusion and chaos.[59]

Read in this way, the riddle is not a matter of the different stages of a life, beginning, middle, and end, but rather an anticipation of Oedipus's own tragic because incestuous end. Who is a son, a brother, a husband, and a father all at once and to the same people? Oedipus. This is, on the one hand, to see the political problem that Oedipus raises. At a moment when the city-state was in the process of consolidating itself as a secular and political entity, the threat of incest revealed the structural vulnerability of any system based on the clarity of differential relations among its participants (sovereign and subject; citizen and slave; husband and wife; mother, father, and child). Marc Shell writes that "the widespread practice of incest would lead to a radical transformation of the body politic since such sexual liberty would restructure kinship relations by destroying the crucial distinction between generations. Teleologically, incest dissolves the *pater* (father) in the *liber* (son) and replaces the patriarchy with a radical egalitarian liberty. It establishes what Tiresias calls 'a grim equality between you and your children.'"[60] In *Oedipus Rex*, this "radical egalitarian liberty" is a *narrative* problem insofar as incest seems to dissolve the causal, generational plot that relies on the division of generations into beginnings, middles, and ends. The incestuous crux of Oedipus's story thus functions as a third and even more esoteric solution to the riddle of the Sphinx, an anti-narrative core that threatens precisely to undo efforts to put the particular and the general into some larger, plotted relation. The riddle thus offers us three solutions that inform the tragic structure of *Oedipus Rex* and contribute to the early narrative theory of Aristotle's *Poetics*: the beginning–middle–end narrative of "man," the self-conscious theoretical act of reflecting on that narrative that is "Oedipus," and the at-once tragic and immanent limit to both narrative and narrative theory that is "incest": Oedipus as the existential confusion of son, brother, husband, and father, beginning, middle, and end.

~

As I have said, that tension between the particular and the general, the local event and the whole of a plot, is a tension essential to Aristotle's understanding of narrative as a system of discrete parts that add up to a significant, coherent, and proportional whole. According to one definition, a tragic perspective emerges when one can see the parts and maybe *feel* the whole, but be unable to put them together, when we come up against that fundamental limit. Deborah Roberts writes that this encounter with the limit is essential to Greek tragedy:

> It is a commonplace of contemporary narratology that we seek to give narrative structures to our lives as well as to out fictions, and that our desire for bounded narratives is in part a way of dealing with our inability to be fully aware of either our own beginning or our own end, let alone what precedes or follows. Greek culture generally, and tragedy in particular, show a concern both with escaping the boundedness of the human perspective (consider the role of oracles) and with establishing boundaries (consider the role of oracles).[61]

Where Roberts and Vernant take this feel for the limit as a philosophical and political aspect of tragedy in Aristotle, we can see, too, that it gets at a tension necessary to maybe every narrative: where we experience a book or a film one page or one frame at a time, it is the fact that these pages and moments are always already part of a greater, single, and in some strong sense timeless whole that allows them to make what sense they do. We can, for instance, see Milton exploring a different but related version of this problem in Book 12 of *Paradise Lost* (1667). After hearing the angel Michael prophetically lay out the whole of human history, Adam responds, "How soon hath thy prediction, Seer Blest, / Measur'd this transient World, the Race of time, / Till time stand fix: beyond is all abyss, / Eternity, whose end no eye can reach."[62] Adam is, in other words, reflecting both at the marvel of the angel's prophecy and, more humbly, at the difference between human and divine points of view; where, from a human perspective, to live in time is to experience one isolated and thus inexplicable event after the other, God's view of time is paradoxically timeless. It is time and transience seen as "fixt," which is to say, it is a story where the real trees of detail are ultimately subordinate to the discursive forest of beginning, middle, and end. We can see a very different but nonetheless related version of this same tension between time and timelessness at the beginning *and* end of the second season of *Breaking Bad* (2009), a story about Walter White, chemistry teacher, meth dealer, and one more who would rather "reign in Hell than serve in Heav'n."[63] The first episode of that season opens on an eerie image of a charred pink teddy bear floating in a suburban pool. As that first episode unfolds, we realize that this image is from events that occur at the chronological end of the season; although we do not know, *someone* already knows where the bear is from, what it means, and what *will have happened* over the course of the next twelve episodes (an instance of what Genette would call narrative *prolepsis*). On the one hand, this is a tease, a lure that keeps us tuning in from week to week: where is the pink bear from? Who tore out its eye? Why has it been burned? On the other hand, it connects the season and the whole show back to the tradition that Aristotle explored in the *Poetics*. The fact that we know that the bear *will* burn, whatever it means, forces us to see the events that individual episodes comprise as part of a larger and very nearly tragic narrative. Walt and Jesse believe that they are free to act, to hustle, to break bad; we know, as anyone versed in the demands of tragedy would, that larger and inexorable forces are at work. In both Milton and *Breaking Bad* we see the same narrative logic that fired Aristotle's imagination. This structural tension between freedom and necessity, between time and timelessness, between narrative and its other, is thus at the heart of Aristotle's account of tragedy's considerable power and, as I will argue, an essential part of narrative theories that rely on an opposition between the what and the how of narrative form.

Aristotle's *Poetics* can in that case be read as an attempt to produce a theory of a genre that, in turn, was its own tragic and theoretical response to a period of political and legal uncertainty. As a result, we can see where a methodological division between events as lived and events as represented would have resonated beyond a local inquiry into literary form; that is, and as Aristotle and Plato both understood, representation had emerged not only as a sharply political problem but also as a form in which the difference between one world and another could be staged. Where, though, for Plato the difference was between a real world of ideal forms and our shadowy experience of it, for fifth-century tragedy and thus for Aristotle, the difference is a historical one, a difference between two only apparently different aspects of one and the same experience: it is, as Vernant points out, the practical, perspectival difference between the past and the present as embodied in uneven legal and political developments that had altered life in Athens. Aristotle's difference is, in other words, a historical difference and a narrative difference; as a result, the *Poetics* models a relation among history, politics, and narrative theory that I want to track in what follows.

2.2 Tragedy, Comedy, and the Cunning of Reason: Hegel and Narrative Theory

> "Begin at the beginning," the King said, very gravely, "and go on till you come to the end: then stop."
> Lewis Carroll, *Alice's Adventures in Wonderland*

In the previous Section I argued that Aristotle's *Poetics* should be read not only as one of the first works of systematic literary criticism but also as an early if not the earliest example of narrative theory, an effort, as I am defining it, to understand narrative in whatever medium as a relation between *story* and *discourse*, between the *what* and the *how* of a given narrative. Furthermore, I imagined two motivations for Aristotle's "discovery" of the story–discourse relation. First, his assertion of the apparent difference between actions and the representation of actions was a tacit response to anxieties about art expressed by Plato in the *Republic*. Where Plato worried that we might confuse aesthetic representations of the world with the world itself, Aristotle assumed that differences between made representations of the world and the world itself would be clear enough; this allowed him to see the difference both as a methodological opportunity and as something other than the hard problem it was for Plato. Second, I argued that we could understand the *Poetics* as a response to a set of historical crises and changes that characterized social and political life in fifth-century Athens and the tragic dramas that these changes inspired. Jean-Pierre Vernant and others have argued for the great tragic dramas of Sophocles, Euripides, and Aeschylus as embodied formal reactions to a shift from one system of beliefs to another, from an idea of a legendary "time of the gods" to the real, increasingly secular, and essentially inconstant legal systems that characterized Athenian democracy. What, in that case, gave fifth-century tragedy its character was its attempt to resolve the historical conflict between two incommensurate systems of value, systems that appear as dramatic conflicts between fate and free will, justice and law, or the "time of the gods" and the "time of men."

We can take this nested set of conflicts as an instance of what, in the *Topics*, Aristotle referred to as a "dialectical problem." Dialectical problems are "questions in regard to which deductions conflict (the difficulty then being whether so-and-so is so or not, there being convincing arguments for both views); others also in regard to which we have no argument because they are so vast, and we find it difficult to give our reasons, e.g. the question whether the universe is eternal or no; for into questions of that kind too it is possible to inquire."[64] Dialectical problems are, in other words, the problems that shape our approaches to other problems; they stand as a kind of structural and structuring limit to what we can and cannot think. We can, with this in mind, say that Athenian tragedies both contain and in fact are themselves "dialectical problems"; they are structured around a divide between two kinds of experience that take the form of ambiguities of character and theme as well as of an ambivalent narrative structure that depends on radically distinct forms of narrative perspective: the perspective of the event or part and the perspective of a narrative whole that both transcends and depends upon the part. And, because they highlight perspectival differences between a partial view of the discrete events that make up a narrative and a synthetic view of the narrative imagined as an organically whole beginning, middle, and end, these problematic tragedies demanded from Aristotle not only an account of narrative development but also and more specifically a theory that would anticipate the difference between story and discourse, which is to say the difference between narrative seen from the level of the event and narrative seen from the level of a whole representation of events.

Given its considerable power, it is striking that this sense of tragic narrative as defined by *conflict* more or less faded from view after Aristotle. Although one reading of Aristotle's *Poetics* emerged as a preeminent aesthetic theory during the Renaissance revival of tragic drama, it did so in a form that tended to overlook Aristotle's central sense of narrative, philosophical, and political conflict in favor of a more static insistence on the so-called unities of action, time, and place; as the French tragedian Pierre Corneille succinctly expressed it in his *Discourses* (1660), "It is necessary to observe unity of action, place, and time; that no one doubts."[65] It was not, in that case, until later that narrative conflict reappeared as central in both Athenian tragedy and in interpretations of Aristotle's interpretation of it. More to the point and for reasons that I will explore in this Section, it took the early nineteenth-century work of the great German philosopher Georg Wilhelm Friedrich Hegel to revive the historical and narrative stakes of Aristotle's implicit account of tragic conflict; as Dennis Schmidt argues, "It is Hegel above all who determines the modern appearance of the ancient question put by the tragic work of art. It is Hegel's legacy that one necessarily confronts when taking up the question of the tragic in the present age."[66] This is, of course, not to say that there are not important works that touch on the nature of narrative between Aristotle and Hegel; one could look to the great eleventh book of St. Augustine's *Confessions*, where he writes that "when a true narrative of the past is related, the memory produces not the actual events which have passed away but words conceived from images of them, which they fixed in the mind like imprints as they passed through the senses."[67] Or one could look to Chaucer's account of tragic plots in "The Monk's Prologue": "Tragedie is to seyn a certain storie, / As olde bookes maken us memorie, / Of hym that stood in greet prosperitee, / And is yfallen out of heigh degree / Into myserie, and endeth wrecchedly."[68] One could add other potential, practical, or incipient theorists of narrative to the list: Dante, Corneille, Racine, Shakespeare, Cervantes, Herder, Defoe, Rousseau, Austen, and so on. That said, even though these and many others have important things to say about narratives and how they work, I want to argue that it is with Hegel and with what Hegel helps us to see in Aristotle that narrative theory *as the analysis of a relation and a conflict between story and discourse* begins to take its recognizable and thus transmissible form.

I will argue that we can trace the inauguration of modern narrative theory as a distinct and emerging field of critical inquiry to Hegel's writing and to subsequent responses to his work; as I suggested in the Introduction, Hegel's turn to narrative should be seen partly as a result of historical events – the French Revolution, the rise of European nationalism, the emergence of Romantic ethnography – that made it necessary to think seriously about the fact that other people, other nations, other social classes can and do make different, competing, and nonetheless coherent narratives out of one and the same set of events. To understand how the same events, the same story could be differently represented in different discursive arrangements required a narrative theory. It was, as I will suggest, partly Hegel's deep commitment to narrative that made it possible and even obvious to look to narrative as an autonomous object of study as well as a potent way to understand life, history, and ourselves. Although Hegel is not an obvious presence in contemporary accounts of narrative theory, we will see in this and subsequent chapters (on Marx and Nietzsche, on Lukács, on Barthes and Genette) the degree to which first- or second-degree debts to Hegel have been crucial to its development and consolidation. I will begin with some of Hegel's comments on tragic narratives and tragic conflict before looking to some of the other narrative forms, techniques, and expectations at which he looks and on which he relies.

~

Like Aristotle, Hegel took tragedy not only as a form of literary narrative but also as a potent form of philosophical thinking. The great Shakespearean critic A. C. Bradley writes that "since Aristotle dealt with tragedy, and, as usual, drew the main features of his subject with those sure and simple strokes which no later hand has rivaled, the only philosopher who has treated it in a manner both original and searching is Hegel."[69] More recently, Julian Young writes that "Hegel's account of tragedy is the most impressive since Aristotle's and has proved to be, in terms of influence on philosophers of tragedy, perhaps even more powerful."[70] Peter Burian, signaling what it was that makes Hegel so important, writes, "If there is one category that overarches [tragedy], it is conflict, the starting-point of all storytelling. 'Conflict' has been a central term in criticism of tragedy only since Hegel's *Vorlesungen über die Ästhetik* of the 1820s, surprisingly, since from our perspective it is in many ways the crucial one."[71] Hegel's view of tragedy is crucial because it both returns conflict to the fore and makes possible a reading of tragedy and of Aristotle's *Poetics* that had arguably gone missing in most neoclassical interpretations of his theory. What Hegel contributed to the analysis of tragedy and what, I would argue, he helps to make visible in the *Poetics* is a theory of tragic storytelling as a theory of *conflict*, which will in turn prove to be intellectually and historically pivotal to the development of narrative theory. It was with Hegel in mind that Lukács could write that "it is generally accepted that the central theme of drama is the collision of social forces at their most extreme and acute point."[72] Recently defining "conflict" as an event that "upsets equilibrium" or as "a clash between the beliefs, desires, and intentions of two characters in a narrative, or between dissonant aspects of a single character," David Herman writes that "for many [narrative] theorists, conflict is a core aspect of narrative, whether it originates from within the characters themselves or from an external agent or impeding force."[73] What is interesting about looking back to Aristotle and then Hegel is to see the degree to which even a fundamental concept like conflict cannot be taken as given within the theory of either tragedy or narrative. That is, once we see Aristotle's opposition of actions and representations of actions in relation to the conflict between the "time of men" and the "time of gods," it becomes possible to see that Aristotle had been a quietly committed and even radical theorist of narrative conflict, a fact that might have been lost had it not been for Hegel's own distinctly modern encounter with the tragic; this is why, despite the long years that separate them, it makes sense both to see Hegel's theory of tragedy as a proper successor to Aristotle's and to see both as prescient theorists of narrative.

That said, Hegel does not in fact offer a single, coherent theory of tragedy; in his many and dispersed comments on Greek tragedy in general and *Oedipus* and *Antigone* in particular, one can see him rather developing a broad account of the *tragic* as a mode rather than as a genre, an account of what J. G. Finlayson describes as "*what it is to be a tragedy* ... it is an ethical and metaphysical theory about those aspects of human experience which tragedies make salient."[74] For Hegel, tragedy reveals something broadly tragic about life insofar as it stages and explores the necessity of conflict and the possibilities for its resolution in history and life; it reveals the degree to which human history, human societies, and human lives are defined and motivated by conflict: conflicts between one individual and another, between one value system and another, between individuals and the state, between how things were, are, and how they might be in the future. Conflict in Hegel takes on what we might call both a *synchronic* and a *diachronic* significance, its significance as a whole, static structure and its significance as something that unfolds within a structure over time (I will say more about these terms in Section 5.3 when I turn to Ferdinand de Saussure). On the one hand, the presence of conflict within a history, a state, a relationship, or a plot understood as a whole and fixed thing is what gives a structure its character, its significant and dynamic form; as we saw in the last Section, Jean-Pierre Vernant argued that the narrative of *Oedipus Rex* took its whole tone – a tone that resonates across the levels of plot, language, and character – from the conflict between past and present that animated it and other Athenian tragedies. We might indeed think here of a musical chord: what gives an E minor chord its character is the sustained and audible tension between different notes; the held harmonic tension, the relation among E, G, and B is what makes the whole chord what it is. On the other hand, because conflict also reveals tensions among social, ethical, and political values, it forces agents to act on behalf of their values from moment to moment; conflict makes narrative insofar as it is a problem or an upset that impels individuals to reveal contradictions, to argue for their values, and to act. This sense of conflict is, perhaps, more melodic than harmonic, as each moment of conflict and change more or less determines what can or should happen next. Conflict is, in that case, both a global aspect of a whole narrative structure and a local force that pushes that narrative forward from within. Conflict is at once the harmonic setting and the melodic line of tragic narrative, which is to say that Hegel uses the idea of conflict to highlight the two different but related levels at which Aristotle saw tragic plots working: at the level of story where the melodic passage from event to event is what matters and at the level of discourse where it is the harmonic relation among events put together in a whole representation that matters. These two orders of significance merge to produce the large aesthetic effect of a given tragedy and, perhaps, of any narrative.

We might think here of Hegel's favorite example, Sophocles' *Antigone*. The story is simple enough: at the end of a civil war fought between Oedipus's sons, Eteocles and Polyneices, both brothers die. Creon, brother-in-law to Oedipus and the current king of Thebes, decides that whereas the first of the sons will be honored with a funeral, the latter, Polyneices, will be posthumously disgraced and denied a proper burial. Polyneices' sister, Antigone, opposes Creon's will and buries her brother; both Creon and Antigone are certain that they are in the right. This conflict between two legitimate but incommensurate values thus sets the stage for the tragic events that follow, including Antigone's suicide. The conflict is thus both the structure of the play and an impetus that drives action within the play. It is at once synchronic and diachronic. What is more, the conflict between Creon and Antigone is powerful precisely because, according to Hegel, neither character is obviously wrong. Creon's refusal to bury Polyneices is a legitimate use of his kingly authority, a decision that he makes both within and for the law. Antigone's desire to meet her filial obligations to her brother is illegal but nonetheless just; it is an imperative that transcends human law and has the approval of the gods if not the state or the king. The conflict between law and justice is not, in that case, a conflict between right and wrong; it is, rather, a conflict between two rights, a fact that gives the play not only its narrative occasion but also what was for Hegel its undeniable ethical force. It is, as Hayden White writes, a conflict "in which two contending rights, two equally justifiable moral principles, become locked in combat in order to determine what the *form* of human life in a specific social incarnation *may* be."[75] The conflict thus both reveals a tragic tension that exists at the structural heart of society – it reveals a society's character – and stands as the cause of the narrated events of Sophocles' play. Conflict is for Hegel both a precondition for individual narrative actions and the whole narrative frame in which those actions become meaningful.[76]

In this sense, *Antigone* embodies a productive ambiguity that, as we saw, Vernant and others took as essential to Greek tragedy and maybe to narrative as such; the conflict between Antigone and Creon is, in other words, another version of a conflict between the "time of men" and the "time of the gods." As I argued in the previous chapter, this tension within the structure of Greek tragedy finds tacit formal expression in Aristotle's account, when he insists on the difference between actions and representations of actions; more than just marking out a difference between two kinds of aesthetic stuff, Aristotle's theory reveals the fact that tragedy not only tells the story of tragic events but also encodes the very experience of tragic conflict within its narrative structure. Margaret Cohen has recently written that "proposing genre as a mode of social expression, Hegel depicts tragedy specifically as the genre that both represents and resolves ethical contradictions in the register of the aesthetic. Hegel thus offers the first materialist account of tragedy, or rather, with his account Hegel founds [a] materialist model of genre."[77] Hegel's sense of tragedy as – among other things – a "mode of social expression" helps to reveal what was always at stake in Aristotle's *Poetics*; it reveals the degree to which Aristotle's and his own account of the tragic are reliant on an idea about conflict that forms an important if unexpected foundation for the development of a narrative theory.

In a recent essay, Peter J. Rabinowitz makes the case for the importance of what he calls narrative *paths*, the idea that, in addition to the two temporalities of story and discourse, we need to consider the possibility of more finely grained or idiosyncratic experiences of time in narrative, experiences that fall somewhere *between* the apparently natural necessity of story-time and the aesthetic freedom of discourse-time: from the perspective of a particular character as opposed to the perspective of narrators or readers, the experience of time and thus the narrative relation of one event to another will often take on a practically idiosyncratic quality. In other words, because characters are embedded in a world of events, they will often encounter those events – as they experience them directly, hear about them, read about them, recover them after amnesia, see them return to the surface after a traumatic experience – in a different but equally "real" order than readers, who are not, after all, embedded in a story world. In a way that recalls the kind of conflict that I am associating with Hegel's post-Aristotelian theory of tragedy, Rabinowitz's notion of the possible plurality of narrative paths is a source of a conflict that seems necessary to narrative as such:

> After all, characters, too, "receive" the events, either by experiencing them directly or by hearing about them second hand, sometimes from the narrator as a narratee but more often in some other way. Rarely do they all do so in the same order or from the same source. Indeed, we could easily reconceptualize dramatic irony as a clash of paths: the clash between Oedipus's path and Tiresias's, for instance, or the clash between the paths of Grace Ansley and Alida Slade, the main characters of Edith Wharton's "Roman Fever." As a result, most narratives turn out on closer examination, to be gardens of fuguing paths.[78]

The point, here, is that Rabinowitz's notion of the experiential path helps to highlight the narrative significance of both Aristotle's and Hegel's reliance on conflict; instead of standing as a third, alternative term to story and discourse, the path activates a tension that exists between them as two aspects of the same system. In other words, part of what motivates Hegel's theory of tragedy is the sense that story and discourse, the time of men and the time of the gods, will always in the end emerge as two aspects of one and the same garden.

I have begun here with Hegel's scattered thoughts on Greek tragedy because they provide a crucial and shaping link between Aristotle and subsequent attempts to engage with the relation among conflict, narrative events, and narrative form. Tragedy is, however, just one of several related narrative genres that Hegel looked to in order to understand the world. Although Hegel is many things, he is, for the purposes of our project, an early and immensely important theorist of narrative. His sense of tragedy's conflict as a clash between seemingly different orders of temporal experience, orders that we can map onto familiar distinctions between justice and law, fate and free will, allows him to imply a theory of narrative levels that will return in several forms in Marx, Nietzsche, Lukács, Barthes, and Genette. What is more, Hegel's sense of the relation between the two levels as a deeply historical difference, as an effect of our own situated place in time, will directly influence some critical and historical claims that underwrite some especially powerful theories of narrative. In these terms, my moves from Aristotle to Hegel and then from Hegel on to Marx, Nietzsche, and Freud represent key moments in the development of thinking about narrative as a dedicated and seemingly self-authorizing mode of inquiry. What interests me here and in the following chapter is how it is that narrative emerged in the midst of a broader philosophical context as a self-evidently obvious category through which to understand literature, history, and life.

~

Like Aristotle before him, Hegel thinks in terms of systems. Beginning in 1807 with the publication of *Phenomenology of Spirit*, Hegel sought across decades to lay out a philosophical architecture that could account organically for the development of and relations among history, art, religion, philosophy, desire, politics, war, nature, and just about everything else. Indeed, the complexity, the obscurity, and the reach of Hegel's writings have both furthered and complicated his enormous influence, a fact that has allowed readers of radically different ideological commitments to claim or to reject Hegel in very different terms; he has been taken as a communitarian conservative, a classical liberal, a neoliberal capitalist, a protocommunist, an existentialist *avant la lettre*, a negative theologian, a belated medieval mystic, a cryptofascist, and so on. If the ultimate sense or consequence of Hegel's enormously complex project can sometimes seem to slip out of reach, it is nonetheless clear that he is a narrative thinker who sees the world and philosophical history in terms of beginnings, middles, and ends; who employs narrative figures and forms to convey his own sense of those histories; and who almost incidentally imagines a post-Aristotelian narrative theory that will prove enormously if tacitly powerful to later literary and critical theorists.

I will focus on the *Phenomenology of Spirit*, a text Marx referred to as "the true birthplace and secret of the Hegelian philosophy."[79] Characterized in its simplest terms, Hegel's *Phenomenology* is an attempt to understand what human history means and how it means it. It follows the development of both history and human consciousness – what he refers to obliquely as *Geist* or Spirit – as it moves from naive and unconscious self-identity, through a middle period of conscious and indeed unhappy division from self, to an endpoint of Absolute Consciousness, a state that manages to combine the happy unity of the first stage with the hard-earned wisdom of the second. It is, more to the point, a perspective from which the whole story – beginning, middle, and end – can be taken in and understood. In *Time and Narrative*, Paul Ricoeur makes explicit the Aristotelian structure of Hegel's thinking; in a passage that resembles the lines from the *Poetics* in which Aristotle treats the relational nature of beginnings, middles, and ends, Ricoeur write that Hegel affirms "that philosophy can attain not only the present, by summing up the known past, taken as the seed of the anticipated future, but also the eternal present, which assures the underlying unity of the surpassed past and the coming manifestations of life."[80] Hegel's is, in other words, a narrative of development that would seek to account for all experience in the Aristotelian terms of a single and whole plot. How, though, does it work? How does one move from one part of the plot to another? What is it that makes any one moment, event, or experience significant? How are we to understand relations among the past, the present, and the future? Is meaning a human illusion, something that we optimistically project on the chaos and contingency of things, or is meaning rather something real and mysteriously immanent to life as it unfolds?

Although these feel like unanswerable questions, they had a particular urgency for Hegel and for a couple of reasons. First, we need to see Hegel's effort in relation to an intellectual context that had been more or less dominated by Immanuel Kant. Like Hegel after and Aristotle long before, Kant offered a more or less complete philosophical system, one that would account for the whole of what we can know about the world and, more importantly, how it is that we can know it. As a result of the ambition, beauty, and power of his system, Kant was the one to beat among the philosophers of Hegel's generation; he is, indeed, the presence that looms largest in Hegel's work (as well, arguably, as in the whole of modern philosophy up to and including the present day). Stated in simplest terms, Kant worked to see the limited and subjective experience of the world in relation to the objective fact of the world itself; to put together a whole picture of human existence was, on the one hand, to see the subject's limited, empirical, sensory engagement with the perception of things and, on the other hand, to know that, beyond the perceiving self, there was an objectively real world of things in themselves:

> We have therefore wanted to say that all our intuition is nothing but the representation of appearance; that the things that we intuit are not in themselves what we intuit them to be, nor are their relations so constituted in themselves as they appear to us; and that if we remove our own subject or even only the subjective constitution of the senses in general, then all constitution, all relations of objects in space and time, indeed space and time themselves would disappear, and as appearances they cannot exist in themselves, but only in us.[81]

To achieve a full account of things, one needs to see the two sides of this problem, to see things as they are alongside what Aristotle might call our representations of those things. Kant refers to these two aspects or substances as *noumena* and *phenomena* and gives us another set of tools with which to think about the relation between stuff and the representation of stuff, a relation that motivated Aristotle and that, as we saw in the Introduction, will have something to do with the more pragmatic distinction between the events and entities that make up a given story and the representations of those events and entities that make up narrative discourse.

I will also return to the relation between Kant's project and narrative theory in Sections 4.2 and 4.3, where I turn to the influence that two distinct strains of neo-Kantianism had on Georg Lukács and Mikhail Bakhtin. Indeed, while a comparison between Kant's system and the methodological terms of contemporary narrative theory might seem merely analogous, we can in fact draw a direct line from Kant, through the neo-Kantian schools of the late nineteenth and early twentieth centuries, to Mikhail Bakhtin, who relied on these concepts in order to develop his own powerfully historical account of narrative genre, and then from Bakhtin to Julia Kristeva, Tzvetan Todorov, and Roland Barthes, figures directly responsible for the midcentury consolidation of structuralist narratology. This will become clearer as we go. For now, however, I want to highlight a double movement that I make throughout this book. On the one hand, I want to argue that the different systems, questions, and problems that I am looking at can be profitably *compared* to the story–discourse relation. This is, in fact, to see narrative theory alongside a whole set of intellectual projects that turn on the relation between events as they occur and what meaning those events might have when seen as part of one or another larger system. On the other hand, I want to make a more direct case for lines of historical influence that connect contemporary narrative theory with modes of historical and philosophical thought that might otherwise seem far afield.

So: Kant wanted to develop a system that put things and ideas, content and form, stuff and representation into a meaningful relation with one another. If, though, Kant's system is synthetic, it did not seek to erase the fundamental difference between ideas and things; while a relation between ideas and things makes knowledge of self or world possible, ideas and things nonetheless remain fundamentally distinct. Although we can deduce the existence of a real world governed by universal laws, we cannot know that world directly because we are creatures of limited, subjective, sensory experience; Kant's system thus relies on both the play of and the ultimate difference between ideas and things. And, because it leaves us more or less stranded on one side of these two apparently incommensurate domains, Kant's system seemed to some to grind to an existential halt. Charles Taylor writes that

> the Kantian world of experience was distinguished from the ultimate reality. It took its shape partly from the subject, from the shape of our minds, and these structures could be explored by transcendental argument; but by the very fact that its shape was partly given by us, it could allow us to conclude nothing about the shape of things as they were in themselves. Such things there must be because we as finite subjects are affected, our intuition receives its content from outside of us; but the nature of this ultimate reality is a closed book to us, and that insurmountably.[82]

This distance between subjective experience and objective reality forms the core of Kant's philosophy; it is both what makes our knowledge possible and what prevents us from knowing things directly.

While my account of Kant's thinking is, of necessity, a gross simplification, it gets, I hope, at what so frustrated Hegel and many of his contemporaries; although it was indeed comprehensive, Kant's system left little or no room for *development*, for a move toward a greater or different knowledge of the world. The world we lived immediately in seemed one of brute sensation, mere inclination, and natural necessary; and, while the world of ideas represented freedom from that necessity, it remained a pure, tantalizing, and finally unattainable thing. Jonathan Rée writes that "if Kant had a weak point, it was probably his attempt to draw a boundary between the straightforward world of everyday objects in space and time, where the human understanding could safely heap up endless treasuries of empirical knowledge, and the perilous, delusive, transcendent world of Ideals – of freedom, reason, *noumena*, and the sublime."[83] As Kafka once said of hope, there was for Kant "plenty of freedom, an infinite amount of freedom – but not for us."[84]

It is, as we will see, in response to what seemed to be the static, elegantly fixed quality of Kant's system that Hegel develops his own intensely narrative account of individual and historical development. Where for Kant ideas in their pure form remained on the other side of a divide, Hegel worked to develop an account of things built around the story of our movement from things to ideas, from brute sensation to absolute knowledge, from necessity to freedom; Lee Congdon writes that "in place of two worlds – phenomenal and noumenal – [Hegel] posited one, the historical. Having thereby eliminated the thing-in-itself, Hegel was in a far better position to realize the systematic ambition of rationalism. He was convinced that history could be grasped as a concrete totality."[85] Hegel, in other words, narrativizes the relationship between things and ideas, casting one as the beginning and the other as the end of a historical masterplot, a story that begins with physical necessity and ends in conceptual freedom; and, because Hegel saw the world and its history as a narrative, he needed a narrative theory to account for it.

~

Hegel's dissatisfaction with the apparent fixity of Kant's system was not his alone. Indeed, Hegel came of age in a period of intense social turmoil, a fact that seemed to give the lie to any overly static account of history and the world. Of utmost importance here was his understanding of the nature and consequence of the French Revolution. Taylor writes that the French Revolution was "the great political event of Hegel's youth, the event against which all his generation had to think out their political philosophy, and had to rethink their stance to the Enlightenment."[86] Tom Rockmore asserts, "With few exceptions, philosophy was late in acknowledging the importance of history. This only occurred [with Hegel] after the eruption of one of the great series of historical events of modern times, the French Revolution."[87] And Susan Buck-Morss writes that "it has long been recognized that Hegel's understanding of politics was modern, based on an interpretation of the events of the French Revolution as a decisive break from the past and that he is referring to the French Revolution in *The Phenomenology of Mind*, even when he does not mention it by name."[88] Like his exact contemporary William Wordsworth, Hegel was a passionate if removed observer of the French Revolution and its aftermath; both were born in 1770 and were eighteen years old when the revolution broke out, a fact that shaped the hopes, anxieties, and the projects of a generation (Beethoven was also born in 1770 and Sir Walter Scott in 1771). As Wordsworth was later famously to write, "Bliss it was in that dawn to be alive / But to be young was very heaven."[89] Hegel cast his own memory of the revolution in similar if less lovely terms: "This was a magnificent dawn. All thinking beings joined in celebrating this epoch. A sublime feeling ruled that time, an enthusiasm of the spirit thrilled through the world, as if we had now finally come to the real reconciliation of the divine with the world."[90] Like Wordsworth, Hegel experienced the revolution at a distance, reading about it in the newspapers as or, rather, just after it happened; indeed, Hegel has often been seen – by Susan Buck-Morss in relation to Hegel's possible contemporary awareness of the Haitian Revolution and by Benedict Anderson in relation to the broader rise of nationalism – as the first philosopher of the newspaper. Indeed, in *Hegel, Haiti, and Universal History*, Buck-Morss argues that Hegel's textual experience of revolutionary distance would have been all the more pronounced in the case of his ambient knowledge of the Haitian Revolution, a political event – both geographically distant and immensely and immediately suggestive – that she sees at the heart of Hegel's daunting and abstract Master–Slave dialectic. In her account, it was the faraway and yet textually proximate fact of *other people's* stories that led to one of his most powerful and, I would suggest, powerfully narrative theories. (I will return to the details of the Master–Slave dialectic in a moment.)

Hegel's distant and yet urgent feel for the French and Haitian Revolutions as narratives to follow and to understand is thus connected to a possibility that I raised in the Introduction, the idea that the rise not of narrative but rather of narrative theory might be associated with a need to understand other people's stories that appears alongside the emergence and consolidation of an international print culture; according to Anderson:

> the significance of this mass ceremony —Hegel observed that newspapers serve modern man as a substitute for morning prayers—is paradoxical. It is performed in silent privacy, in the lair of the skull. Yet each communicant is well aware that the ceremony he performs is being replicated simultaneously by thousands (or millions) of others of whose existence he is confident, yet of whose identity he has not the slightest notion.[91]

To read about a revolution at a distance, as something that occurs, in the words of Mary Favret, "beyond the reach of eyes and ears, somewhere else, over there," is, in that case, to engage in an ideological and imaginative reconstruction of events that requires us to accept the existence of other people and thus of other people's experience of events (other relations between story and discourse); it requires us to recognize, in other words, that different discursive representations of the same sequence of events is not only possible but also inevitable.[92] Rebecca Comay suggests that Hegel's experience of revolution at a distance indeed forced him to confront the difference between what one knows about history and the fact of history itself: "The German encounter with the French Revolution is an extreme case of the structural anachronism that afflicts all historical experience. The clocks are never synchronized, the schedules never coordinated, every epoch is a discordant mix of divergent rhythms, unequal durations, and variable speeds."[93] Divergent rhythms, unequal durations, and variable speeds: it is not for nothing that Hegel's experience of history sounds a lot like a narrative relation based on the temporal difference between events as they occur and the representation of events. Andrew Cole writes in similar terms that, for Hegel, "the present is always peculiarly uneven and inherently dialectical—a present exhibiting every day some new contradiction or break that may take seconds, hours, or years to notice. Hegel offers up a theory of historical unevenness that accommodates all scales of time, all durations from the instant to the larger period or episteme."[94]

In addition to the conditions under which he observed it, the French Revolution had an effect on Hegel also because of how it both began and ended. The early enthusiasm of the French Revolution, its overthrow of a seemingly intractable *Ancien Régime*, and its initial promise of universal *Liberté, Egalité,* and *Fraternité* seemed to Hegel and many others not only to inaugurate a set of specific political and democratic improvements but also to instantiate the Enlightenment ideal of radical human freedom that could transcend specific political oppression and, more broadly, natural necessity. In these terms, the Revolution looked initially like a practical response to Kant's antinomies, his sense that real freedom must sit on the far side of an existential divide. If, however, the Revolution began in hope, it quickly collapsed into the disappointment of the Terror, the late period of the Revolution during which thousands died under the guillotine. This period of grotesque violence ended Hegel's hopes for the Revolution and, indeed, hastened the collapse of the Revolutionary government and the concomitant rise of Napoleon as the emperor of France and, for a time, much of the world. Part of the problem for Hegel was the oddly neutral quality of the Terror's violence; Comay writes that "terror institutionalized itself as the official order of the day. At this point, the scene of suffering, formally contained in Aristotelian tragedy, threatened to pervade the totality of the spectacle. At this point, too, the radiant transparency of the revolutionary festival gave way to the perfunctory, banal nonspectacle of the guillotine."[95] Hegel was particularly struck with the curiously dispassionate character of the executions, acts that seemed to have robbed death – and thus life – of its deep meaning, rendering it "a death which has no inner scope and represents no fulfillment, for what is negated is a point void of content, that of the absolutely free self; it is thus the coldest, flattest death, with no more significance than cutting through a cabbage head or throwing back a draught of water."[96] James Schmidt writes that "one of the central themes of Hegel's account of the Terror is that murder is, ultimately, a rather unsatisfying experience," an experience that, because it was denied texture or particularity, lacked narrative significance.[97] Death by guillotine was, in other words, a death denied not only spectacle but also the dignity of story, a death removed from its place of privilege in the beginning, middle, and end that had been a whole and wholly human life.

~

Walter Benjamin takes up exactly this implied connection between the particularity of death and the possibility of narrative closure in his 1936 essay "The Storyteller": "Yet, characteristically, it is not only a man's knowledge or wisdom, but above all his real life—and this is the stuff that stories are made of—which first assumes transmissible form at the moment of his death. Just as a sequence of images is set in motion inside a man as his life comes to an end—unfolding the views of himself in which he has encountered himself without being aware of it—suddenly in his expressions and looks the unforgettable emerges and imparts to everything that concerned him that authority which even the poorest wretch in dying possesses for the living around him. This authority is at the very origin of the story."[98] Garrett Stewart takes up this relation between death and meaning both at the level of the individual sentence, which is to say the level of style, and at the level of whole plots: "This is the narratological hold death has over any text. The idea of death, otherwise known as the sense of an ending, becomes the inevitable incarnation of plot in the world of sheer story, the imposition of discourse on the course of random account, of form on the amorphousness not of death but of life without it."[99] With the reduction of death to an essentially trivial and thus non-narratable event, the Terror threatened for Hegel to drain both life and death of their respective capacities for narrative sense; as Aristotle knew, without a meaningful end, the beginning and middle of a life couldn't mean much. This is what the mechanical, rote nature of the guillotine seemed to do; it made it impossible to see an individual's death as giving an individual's life its own idiosyncratic structure. The failure of revolution and its fall into terror emerged, in that case, as an *anti-narrative* force, as a denial of meaning in and of itself.[100]

In *The Death-Bound Subject: Richard Wright's Archeology of Death*, Abdul JanMohamed builds on the Hegelian correlation of a good and discrete death and the forming possibility of narrative closure to explore the narrative and stylistic effects of a culture of social and literal death associated with slavery and its aftermath in the American South: "Whatever the changes in the status of power or honor or other aspects of sociocultural condition of the descendants of slaves, historical records and subjective testimony leave little doubt that lynching continued to play the dominant role in the political suppression of black Americans in the South."[101] JanMohamed looks to some of the large conceptual and local narrative effects that this other, pervasive relation to literal and social death had on African American culture in general and on Richard Wright's novels and stories in particular. For instance, he reads a sentence from Wright's "Bright Morning Star," the final story in *Uncle Tom's Children*, as enacting a painful sequence "produced by the unrelenting containment and penetration of life by death": "But her fear was a quiet one; it was more like an intense brooding than a fear; it was a sort of hugging of hated facts so closely that she could feel their grain, like letting cold water run over her hand from a faucet on a winter morning."[102] "The syntactic structure of the above quotation aesthetically mirrors the process of discovering the structure of the culture of social-death. The sentence, a series of short clauses moving from abstract definitions of emotions to increasingly concrete representations and, finally, ending with a concrete and apt, if paradoxical, simile, accurately maps the development of Wright's short stories."[103] Because, in other words, death in the African American tradition stands not as the terminal point of an otherwise progressive narrative but rather as a possibility or a condition that permeates experience, it reshapes and revalues narrative expectations, narrative values, and narrative forms within that tradition. For JanMohamed, the culture of death routinized a form of social and narrative failure that Hegel associated with the French Revolutionary Terror and that had a deep effect not only on African American lives but also on the forms of narrative discourse that those lives could take.

Part of what Hegel took from the Revolution was a personal and political need to save the significance of the Revolutionary "dawn" in spite of the apparently meaningless because anti-narrative dejection of the Terror.

Although the guillotine revealed crucial contradictions within the Revolutionary project, Hegel nonetheless wondered if there was a story to tell that could both save the Revolution and reveal the Terror, while terrible, as part of some larger, more sensible plot. Was there, in spite of the calculated violence of the guillotine, a narrative that could recover the dignity of the individual death and thus the individual life? Was there something to learn from the Terror? Was it possible, as Georg Lukács puts it in *The Historical Novel*, "to demonstrate the necessity of the French Revolution, to show that revolution and historical development are not opposed to one another"?[104] Was there, in other words, a way to see the Terror not as a grotesque and exceptional failure but rather as an event that would, in time, be revealed as an important if bloody part of a larger story of human liberation? Does any historical event have meaning or is it all, as someone once said, "just one damned thing after another"? Could history be, as Karl Mannheim puts it, "pursued in a manner which will see in the sequence and co-existence of phenomena more than mere accidental relationships, and will seek to discover in the totality of the historical complex the role, the significance, and meaning of each component element"?[105] Philosophy appeared for Hegel as a possible response to a time that had been put out of joint; Comay writes that, "This is why the French Revolution will remain the burning center of Hegel's philosophy: the event crystallizes the untimeliness of historical experience. The task of philosophy is to explicate this untimeliness."[106] Or, as Fredric Jameson puts it, "The experience of defeat of the various revolutionary movements in this period has a paradoxical consequence: it does not discourage its followers theoretically, but rather intensifies their attempts to conceptualise that mysterious historical moment which is the passage from one system to another."[107] The question – is it possible to resolve the local contradictions of the past and the present in terms of some larger process or narrative – provides, as we will see, one important and influential basis of Hegel's project and its reliance on a particular account of narrative.

~

I want now to show how Hegel's attempts to deal both with the antinomies of Kant's system and with questions raised by the French Revolution led him to develop a general theory of narrative. The heart of this theory is what Hegel famously called the *dialectic*, a process that could, on the one hand, allow for the productive mingling of things and ideas, the objective and the subjective, necessity and freedom and, on the other, account for the fact and ultimate significance of events within the whole frame of historical change. At its most basic, the dialectic for Hegel is a narrative explanation for the fact that systems and things that seem or seemed complete can and in fact must change in unexpected and sometimes violent ways. The dialectic moves in three stages: with the first stage, we see a state of affairs as complete, as fully grown, as fulfilled; as with Kant's system or with things as they were before the French Revolution, this stage seems complete in itself and thus incapable of alteration. With the second stage, some new event or idea or argument calls the completion of things into question; where it had appeared that a world or state of affairs had reached the end of its story, some new piece of information forces us to admit the reality of incompletion and thus the possibility or necessity of change. This is a moment of upset, violence, and confusion; it is what Hegel calls *negation*, where an old state of affairs is transformed or destroyed or forced to confront an internal limit. With the third stage, we manage to think things – or things somehow manage to "think" themselves – into a position where old ideas come meaningfully to coexist with new ideas; where negation had seemed like the simple destruction or death of the past, it is revealed in time as, in fact, the new emergence of the past within the present or future, a present or future capable of thinking an old world in productive relation to the new. Paul Ricoeur writes that, "for the philosopher what counts about the past are those signs of maturity from which shine a sufficient clarity concerning what is essential. Hegel's wager is that enough meaning has been accumulated for us to decipher in them the ultimate end of the world in its relation to the ends and the material that assure its realization."[108] It is not merely that the past exists as a material cause that makes the present and future possible; it is also that the past sometimes appears as proof that it and the rest of history are parts of a larger and coherent whole. The apparently meaningless stuff of the past is revealed in the present as events that will come significantly together in the future to form a whole plot. The future, in other words, *makes* the past, just as the past leads to the future. Hegel's dialectic is, in that case, one especially potent version of a broadly Romantic scheme that Geoffrey Hartman associates with the idea of "anti-self-consciousness": "To explore the transition from self-consciousness to imagination and to achieve that transition while exploring it (and so to prove it still possible) is the Romantic purpose I find most crucial."[109] The dialectic is, in other words, a concentrated expression of the relation between beginning, middle, and end; it is a minimal instance of what Aristotle would call plot.

Much of the explanatory power of the dialectic comes from the fact that it is endlessly scalable, that it works in the same way at its lowest as well as its highest level of abstraction, from a moment in time all the way up to history as a grand narrative whole. Wherever we see change, we will see the dialectic at work. Indeed, Hegel finds it in the development of political institutions, in Christianity, the history of art, the theory of history, the meaning of violence, and the fact of love. It was also, as we saw, the basis of his theory of tragic conflict: tragic narratives begin with a conflict between the way things are and an act or idea that cannot make sense within that status quo, as a result, "The *collision* arises, as we are now considering it, in an act of *violation*, which is unable to retain its character as such, but is compelled to find a new principle of unity; it is a change in the pervasively existent condition of harmony, a change which is still in process."[110] Hegel goes on to say that this three-part story helps to account for the fact that many of the great tragedies form trilogies that enact this logic at an even larger level; they are instances of the dialectic nested within other instances of the dialectic, which are themselves situated within still other instances of the dialectic. In the end, Hegel's whole philosophy turns on the idea that, beginning with consciousness itself, every-thing at whatever scale should be understood in the precisely narrative terms of beginning, middle, and end.

One of the best-known examples of this three-part program appears in the *Phenomenology of Spirit* as Hegel's famous dialectic of "Lordship and Bond-age," his starkly narrative account of one origin of human society and human history. In what follows, I draw on Alexandre Kojève's gloss on this section of the *Phenomenology* both because it helps to clarify some of Hegel's terms and because this version will, as I will go on to say, have a direct and profound influence on some of the main figures in literary, critical, and narrative theory. (The terms "Master" and "Slave" instead of "Lord" and "Bondsman" come from Kojève's *Introduction to the Reading of Hegel*.) The Hegel lectures Kojève gave in Paris from 1933–1940 were crucial to the development of several important intellectual movements; Andrew Cole writes that "Kojève had effectively kicked off the Hegelian renaissance in France with his lectures at L'École Pratique des Hautes Études beginning in the late 1930s. These lectures were heard and/or absorbed by the likes of Georges Bataille, André Breton, Alexandre Koyre, Jacques Lacan, Emmanuel Levinas, Maurice Merleau-Ponty, Raymond Queneau, Jean-Paul Sartre, and Eric Weil," several of which figures will come together to form an important backdrop for events and ideas discussed in Sections 6.1, 6.2, and 6.3.[111]

Part of the success of Kojève's lectures comes from the fact that they revealed Hegel not only as a great philosopher but also as a gifted if sub-merged narrative artist; Vincent Descombes writes that, "Alexandre Kojève was a very talented story-teller. In his commentaries, the austere Hegelian *Phenomenology* turns into a kind of serialized philosophical novel, where one dramatic scene follows another; picturesque characters come face to face, reversals of situation keep up the suspense, and the reader, avid to know the end of the story (or history), clamors for more."[112] One could say that, in the same way that Hegel's theory of tragedy helped to reveal a theory of narrative conflict that was obscured but already at work in Aristotle, Kojève's lectures helped to reveal an essential narrativity that was, once again, obscure but always already at work in Hegel. That narrativity is, as I have been suggesting, an element of both Hegel's method and his style. (And, once again, Kojève plays a key role in narrative theory's history insofar as he allows us to go from Kant, to Hegel, to Kojève, to Bataille and Lacan, to Barthes and other figures at the journal *Tel Quel*, to the founding moment of structuralist narratology, to the disciplinary consolidation of the questions and terms that we still associate with narrative theory as such. I'll come back to this provisional line of succession in later chapters and look particularly at the tacit appearance of Kojève via Lacan in the thinking of Roland Barthes.)

Hegel's story is, in its way, simple. Human beings and animals share a capacity to desire, which Hegel understands as a motive emptiness or lack or want that forces them to act, to seek out and to consume (to destroy or to transform) objects necessary to their survival: "Born of Desire, action tends to satisfy it, and can do so only by the 'negation,' the destruction or at least the transformation of the desired object: to satisfy hunger, for example, the food must be destroyed or, in any case, transformed."[113] For animals, desire is simple and finite: when hungry or cold, the animal "desires" food or warmth. When an action allows those desires to be met, the desires disappear and the animal sinks back into the "savage torpor" of unselfconsciousness, a state in which the animal will remain until hunger or cold once again rouse the animal into a condition of sensation and desire. Hegel refers to this bare and ephemeral state of self-awareness as the "sentiment of self," a minimal and temporary self-consciousness that is finally only an awareness of physical need. Where humans differ from and surpass animals is in the nature of their desire: "All the Desires of an animal are in the final analysis a function of its desire to preserve its life. Human Desire, therefore, must win out over this desire for preservation. In other words, man's humanity 'comes to light' only if he risks his (animal) life for the sake of his human Desire."[114] Because animal consciousness is defined by its immediate, flickering relation to the appearance, satisfaction, and temporary cessation of desire, human desire must differentiate itself from animal desire in terms both of its object and the possibility of its satisfaction. To be human, one must desire something other or more than life itself. What would make a human risk his or her life? What desire could trump the desire to survive? For Hegel, the desire that overcomes the desire to live is the desire for *recognition*, the desire to have one's own desire and one's own capacity to desire (which is to say, one's capacity for change and growth) *recognized* by another; and because this desire for recognition is a desire that overrides the finite desire of animals, it is essentially human: "Therefore, to desire the Desire of another is in the final analysis to desire that the value that I am or that I 'represent' be the value desired by the other: I want him to 'recognize' my value as his value. I want him to 'recognize' me as an autonomous value. In other words, all human, anthropogenetic Desire—the Desire that generates Self-Consciousness, the human reality—is, finally, a function of the desire for 'recognition.'"[115]

Hegel goes on to imagine the origin of human Self-Consciousness in the form of a violent and unembellished fable, a narrative with the barest architecture of beginning, middle, and end: once upon a time, one human being met another. Each seeing that the other was of the same species, each demands that the other recognize the humanity of his or her desire at the expense of the other's desire; each demands to be recognized by someone who won't demand recognition in return. A fight to the death necessarily ensues: "to speak of the 'origin' of Self-Consciousness is necessarily to speak of a fight to the death for recognition."[116] It has to be "to the death," because it is only in the willingness to allow the desire for recognition to trump the desire for survival that one can prove one's humanity, which is to say one's ability to overcome animal desire and thus to be free from brute necessity. The battle continues until one of three things happen. If both individuals die, the story comes to an obvious and sudden end. If one of the combatants dies, the story comes to a different but related end; although there is a winner of the fight, the stark setting of Hegel's story means that there is no one else there to see the fight and thus to recognize the winner or the winner's desire. Victory requires witness, and with the loser goes the only possible witness; consequently, the desire for recognition is not met. The third outcome is the one that interests Hegel: instead of fighting all the way to the death, one of the combatants experiences *the fear of death* and thus surrenders, giving up his or her claim to recognition in order to satisfy the simple animal desire for life. At this point, the winner, whose desire has been recognized, becomes the Lord, and the loser, whose desire is not recognized, becomes the Bondsman and has to serve the Lord or once again risk his or her life, which he or she, having experienced the fear of death, will not do. That would seem to be the end of the story, but as Hegel tells it, yet another dialectical turn takes place.

Because the Bondsman serves the Lord, which is to say because the Bondsman satisfies all of the Lord's animal needs as well as his or her desire for recognition, the Lord and the Bondsman develop very different relationships to the wider world of things. Because his or her desire for recognition has been ostensibly met, the Lord learns nothing more and does nothing more; paradoxically, victory over the Bondsman has not only met the Lord's desire for recognition but also turned that desire into something like an animal desire insofar as it has been satisfied and thus brought to its narrative conclusion. In Hegel, human desire is a narrative principle that moves things forward; once movement stops, desire loses its essential and characteristic negativity and thus its relation to real freedom. With the satisfaction of desire, one's story comes to an end. Because, however, the Bondsman needs to serve the Lord, he or she needs *as a subject* to continue to confront and to negate (which is to say to transform and to use) an entire world of things: "The Slave, in transforming the given World by his work, transcends the given and what is given by that given in himself; hence, he goes beyond himself, and also goes beyond the Master who is tied to the given which, not working, he leaves intact."[117] What's more, because the Bondsman never wanted to be the Bondsman, he or she retains an unsatisfied desire *to be something else*, a fact that sustains the Bondsman's human capacity for narrative, which is to say, his or her transformative relation to the world. In the service of the Lord, who cannot change because he or she no longer desires (his or her ultimate desire for recognition has been met), the Bondsman gradually "masters" all the stuff of the world and is revealed in the end as the true master, the figure who has not overcome an adversary but has rather brought the whole of the external world into a productive, subjective relation with the self. At this point, the content of the true human struggle – the struggle to resolve the ultimate difference between self and other, nature and culture, subject and object – is revealed. At this point, when the ultimate differences between the experience and the idea, the is and the ought are resolved, the dialectical narrative comes to its ultimate end, and Kant's apparently insoluble antinomies are overcome: "the interaction of Master and Slave must finally end in the 'dialectical overcoming' of both of them."[118]

I have taken the time to rehearse Kojève's reading of Hegel's dialectic of Lordship and Bondage for a few reasons. First, as I've already suggested, Kojève's reading of this passage will turn out to be important in later chapters as we turn to structuralist and post-structuralist versions of narratology. Second, it offers us another look at Hegel's storytelling, the fact that in order to account for the necessarily social and historical nature of human consciousness and human desire, he turns to legend and fable. Hegel sees, in other words, that certain aspects of history and life are best and maybe necessarily represented as a motivated relation between part and whole, between discrete events and events as they come together to form a whole narrative. What's more, the fact that Hegel brings together the abstractions of the dialectic with a stripped-down but nonetheless evocative narrative account of conflict, violence, desire, hope and, ultimately, triumph over adversity helps to make visible an important quality of his method.

We could, for instance, reread Kojève's reading of Hegel's account of "Lordship and Bondage" in terms of three related types of narrative response identified by the James Phelan. Because Phelan follows Wayne Booth (whom I will discuss in Section 4.1) in seeing narratives as rhetorical acts, he understands them as implying some combination of three different narrative "components" that invite particular kinds of interest on the part of readers (the mimetic, the thematic, and the synthetic): "Responses to the mimetic component involve an audience's interest in the characters as possible people and in the narrative world as like our own, that is either our actual world or one that is possible given what we know and assume about the actual world"; "responses to the thematic component involve an interest in the characters as representative of classes of people . . . and in the cultural, ideological, philosophical, or ethical issues being addressed by the narrative"; and "responses to the synthetic component involve an audience's interest in, and attention to, the characters and to the large narrative as a made object."[119] Although each of these components is present in all narratives, they appear in different proportions, a fact that helps to give different narratives their particular characters: "Some narratives are dominated by mimetic interests, some by thematic, and others by synthetic, but as a narrative develops, it can generate new relations among those interests. In most realistic narratives, for example, the audience has a tacit awareness of the synthetic while it focuses on the mimetic and the thematic components."[120] While, in other words, a reader is paying attention to what's happening to different characters at a given moment, he or she will anticipate that part's relation to a synthetic beginning, middle, and end; an awareness of an end and thus the narrative as a whole will inflect, however dimly, a reader's experience of the present moment.

From one point of view, we might see Hegel's story of Lordship and Bondage in merely "thematic" terms insofar as he presents it explicitly as a kind of allegory of historical development according to the logic of desire and dialectical conflict that the story captures; the "point" is not to tell someone's story but rather to make visible relations and modes of development that he sees at work in history as such. Although personified, the forces represented by Lord and Bondsman are not characters in the same way Jane Eyre or Willy Wonka are characters. From this perspective, Hegel's story wouldn't be a narrative so much as what the philosopher Jean-François Lyotard refers to as a "Grand Narrative"; Marie-Laure Ryan writes that, "Grand Narratives, also known as metanarratives, are global explanatory schemes that legitimize institutions, such as the practice of science, by representing them as necessary to the historical self-realization of an abstract or collective identity, such as Reason, Freedom, or the State. Hegel's and Marx's philosophies of history are prototypical examples of Grand Narratives."[121] According to Ryan, Grand Narratives "can only be called narrative in a metaphorical sense, because they do not concern individuals and do not create a concrete world."[122] Left, then, at the level of the "thematic," Hegel's story of the Lord and Bondsman might seem to fall short of authentic narrativity. Seen, however, through Kojève's more dramatic presentation, it becomes clear that Hegel is in fact bringing together each of Phelan's three components. At the same time that his story offers an explicitly "thematic" attempt at typifying larger historical and philosophical ideas, it also encourages us to see those ideas in the context of a bare but nonetheless possible world, a more or less "mimetic" context in which the abstract ideas of desire and conflict take on an immediate sense of urgency and relevance; the fact that Hegel's story is also about desiring, eating, and fighting gives what might otherwise remain "grand" a gritty and felt texture, a sense of drama that involves his reader in a way that the merely thematic couldn't. And, because Hegel's story is and is offered by Kojève as an especially representative part of the *Phenomenology*, it not only forces us to think through the relation between it and Hegel's larger project but also – given the nature of that project – encourages us to see it an argument about the conditions that make narrative synthesis possible in the first place. Hegel's allegory works in part because of its efforts subtly to manage three different but related modes of narrative address; he manages, in other words, to use narrative in order to produce a productive synthesis of the abstract and the concrete, a goal that underwrites all of his work.[123]

Hegel's story thus highlights a necessarily reciprocal relation between narrative and desire that will be important to some of our later figures. As we've seen, desire emerges in Kojève's account of Hegel as a motive force that powers the dialectic and pushes beginnings towards ends; it is because the self is driven forward by desire that the self takes on an identity in and only in narrative time: "it will be (in the future) what it has become by negation (in the present) of what it was (in the past), this negation being accomplished with a view to what it will become."[124] In a sense, Kojève anticipates someone like Peter Brooks, who makes the relation between plot (as beginning, middle, and end), desire, and the dialectic into the cornerstone of his own theory of narrative and "narrative desire": "We can, then, conceive of the reading of plot as a form of desire that carries us forward, onward, through the text. Narratives both tell of desire—typically present some story of desire—and arouse and make use of desire as dynamic of signification."[125] As we will see later, desire in several of its forms and in terms that come more or less directly from Hegel will indeed become a central concept in the consolidation and development of narrative theory (indeed, I'll come back to Brooks and narrative desire in Section 3.3).

~

I began this section with a discussion of Hegel's theory of tragic conflict and its relation to Aristotle. Hegel helped both to account for an essential relation between conflict and narrative in tragedy and to reveal the degree to which a theory of narrative as conflict was already implicit in Aristotle's *Poetics*. I want now to turn from the tragic in order to introduce a different narrative form, one that Hegel not only took as modern answer to tragedy but also as a model for his *Phenomenology*: the *Bildungsroman*, or the novel of development. That is, while Hegel understood tragedy as the narrative form that laid bare the necessary relation between conflict and narrative action, he also believed that authentic tragedy was only truly possible in its native context of ancient Greece, where a conflict between the individual and a coherent community could be clearly delineated; for Hegel, those days were over: "it is not difficult to see that ours is a birth-time and a period of transition to a new era."[126] This sense of Greek culture as a lost or alien alternative to modern life will return in later Sections (4.2 and 4.3) as different figures – most notably Lukács and Bakhtin – use the example of Greek epic as a genre against which to delineate the particular character of modern narrative and modern narrative genres.

Indeed, as opposed to the classical austerity of tragedy, the novel emerged for Hegel as a narrative form better suited to address the self-conscious complexities of modern life; the widening and internal differentiation of the modern world makes it difficult if not impossible to reduce any problem to a simple conflict between two alternatives. This is why, for Hegel, the ascetic directness of an Antigone or an Oedipus is replaced first with the inscrutably melancholic vacillations of a Hamlet and later with the prosaic confusion of Goethe's Wilhelm Meister, characters who long for the simplicity of a hard but clear conflict but are instead faced with a spreading complexity, with the bad infinity of too many choices. Terry Eagleton writes that, "The problem for Hegel is that, given the grievous complexity and contradiction of social conditions, knowledge of the whole can no longer be spontaneous. ... We have left behind ancient Greece, a society which Hegel likens to an artifact, where a spontaneous knowledge of the whole was still routinely available."[127] Instead of reducing conflict to a tragic because static division between two equally valid positions, the novel instead "tarries" in the negative space of a narrative complexity that stands between the beginning and the end of the story that Hegel describes. This is why, as Jonathan Rée points out, "Hegel's attempt to recount the internal history of Spirit's experience in the *Phenomenology* stretched the resources of early nineteenth-century literary narrative to their limit."[128] While the modern novel draws dialectically on all of the narrative forms that came before (classical epic as well as tragedy and comedy), it foregrounds the character of narrative as a form and a process in a way that sets the stage for subsequent theories of narrative.

As we saw with his fable of Lordship and Bondage, Hegel's *Phenomenology of Spirit* is itself a strange and intense work of literary imagination; M. H. Abrams calls it, "one of the most original, influential, and baffling books ever written."[129] Walter Kaufmann writes that, "The *Phenomenology* is certainly *unwissenschaftlich*: undisciplined, arbitrary, full of digressions, not a monument to the austerity of the intellectual conscience and to carefulness and precision but a wild, bold, unprecedented book that invites comparison with some great literary masterpieces."[130] While much of its originality is a result of its startling claims about the nature of consciousness, the course of history, and the ends of philosophy, the *Phenomenology* is also strikingly innovative in its form. Rather than simply offering arguments, Hegel lays out his case for a motivated relation between ideas and things as a crowded kind of drama, a tragicomic and novelistic narrative of conflict, reconciliation, and development populated by a range of more or less allegorical figures, among them the master, the slave, the unhappy consciousness, the beautiful soul, and so on. I say *more or less* allegorical because, while these figures do stand in for this or that argument about the nature and the progress of self-consciousness, they often seem somehow to exceed their explanatory function and to take on an oddly novelistic density. Judith Butler compares Hegel's figures to cartoon characters who "always reassemble themselves, prepare a new scene, enter the stage armed with a new set of ontological insights—and fail again."[131] Or, as the young Marx wrote while comparing Hegel's achievement to the philosophical systems of the ancient Greeks: "It is essential that philosophy should ... wear character masks."[132] Hegel's *Phenomenology* is thus *both* a theory of narrative, of the ways in which historical change appears as the dialectical result of conflicts between apparently stable societies and new events and ideas, *and* a narrative in and of itself, a novelistic representation of the dialectic's passage from innocence, through experience, to achieved or "absolute" wisdom.

As I said, Hegel's book has often been compared particularly to the *Bidungsroman*, or the novel of development. Rée writes that, "The *Phenomenology* is, as has often been noticed, a kind of *Bildungsroman*, a story of a wayfaring consciousness called Spirit, traveling from what Hegel calls its 'natural' state, along a road which, though it passes through all sorts of deceptions and disappointments, leads ultimately to 'absolute knowledge.'"[133] For Martin Jay, the *Phenomenology* is "the record of the Subject's formation, a kind of *Bildungsroman* of the Absolute. The historical totality was this a self-reflexive one: the subjective totality at the beginning of the process recognized as itself the objective totality at the end."[134] M. H. Abrams writes that, "Josiah Royce passingly remarked a half-century ago that Hegel's *Phenomenology* was akin to the contemporary *Bildungsroman*. We can be more precise and more circumstantial. By a remarkable feat of invention, Hegel composed the *Phenomenology* as a *Bildungsbiographie* which is in a literal sense a spiritual history."[135] Royce's key example was Goethe's *Wilhelm Meister's Apprenticeship* (1795), a work considered by Hegel's Romantic contemporaries to be one of the great achievements of its time and that does seem to have provided Hegel with a kind of model. That said, although he had the utmost respect for Goethe, Hegel was not a fan of *Wilhelm Meister*, which he thought overly prosaic. Where the great tragedies and epics allowed us really to see conflicts that lie at the heart of experience, Hegel thought that novels like Goethe's provided a modern, bourgeois audience with a more or less accurate and thus unenlightening representation of itself: "They involve a young person who sows wild oats, gets involved in all kinds of escapades, but then gets a partner, settles down, possibly has a family, and falls into the typical worries of the bourgeois household, and the protagonist 'becomes as good a Philistine as the others.'"[136] Given his distaste for the novel's content, it is all the more striking that, as Royce, Abrams, Jean Hippolyte, and others have argued, Hegel draws so obviously on its form for the narrative development of his own *Phenomenology of Spirit*.

Although the *Bildungsroman* is often discussed in terms of a dialectical plot, one that takes a protagonist from a beginning state of naive innocence, though a middle education by error, to some sadder and wiser state of final maturity, the genre is also marked by its own necessary relation between story and discourse, between the events that make up the content of a novel and the way in which those events are aesthetically arranged and presented at the level of narrative form. In *The Way of the World: The Bildungsroman in European Culture*, Franco Moretti casts the classical *Bildungsroman* as a genre that enacts the hard-won synthesis of an individual's desires and experience and the ethical and cultural imperatives of society at large. As opposed, though, to simply imposing the latter onto the former, the *Bildungsoman* presents this synthesis as a *narrative* of development: to grow up in the *Bildungroman* is to learn really and truly to want what society wants, to find oneself and one's desire ultimately "at home" in one's world. Georg Lukács put the case this way: "...the decisive point in the education of Wilhelm Meister consists precisely in his abandonment of a merely internal, merely subjective attitude towards reality and his working towards an understanding of objective reality and an active participation join reality just as it is. *Wilhelm Meister* is an educative novel: its content is the education of man for a practical under-standing of reality."[137] The point here is that the *Bildungsroman* seeks to resolve terms that were opposed in Kant: the internal world of subjective experience and the external world of the world as it objectively but unknow-ably is; this is something that Hegel recognized in Goethe's project and adapted – at the level of form if not content – for his own purposes in the *Phenomenology*.

Although this process is represented in many different ways in and beyond the novel, what narrative had especially to offer is the way that it can manage the relation between what I've been calling *story* and *discourse* in order formally to encode this relation; Moretti, using Russian Formalist terms to which we will return in Section 5.2 (*fabula* for "story" and *sjuzhet* for "discourse"), makes the case:

> *Fabula*, in other words, is the story "as it is": established, unchangeable, independent of enunciation. *Sjuzhet* is a way of evaluating the story, dissecting it according to specific viewpoints and values: it is a perceptual schema, an implicit "comment" projected on to the "facts." Well, what happens to these two narrative modes in [*Wilhelm Meister's Apprenticeship*]? During the narration they are as distant from one another as possible: it is *sjuzhet* and the differentiation of viewpoints that dominate. But at the end of the narration they coincide perfectly; or rather, *sjuzhet* must renounce its characteristic features and bow to the super-individual necessity embodied within the reconstruction of the *fabula*.[138]

The formal difference between story and discourse thus does a couple of things for the *Bildungsroman* and for Hegel. First, insofar as story appears as the given material of a narrative, as that which simply "is what is," and insofar as discourse appears as a space in which that given might be more or less freely managed, rearranged, or interpreted, the formal divide between them can, in Moretti's view, stand in for the thematic divide between necessity and freedom that sits at the heart of both Kant and Hegel's respective projects. Where Kant saw them as philosophically and statically incommensurate (*noumena* and *phenomena*), Hegel animated their relation, turning the history of the world into a dialectical movement from one to the other (from necessity to freedom, from the is to the ought, from nature to the idea). We could see this now in terms of a turn from one mode of analysis to another, from the "substance dualism" of Kant to the "aspect dualism" of Hegel. That is, instead of seeing the world as made up of two entirely different kinds of stuff, Hegel wants to see the apparent doubleness of things as an effect of a historically specific limit to our perspective in relation to things. What, in other words, look like antinomies or opposed substances (the ideal and the real, the is and the ought, freedom and necessity, etc.) are in fact different aspects of one and the same stuff; and the story of history that Hegel tells is the history of coming to terms with that fact: that what looks like two is in fact one. As I will suggest later, this move from the two to the one has important consequences for story and discourse.

Second, with the end of the novel and the narrative closure it brings, the distance is at last erased; where, in other words, discourse can do what it will with the narrative given of story as long as the plot continues to unfold, with a novel's end the discourse is, precisely because it is over, just as fixed in form as the story ever was. With narrative's conclusion, the distance between two modes that had been necessarily distinct collapses into a new and conclusive unity. The dialectical, motivating conflict between story and discourse comes at last to an end and, with it, the novel does, too. Frederick Beiser writes that, "The dialectic will go on until we reach the absolute whole, that which includes everything within itself, and so cannot possibly depend upon anything outside itself. When this happens the system will be complete, and we will have achieved knowledge of the absolute."[139] This was not just a way to imagine history's meaning in relation to history's putative end; it was also a way after Aristotle to imagine in the ultimate synthesis of story and discourse a way of resolving the relation between the "time of men" and the "time of gods"; Rée writes that, "Like any other journey-story, the *Phenomenology* works by playing on the contrast between the bounded perspective of the traveller, and a bird's-eye view, or map, of the journey as a whole."[140] Narrative, seen from Hegel's point of view, formalized his hopes for a larger reconciliation between the parts and the whole of human history: beginning, middle, and end.

~

We saw in the previous chapter that Aristotle offered one of the earliest accounts of the story–discourse relation, making clear a distinction between actions and the whole representation of actions that come incompletely together to form a tragedy. I argued that one way to understand Aristotle's insistence on this distinction was to look to a similar split that characterized fifth-century tragedy, a split between a "time of men" and a "time of the gods" that in turn stood as a response to social and political changes that were occurring in Athens at the time. As a result, Aristotle was committed not only to the difference but also to the conflict between these two ideas; I began this chapter arguing that, although it had fallen out of view in the years between, Hegel's sense of tragedy and its relation to dialectical thinking allowed him to see and to recover Aristotle's own theory of conflict and to apply it to the experience of modern life. With Hegel's turn to the novel form, we now get a different but related sense of things. As Moretti points out, the *Bildungsroman* is built around the more or less opposed presence of different values that must exist – at least at first – in conflict: how things are and how they ought to be; innocence and wisdom; fact and value; necessity and freedom; the world of things and the world of ideas. Where the novel form differs from tragedy is that, instead of formalizing conflict as insoluble, it works to imagine the possibility of an ultimate synthesis of two apparently incommensurate concepts. Where, however, tragedy used the difference between story and discoulrse to crystalize conflict in the form of what Aristotle called a dialectical problem, Hegel adapts the form of the *Bildungsroman* to philosophy in order to put story and discourse in a developmental or dialectical relation with one another; although he denies the content of *Wilhelm Meister's Apprenticeship*, Hegel nonetheless sees that the logic of the *Bildungsroman*, insofar as it turns on the coming together of story and discourse, is ideally suited to the work of representing the dialectic and thus the whole of history in action.

I've argued here that we can understand Hegel's engagement with Aristotle and Kant in terms of his effort to use narrative forms – the tragedy, the novel, and others – in order to lay bare and to advance the problems of philosophy. For Hegel, philosophy's greatest challenge was to see how the distance between ideas and things – a distance that Kant took as absolute – might be bridged. In order to think through that effort, Hegel drew on a number of different narrative models and developed an account of the world that sought to explain how an apparently stable condition or division could be upset by the negating introduction of new ideas, events, and possibilities. This process is what Hegel refers to as the dialectic, and it is itself an essentially narrative theory. Hegel's philosophy and his reaction to the world-shattering experience of the French Revolution initiated what we might call a narrative turn in intellectual history. Because Hegel not only thought about narrative but also identified narrative as the means by which we could understand history and consciousness, he made it all but inevitable that subsequent thinkers and critics would have to come to terms with one or another theory of narrative. And so it went.

Chapter 3

Lost Illusions

Narrative in Marx, Nietzsche, and Freud

> The curtain rose again, a lantern was lowered from the ceiling, and firemen and stage carpenters departed on their rounds. The fairy scenes of the stage, the rows of fair faces in the boxes, the dazzling lights, the magical illusion of new scenery and costume had all disappeared, and dismal darkness, emptiness, and cold reigned in their stead. It was hideous.
>
> Honoré de Balzac, *Lost Illusions*

I argued in the last section that Hegel is important to narrative theory for a few reasons. I suggested that Hegel sought to engage with the two great events of his early intellectual life – his encounter with Kant and the fact and idea of the French Revolution – in terms of a philosophical system that depended on narrative form (a relation between story and discourse) in order both to link aspects of life that a previous generation of philosophers took as fundamentally different in kind and to imagine a version of history that could make productive sense of historical events that would otherwise seem hateful or absurd. Dennis Schmidt writes that Hegel's "turn to the topic of tragedy, now in order to develop a theory of the tragic" – and, I would add, a theory of narrative – "has above all these dual motivations: the effort to think through the end of philosophy as metaphysics, which Kant first made a necessary concern, and the effort to think the radical transformation in history and the idea of freedom that is announced by the French Revolution."[1] First, Hegel's narrative method thus allowed him to imagine an ultimate synthesis of ideas and things, form and content, a synthesis that Kant and others saw as impossible; and, second, imagining history not as a series of unrelated events but rather as a whole and organic system governed by a single dialectical logic allowed him to see events such as the French revolutionary Terror of 1793 as something other than a waste of life, time, and potential. Thinking of history as an encounter between the experience of life as it mysteriously unfolded and the idea of life as a whole, intentional, and significant plot gave Hegel a way both to understand the

76

consequence of an otherwise tragic divide between freedom and necessity and to treat history and its various contents as available to analysis and interpretation. Although it could often seem or rather feel otherwise, history seen as an unfolding beginning, middle, and end would turn out at last to have made sense; imagined from the point of view of an ideal and supra-historical reader looking back from history's end, the world and its events would be just as comprehensible or, rather, as interpretable as any novel or play. Paul Ricoeur writes that these two points of view, the scene looked at from within and the scene observed from outside or from its end, give the same events an entirely different character: "From the point of view of the individual," history "is the history of a failed project." He continues, "It is only from the point of view of the higher interests of freedom and its progress" that failure "may appear as significant."[2] When seen from the right point of view, even the ugliest events would reveal themselves as essential, as historical counterparts to Anton Chekhov's famously well-wrought rifle: "Remove everything that has no relevance to the story. If you say in the first chapter that there is a rifle hanging on the wall, in the second or third chapter it absolutely must go off. If it's not going to be fired, it shouldn't be hanging there."[3] Hegel's immense hopes for history and philosophy forced him to develop a working method that prefigures and influences narrative theory's foundational distinction between story and discourse as the source of narrative's capacity to mean as well as its apparently necessary relation to human life. In other words, once he imagined individual events as making sense only within the context of a whole historical sequence, he needed a theory that could come to terms both with narrative development and with the apparent senselessness of individual events, both with the event as an isolated or contingent moment in empty time and with the event as a significant part of a narrative whole; he needed, in other words, a theory that could account at once for the difference and the relation between two different aspects of the same historical experience, levels that anticipate and, I will argue, influence the development of the story–discourse relation and thus narrative theory.

Because Hegel thus focused on a version of narrative as his primary object of study and modeled the shape and method of his philosophy on available narrative forms (tragedy, myth, the *Bildungsroman*, etc.), his work revealed a narrative force already at work in precursors including Aristotle and set the stage for the emergence of narrative as a newly central idea in the history of philosophy as well as in the philosophy of history. Although others had of course discussed narrative before he did, Hegel made it seem self-evident that a narrative approach was necessary to understand aesthetic experience, historical events, human psychology, and life itself; this idea remains current today as political strategists, cognitive therapists, and business consultants stress the importance of having "a good narrative" or of "controlling the narrative."[4] Part of Hegel's legacy is felt, in other words, in our broad cultural faith in narrative's shaping power, in our shared sense that difficult or painful experiences and ideas can be made manageable and productive by situating them within a narrative, and that it is sometimes more important, perhaps, that a narrative be coherent and comforting than that it be true. (See the Introduction for a brief discussion of the so-called "narrative turn" in the humanities and social sciences.) Once again, part of my argument here is that, as self-evidently important as narrative is to life, we need also to ask both when and why that became an assertion we could so confidently make.

In this chapter, I will argue that Hegel's example offered a different kind of inspiration to a group of nineteenth- and early twentieth-century writers whose work would also go on in several ways to influence the first and subsequent generations of narrative theorists. I want, in other words, to look at three figures who implicitly or explicitly take up Hegel's focus on narrative as fundamental to understanding life, history, and society but who also call attention to narrative's limits as a tool with which to understand the world and our place in it. What is more, in looking at how Karl Marx, Friedrich Nietzsche, and Sigmund Freud implicitly and explicitly accepted, developed, and challenged Hegel's reliance on narrative, I want to explore another set of terms that will come to shape later narrative theories; because Marx, Nietzsche, and Freud worked in distinct fields, they each activate a different set of questions and answers about narrative's capacity to order human experience. As was the case in the previous two chapters, I cannot hope to cover Marx, Nietzsche, and Freud; I want, rather, to focus on some ways in which their respective encounters with narrative's post-Hegelian prestige contributed and continues to contribute to later thinking about narrative and its discontents.

Why discontents? In his *Freud and Philosophy*, Paul Ricoeur famously sees Marx, Nietzsche, and Freud as unknowingly meeting to form a more or less coherent "school of suspicion."[5] For Ricoeur, *suspicion* names one of two general approaches toward interpretation; *reminiscence* names the other. In terms of the latter: there is the reader who seeks to bind things up and draw them together, to "remember" ways in which past events or apparently stray details emerge as significant in relation to a present act of interpretation. We can think again of Hegel's effort to show how the French Revolution was not simply a random and disappointing event but rather a moment that would ultimately *have made sense* within the larger story – the beginning, middle, and end – of world history. (We should think of *re-membering* as a productive alternative to *dis-membering* or breaking apart.) As I said, Ricouer refers to the effort to merge and to bind different experiences and things into larger, more comprehensive systems as characteristic of an interpretive "school of reminiscence." Hegel, because his system depends on imagining an end-of-history position from which it would be possible to remember and thus reconstitute *everything* that ever happened, is perhaps the grand master of reminiscence; in a deep and maybe more than human sense, memory and remembering are everything to Hegel. At the end of the *Phenomenology*, he makes the importance of what we might call a narrating memory clear: "The *goal*, Absolute Knowing, or Spirit that knows itself as Spirit, has for its path the recollection of the Spirits as they are in themselves and as they accomplish the organization of their realm. Their preservation, regarded from the side of their free existence appearing in the form of contingency, is History."[6] Hegel, in other words, needs to imagine a narrative perspective from which the apparently contingent events of the past could be *re-membered* into a whole, organic, and coherent narrative that he calls History.

If, however, there are those readers, there are also interpreters who do not build things up but, rather, break them down: readers who call apparently whole stories into question, to reveal them as comforting but ultimately false accounts of matters as they really are; Ricoeur refers to these as members of the "school of suspicion." This other attitude toward narrative is a double one; while the suspicious critic works to undermine available narratives, he or she does so precisely because he or she recognizes narratives as so powerful. As I said in the previous chapter, we can see Hegel's turn to narrative as an aspect of a larger need to recognize, to analyze, and to understand if not to share other people's narrative accounts of the same events (a war, a revolution, a birth, a marriage, a death); in this way, Hegel's sense of the related power and fragility of narrative needs to be seen alongside the emergence of ideology as an important historical concept. In *Ideology and Utopia*, Karl Mannheim identifies the conceptual emergence of ideology with Napoleon's dismissal of adversaries as mere "ideologists," people whose stories about the world were coherent but unreal: "During the nineteenth century, the term ideology, used in this sense, gained wide currency. ... Henceforward the problem implicit in the term ideology – what is really real? – never disappeared from the horizon."[7] As I have said, for Hegel and for others, the emerging problem of ideology was a problem of narrative, a potentially tragic conflict among equally coherent discursive representations of events. This is where suspicion comes in: once you see that narratives or ideologies can organize and direct life while remaining only partially true or, indeed, entirely untrue, you need a theory of narrative in order methodologically to sort out what is what. You need a way to separate truth from illusion. (This is, of course, what one version of the nineteenth-century European novel – *Madame Bovary* (1856), *Great Expectations* (1861), *Père Goriot* (1835) – is all about: the gradual or sudden unraveling of the stories we tell ourselves about how things are or how they should be.) "Suspicion" thus names a mix of piety and impiety toward narrative, a sense that we need to call narratives into question precisely because we need them so much. The "school of suspicion" thus takes up the tools of Hegelian reminiscence in order not only to instruct but also to undo false or incomplete narratives. We could just as well refer to this as the school of disillusion or, as Balzac would have it, the school of "lost illusions."

I want to argue here that part of what joins Marx, Nietzsche, and Freud together into a loose but powerful school is the fact that each of them took up the conciliatory terms of Hegel's narrative theory *both* as a way to engage with history, the relation among things, and the nature of human experience *and* as the first step of an importantly critical project. Where, in other words, Hegel moved conceptual mountains to tell a coherent story, to reveal an order behind what he called the "slaughter-bench" of history, Marx, Nietzsche, and Freud worked variously to upend, invert, and mobilize Hegel's method in order to develop distinct critical approaches to narrative, approaches that might, ideally, allow one to differentiate between the false and the true. As I have suggested, what makes Hegel so important to narrative theory is also what makes him important to thinking about ideology; once one sees how individuals, classes, cultures, or nations *think* as historical and thus contingent, it becomes possible to subject those ways of thinking to criticism, to unveil them as just one perspective among many, as the illusion of an individual or a group. Taken together, Marx, Nietzsche, and Freud represent the next step in our prehistory of narrative theory because they use narrative not only to put things together – although they do that, too – but also to take them apart.

3.1 Karl Marx: First as Tragedy

Karl Marx begins "The Eighteenth Brumaire of Napoleon Bonaparte" with a famous and gnomic observation about Hegel and the essentially narrative character of history: "Hegel remarks somewhere that all facts and personages of great importance in world history occur, as it were, twice. He forgot to add: the first time as tragedy, the second as farce."[8] The line is characteristically compressed, joining complicated ideas about history and the philosophy of history with the deceptively throwaway wit that distinguishes much of Marx's writing in "The Eighteenth Brumaire." The self-consciously casual reference to Hegel immediately puts the essay in a tonal range somewhere between the high and the low, the willfully arcane and the coolly pragmatic; here, Marx plays both professor and operator. The assertion, obviously absurd, that everything happens twice, encourages us to imagine history as organized and intentional, as a narrative written by *someone* that follows or reaches after the clarity of aesthetic design (repetition produces a pattern and patterns are evidence of intention); and the association of that aesthetic design with recognizable narrative genres – tragedy and farce – signals the essay's more broadly comparative mode, its commitment to tracking not only the character of historical events but also how they might merge or mean something entirely different in tragedy or farce or comedy or satire. Although it is a joke, the line nonetheless encourages us to take seriously the idea that history *is* in and of itself a form of narrative, which is to say an arranged representation of events; the line thus takes up, albeit with a kind of sardonic reticence, some of the narrative claims for history and memory that we have already seen at work in Hegel.

Written in the immediate wake of the history it describes, Marx's essay picks up a number of threads suggested by that opening line: it offers a trenchant and often satirical analysis of contemporary events in France and, more particularly, of the passage from the Revolution of 1848 to Louis Bonaparte's successful coup d'état in 1851; it acknowledges the real but roundabout influence of Hegel's thinking about narrative and history on Marx's whole project; it makes a quiet case for the necessary relation between two levels of history – real history *as* the history of class struggle and history *as it appears* in the form of political and cultural representation – and, most importantly for our purposes, it relies on an idea about the essential narrativity of events that connects Marx's thinking about history and history writing to the longer history that I have been tracking. Put simply, because he begins his essay on Louis Bonaparte and the Revolution of 1848 with a gesture toward two distinct narrative genres – tragedy and farce – Marx encourages us to think about how individual events can join into more meaningful and plotted wholes, how the apparently absurd fact of history as it happens seems somehow to add up *after the fact* into an inherently meaningful and coherent plot. As a result, Marx encourages us to look back to Aristotle and Hegel, from whom he takes ideas about the logic and the character of plots, and forward to the many theorists of narrative who owe an implicit or explicit debt to Marx's thinking about narrative, history, and culture.

Marx is indeed a narrative thinker who relies on a structured play between events and the representation of events as well as among beginnings, middles, and ends in many of his most important works. These relations are present in the opening sections of *Capital* where Marx manages to give his account of the dialectical development of value from its simple to its expanded, general, and money forms the urgency and narrative drive of an adventure story or a *Bildungsroman*. They are also present in the more overtly narrative form of *The Communist Manifesto*, which pits the restless, destructive, and inconclusively Faustian momentum of bourgeois desire against the proletariat as a class representative of revolutionary and narrative closure: "Let the ruling classes tremble at a Communistic revolution. The proletarians have nothing to lose but their chains. They have a world to win. Working Men of All Countries, Unite!"[9] In this sense, the two great classes of Marx's theory represent not only the last phase of a historical struggle that seemed to Marx to have reached the verge of its own narrative conclusion but also the necessary conflict between what Peter Brooks (following Jacques Derrida) refers to as "force" and "form," principles that he takes as essential to and at odds in every narrative:

> My study, then, while ever resting its case on the careful reading of texts, intends to take its stand beyond pure formalism, attempting to talk of the dynamics of temporality and reading, of the motor forces that drive the text forward, of the desires that connect narrative ends and beginnings, and make of the textual middle a highly charged field of force. "Form fascinates when we no longer have the force to understand force from within itself," Jacques Derrida has written in criticism of the formalist imagination of structuralism. I am not certain that we can ever "understand" force (nor does Derrida claim to), but it ought to be possible to recognize its place in narrative, and to find ways of talking about our experience of reading narrative as a dynamic operation, consuming and shaping time as the medium of certain meanings that depend on energy as well as form.[10]

In Brooks's account, "force" is a pure manifestation of desire, as a motive energy that forces plots forward; that pushes against boundaries; that wants, needs, and uses up more and more meaning; and that pits itself against the possibility or inevitability of closure; "force" is a fascination with change for its own sake, a fascination that Marx took as essential to the bourgeois character:

> Constant revolutionizing of production, uninterrupted disturbance of all social conditions, everlasting uncertainty and agitation distinguish the

bourgeois epoch from all earlier ones. All fixed, fast-frozen relations, with their train of ancient and venerable prejudices and opinions, are swept away, all new-formed ones become antiquated before they can ossify. All that is solid melts into air, all that is holy is profaned, and man is at last compelled to face with sober senses his real conditions of life, and his relations with his kind.[11]

"Form," on the contrary, refers to the desire *for* closure, to the paradoxically narrative desire for desire's and thus narrative's end; it is the urge toward a perspective from which a story can be seen as whole, coherent, and finished; it is, in other words, a desire that Marx associates with his revolutionary class, with the idea of history as something that can and should come to an end. In a way that thus reproduces the logic of Hegel's fable of "Lordship and Bondage," the proletariat's work for the bourgeoisie will lead dialectically to its final victory and thus to the conclusion of a narrative that had been defined by a conflict between classes: "What the bourgeoisie therefore produces, above all, are its own grave-diggers. Its fall and the victory of the proletariat are equally inevitable."[12] In Marx's account, the proletariat is the class of closure and thus the class of narrative form as opposed to force; the class struggle is, in other words, not only a narrative but also an implicit narrative theory, which is to say an account of the conflict between two motives or desires that Brooks takes as essential to narrative as such.

More to the point, Marx's account of history depends on the idea that different classes have different stories to tell about the way things are, and that the goal of criticism is to strip those stories down until we reach something like a truth; Hayden White writes that "the relation between the form and the content of any social phenomenon in any specific historical situation, Marx argues here and elsewhere, is a product of a conflict between specific class interests as they are envisaged and lived by a given class."[13] And Fredric Jameson writes,

> The most influential lesson of Marx – the one which ranges him alongside Freud and Nietzsche as one of the great negative diagnosticians of contemporary culture and social life – has, of course, rightly been taken to be the lesson of false consciousness, of class bias and ideological programming, the lesson of structural limits of the values and attitudes of particular social classes, or in other words of the constitutive relationship between the praxis of such groups and what they conceptualize as value or desire and project in the form of culture.[14]

Put differently, particular classes will arrange the materials of life into narratives that more or less reflect or support their interests insofar as those interests are defined against those of other, competing classes; criticism, in that case, is the effort not only to compare those narratives but also to understand the conditions and relations that made them possible in the first place. We should, as I argued in the Introduction as well as the last chapter, see Marx's comparative approach to differently classed narratives as emerging from the same context that produced Hegel's deeply narrative sense of history and the stories other people tell. The related ideas that individual narratives can and should be analyzed down to their base, that events are made meaningful by their arrangement into politically motivated discourse, and that the best way to break narratives down is to recognize them as a relation between different levels are at the heart of Marx's project and will go on directly to influence some of our later figures: Lukács, Bakhtin, the Russian Formalists, Kristeva, Lévi-Strauss, Barthes, Genette, and others.

~

But, to return to "The Eighteenth Brumaire," what does it really mean to say that history happens "the first time as tragedy, the second as farce"? What does it mean to say that the same event or the same kind of event – in this case a revolution – can occur a second time but only in a different generic form? In one sense, Marx is offering a comparative and critical evaluation of two moments in history, casting the French Revolution of 1789 as a tragedy (a noble, consequential, well-formed event) and the French Revolution of 1848 as a farce (a ridiculous but nonetheless deadly joke). We have already seen that Hegel understood the French Revolution of 1789 as essentially tragic; beginning in optimism, hope, and a celebration of distinctly human potential, the revolution devolved into the violence and waste of the Terror. Because it revealed both the huge potential of human events and how that potential could be squandered, the revolution was tragic in a sense that A. C. Bradley, a literary critic directly inspired by Hegel, lays out in *Shakespearean Tragedy*: "'What a piece of work is man,' we cry; 'so much more beautiful and so much more terrible than we knew! Why should he be so if this beauty and greatness only tortures itself and throws itself away?' We seem to have before us a type of the mystery of the whole world, the tragic fact which extends far beyond the limits of tragedy."[15] For Hegel and then for Marx, the first French Revolution thus followed a certain narrative pattern, embodying a tragic order that both relied on and called into question the right relation among beginnings, middles, and ends. Rebecca Comay writes of both Hegel and Marx that "the encounter with the French Revolution introduces anachronism – trauma itself – as a henceforth ineluctable feature of historical and political experience."[16]

Marx saw the French Revolution of 1848 as farce rather than tragedy for a number of reasons: because of the low cunning of Napoleon's itinerant nephew, Louis Bonaparte; because of the fecklessness of politicians who capitulated to his demands; and because of the nearly slapstick character of the events that led from the Revolution in 1848 to Bonaparte's coup d'état in 1851. What, however, made events truly farcical was their staged and inauthentic relation to the earlier revolution; according to Marx, the nephew dressed up his ambition in the more authentically tragic style of 1789 and thus beguiled the whole of France with an ersatz and absurd performance of tragedy as opposed to the thing itself: "A cunning old roué, he conceives popular history and high politics and finance as comedies in the most vulgar sense, as masquerades where fine costumes, words and postures serve only to mask the most trifling pettiness."[17] Farce is, in that case, what happens when absurdity or brute self-interest appears dressed in tragedy's Attic style, when the roundabout and tenuous relation between uncle and nephew is given the full Oedipal consequence of a relation between father and son. Marx thus understands the difference between the two historical events in narrative terms, as the difference between the more or less self-conscious way in which events were arranged into and thus given significance as whole plots.

Tragedy and farce thus name different ways of ordering the same events into differently significant narrative wholes: where tragedy is, as we know from Aristotle and Hegel, determined by the deeply reciprocal relation among its tensions, its conflicts, and the whole structure of its plot, farce is characterized by the serial disconnection of its events and thus its essential absurdity: farce is funny because farce does not add up. In an essay that touches on the place of farce in the logic of "The Eighteenth Brumaire," Stephen Tifft writes, "'Farce' in [its] colloquial sense denotes a breakdown of rational behavior, a state of failure and confusion in which unseasonable motives are pursued with tactical purblindness matched only by a self-defeating automatism of execution."[18] Farce is, in this sense, neither tragic nor exactly comic; as opposed to trading one form of synthesis for another, farce elevates a resistance to synthesis into a paradoxical end of its own. Marx's invocation of tragedy and farce evokes the difference between disparate but equally persuasive accounts of how more or less the same events hung together.

On the one hand, Marx's sense of tragedy and farce as two ways of arranging similar or the same events into differently significant narrative forms needs to be understood in terms of his avowed role as a historian and thus a narrator of 1848–1851. In his 1869 preface to the second edition of "The Eighteenth Brumaire," he casts the difference between his and other accounts explicitly in terms of narrative strategy: "Victor Hugo confines himself [in his *Napoleon le petit*] to bitter and witty invective against the responsible producer of the *coup d'état*. The event appears in his work like a bolt from the blue. He sees in it only the violent act of a single individual. . . . I, on the contrary, demonstrate how the class struggle in France created circumstances and relationships that made it possible for a grotesque mediocrity to play a hero's part."[19] The difference between Marx and Hugo comes down to their different understandings of the relation between events and how events can or should be discursively ordered into narrative wholes; it is, in other words, the difference between two ways of thinking about the means and ends of narrative form. Marx thus anticipates Hayden White's discussion of the relation between history and genre in *Metahistory: The Historical Imagination in Nineteenth-Century Europe*, where he argues that every history, which is to say every account of history, is "a verbal structure in the form of a narrative prose discourse that purports to be a model, or icon, of past structures and processes in the interest of *explaining what they were by representing them*."[20] The historian, in other words, deals with a range of historical events by choosing one or another narrative genre to guide the selection and arrangement of those events into a coherent and significant form; according to White, the great historians Michelet, Ranke, Tocqueville, and Burckhardt each adopted a different generic mode in order to make sense of events: romance, comedy, tragedy, and satire. As a result, different historians' accounts of the same events look different and will, indeed, mean different things.

A tragic narrative about a revolution or military campaign might, in other words, begin in the middle of things, with a moment when latent conflicts within a party or group had just begun to rise to the surface, when optimism about a new way of life had begun to give way to anxieties about the insoluble difference between two apparently valid ideas about the good and the true; beginning discursively at the middle might allow the beginning and ending of the events to be cast in greater relief – as is the case in *Oedipus Rex*, where we begin the narrative with Oedipus already on the throne, we look back to the heroic and hopeful events that put him there, and we end as hope turns to disappointment, heartbreak, and violence. A farcical narrative of the same events might rather ignore the significant relation among events in order to focus on what we might see as a permanent present of absurdity, vanity, and fecklessness. We might think here of Charlie Chaplin's *The Great Dictator* (1940) and a tension that falls between the film's bare and frankly unconvincing plot and the brilliant energy of its farcical set pieces. Although it is clear that Chaplin wanted to make sense of world events in 1940, to put them in some kind of progressive historical order, the film's power results rather from its more purely critical moments, the scenes where plot is subordinated to the anarchic and antinarrative force of slapstick and farce. In other words, although a tragic and a farcical treatment might draw on the same events, they would select and arrange those events differently at the level of discourse to produce very different results. In this sense, we can see Marx's evocation of tragedy and farce at the beginning of his essay as a historian's moment of methodological self-consciousness, as Marx's effort to acknowledge the degree to which he was about to *make* history into one whole, significant, and politically organized representation of events as opposed to another.

~

What is most striking about the opening lines of "The Eighteenth Brumaire of Napoleon Bonaparte" is not or at least not only that they reveal generic choices available to the historian; it is rather that they attempt to capture the generic character of the events themselves. Marx is not only reflecting on the possibility that the events of 1789 or 1848 could be differently narrated by different historians in one or another ideologically distinct way; he is also suggesting that the two revolutions each had their own *essentially* generic character: if 1789 *was* tragedy, 1848 *was* farce. Marx seems, in other words, to suggest that history is not only available to narrative but also a form of narrative in and of itself. What does it mean to see history as narrative? On the one hand, this leads us back to the idea that history needs to be understood both from the perspective of those living in it (the perspective of events) as well as from the perspective of someone looking back at the whole plotted course of history (the perspective of those events as they merge into a beginning, middle, and end); in both Aristotle and Hegel, we saw that history can be understood as a kind of narrative if we accept a difference and a relation between the moment-to-moment experience of history lived from within and history as it will appear to someone viewing it from its outside or end, a difference and a relation between what we referred to in the chapter on Aristotle as the time of men and the time of the gods. For Fredric Jameson, this necessary play between intrinsic and extrinsic narrative perspectives is at the heart of Marx's interpretive project:

> Only Marxism can give us an adequate account of the essential *mystery* of the cultural past, which, like Tiresias drinking the blood, is momentarily returned to life and warmth and allowed once more to speak, and to deliver its long-forgotten message in surroundings utterly alien to it. This mystery can be reenacted only if the human adventure is

one; only thus … can we glimpse the vital claims upon us of such long-dead issues as the seasonal alteration of the economy of a primitive tribe, the passionate disputes about the Trinity, the conflicting models of the *polis* or the universal Empire, or, apparently closer to us in time, the dusty parliamentary and journalistic polemics of the nineteenth-century nation states.[21]

It is, in other words, because Marx sees history as a whole and single narrative ("the human adventure is one") that he can imagine a perspective from which all of its apparently disparate moments will not only make sense but also make sense in relation to each other. For Marx, who saw history as the history of a class struggle that would culminate in proletarian revolution ("The history of all hitherto existing society is the history of class struggles"), events needed always to be seen from two perspectives – the intrinsic and apparently tragic perspective of events as they are experienced on the ground and the extrinsic, maybe fantastic, and finally comic perspective as history as it would be seen from its end.[22]

Indeed, Hayden White casts Marx's double vision, his interest in the event as discrete event and the event as a necessary part of a larger whole, in terms of a nested relation between tragedy and comedy: "Marx employed the historical process in two modes, Tragic and Comic, simultaneously, but in such a way as to make the former emplotment a *phase* within the latter, and so as to permit himself claim the title of a 'realist' while sustaining his dream of a utopian reconciliation of man with man *beyond* the social state."[23] This is another reason why Marx characterizes 1848 as *farce*; as opposed to comedy's drive toward an ultimate, synthetic end, farce refuses narrative closure, focusing instead on the isolated, absurd, and slapstick (which is also to say the violent) charm of events in and of themselves. In Marx's account of 1848, the nephew's genius is best expressed in his ability temporarily to short-circuit the logic of historical development; because his rise to power represents an anachronistic disturbance in the larger logic of capitalist development and bourgeoisie self-interest, it functions as a minor but nonetheless consequential rejection of history's innate narrative sense; and because Marx sees the nephew as a clever opportunist as opposed to a sign of the times, he sees him, at last, as the farcical, antinarrative exception that disastrously proves the narrative rule.

This is where Marx's debt to Hegel is most important and most vexed; White writes that "Marx's aim as a writer was to clarify the relation of content to form in a way that he thought, correctly I believe, was consistent with Hegel's dialectical method of analysis, although – in his view – Hegel had got the form–content distinction wrong way about."[24] Like Hegel, Marx sees history as moving through a beginning and middle toward a synthetic narrative end; unlike Hegel, Marx sees history's narrative as governed not by a supernatural entity like Spirit or *Geist* or Absolute Knowledge but rather by the wholly and importantly limited human acts and thoughts of those who participate in it: "Men make their own history, but they do not make it as they please; they do not make it under self-selected circumstances, but under circumstances existing already, given and transmitted from the past."[25] We make our own history because we are an active and organic part of it; we cannot "make it as we please" because we are, at last, only a part of it, because we show up in the middle when a lot of things have happened and there are a lot more in store. As Frank Kermode puts it, "Men, like poets, rush 'into the middest,' *in medias res*, when they are born; they also die *in mediis rebus*, and to make sense of their span they need fictive concords with origins and ends, such as give meaning to lives and to poems."[26] Marx's theory is, in other words, a narrative theory because it relies on the comparative analysis of the different ways in which different narrative genres – tragedy, comedy, farce, etc. – can ideologically arrange the same real events into differently significant plots.

Margaret Cohen, in her *The Sentimental Education of the Novel*, has recently gestured toward Marx's implicit account of the shaping power of narrative genre; drawing on a Marxian strain within the work of the sociologist Pierre Bourdieu, she writes that

> genre is a position. Genre designates the fact that writers share a
> common set of codes when they respond to a space of possibles, a
> horizon formed by the literary conventions and constraints binding any
> writer at a particular state of the field. Or better, when they resolve the
> space of possibles, for this space of possibles is dynamic, taking the form
> of "problems to resolve, stylistic or thematic possibilities to exploit,
> contradictions to overcome, even revolutionary ruptures to effect"; it
> constitutes a literary problematic that interacts with factors on the level
> of the whole social formation to shape textual poetics.[27]

Beginning with this sense of genre as a social as well as an aesthetic *position*, as a configuration of conventions and, potentially, reactions to or against conventions, Cohen offers a revaluation of the French nineteenth-century novel as a *narrative genre*, which is to say a series of positions taken up, advanced, or put down within what was a wide, contested, and essentially sentimental field. Looking to a massive archive of now more or less unread nineteenth-century novels, many of them written by women, Cohen shows how apparently representative realist texts by Balzac and Stendhal need rather to be seen as emerging out of a wide and now more or less forgotten field of sentimental literature, a fact that makes clear the degree to which any given novel is itself a position taken in relation to a whole social world and, in this case, a world largely and frankly organized around questions of gender that have often gone missing from standard accounts of French literary history. From this point of view, the sentimental novel, a genre that represents a necessarily gendered position taken in relation to the world and that also embodies that position in the ways it organizes events in relation to one another as narrative discourse, is revealed as essential not only to the rise of the realist novel but also to the whole imaginative structure of postrevolutionary life in France. Using, in other words, an explicitly post-Marxian take on the analysis of narrative genres, Cohen is able to show how the sentimental novel, which is – like tragedy and farce – a particular arrangement of story and discourse, reveals ways in which nineteenth-century French culture used a particular narrative form connected to the experience of women and women writers to present itself to itself.

~

Marx's reliance on narrative genre leads us to another important and influential aspect of his thinking about history and narrative: his understanding of the relation between *base* and *superstructure*, between, in other words, the essential and necessary and material events of history and the different and more or less distorted expressions that those events take as they are lived and understood in politics and culture. Although Marx did not say much about these terms, his few comments have been important to and controversial in the development of Marxian thinking after Marx. In the "Preface to *A Contribution to the Critique of Political Economy*," Marx writes that

> in the social production of their existence, men inevitably enter into definite relations, which are independent of their will, namely relations of production appropriate to a given stage in the development of their material forces of production. The totality of these relations of production constitutes the economic structure of society, the real foundation, on which arises a legal and political superstructure and to which correspond definite forms of social consciousness. The mode of production of material life conditions the general process of social, political and intellectual life.[28]

Crudely put, Marx's point is that the analysis of a society must assume the more or less coordinated presence of two different but related levels. On the one hand, there is the economic *base*, the particular and material "relations of production" that govern the forms labor takes, the struggle between different classes, and, more broadly, the character of social life at a given moment in time. On the other hand, there is the *superstructure*, a level of legal, political, and cultural activity that reflects and "supports" the material logic of the base, while also existing at a significant remove from it. That is, while Marx understands the base as ultimately determinate of what appears at the level of superstructure, the structural distance and temporal gap between base and superstructure are nonetheless historically significant:

> The changes in the economic foundation lead sooner or later to the transformation of the whole immense superstructure. In studying such transformations it is always necessary to distinguish between the material transformation of the economic conditions of production, which can be determined with the precision of natural science, and the legal, political, religious, artistic or philosophic – in short, ideological forms in which men become conscious of this conflict and fight it out.[29]

While, in other words, the logical status of the base is always the ultimate cause of changes that occur at the level of superstructure, the fact that those changes can occur "sooner or later" makes them immensely hard to track, to diagnose, and to understand; and while history's struggles between classes will ultimately come down to the character and shape of the "relations of productions," real and consequential fights over what those relations are and what they mean will almost always take place at the experiential level of the superstructure: in courts, in elections, and in the countless exchanges, representations, contests, and quarrels that constitute culture. (The farcical, anachronistic nephew is, we might say, a lived instance of the "sooner or later.") In his great essay "Ideology and Ideological State Apparatuses," Louis Althusser highlights the topographical and thus the relational nature of base and superstructure:

> We can therefore say that the great theoretical advantage of the Marxist topography, i.e. of the spatial metaphor of the edifice (base and superstructure) is simultaneously that it reveals that questions of determination (or of index of effectivity) are crucial; that it reveals that it is the base which in the last instance determines the whole edifice; and that, as a consequence, it obliges us to pose the theoretical problem of the types of "derivatory" effectivity peculiar to the superstructure, i.e. it obliges us to think what the Marxist tradition calls conjointly the relative autonomy of the superstructure and the reciprocal action of the superstructure on the base.[30]

So, even though the superstructure needs at last to be understood as "only" a representation of economic events, the practical experience of history, struggle, and identity will take place almost entirely at the level of the superstructure; and, because the superstructure is "relatively autonomous," because it sometimes lags behind or gets ahead of events as they unfold at the level of the base, the superstructural "representations" of those events both demand and offer a variety or interpretations, different possibilities for construing the ultimate meaning of history.

As I have already suggested, the variable temporal logic of base and super-structure – its *sooner-or-later* quality – is one of the relation's most compelling and troubling aspects. (It also recalls – significantly, I think – the paradox of "which comes first, story or discourse" that I discussed in the Introduction.) What, after all, can it mean that one aspect of our shared historical experience seems to slip like an oversized suit back and forth over the events themselves? What hope do we have of seeing history if history not only moves but also moves contrapuntally against itself? A powerful and succinct description of the complex timing of the superstructure appears in Raymond Williams's "Base and Superstructure in Marxist Cultural Theory." Williams argues there that, whatever its ultimate nature, what is important to the historian and cultural critic about the relation among these levels is the fact that the discursive experience of history can often appear "out of joint" with history itself, reaching back to old modes (the *residual*), anticipating changes that have not yet been realized (the *emergent*), and, sometimes, fully expressing the spirit of a moment (the *dominant*). (As we will see in Section 6.3, the play between residual and dominant in Marx anticipates – again, significantly – Genette's thinking about what he calls narrative *anachronies*.) What Williams reveals at the heart of Marx's system is an essentially and complicatedly narrative relation between events as they occur at the level of the base and the representation of those events at the level of the superstructure; the relation demands that a reader negotiate the different ways in which a given culture variously, imperfectly, productively, and sometimes dishonestly manages the stable, but ultimately inscrutable fact of history as history or, to use Fredric Jameson's famous phrase, of history as "what hurts": for Jameson, history *as it is* as opposed to how it looks "is what refuses desire and sets inexorable limits to individual as well as collective praxis, which its 'ruses' turn into grisly and ironic reversals of their overt intention. But this History can be apprehended only through its effects, and never directly as some reified force."[31] History is, in other words, what lies illegibly on the other side of its own representation.

Put in the terms I have used throughout, the difference between base and superstructure anticipates and feeds into and helps to activate narrative theory's story–discourse relation. What gives both narratives and societies their significant, which is to say interpretable character, is an essential difference between levels, one that is most visible at points where they are most temporally at odds. This might seem to be a provocative analogy between two finally unrelated or distantly related systems; as I will argue later, I want rather to see both as structurally related and historically specific antinomies that link our shared interest in narrative to other relations characteristic of modern life. The resonance between Marx's theory of history as the relation between levels and narrative theory as the analysis of the relation between story and discourse might be the result of a shared relation to a more broadly narrative moment, one that – as we have seen – Marx imagined as coming to a kind of end with the end of that moment's most important, defining narrative: the narrative of class struggle. What, in other words, characterizes the proletariat's particular relation to the class struggle is the fact that it is in a position to see clearly what the class struggle meant; and history seen clearly is a history without need of representation, superstructure, or discourse. It is a history that must exceed the generic terms of tragedy or farce; it is a history as something other than narrative. Marx's thinking about history, narrative, their relation, and their possible ends will, as we will see, directly shape some of the most important narrative theorists, from Georg Lukács and Mikhail Bakhtin to Roland Barthes and Claude Lévi-Strauss, who once wrote that he "rarely broached a new sociological problem without first stimulating my thought by rereading a few pages of *The 18th Brumaire of Louis Bonaparte*."[32] In each case, these theories are governed by the sense both that the story-discourse relation is necessary to historical and ideological analysis and that that relation is itself a historically specific concept. As we will see, the forms that that doubled sense of things take will in each case owe something explicit to Marx and his theory of narrative.

3.2 Beyond Story and Discourse: Friedrich Nietzsche and the Limits of Narrative

After Aristotle and Hegel, Friedrich Nietzsche is the next great theorist of tragedy; and, although he mentions neither by name in *The Birth of Tragedy* (1872), he nonetheless builds on their related senses of tragedy as a split genre (for Aristotle split between actions and representations of actions, and for Hegel between the varied but always apparently antithetical terms of the dialectic). What is more, like Aristotle, Hegel, and, later, Marx, Nietzsche understands this split in terms that are presciently narrative or, rather, *narrative theoretical*; for Nietzsche, tragedy is simultaneously defined by a difference and a relation between narrative levels, between things and the arrangement of things that join to motivate the content and the form of Greek tragedy. *The Birth of Tragedy* is, of course, a strange book (Nietzsche later called it "an impossible book"); it blends scholarly rigor, the enthusiasms of a fan, and an inflated style that anticipates his later and wilder works (Alexander Nehamas refers to Nietzsche's as a "thick style").[33] It is also an intensely literary work that draws on a range of poetic and rhetorical techniques in order to go beyond the academic protocols of philosophy, history, and classical philology. At the heart of Nietzsche's project is his account of tragedy as kind of narrative that draws attention to the relation between life and the forms that life takes when we attempt to represent it from one or another point of view; tragedy is thus an example of what Nietzsche takes as a more general if paradoxical drive to put a real and unruly life into some kind of order while nonetheless preserving exactly those qualities – its bracing unruliness and its almost overbearing sense of reality – that make it worth living. Like Aristotle and Hegel before him, Nietzsche thus understands tragedy as essentially if paradoxically mimetic, as an effort to convert the stuff of life into a representational beginning, middle, and end. What he adds to both is his sense that Greek tragedy succeeds because, at the same time that it seeks to put experience into some kind of order, it also celebrates a disorder that refuses the consolation of narrative coherence; for Nietzsche, Greek tragedy manages to capture a living, motive tension between narrative and its discontents.

In part, this double sense of tragic narrative is an early expression of the genealogical method that characterizes Nietzsche's most important works, his effort to show that, behind every officially sanctioned historical point of origin, there is always another hidden or disavowed beginning, another story or stories suppressed in the name of an official social or political interest; in "Nietzsche, Genealogy, and History," Michel Foucault writes that, where methodological faith in any single origin shuts down inquiry, "the genealogist needs history to dispel the chimeras of the origin. ... He must be able to recognize the events of history, its jolts, its surprises, its unsteady victories and unpalatable defeats – the basis of all beginnings, atavisms, and heredities."[34] Pursued perhaps most consistently in *On the Genealogy of Morals* (1887), Nietzsche's favored method is thus a philosophical critique of historical plots, of the idea that history can or should be reduced to one or another beginning, middle, and end.

In *The Birth of Tragedy*, he thus begins with a critique of what he took as the official, scholarly account of the origin of Greek tragic drama in the achieved, mature, and calm aesthetic and political disposition of fifth-century Athens: "In order to understand this, we need to dismantle the artful edifice of *Apolline culture* stone by stone, as it were, until we catch sight of the foundations on which it rests."[35] As opposed to this overly simple story (an Athenian sense of proportion and calm represented by the god Apollo leads to the aesthetic achievements of the great tragedians), Nietzsche offers a complex, contradictory, bifurcated account of the birth of tragedy, a frayed narrative that relies on an ambivalent relation between what he takes as two essential human drives: a Apollonian drive toward order, beauty, individuation, and the just proportions of sculpture and a Dionysian drive toward intoxication, desire, disindividuation, and the presymbolic force of music:

> Their two deities of art, Apollo and Dionysos, provide the starting-point for our recognition that there exists in the world of the Greeks an enormous opposition, both in origin and goals, between the Apolline art of the image-maker or sculptor and the imageless art of music, which is that of Dionysos. These two very different drives exist side by side, mostly in open conflict, stimulating and provoking one another to give birth to ever-new, more vigorous offspring in whom they perpetuate the conflict inherent in the opposition between them, an opposition only apparently bridged by the common term "art" – until eventually, by a metaphysical miracle of the Hellenic "Will," they appear paired and, in this pairing, finally engender a work of art which is Dionysiac and Apolline in equal measure: Attic tragedy.[36]

Greek tragedy thus manages a delicate, beautiful, and ultimately doomed compromise between opposed forces as they appear in dramatic form; tragedy is, in other words, an aesthetic embodiment of the structuring tension that exists between the Dionysian disorder of life *as it is* and the Apollonian order of life as it is partially represented in discrete images of that life: "The Apolline Greek ... was bound to feel more than this: his entire existence, with all its beauty and moderation, rested on a hidden ground of suffering and knowledge which was exposed to his gaze once more by the Dionysiac. And behold! Apollo could not live without Dionysos."[37] And, insofar as the encounter between Dionysus and Apollo takes place within and, indeed, as the narrative form of Greek tragedy, it helps us to see both the power and the limits of the forms with which we try to order experience.

~

The complexities of Nietzsche's argument are partly a counterintuitive response to the discipline of nineteenth-century philology. In 1872, when *The Birth of Tragedy* first appeared, Nietzsche was a bright light in the world of classical philology, having secured a position at the University of Basel in Switzerland four years earlier at only twenty-four. Philology is the study of language and culture as it appears in writing; it draws on comparative linguistic analysis, literary criticism, and cultural history and demands from practitioners a daunting command of languages, historical fact, and scholarly method. James Turner has recently written that "the word philology in the nineteenth century covered three distinct modes of research: (1) textual philology (including classical and biblical studies, 'oriental' literatures such as those in Sanskrit and Arabic, and medieval and modern European writings); (2) theories of the origin and nature of language; and (3) comparative study of the structures and historical evolution of languages and of language families."[38] In an influential essay calling for a "return to philology," Edward Said writes that "philology is, literally, the love of words, but as a discipline it acquires a quasi-scientific intellectual and spiritual prestige at various periods in all of the major cultural traditions, including the Western and the Arabic-Islamic traditions that have framed my own development. ... All these involve a detailed scientific attention paid to language as bearing within it a knowledge of a kind entirely limited to what language does and does not do."[39] According to Leo Spitzer, one of its last great representatives, philological interpretation works in a "circular" fashion,

> a legitimate means available to the humanist or to the historian, whether his background is linguistic or literary, who wants to understand a human phenomenon. When he notices a peculiarity – and it may or may not be linguistic – he assumes its origin to be psychological and verifies his hypothesis against other such peculiarities: his path is a continual movement between indication and deduction, a coming and going from detail to essence and back from essence to detail.[40]

The philologist tacks hermeneutically between the general and the particular in order to understand how culture and history produced their many words and how those words, in turn, helped to shape, to color, and, indeed, to produce history and culture as phenomena available to interpretation.

While Nietzsche understood that he was pushing against the traditional boundaries of his field (as he expected, his work caused a minor academic scandal and he left his post at Basel shortly after), he nonetheless continued to see himself fundamentally as a philologist, which meant for Nietzsche as it did for Spitzer inhabiting a critically circular path between apparently opposed values and ideas: not only particular and general but also good and evil, nature and culture, order and disorder, the ancient and the modern, image and music,

Apollo and Dionysus. He indeed imagined that the circular path of *The Birth of Tragedy* could advance philology to a kind of intellectual fruition; as he wrote the year before publishing his book, "I observe how my philosophical, moral and scholarly endeavors strive towards a single goal and that I may perhaps become the first philologist ever to achieve wholeness."[41] In practice, this meant that *The Birth of Tragedy* tends to move both synthetically if somewhat mysteriously between moments of empirical particularity – early Greek ritual, the nature of the tragic chorus, the fate of Oedipus – and broadly speculative claims about human life and the nature of value, a synthetic methodological tendency that seeks to reproduce the whole doubled structure of tragedy itself. Ancient Greece is thus both an object of study and a methodological model for Nietzsche, and Greek tragedy is great because it is a narrative form capable of resolving – however delicately – oppositions that Nietzsche took as fundamental not only to Greek but also to all human life, the opposition between Dionysus and Apollo, music and sculpture, nature and civilization, feeling and reason, violence and calm, dissolution and individuation, content and form, and, in the narrative terms I have been using, events and the shape those events take in a culture's imagination or memory; it is also great because it offered Nietzsche a prototype of a critical method that he would develop and refine for the rest of his life: Silk and Stern write that "as far as Nietzsche is concerned, we can learn true philosophy from tragedy."[42]

~

Nietzsche makes his argument about the tragic conflict between and the resolution of these forces in genetic, philosophical, and aesthetic terms. Although, as I have said, scholarship had tended in his view to see Greek culture and Greek tragedy as expressions of an exclusively Apollonian tendency toward definition and clarity – "profound delight, and a joyous necessity" – Nietzsche argues that the dreamlike calm of Greek art was in fact a later response to an earlier and more fundamental experience, one associated with religious ritual, with sexual excess and intoxication, with the prelinguistic power of music, with a violent and self-destructive Dionysian tendency that he saw at the very heart of ancient Greek culture: as opposed to Apollonian calm, the Dionysian artist "has become entirely at one with the primordial unity, with its pain and contradiction, and he produces a copy of this primordial unity as music, which has been described elsewhere, quite rightly, as a repetition of the world and a second copy of it; now, however, under the influence of the Apolline dream, this music in turn becomes visible to him as in a symbolic dream-image."[43] Greek tragedy is thus a product of and response to our encounter with a natural world that both resists and demands several layers of aesthetic representation. Faced with what Nietzsche refers to as a violent, disindividuating, and "primordial" oneness at the heart of things, the Greek sought first to capture that oneness in the form of music and then to contain what was both seductive and horrifying about the possible loss of self within the ordered and dreamlike fabrications of Apollonian image making; the Greeks sought also to allegorize or, indeed, *to image* that process in the form of an increasingly elaborate mythology of fickle gods and goddesses at war over competing aspects of life: light and dark, life and death, reason and feeling, love and lust, and so on.

Tragedy stands, then, as a concentrated expression of this larger cultural logic; because, Nietzsche argues, it begins in the unstructured form of the choral song before being elaborated into full visual and dramatic spectacle, Greek tragedy stages both in its history and in its structure the larger conflict that characterizes Greek culture, the conflict between the primal and inhuman violence of the natural world and a human idea – an illusion, if you will – about the world that is both an answer and antithesis to that violence. Tragedy offers a concentrated instance of the tenuous, fragile compromise between order and disorder that allowed the Greek "to be able to live" in the face of Dionysian knowledge. What is more important for us is the necessarily narrative form that this compromise takes in *The Birth of Tragedy*. It is significant that Nietzsche sees a narrative form as opposed to a more recognizably philosophical style as offering the most workable and most wise response to the conflicts and contradictions that underwrote Greek life and, indeed, life in general. Because, in other words, tragedy foregrounds the structuring difference between events and the representation of events, it allows Nietzsche to reflect on the motivating dissonance between things as they are and things as they seem to be; it allows him, in other words, to do a kind of philosophy. This is a consequence of the very structure of tragic narrative, which is, as Aristotle saw, built around and expressive of a fundamental and particular conflict between actions and the representation of actions.

The divide between the Dionysian and the Apollonian aspects of tragedy thus more or less corresponds to the productive difference between discrete actions or events and the aesthetic arrangement of those actions or events into whole representations, a difference to which Hegel turned in order to understand and to motivate a conflict between ideas and things that had reached an alarming and seemingly sterile kind of conclusion in Kant. In both cases, a *relation* between events and the schemes we employ to give events their significance, their order, their direction became itself the object of critical analysis; a critical philosophy thus emerged as the effort not to understand events or representations in and of themselves but rather to understand how the active relation between the two could give art, history, and life what meaning they have. For Nietzsche, the Dionysian and the Apollonian are also distinct representational levels, with the Apollonian *image* standing as an ordered and clarifying representation of a more primordial Dionysian experience; Nietzsche's mythic confrontation between these gods is, in other words, a way to allegorize two aspects of tragedy: the *what* and the *how* of tragic narrative form.

This is perhaps why Nietzsche takes care to identify the moment of tragedy's birth with the invention of the tragic chorus. As opposed to earlier commentators who saw the Greek chorus either as a figure for the political relation between the people and the state in ancient Athens or as a sort of "ideal spectator," a stylized expression of what the tragedian hoped and expected from his real audience, Nietzsche instead sees the chorus in structural terms, as "a living wall which tragedy draws about itself in order to shut itself off in purity from the real world and to preserve its ideal ground and its poetic freedom."[44] The dividing line of the chorus functions, in other words, as a formal border that allows the tragedian to draw a sort of *magic circle* around one part of reality in order to cast that part as an autonomous and aesthetic whole; Johan Huizinga writes that, like the playground, the card table, the stage, and the screen, the magic circle marks off "temporary worlds within the ordinary world, dedicated to the performance of an act apart."[45] This is all the more important because, as Nietzsche understands it, what the tragedian wants to represent and provisionally to contain is the more or less unrepresentable Dionysian experience of life itself: "The metaphysical solace which, I wish to suggest, we derive from every true tragedy, the solace that in the ground of things, and despite all changing appearance, life is indestructibly mighty and pleasurable, this solace appears with palpable clarity in the chorus."[46] The chorus allows the raw stuff of life, nature, and desire to take temporary form as a bound and thus more or less safe aesthetic experience. As we will see in Section 4.1, Henry James similarly defined narrative art as the drawing of a circle around some part of a life defined by its tendency to resist reduction to one or another formal representation:

> Really, universally, relations stop nowhere, and the exquisite problem of the artist is eternally but to draw, by a geometry of his own, the circle within which they shall happily *appear* to do so. He is in the perpetual predicament that the continuity of things is the whole matter, for him, of comedy and tragedy; that this continuity is never, by the space of an instant or an inch, broken, and that, to do anything at all, he has at once intensely to consult and intensely to ignore it.[47]

For Nietzsche as for James, the narrative act is a self-conscious and ironic act of enclosure, a knowingly limited and indeed paradoxical effort to represent a part of life as a whole within the self-consciously partial confines of this or that narrative form.

The productive limits of this model become especially clear in Nietzsche's account; while the forms of tragedy can, at their best, manage a bound and ephemeral representation of life itself, when the viewer finally turns away from the magic circle of the chorus and back to the inauthentic world of everyday things, he or she does so with a sense of disgust: "But as soon as daily reality re-enters consciousness, it is experienced as such with a sense of revulsion; the fruit of those states is an ascetic, will-negating mood."[48] The play between the magic circle of tragic narrative, a circle that gives us a real, if managed look at life itself, and the empty absurdity that exists beyond that circle leads in two related directions: on the one hand, it can convey an awful and debilitating knowledge, the knowledge of an Oedipus or a Hamlet; on the other hand, it leads, in the best case, away from despondency towards more and more art: "Art alone can re-direct those repulsive thoughts about the terrible or absurd nature of existence into representations with which man can live."[49] Although there is much to say about Nietzsche's sense of the capacities and limits of aesthetic consolation, I want to highlight the simple fact that his account of the chorus and its formal relation both to the content of a given tragic narrative and to the world beyond that content is cast in terms of *narrative technique*; like James and, as we will see, Lukács, Genette, and others, Nietzsche attempts to capture a moment at which the external or preconditional *making* of narrative form becomes internally and ironically available as its own kind of narrative content. And that is what the chorus is for Nietzsche: the place in tragedy where form and content, image and music, inside and outside threaten, at last, to become one and the same.

Taken further, we might see in Nietzsche's emphasis on the threshold quality of the chorus a version of a narrative figure that Gérard Genette refers to as *metalepsis*, or the transgressive crossing or short-circuiting of narrative levels. Under "normal" conditions, narratives rely on a structuring difference between what Genette sees as an "outside" *extradiegetic* level from which a narrator retrospectively narrates events and an "inside" *diegetic* level at which those events occur: "We will," he writes, "define this difference in level by saying that *any event a narrative recounts is at a diegetic level immediately higher than the level at which the narration act producing this narrative is placed*."[50] We might think of a narrative like *Jane Eyre*. Although the whole of Brontë's novel is *about* Jane and the story of her development, experiences, and eventual marriage, the novel in fact relies on two structurally different

Janes, the narrated or *diegetic* Jane, whom we follow from childhood up to and beyond her marriage to Rochester, and the narrating, remembering *extradiegetic* Jane, who has already had all of those experiences and can thus remember and assemble them into coherent narrative form. While the difference between the two levels remains necessary to our understanding of the novel, Brontë calls different kinds of attention to the structure at work, sometimes allowing the extradiegetic Jane's narration to shift from the past into the present tense at moments of emotional intensity; as I said previously, Genette refers to these moments of shifting from one to another level as metalepses. When, for instance, Rochester enters a room in a midst of an otherwise boring party, the novel's voice shifts suddenly from the past to the present tense, inserting, as it were, the present narrating Jane temporarily and impossibly into the midst of the narrated Jane's past experience: "He comes in last: I am not looking at the arch, yet I see him enter."[51] Although they can be confusing, Brontë's occasional and intentional lapses help paradoxically to underscore the structural difference between the diegetic narrated world and the extradiegetic instance of narration.

Indeed, for Genette, such instructive lapses in the ordering difference between narrative levels both have local significance (in the case of *Jane Eyre*, they are an index of emotional intensity) and stand more broadly as exceptions that prove the structural rule: "All these games, by the intensity of their effects, demonstrate the importance of the boundary they tax their ingenuity to overstep, in defiance of verisimilitude – a boundary that is precisely the narrating (or the performance) itself: a shifting but sacred frontier between two worlds, the world in which one tells, the world of which one tells."[52] An instance of metalepsis is thus powerful because it threatens to collapse a structurally necessary duality into one. This takes us back to Nietzsche and the chorus. Because the chorus stands all at once as a kind of surrogate for extradiegetic narration, as a representative of an equally extradiegetic ideal spectator, and, finally, as an agent or voice diegetically present alongside the other characters of a given tragedy, it exists as a fundamentally metaleptic figure, a figure for both the exception and the rules of narrative. On the one hand, this is to see Nietzsche's understanding of the chorus as of a piece with what Silk and Stern identify as his broadly associative, "centripetal," or, as they also put it, "metaleptic" style: "His imagery is not thematic in any ordinary sense, but much of it is intensely centripetal: he presents a long string of isolated images, a surprising number of which are drawn directly from the underlying concerns of his book."[53] Nietzsche, in other words, uses a loose and apparently under-motivated network of images – stones, sunshine, masks, etc. – in order to create stylistic as opposed to argumentative ties between one part of his book and another. On the other hand, it is to see that Nietzsche's theory of tragic form relies on, anticipates, and metaleptically undermines one of narrative theory's foundational concepts: a distinction between diegetic and extradiegetic narrative levels on which all narrative relies.

~

The problem with all of this is that Nietzsche finally understands the representational relation between Dionysus and Apollo not as a representation of the world but rather as itself a second-order representation of a representation of a world: "Philosophical natures even have a presentiment that hidden beneath the reality in which we live and have our being there also lies a second, quite different reality; in other words, this reality too is a semblance."[54] That is, while readers have sometimes taken Nietzsche's comments on the Dionysian to reflect his belief that one could tap directly into the ultimate and primal state of things, Nietzsche in fact understood Dionysian music as at last only another if closer representation of nature's "primordial oneness." James Porter writes that Nietzsche adapted this idea of tragedy as an Apollonian representation of a Dionysian representation of something else from the post-Kantian philosopher Friedrich Albert Lange, who wrote that "the true nature of things, the ultimate cause of every appearance, is not only unknown to us, but the concept of it is no more and no less than the last strange product of an opposition that is conditioned by our organization; nor do we even know *whether this opposition has any meaning outside of our experience.*"[55] As opposed to Hegel's effort to find a way to bridge Kant's absolute gap between ideas and things, Lange doubles down, arguing not only that the world is fundamentally unknowable but also that its unknowability is its essential and essentially tragic fact. For Nietzsche this means that *even* Dionysos, *even* the most raw and violent experience available to us, is in the end only a representation of what cannot be represented; Porter writes, "The problem can be simply stated. Being (reality, truth, 'the ground of our being,' 'the eternally suffering and contradictory primal unity,' *das Ur-Eine*, or the One Will) is seemingly accessible in brief, unmediated glimpses (tragic knowledge is predicated on this possibility), but in point of fact no glimpse of reality can be had except through the filtering and distortive agency of appearances."[56] In *Nietzsche and Metaphor*, Sarah Kofman asserts that "we can have only representations of the essence of things, since we ourselves, and the universe along with us, are only images of this completely 'indecipherable' innermost essence."[57] Because, in that case, the Apollonian image is a representation of Dionysian stuff, and because that stuff is in itself a representation of a level of existence that stands outside and beyond human knowledge, Nietzsche's system is built on a recursive layering of representations, a metaphor of a metaphor or a mimesis of mimesis that both draws on Aristotle's example and calls sharp attention to its limits as a theory of both narrative and life. As we shall soon see, Nietzsche's third layer anticipates the narratologist A. J. Greimas's identification of the three stages necessary "to achieve the construction of cultural objects"; below, as it were, *the surface structures*, which correspond roughly to story, and *the structures of manifestation*, which correspond roughly to discourse, there are *the deep structures*, "which define the fundamental mode of existence of an individual or a society. . . . As far as we know, the elementary constituents of deep structures have a definable logical status."[58] I will return to Greimas and the idea of narrative deep structure in Section 5.1.

At the same time that Nietzsche praises the Greek capacity to represent the tension between life and death, light and dark, story and discourse in the narrative form of tragedy, so is he committed to calling attention to what can never find a meaningful place within tragedy, history, or human experience: "Now no solace has any effect, there is a longing for a world beyond death, beyond the gods themselves; existence is denied, along with its treacherous reflection in the gods or in some immortal Beyond."[59] Faced with an idea of a radically natural world that would reject even the darkest and most violent forms of representation, the individual has two choices; first, says Nietzsche, he or she can follow in Hamlet's footsteps and choose inaction as a radical and self-defeating response to the absurdity of a life that denies the possibility of meaning; second, and this is Nietzsche's solution, he or she can accept the ultimate inadequacy of narrative but take that inadequacy as an opportunity to narrate one's life and one's world *as one would have it*. Nietzsche's confrontation with the ineffable thus led him to an original understanding of the creative nature of philosophy; according to Kofman, "The 'imagination' plays as important a role in philosophy as it does in poetry. '[The philosopher] knows in that he invents, and he invents in that he knows.' The imagination allows one to grasp analogies; reflection intervenes only after the event to replace them with equivalences, to replace successions with causal relations, and to being the measure of the concept to bear. Philosophy is a 'continuation of the *mythical drive*.'"[60] Philosophy, as described here, is a self-consciously literary effort to put life into some kind of order; it is the effort to arrange events into a self-consciously provisional whole made up of causes, effects, equivalences, patterns, beginnings, middles, and ends. Philosophy is, in other words, both a form of narrative and a narrative theory, an effort to relate story to discourse while nonetheless recognizing the definite and human, all-too-human limits of that effort. The failure of narrative fully to represent life results in a vexed but joyous responsibility; if narratives cannot describe life as it is, they just might able to make or remake the world as we would have it. Crucially, for Nietzsche this act of making is an act of interpretation, the selective and thus productive arrangement and evaluation of events.

As we saw with Marx, Nietzsche develops a system that at once refuses and embraces narrative. He refuses narrative insofar as society offers certain stories as simply and absolutely true, stories that create false values, limit human potential, and prevent us from seeing or even imagining a primal and *living* experience of life that stands over and above our efforts and ability to account for that life; at the same time, he embraces narrative insofar as the absence of any single story both allows and demands that we accept the responsibility of narrating life for ourselves, of making sense of experience in the absence of any transcendental guarantee, of saying *thus I willed it*.[61] This, he suggests, is what the Greeks understood when they managed a represented relation between order and chaos in the form of the great works of Attic tragedy and imagined the genre as one that could help us to look into the heart of things and yet nonetheless live. A few years later in "On the Use and Abuse of History for Life" (1874), Nietzsche extended his analysis of tragedy's relation to what it would but cannot represent to the narrative drive of history in general; as opposed to the two main schools of historical reckoning – a "monumental history" that codifies the past and distorts life in the service of a present status quo and an "antiquarian history" that values the past over the present and thus chooses death over life – Nietzsche offers "critical history" as the kind of history that can best deal with life *as* life: "In order to live, he must possess, and from time to time employ, the strength to shatter and dissolve a past; he accomplishes this by bringing this past before a tribunal, painstakingly interrogating it, and finally condemning it. But every past is worthy of being condemned – for this is simply how it is with human affairs: human violence and weakness have always played a powerful role in them."[62] To live is not to cover up the past and the present with the comfort of one or another narrative; it is to see both that we cannot narrate away the tragic experience that Nietzsche associated with the Dionysian and that, even so, we cannot live without narrative either. This tragic tension between the need to narrate and the constitutive limits of narrative is not only at the heart of Nietzsche's view of Greek tragedy; it is also the critical knowledge or, as he puts it in *The Birth of Tragedy*, the Dionysian wisdom that one needs in order to live.

Looking back on the time of its composition, Nietzsche later understood his book as one that had its own complicated relation to the present experience of war and violence and their shaping influence on life:

> Whatever underlies this questionable book, it must be a most stimulating and supremely important question and, furthermore, a profoundly personal one – as is attested by the times in which it was written, and in spite of which it was written, the turbulent period of the Franco-Prussian War of 1870–1. While the thunder of the Battle of Wörth rolled across Europe, the brooder and lover of riddles who fathered the book was sitting in some corner of the Alps, utterly preoccupied with his ponderings and riddles and consequently very troubled and untroubled at one and the same time, writing down his thoughts about the Greeks.[63]

As remembered here, *The Birth of Tragedy* was itself a tragic response to war. Just as the Greeks used the tenuously dialectical form of tragedy to manage the difference between the Dionysian desire for violence and the Apollonian rejection of violence, so did Nietzsche's book emerge as a way simultaneously to move toward and to escape from the enormity of war. Nietzsche looked back on his book as formal compromise between the unbinding, terrible, but, for him, liberating excess of violence and the need to come aesthetically to terms with that violence; like the Greeks, he saw the war as an invitation to understand how one can use art to live against, through, and with strife.

Nietzsche did not in fact remain hidden away in the mountains during the war; faced, rather, with the prospect of an event that he already imagined as offering terrible proof of the "primordial oneness" he had been looking for, he volunteered as a medical orderly: "Nietzsche spent a mere two weeks in September at the western battlefields. He witnessed the dead being gathered from the fields, and he accompanied a transport of the wounded."[64] The experience, although brief, helped to shape Nietzsche's life and thought. He contracted dysentery and diphtheria at the front, which contributed to the health problems that both plagued his later life and fueled his thinking about the necessary relations among sickness, health, and culture. More importantly, the experience of war seen close up provided him with a model for thinking about a violence that would both resist representation and give shape to the rest of a culture. Unlike Hegel, who looked to history as a whole narrative that could make retroactive sense of the violence of the French Revolutionary Terror, or Marx, who saw the class struggle as a narrative that would, in the end, resolve the tragic contradictions of life under capitalism into the comic resolution of proletarian revolution, Nietzsche saw the violence of war and human aggression as a thing ultimately resistant to narrative, as an experience that would in every case give the lie to the comforting stories we tell ourselves about the past and the present. Instead, though, of seeing this primal aggression as an excuse for nihilism, Nietzsche took it, however perversely, as an opportunity and a responsibility.

It was an opportunity because the destabilizing fact of a primal and violent chaos put the tragic poet or the philosopher in a position to *make* life meaningful as he or she willed it. The process of turning life into narrative was itself the source of life's meaning. This was apparent in the Greek effort to represent myths, which sought self-consciously to represent an unrepresentable "primordial oneness" in the dialectical form of particular tragedies. It was also present in what Nietzsche understood as the historian's responsibility both to respect the unnarratable limits of life itself and *nonetheless* to find provisional, procedural modes of narration that could make that life livable. It is this bind, the fact that Nietzsche sees life as a thing that cannot be narrated but must be narrated, that makes him important to narrative theory. He is, in a way that will inform the most powerful narrative theories and that stands as a culmination of a tragic theory of narrative that I have been trying to develop, for and against narrative.

3.3 Sigmund Freud: Narrative and Its Discontents

Like the other figures I have described in this section, Sigmund Freud built a theory of great complexity and explanatory power around what seems a basic human need to narrate, a need to put life's events into order. With this – and like Marx and Nietzsche before him – Freud takes over an urge toward historical reckoning that Hegel had developed in response to his reading of Kant, his experience of the successes and failures of the French Revolution, and his resulting theory of tragic conflict. Freud's lifelong project, psychoanalysis, is in its way also a historical project, the effort to understand how the past, present, and future of an individual life might add up to something significant. Patients traveled to Freud's office in late nineteenth- and early twentieth-century Vienna when it seemed that their lives no longer held together, when they could not understand their pasts, manage their relations with others, or parse how their incomplete understanding of self and desire appeared in the at-times-debilitating form of neurotic symptoms. In response to this inability to make sense, Freud encouraged his patients to talk, to free associate, to cast their feelings, experiences, and anxieties in linguistic or, we might say, textual forms. This is why one of Freud's earliest patients referred to psychoanalysis as a "talking cure"; if it worked, it worked because it encouraged both analyst and patient to narrate, to read, and perhaps to revise the memory of past events in relation to the present and future.

This therapeutic and critical reliance on talk, on stories, on narrative is one that stretches from the beginning to the end of Freud's work, from his first efforts to encourage his patients to make sense of their lives and problems by talking about them to his late reflections on the relation among beginnings, middles, and ends that drove his wildest and most disturbing reflections on the interminable and essential conflict between the forces of life and death. Indeed, many of Freud's most important concepts rely on an implicit theory of narrative form: the idea that a child must pass more or less "successfully" through oral, anal, phallic, and genital stages of development; that the Oedipal scene is a threshold or narrative middle that everyone needs somehow to cross; that the story of psychosexual development is only meaningful because its infantile beginning is separated from its mature end by the middle barrier of what he calls the "latency period"; that an obscurely narratable process allows the ego to emerge out of the chaos of raw biological instinct; and that there is an idiosyncratic path that we all must follow and in our own way on the way from life to death.[65] In each of these cases, Freud imagines human life as a partial and inherently fraught process of arranging the events of individual and collective human lives into a more or less significant form.

~

As was the case with both Marx and Nietzsche, Freud relies on a highly literary sense of Greek tragic narrative that draws on the long history of thinking about the genre that, once again, goes back to Hegel's ideas about the necessary relation between tragedy and conflict as well as Aristotle's work on tragedy as an exemplary form of plotted representation. Freud and Josef Breuer referred to their earliest efforts to treat hysteria as a *cathartic* method, a term that connects their early efforts to uncover a patient's painful "residues or reminiscences" to what Aristotle saw as the central emotional effect of a successful tragic drama, its ability to reveal and thus to purge pity and fear.[66] In the *Three Essays on the Theory of Sexuality* (1905), Freud compares the child's wonder about "where babies come from" to Oedipus's famous riddle: "This, in a distorted form which can easily be rectified, is the same riddle that was propounded by the Theban Sphinx."[67] Most famously, Freud cast his central theory of psychosexual development in terms of Oedipus's fateful encounter not with the Sphinx but rather with his own father and mother; he writes in *The Interpretation of Dreams* (1899) that the haunting effect of Sophocles' play can be attributed to the fact that it reflects the terms of a conflict that Freud took as a repressed and universal aspect of human development: "His destiny moves us only because it might have been ours – because the oracle laid the same curse upon us, perhaps, to direct our first sexual impulse towards our mother and our first hatred and our first murderous wish against our father."[68] Julia Reinhard Lupton writes that "for Freud, *Oedipus the King* staged a fundamental plot of human desire and development, the crystalline clarity of its dramatic action bearing the structural stamp not only of literary art, but also of ritual and archetype."[69] Freud's masterplot thus reveals his reliance on narrative as a model both for the dynamic relation among different developmental stages as well as for the ways in which different levels of psychic life are related to and inform one another.

We should also consider the more technical role that the Oedipal complex plays in Freud. When, in Freud's account, the father blocks the child's erotic access to the mother, it results in a first and formative *repression*. (As others have pointed out, in the case of *Oedipus Rex*, the father does not in fact manage to block the child's access to the mother, which is strange proof that if there is anyone who does not suffer from the Oedipus complex, it is Oedipus!) According to Freud, the child, despite accepting the father's prohibition, refuses at some level to part with the object of his or her desire; for Freud, people are essentially "incapable of giving up a satisfaction [they] had once enjoyed."[70] As a result, the child finds a way at once to give up and to preserve the prohibited object; the child, in other words, engages in a first *repression*, the act, as Freud understands it, of at once pushing a proscribed wish or idea or desire out of consciousness and preserving it *elsewhere*; as Freud expresses it, "The essence of repression lies simply in turning something away, and keeping it at a distance, from the conscious."[71] In a manner that recalls the terms of Hegel's dialectic, repression both overcomes and preserves the repressed wish. Fine: but where does the repressed idea go? It is at this point in his argument that Freud develops one of his most important and surprising concepts, one that we today take for granted but that fundamentally changed how one could think about the mind, its history, and its relation to desire. When ideas are repressed, says Freud, they are preserved in the other space of the *unconscious*, which is one part of a newly constituted and internally divided psychic apparatus and serves as a hidden but nonetheless present reservoir of all the things that we have had to give up but cannot give up. According to Freud, the establishment of the unconscious thus emerges as part of a larger effort to manage our essential and biological drive toward the increase of pleasure and decrease of pain in relation to the demands of a real, material, and social world that forces us to delay and sometimes to deny gratification; the unconscious is thus a complicated solution to the problem posed by the difference between what the *pleasure principle* wants and what the *reality principle* demands. It is, however, a necessarily incomplete solution; because the contents of the unconscious are displaced but not destroyed, they continue to exert a pressure on and to enter conscious life – albeit in disguised form – appearing as dreams, slips, jokes, and symptoms. To sum up the process: the Oedipal conflict between the father and child over erotic access to the mother forces the child to repress his or her desire for the mother; as a result of that first Oedipal repression, which is the result of his or her reluctance to part ways with an anticipated or remembered pleasure, he or she constitutes the unconscious, which will come to serve as a reservoir for all subsequent repressed desires, ideas, and wishes. And, because the unconscious exerts a dynamic pressure on the normal functions of conscious, waking life, its contents will continue to reappear in the disguised form of dreams, jokes, slips, omissions, neurotic symptoms, and so on.

So far, so good. But why think of the emergence of the unconscious out of the Oedipal complex as having some relation to narrative theory? What, other than the fact that it derives its name from Sophocles' tragedy, makes this turn of events significant for the analysis or understanding of narrative? The answer is related to Freud's sense of what separates the newly constituted unconscious from the ordinary operations of consciousness. In *The Interpretation of Dreams*, Freud differentiates between the rules that govern the development and association of ideas in waking, conscious life and those that govern the unconscious world of dreams. The conscious mind organizes, regulates, and *binds* thought in terms of certain temporal and causal rules: one thing needs to occur before or after another, two things cannot occupy the same point in time or space, there is a necessary relation and difference among beginning, middle, and end of a thought or sequence of events. Freud refers to these binding rules as *the secondary processes*. Where, however, the conscious, secondary processes order thought and experience, the unconscious is rather *unbound*; its very different rules, which Freud refers to as *the primary processes*, allow for relations among ideas that would seem impossible or dangerous in waking life. In the unconscious, ideas can be stacked allusively or metaphorically or interchangeably on top of one another (what Freud calls *condensation*); they can take on disguises, with significant things appearing as insignificant, or vice versa (what Freud calls *displacement*); their causal order can be inverted, reversed, or shuffled in any number of ways. As with Marx's account of base and superstructure, the two levels of the Freudian mind are both absolutely related and apparently at temporal and causal odds with one another; like the superstructure's relation to the base, unconscious material can outpace or lag behind, can have an emergent or residual relation to consciousness, a fact that Freud acknowledges in the twisty last lines of *The Interpretation of Dreams*:

> And the value of dreams for giving us knowledge of the future? There is of course no question of that. It would be truer to say instead that they give us knowledge of the past. For dreams are derived from the past in every sense. Nevertheless the ancient belief that dreams foretell the future is not wholly devoid of truth. By picturing our wishes as fulfilled, dreams are after all leading us into the future. But this future, which the dreamer pictures as present, has been moulded by his indestructible wish into a perfect likeness of the past.[72]

In dreams as well as in narrative discourse, the barriers among past, present, and future can break down. As Genette might put it (or as he *will have* put it in Section 6.3), the unconscious is defined by a logic of *anachrony*.

This is why Freud refers in *Civilization and Its Discontents* (1930) and elsewhere to the unconscious as essentially *timeless*: where the conscious mind puts matters in order and insists on the difference between before and after as well as cause and effect, in the unconscious everything can seem to happen at once. Freud goes on to compare the timelessness of the unconscious to a fantastical image of Rome, where all of its various historical phases and stages are not only all equally present but also present in one and the same physical space: "Now let us, by a flight of the imagination suppose that Rome is not a human habitation but a psychical entity with a similarly long and copious past – an entity, that is to say, in which nothing that has once come into existence will have passed away and all the earlier phases of development continue to exist alongside the latest one."[73] To analyze a whole mind is, in that case, to engage with the productive, mobile, and ultimately mysterious relation between two differently ordered aspects of psychic life, two different aspects of the same system that correspond with other apparent antinomies I have been tracing.

In *The Interpretation of Dreams* the difference and the relation between these two aspects of mental functioning, the primary and the secondary processes, make dreams both possible and interpretable. Although the system seeks to keep what has been repressed in the unconscious, that content "wants" to re-enter conscious, waking life so that it can be realized in practice as well as in the realm of unconscious fantasy and so exerts a constant pressure on the line that stands between conscious life and the unconscious, between the secondary and the primary processes. As I said before, although the system is mostly capable of keeping repressed desires at bay, the fact that ideas are differently and promiscuously associated, stacked, displaced, and disguised within the unconscious means that those repressed desires can at times of psychic weakness or distraction – during sleep, when one is under stress or intoxicated – cross the threshold into waking life as slips, symptoms, or dreams. Freud's theory of the dream and the interpretation of dreams thus relies on the relation between what appear as two kinds of stuff, the unbound, disordered stuff of the unconscious – what he calls *latent content* – and the bound, ordered, structured stuff of conscious, waking life – what he calls *manifest content*. What makes the dream meaningful is in that case the *relation* between these two kinds of stuff – latent and manifest – and the different processes – primary and secondary – that govern them; and what is true of the dream, what Freud called "the royal road to the unconscious," is true of psychic life in general: what makes psychic life significant to the tools of psychoanalytic interpretation is the fact that everything we say or do is inflected by the relation between the latent and manifest aspects of our psychic lives.

It is important to underscore that, while they might appear and are, in fact, often treated as if they were different in kind, the latent and manifest are in fact two *aspects* of one and the same psychic system. This once again connects Freud to the other figures I have treated. What separates Hegel from Kant is precisely the fact that, where Kant saw ideas and things – or the *phenomenal* and the *noumenal* – as different in kind, Hegel recast the system so as to allow the only apparent difference between different aspects of life to be overcome *in time*. Hegel's system is a narrative system because he imagines the resolution of apparent contradictions as the result of an ongoing and progressive developmental narrative. This treatment of differences as aspectual as opposed to substantive oppositions means that neither one nor the other of the terms can be treated as fundamental. In the same way that both the Apollonian and the Dionysian aspects of experience revealed themselves as representations of a deeper and paradoxically unrepresentable natural order, so is it the case that the seemingly essential difference between consciousness and the unconscious should be more properly understood as a contingent if crucial psychic development, a development that Freud worked again and again to pinpoint and to understand; and because the difference between the two is contingent or, one might say, historical, it is also a difference that can be overcome in time. It is this unlikely possibility of overcoming difference that gives the Freudian psychic apparatus its narrative and thus interpretable character.

Attentive readers will have anticipated that I see the relation between these two aspects of psychic life as analogous to the story–discourse relation, a relation that I take as coterminous with traditional forms of narrative and that appears in important and anticipatory forms in the prehistory of narrative theory that I have been working to establish here. In the same way that events merge with the representation of events to form a tragic plot (Aristotle), or in the way that events as they are experienced join with events as they are seen or imagined from some future perspective to become significant (Hegel and Marx), or in the way that a Dionysian life force both meets and resists the shaping imposition of Apollonian aesthetic to form tragedy (Nietzsche), so does the latent content of the unconscious both exceed and find incomplete but necessary expression *in relation to* the bound and ordered forms of manifest content. Freud's identification of latent and manifest contents as two aspects of psychic life is a recognition both of the ways in which we need narratives to arrange matters in some kind of meaningful – which is to say interpretable – order and the necessary limits of those narratives. Importantly for Freud, this process is not a simple matter of decoding the manifest content in order to reveal a more fundamental latent truth lying beneath; as opposed to seeing dream interpretation as the unveiling of latent truths, Freud writes, "At bottom, dreams are nothing other than a particular form of thinking, made possible by the conditions of the state of sleep. It is the dream-work which creates that form, and it alone is the essence of dreaming – the explanation of its peculiar nature."[74] Henry Sussman writes that "dreams become intelligible not through the application of a fixed key to their code but through the negative relations that define the great laws of the unconscious: repression, displacement, condensation, substitution, regression, and deferral."[75] The point is that the difference between latent and manifest – between the surface and the depth of the dream, between symptom and trauma, between what life seems to be and what it really is – is a heuristic difference for Freud; instead of naming a substantive divide within psychic life, latent and manifest once again name two aspects of the same system. Fredric Jameson asserts:

> Interpretation proper . . . always presupposes, if not a conception of the unconscious itself, then at least some mechanism of mystification or repression in terms of which it would make sense to seek a latent meaning behind a manifest one, or to rewrite the surface categories of a text in the stronger language of a more fundamental interpretive code. . . . But above and beyond the sheer fact of mystification, we must point to the supplementary problem involved in the study of cultural or literary texts, or in other words, essentially, of narratives: for even if discursive language were to be taken literally, there is always, and constitutively, a problem about the 'meaning' of narrative as such.[76]

Psychic life is thus both meaningful and mystified, wholly profound and entirely limited as a result of the play between latent and manifest or, as

I have been suggesting, as a result of a relation between the story and the discourse that gives both narrative and life their practical but tenuous significance.

~

All of this takes us back to Freud and tragedy. I have argued that we can trace Freud's interest in and reliance on tragedy as a model in a number of ways: in references that appear throughout his work, in the centrality of conflict to his theory of mental functioning, in his fraught relation to beginning, middles, and ends. I want, however, to make another claim about the relation between tragedy and psychoanalysis. Part of what characterizes Marx's and Nietzsche's use of tragic models was the degree to which both saw them as fruitful but ultimately partial. For Marx, tragedy represented one aspect of history, the perceived character of events as they are experienced but not necessarily as they really are; seen from the end of the class struggle, all of those tragic events would turn out to have been moments within a larger and, indeed, totalizing comic narrative. The larger dialectical nature of history's plot would eventually resolve and make sense of what had seemed random, brutal, ideologically limited, or just plain bad. For Nietzsche, the limits of tragedy work differently. As I said in the previous section, Nietzsche understood tragedy as the embodied conflict between two forces essential to human life, the Apollonian urge toward order, shape, and reason and the Dionysian urge toward chaos, unbinding, and feeling. If we take that divide to be Nietzsche's final word on the tragic, we would say that tragedy is in fact a perfectly comprehensive genre because it managed, in a way that nothing else could, to draw together the two defining poles of human experience. Because, however, Nietzsche in fact understands even the Dionysian elements of tragedy as *representations* of something still more primal and indeed unrepresentable, his philosophy starts, as it were, where tragedy stops. Instead of treating this lack of guarantees as cause for despair, Nietzsche takes it as an opportunity to narrate, to give meaning to one's life as one sees fit; Jacques Derrida refers to this sense of opportunity as "Nietzschean affirmation – the joyous affirmation of the freeplay of the world and without truth, without origin, offered to an active interpretation."[77] If Marx saw tragedy as an incomplete aspect or part awaiting resolution within history's whole comic plot, Nietzsche sees tragedy both as an encounter with an essential discord and as an ecstatic opportunity. In both cases, a theory of tragedy provides the basis for a theory of narrative that, in turn, leads the one to imagine the whole of significant human history as a large comic plot and the other to see plots as necessary if paradoxical responses to a life that exceeds plot all on its own.

Freud, however, is and, more to the point, *became* a resolutely tragic thinker; indeed, Freud occupies an appropriate end and limit to that effort to think through the relation between narrative and the tragic that I have been tracing and that began with Aristotle's *Poetics*. While tragedy is only one among many kinds of narrative, it plays a powerful, heuristic role in Aristotle, Hegel, Marx, Nietzsche, and Freud because of the way it forces us to confront and to consider the urge toward and limits of narrative as an organic whole that comprises both beginning, middle, and end and of a structuring relation between story and discourse, between events and the aesthetic representation of events. Hegel is especially important here because of his insistence on the relation between tragedy and conflict, a relation that both helped to highlight critical aspects of Aristotle's account that had been overlooked by neoclassical interpreters such as Corneille and Racine and encouraged later readers to look to the genre for the ways in which its thematic engagement with filial and social conflict found formal expression in a way that made visible a dialectical tension between aspirations toward wholeness and the impossibility of wholeness that is essential to tragedy. The tradition that I have been working to understand found the beginnings of a more systematic narrative theory in tragedy because of the way the genre reveals problems and contradictions inherent to narrative relations among beginning, middle, and end; between part and whole; and between story and discourse. Because tragedy is about fundamental conflicts between freedom and necessity, the laws of the heart and the laws of the state, how things are and how they ought to be, it is a genre particularly suited to address tensions and contradictions that are present in all narratives. This tragic approach to the theory of narrative is nowhere more evident than in Freud.

~

From the very beginning, Freud understood the ideal work of psychoanalysis as the resolution of conflicts that threatened to upend or to undo a potentially whole psychic life. The conflicts of psychoanalysis are many: conflicts between the conscious mind and the unconscious; between the manifest and latent content of the dream; between the polymorphous urges of infantile sexuality and the social, heteronormative demands of sexual maturity; between the ego and the ego ideal; between what the Id wants and what the ego knows that it should and can have; and, ultimately, between the life of the ego and what Freud would in time call the death drive. Introduced in *Beyond the Pleasure Principle* (1920) and developed in later texts such as *Civilization and Its Discontents* and *The Ego and the Id* (1923), the death drive offered an answer to two related questions that troubled psychoanalysis from the start: first, where does the ego originate and does it have a history? And, second, how is that we are capable of causing ourselves a kind of pain that seems to oppose what Freud had taken as the fundamental law of psychic life, namely, the pleasure principle? It is with these questions in mind that Freud begins – in such essays as "On Narcissism: An Introduction" (1914) – to imagine a set of desires or instincts that predate the consolidation of the ego; and, because the psychic apparatus never forgets a pleasure, it must remember and continue to want things that not only predate but also threaten the ego. It was with this late speculative turn that Freud arguably offered his most radical theory of narrative, one that, as Peter Brooks sees it, follows the path of every living thing from a purely potential and thus quiescent once-upon-a-time; through the agitated, narrative middle of a life lived; to the same-but-different quiescence of happily-ever-after: "Between these two moments of quiescence, plot itself stands as a kind of divergence or deviance, a postponement in the discharge which leads back to the inanimate. For plot starts (or must give the illusion of starting) from that moment at which story, or 'life,' is stimulated from quiescence into a state of narratability, into a tension, a kind of irritation, which demands narration."[78] Brooks refers to this pattern and desire as Freud's masterplot: "His boldest intention may be to provide a theory of comprehension of the dynamic of the life span, and hence of its narrative understanding."[79] Freud's theory of the drives thus allowed him to project onto and beyond the human life a beginning, middle, and end that could give life its meaning.

Of course, Freud's terms have their own conceptual and historical baggage; although immensely powerful, his models often are wrapped up with frankly appalling ideas about sexuality and desire that require more than a little disentangling. For instance, in "Coming Unstrung: Women, Men, Narrative, and Principles of Pleasure," a response to *Reading for the Plot*, Susan Winnett points to the ways in which Brooks fails to acknowledge how his Freudian metaphors for plot and for the satisfactions of plot might in fact reproduce an exclusively male model of sexual pleasure: "Brooks's articulation of what are ultimately the Oedipal dynamics that structure and determine traditional fictional narratives and psychoanalytic paradigms is brilliant, and it reminds us, in case we had forgotten, what men want, how they go about trying to get it, and the stories they tell in that pursuit."[80] Winnett shows, in other words, the degree to which not only Brooks and Freud but also the larger apparatus of narrative theory should be examined in relation to its gender biases; she proposes in her essay to develop a model of narrative based instead on the pattern of feminine experience and feminine pleasure, one that could lead to "an economy in which another consideration of the relations among beginnings, middles, and ends would yield radically different results."[81] Winnett thus provides a useful alternative, at once feminist and formal, to a model that can seem all too blunt; with this, her essay stands as an engaged response to Susan Lanser's influential call for a "feminist narratology": "The most obvious question feminism would ask of narratology is simply this: upon what body of texts, upon what understandings of the narrative and referential universe, have the insights of narratology been based? It is readily apparent that virtually no work in the field of narratology has taken gender into account, either in designating a canon or in formulating questions and hypotheses."[82] Writing sometime after the initial consolidation of feminist narratology, Robyn Warhol summed up some of the directions it had taken after Lanser's call:

> Feminists interested in narrative theory borrowed the feminist-epistemological critique of objectivity from the social and natural sciences to object that systems of meaning are never neutral, and that they bear the (gendered) marks of their originators and their receivers. Furthermore, feminists have always been interested in significance, in both the linguistic and historical senses of that word. Hence, feminist narratologists never tried to replace the structuralists' systems with alternative macrosystems of their own. Instead, feminist narratology focused on two kinds of projects that relied more on both close reading and historical context that structuralism ever did. There were: (1) finding examples of narrative written by women that posed challenges to the categories of classical narratology, and referring to historical context to account for (the significance of) the gendered differences they observed; and (2) "reading in detail," as Naomi Schor memorably called it, applying the analytic categories narratology made available to scrutinize texts very closely and arrive at gender-conscious interpretations of narratives.[83]

More recently in *No Future: Queer Theory and the Death Drive*, Lee Edelman links Freud's model of the death drive, its relation to the possibility and ultimate psychic limits of narrative form, and what he calls "queer negativity" in order to imagine queer sexual identity as attaining "an ethical value" in relation to its structuring or, rather, unstructuring rejection of the ameliorative futurity of narrative form: "Far from partaking of this narrative movement toward a viable political future, far from perpetuating the fantasy of meaning's eventual realization, the queer comes to figure the bar to every realization of futurity, the resistance, internal to the social, to every social structure or form."[84] Edelman, in other words, associates queerness with the drive because both represent forms of desire that resist the normalizing pressure of social or political scripts that would put every form of desire to work for particular social or political ends; linking queer desire to the negativity of the drive is a way to figure its resistance to narrative limits imposed by a socially prescribed account of pleasure and its "appropriate" ends:

> Politics, that is, by externalizing and configuring in the fictive form of a narrative, allegorizes or elaborates sequentially, precisely *as* desire, those overdeterminations of libidinal positions and inconsistencies of psychic defenses occasioned by what disarticulates the narrativity of desire: the drives, themselves intractable, unassimilable to the logic of interpretation or the demands of meaning-production; the drives that carry the destabilizing force of what insists outside or beyond, because foreclosed by, signification.[85]

The socially impossible but nonetheless and even especially real pleasure – what, as we will see in Section 6.2, Roland Barthes, following Jacques Lacan, refers to as *jouissance* – represented by the drive thus figures a limit to the official forms that subjects and stories can take. We will soon return to the question of narrative, gender, sexuality, and different economies of pleasure in relation to Kristeva, Barthes, and Genette.

Late in his career, Freud wrote an essay, "Analysis Terminable and Interminable" (1937), in which he imagined a complete psychoanalytic process as one explicitly structured around the Aristotelian presence of a beginning, middle, and, most importantly, an end. Freud imagined an authentic *end* to analysis in admittedly ambitious terms:

> What we are asking is whether the analyst has had such a far-reaching influence on the patient that no further change could be expected to take place in him if his analysis were continued. It is as though it were possible by means of analysis to attain a level of absolute psychical normality – a level, moreover, which we could feel confident would be able to remain stable, as though, perhaps, we had succeeded in resolving every one of the patient's repressions and in filling in all the gaps in his memory.[86]

The end of analysis would, in other words, fully resolve the repressions and psychic conflicts that gave rise to the psychic apparatus as such; if, in other words, analysis were able to do away with repression, it would be able to do away with the unconscious, which is itself an effect of repression; and, without an unconscious, psychic life would no longer be structured around the difference between the primary and secondary processes and thus could not generate the significant tensions between latent and manifest that give the dream and the whole of psychic life their meaning. This collapse of manifest into latent would amount, in that case, to something like the highest hopes for Marx's proletarian revolution, as a moment when a culture or an individual's fundamental structuring conflicts would give way to a larger homogeneous unity. Were this the case, a successful analysis would have to end because the patient would, in a strong sense, have become unreadable. The end of analysis would represent a collapse of latent and manifest that would result in something other than narrative or psychic life as we know it. Freud goes on in his essay to lay out several reasons why this version of the end of analysis would be impossible as well as why analyses will always turn out to be practically interminable: sometimes the constitutional as opposed to accidental factors that produce neuroses are simply too strong to undo; it appears to be in the nature of the unbound energy related to the primary processes to exceed and resist the binding efforts of the ego; the analytically necessary experience of transference muddies the difference between analysis and life in a way that cannot be fully managed; and the death drive, because it is finally biological as opposed to psychic, precedes and thus trumps even the most energetic analytic efforts. In a way that anticipates and allows for Edelman's association of queer theory with the death drive, Freud ultimately understood that analysis and, indeed, life were defined by their essential resistance to Aristotelian ends; they are interminable, which is to say resistant to narrative form as such.

One can trace some of this turn to Freud's experience of the First World War. Where prior to 1914 his system was indeed built around the sense that human lives were in one complicated way or another governed by the *pleasure principle*, by an urge toward erotic contact and the production of *more* life, the fact of the war and its profound waste seems to have changed his mind. Beginning with "On Narcissism" in 1914 (not to mention "Thoughts for the Times on War and Death" in 1915), Freud's essays increasingly explore ways in which psychic life appears to be not only pitted against itself but also and at some fundamental level committed paradoxically to self-destruction; at the same time that we feel impelled to move forward, to experience more, to make connections with others and with the world, something in us, something that works deeply and undeniably against narrative, wants to undo those connections, to shatter any attempt to stitch life together into a whole narrative. This death drive, as Freud calls it, reveals ultimate limits to whatever stories we might tell. Although we might want to imagine life as organized according to a relation among beginnings, middles, and ends that could, as with Hegel and Marx, cast the locally tragic experience of conflict as part of a larger and more meaningful comic plot, Freud's ultimate resistance to an end that could confer retroactive significance onto beginnings and middles stands as a strong limit to narrative's ability to *make* sense. It is this fact, that Freud joins an intensely and brilliantly narrative method to a deep and mournful resistance to narrative, that gives his work its terrifically and even corrosively powerful skepticism and that allows it at last to stand as a profound, influential, and tragic theory of narrative.

Chapter 4

Epic, Novel, Narrative Theory

Henry James, Georg Lukács, Mikhail Bakhtin, and Erich Auerbach

If we want life itself, here surely we have it.
Virginia Woolf, "Modern Fiction"

I have worked thus far to lay out a partial and speculative prehistory of narrative theory, a necessarily incomplete but hopefully suggestive account of several related moments that contribute to the sense that narrative ought to be understood not only as an aspect of some texts but also as an object worthy of study in its own right, as a lens through which we tend to see life, history, and the world. From one perspective, the Bible, the *Iliad*, a folk song, a sensational report, a tragedy, and a joke are narratives, to be sure, but they are also many other things. From another perspective, the one that I've been trying to understand, the narrative aspect of these objects emerges as their fundamental, defining quality, as what in another context the linguist Roman Jakobson might have called their "dominant, determining function."[1] Indeed and in ways that can be hard to see now that the position has become more or less naturalized, narrative has emerged as an essential, maybe *the* essential characteristic of a meaningful human life; it seems, in other words, to have become self-evident that many apparently unrelated aspects of life – psychology, politics, science, history, and so on – can and should be understood as forms of narrative. Marie-Laure Ryan writes that, "In the past fifteen years, as the 'narrative turn in the humanities' gave way to the narrative turn everywhere (politics, science studies, law, medicine, and last, but not least, cognitive science), few words have enjoyed so much use and suffered so much abuse as narrative and its partial synonym, story."[2] In order to trace the beginnings, development, and consequences of this expansion, I went back to Aristotle and then moved up through Hegel, Marx, Nietzsche, and Freud in order to account for some of the conditions that led to and made possible the development of a coherent and recognizable narrative theory, which is to say a more or less continuous and self-conscious effort to think about narrative as not only an aesthetic reaction to but also an essential condition of human life.

As a result of starting with these few major figures, we are now able to make some related observations about the character and development of narrative theory. Although there are many ways to think about the many kinds of narratives, I want to think about *narrative theory* – as opposed to narrative – in terms of a few more or less shared qualities.

1. Narrative theories deal with what Aristotle referred to as *plot*, that is, the relation between the different constituent parts of a narrative, namely the beginning, middle, and end. As I suggested, what Aristotle took as a structural aspect of a successful tragedy becomes in Hegel, Marx, Nietzsche, and Freud a way to variously understand the significance, direction, and coherence of histories, political struggles, accounts of culture, and individual lives.

2. Narrative theories deal with the enabling difference and relation between events (real or imagined) and the aesthetic representation of those events, a difference that was variously present in Aristotle, Hegel, Marx, Nietzsche, and Freud and that, as I suggested in the Introduction, we can cast as the difference between *story* and *discourse*.

3. Narrative theories often both address the capacities of narrative to give meaning and order to events *and* to explore how those capacities seem inevitably to come up against certain apparently necessary limits; these theories sometimes show us what narrative both can *and* cannot do.

4. Narrative theories seem to emerge in response to periods of social transformation or social crisis; they emerge when the relation between events and the shared meaning of events seems to have become strained and thus visible.

This last point is the most tendentious of the four; as I suggested in the Introduction, it has seemed to me worthwhile to think about the different appearances of narrative theory in terms of a possible relation between their exoteric and esoteric senses. That is, while all of the works I discuss here are *about* narrative, it seems to me that they are also coded responses to their own moments in time, particularly when those moments are politically or socially fraught. In some cases, this is doubleness is merely symptomatic; in others, it is the result of a calculation on the part of writers and thinkers who wanted to say what might have been personally difficult or politically impermissible to say out loud.

Aristotle's narrative theory in the *Poetics* is, I suggested, partly a response to legal and political shifts in Athens that led both to the tragic image of a gulf between *the time of men* and *the time of the gods* as well as to an allegorical foregrounding of the difference between discrete events and the meaningful arrangement of those events into the whole representation that Aristotle calls *plot*. In Hegel, the lived experience of political turmoil and disappointment in the form of the French Revolution and the Napoleonic Wars led to the development of a dialectical theory in which apparently tragic, which is to say apparently meaningless, events would become meaningful *in time*; what's more and as I argued, the new nationalisms that appeared alongside the French Revolution demanded new modes of imaginative engagement with other people, other ideas or ideologies, and other epochs. In other words, just as historians of the nation state argue that the French Revolution led those of Hegel's generation to a different awareness of the particularity of national and historical consciousness, so, I'm arguing, did it demand a mode of analysis that could not only attend to the radical particularity of different stories about the past and present but also understand what all of those particular stories could have *structurally* in common.[3] Necessity, ability, and luck in other words came together to make Hegel an especially strong representative of a larger narrative turn in history, philosophy, ethnography, etc. In Marx, Nietzsche, and Freud, each of whom lived and worked in this explicitly post-Hegelian intellectual context, the ubiquity of narrative as a necessary conceptual horizon led both to an effort to narrate political, social, and personal experience at times of violent instability (the failed European revolutions of 1848 for Marx, the Franco-Prussian War for Nietzsche, and the First World War for Freud) and to a paradoxical conviction that these narratives work best precisely when they are brought close to or past their limits, caught in the midst of failure, or revealed as illusory. By looking at these different and differently motivated theories of narrative as part of the same, long critical project, I want, as I suggested in the Introduction, to think not only about what narrative theory is and how it works but also about *why* it takes the shape it does at different moments in time and how each new major statement builds on the strengths and the limits of what came before. I want to look at the punctuated and often contingent history of narrative theory both as an unfolding effort to engage with the stories we tell ourselves about ourselves and as a sometimes tacit series of encounters with the limits of narrative as an effort to manage or to explain some of what's most difficult about life and history.

I'll turn in this and the next section to a handful of twentieth-century critics who take up this critical project and also take narrative as a primary object of study but who are able to do so in a more self-conscious, institutionally visible way. Where it took some interpretive work to see the early figures as part of the prehistory of narrative theory, the figures I'll discuss are more obviously associated with some of the different forms of narrative theory: Russian formalism, the theory of the novel, dialogism, structuralist narratology, etc. In the twentieth century, narrative theory thus begins to emerge as a complex, developing but more or less coherent and institutionally viable area of study; the figures I'll focus on from here could, in other words, take it more or less for granted that narrative was not only an aspect of life but also a privileged means by which to account for the significance and shape of that life. In what immediately follows I'll look to a few figures who approach the theory of narrative via a particular genre: the novel. In each of the four cases that follow – Henry James, Georg Lukács, Mikhail Bakhtin, and Erich Auerbach – the novel emerges as an especially important because especially *historical* form of narrative, a form that allows each of these figures to reflect on general aspects of narrative that once again count on an implied theory of story and discourse while also looking at ways in which the novel as a historically specific form of narrative allows us to engage in what I'll call *the comparative analysis of narrative forms*, a type of critical analysis that does much to shape the methods, the practices, and the assumptions of narrative theory.

4.1 Relations Stop Nowhere: Henry James and the Forms of the Novel

Between 1907 and 1909 Henry James wrote a series of prefaces for the twenty-four volumes of the New York edition of his novels and tales. These prefaces, associated as they were with his self-consciously late effort to assemble, to revise, and to *explain* his life's work, amounted to a single, more or less continuous, deeply sustained critical performance, one that bears comparison to Aristotle's *Poetics* in terms of its methodological focus, critical intensity, and lasting influence; indeed, in a letter to William Dean Howells, James wrote that the prefaces "are, in general, a sort of plea for Criticism, for Discrimination, for Appreciation on other than infantile lines—as against the so almost universal Anglo-Saxon absence of these things; which tend so, in our general trade, it seems to me, to break the heart. ... They ought, collected together, not the less, to form a sort of comprehensive manual or *vademecum* for aspirants in our arduous profession."[4] Indeed, James's prefaces make up, both as a result of their influence and in their own terms, an important part of the development of novel and narrative theory. More to the point, James's prefaces offer one of the most thorough arguments for understanding narrative as *technique*, for appreciating how an author selects his or her materials, arranges those materials into an aesthetic whole, manages the relation between different characters and plot as they appear in that whole narrative, and, maybe most centrally, enlivens those represented materials and events in relation to one or another explicit or implied point-of-view. Often boiled down to the bald workshop adage, "show, don't tell," James's prefaces to the New York edition offer both a celebration of the craft of fiction and practical advice for the aspiring writer.[5] In this way and with their pragmatic attention to the particular details of a narrative, the prefaces should be taken as a sustained and inductive work of narrative theory, a deeply critical, personal, and theoretical engagement with the possibilities and the limits of narrative fiction.

In the preface to *The Ambassadors* James calls attention to a particular type of minor character, which he calls a *ficelle*, a French term for "a string used to manipulate a puppet, or more broadly, any underhand trick."[6] For James, the term names a type of character whose role in a narrative is almost purely functional; an author introduces a *ficelle* not as a necessary and organic part of the plot but rather as means of providing necessary exposition, of moving the plot mechanically forward, or of drawing rough and ready thematic antitheses; the *ficelle* is, indeed, a cheap but effective and maybe unavoidable trick. As a result, the *ficelle*'s real relations to other characters and thus to the plot as a whole are tenuous or, indeed, practically nonexistent. That is, where more necessary characters give and take meaning from a fictional community of other characters, where they are or ought to exist in a reciprocal relation to their fictional worlds, merely functional characters like the *ficelle* are cogs in a narrative machine; they are agents or objects of narrative exchange and thus represent the labor (as, perhaps, opposed to craft) of fiction at its least organic. As a result, these characters tend, once they have fulfilled their function, to be lost, abandoned or forgotten. Denied the rich and organic presence of a protagonist, they are examples of what Alex Woloch refers to as the "workers" or "eccentrics" of fiction: "In one case, the character is smoothly absorbed as a gear within the narrative machine, at the cost of his or her own free interiority; in the other case, the minor character grates against his or her position and is usually, as a consequence, wounded, exiled, expelled, ejected, imprisoned, or killed (within the *discourse*, if not the *story*)."[7] In either case, the *ficelle* is a point where the narrative machine *as* machine reveals itself; the *ficelle works* and, because it works, it alerts us to the strings pulled behind any apparently seamless act of narrative representation. (We might think here of Edgar Allan Poe's roughly contemporary and self-consciously profane essay "The Philosophy of Composition" (1846), where he reveals "the wheels and pinions—the tackle for scene-shifting—the step-ladders and demon-traps—the cock's feathers, the red paint and the black patches, which, in ninety-nine cases out of the hundred, constitute the properties of the literary *histrio*.)"[8]

James's great example of such a character is Maria Gostrey, who appears early in *The Ambassadors* as a beguiling but random love interest for the novel's protagonist and narratorial surrogate, Lambert Strether; as James admits in his preface, Maria exists almost solely to give Strether the opportunity to talk to someone about himself and thus to provide a reader with necessary plot exposition; James writes that, "Her function speaks at once for itself, and by the time she has dined with Strether in London and gone to a play with him her intervention as a *ficelle* is, I hold, expertly justified."[9] James goes on to say that while the practical function of the *ficelle* is clear, her appearance was in this case an unexpected but real source pleasure for both the author and the discriminating reader: Maria-as-*ficelle* "shows us afresh how many quite incalculable but none the less clear sources of enjoyment for the infatuated artist, how many copious springs of our never-to-be-slighted 'fun' for the reader and critic susceptible of contagion, may sound their incidental plash as soon as an artistic process begins to enjoy free development."[10] James's play between a spring as a natural and seemingly spontaneous figure for poetic inspiration—"that from the secret springs of that dark fountain rose" (Shelley)—and a spring as "an elastic contrivance or mechanical device" (OED) seems intentional here. Indeed, what James loves about a *ficelle* is the art required to conceal the puppet's strings, the craft needed to make what is avowedly artificial look necessary and natural; he loves it because it allows him to indulge in craft for its own sake and, in fact, to show off a little.

What's more, because she is a *ficelle*, which is to say an index of craft appreciated and even loved for its own sake, Maria Gostrey seems also strangely to exceed her place as a mere narrative function and indeed to become an object of desire for James almost as much as for Strether. She appears in his preface as a "living" representative of freedom, play, erotic interest, and "fun." Despite her status as a mere trick, Maria seems in the preface maybe to have seduced James, a fact that undermines what we would take to be the natural difference between worlds within and without a given narrative. This is just one of many points in the prefaces where James seems to imagine his characters as having come weirdly and excessively to life, a fact that anticipates a point of contact between James and Bakhtin, who, as we will see, saw Dostoevsky as unique because he somehow allowed his characters to live and think independently of an author's potentially totalizing and monologic point of view. The *ficelle* thus stands as one of several points in James's thinking where the pleasurable experience of narrative technique *as* technique brings narrative's doubled status as content *and* form, instrumental *and* aesthetic value, story *and* discourse to the fore; put differently, the idea that the *ficelle* emerges both as a functional means to an end – the production of a narrative as a coherent whole – and as pleasurable end-in-itself helps to reveal a paradox that James seems to take as essential to narrative, the paradoxical and maybe incommensurate pleasure that he takes both from the parts of a novel insofar as they add up to some greater whole and from those parts for their own partial sake.

This double sense of narrative technique as both a means to an end and an end unto itself begins to get at the complicated, ambivalent nature of James's broader sense of narrative potential. For instance, we can see this ambivalence at work in his account of how whole narratives do and don't come together around a particular middle or center:

> ... perversely, incurably, the centre of my structure would insist on placing itself *not*, so to speak, in the middle. It mattered little that the reader with the idea or the suspicion of a structural centre is the rarest of friends and of critics—a bird, it would seem, as merely fabled as the phoenix: the terminational terror was none the less certain to break in and my work threaten to masquerade for me as an active figure condemned to the disgrace of legs too short, ever so much too short, for its body. I urge myself to the candid confession that in very few of my productions, to my eye, *has* the organic centre succeeded in getting into proper position.[11]

James's point is, at first glance, simple enough; because novels, unlike traged-ies, are often very, very long, it can be hard to keep their beginnings, middles, and ends in the right kind of aesthetic proportion: ends get rushed, begin-nings seem abrupt or forced, middles linger and stall. If the novel is, as James claimed, sometimes a "large, loose, baggy monster," we need to see that figure's monstrosity against Aristotle's image of a proper plot as a creature that is neither too large nor too small: "Beauty," Aristotle observes, "is a matter of size and order, and therefore impossible either in a very minute creature [...] or in a creature of vast size."[12] That said, the terms in which James makes his related compositional point are, on closer inspection, far more complex. He not only reflects here on the material length of the novel but also suggests a relation between the middle, a more or less physical point standing somewhere and somehow between a syntactic beginning and end, and a "structural center," a source of significant or *semantic* as opposed to syntactic coherence. The point here is that the middle and the center are not at last the same thing and that forcing them together reveals some of what's mysterious about narrative form. How, after all, is it that the content and the form of a narrative can come together to produce both the proportional matter of a given narrative and the real experience of meaning? Can narrative technique – the right placement of a narrative middle – somehow result in the discovery of an organic center, which is to say a point around which events or life could appear as ultimately meaningful? James admits that, while the coincidence of middle and center is his goal, it is one that remains out of reach: "I urge myself to the candid confession that in very few of my productions, to my eye, *has* the organic centre succeeded in getting into proper position." James thus both holds this convergence of significant center and narrative middle both as an aesthetic ideal and a practical impossibility; life will not be reduced to one or another form, and it is the artist's job both to try nonetheless to manage the trick and to make his or her inevitable failure into part of the "fun." After all, what makes the phoenix beautiful is precisely and paradoxically the fact that we will never ever see one. Just as the *ficelle's* pleasurable confusion of technical means and ends points to a contradiction immanent to the affective experience of narrative form, so does the non-identity of middle and center display the necessity of technique while also alerting us to the inevitability of its necessary and, again, pleasurable failure. If, that is, we *seem* to want a narrative that perfectly manages the relation between means and ends, middle and center, story and discourse, what we *in fact* love are narratives when they fail. The love of difficulty, of work, of cheap tricks, noble failures, and beautiful mistakes is at the very heart of James's thinking in the prefaces.

The necessary non identity of middle and center also points towards a larger question for James, the question of how narrative ultimately gives form and thus meaning to the stuff of life. This problem appears in the very first of James's prefaces, the preface to *Roderick Hudson*:

> Really, universally, relations stop nowhere, and the exquisite problem of the artist is eternally but to draw, by a geometry of his own, the circle within which they shall happily *appear* to do so. He is in the perpetual predicament that the continuity of things is the whole matter, for him, of comedy and tragedy; that this continuity is never, by the space of an instant or an inch, broken, and that, to do anything at all, he has at once intensely to consult and intensely to ignore it. . . . The prime effect of so sustained a system, so prepared a surface, is to lead on and on; while the fascination of following resides, by the same token, in the presumability *somewhere* of a convenient, of a visibly-appointed stopping-place. Art would be easy indeed if, by a fond power disposed to "patronize" it, such conveniences, such simplifications, had

been provided. We have, as the case stands, to invent and establish them, to arrive at them by a difficult, dire process of selection and comparison, of surrender and sacrifice.[13]

To put it schematically: James suggests first that "life," the matter out of which he forms his narratives, is naturally continuous, unbroken, and total. He then goes on to suggest that any effort to form that life, to give it a meaningful shape will amount to an imposition, a limitation of the full scope and, thus, the ultimate if ineffable significance of things: "Really, universally, relations stop nowhere." The idea that the novelist must, "by a geometry of his own," draw a circle around some part of the whole of life in order to give it shape and a significance thus rhymes both with Nietzsche's sense of the chorus as providing tragic narrative with a kind of metaleptic magic circle and, as we will see, with Lukács' discussion of the novel's biographical form, with its tendency to adopt the shape of an individual life not because individual lives are necessarily the most important thing but rather because the novel needs what James calls "a geometry," and the sequence of birth-life-death has tended to provide the novel with that geometry. The novel, in that case, emerges for James not only as a representation of some part of life but also as a record of the labor that went into producing that representation, a record of a "difficult, dire process of selection and comparison, of surrender and sacrifice." We are encouraged, in other words, to attend both to what the circle of James's art contains and to the circle itself.

For James, the drawing of that circle takes a particular, technical form; as opposed to a metaleptic chorus or the biographical shape of an individual life, it is an individual *point of view* that lends narrative significance to life in James's fiction. James's discussion of point of view over the course of the prefaces is indeed probably his most significant and controversial contribution to narrative theory; as Robert Scholes and Robert Kellogg write, "The problem of point of view was largely neglected in literary criticism before the advent of Henry James."[14] Indeed, James's reliance on a single organizing consciousness, on the directing presence of an intelligent watchful mind through which to "see" the material of a narrative is essential to his whole project. For instance, in the preface to *The Princess Casamassima* he casts his reliance on a single character's point of view as an enlivening and necessary "intimacy": "Intimacy with a man's specific behavior, with his given case, is desperately certain to make us see it as a whole – in which event arbitrary limitations of our vision lose whatever beauty they may on occasion have pretended to. What a man thinks and what he feels are the history and the character of what he does; on all of which things the logic of intensity rests.

Without intensity where is vividness, and without vividness where is present-ability?"[15] Seen from the perspective of an intelligent individual mind, life takes on an intensity, a shape, a form, and thus a meaning it couldn't otherwise have. For James, narrative form doesn't simply capture meaning; form rather makes meaning possible in the first place. J. Hillis Miller writes in a related context that, "As Henry James understood, form is meaning."[16]

This is partly a practical matter for James, a methodological principle that guides him as he imagines or selects events at the level of story that should, can, and will appear at the level of discourse. In these terms, James anticipates later discussions of what is called *focalization*, a term that, as H. Porter Abbott puts it, "refers specifically to the lens through which we see characters and events in the narrative."[17] Gérard Genette introduced the term in an effort to under-stand the narrative management of *mood*, or "the regulation of narrative information," which usually amounts to the ways in which information is selected and presented in relation to an explicitly or implicitly named perspec-tive, one that may or may not be associated with a narrator.[18] In the case of first-person narratives like *Great Expectations* (1861) or *Bridget Jones's Diary* (1996), it is easy to see that most if not all of what we see has been focalized through Pip's or Bridget's perspective; we see, hear, or feel more or less what Pip or Bridget see, hear, or feel. In the case of third-person narratives like *Middlemarch* (1871) or *Gravity's Rainbow* (1973), information might seem to be differently or serially or partially or paradoxically focalized through a number of character-perspectives; and some narratives can seem even to be at least partly *unfocalized* through any character at all. Although we can "hear" someone speaking, what individual character could see enough to *see* some-thing as abstract as Hardy's great and distant description of the heath in *The Return of the Native* (1878): "The place became full of a watchful intentness now; for when other things sank blooding to sleep the heath appeared slowly to awake and listen. Every night its Titanic form seemed to await something; but it had waited thus, unmoved, during so many centuries, through the crises of so many things, that it could only be imagined to await one last crisis—the final overthrow."[19] Genette thus differentiates between several types of focalization: in the case of what he calls *internal focalization,* a narrative more or less organizes itself around the conceptual or emotional perspective of a particular character or of several characters; in the case of *external focalization,* that perspective is limited to "the characters' external behavior (words and actions but not thoughts or feelings)."[20] (As we will see, subsequent narrative theorists have used the terms *internal* and *external focalization* in a very different sense.) Genette also names the real or theoretical absence of perspective, cases of *zero focalization* where a narrative seems to be narrated from a "nonlocatable, indeterminate perspective or conceptual position," as sometimes seems the case with an omniscient narration that can seem to see everything and thus be both everywhere and nowhere.[21] As he puts it in *Narrative Discourse Revisited*, "it seems to me that classical narrative sometimes places its 'focus' at a point so indefinite, or so remote, with so panoramic a field (the well-known 'viewpoint of God,' or of Sirius, about which people periodically wonder whether it is indeed a point of view) that is cannot coincide with any character and that the term nonfocalization, or zero focalization, is rather more appropriate for it."[22]

With these few distinctions in hand, narrative theorists have gone deeply and controversially into the relation between "who sees or perceives" and "who speaks." Especially important here is Mieke Bal's critique of Genette's terms in her *Narratology: Introduction to the Theory of Narrative*, a book that put important pressure on Genette's scheme and thus helped to reopen the question of narrative perspective: as opposed to imagining a hard difference between instances of focalization where narrative attention is routed through a particular character's point of view and instances where focalization is absent (what Genette referred to as *zero focalization*), Bal sees a continuum between cases of *character-bound focalization* (which she calls *internal focalization*), which limit themselves to what one or another character within a story can see or feel, and cases of *external focalization*, where "an anonymous agent, situated outside the fable [or story], is functioning as a focalizor."[23] Because Bal sees focalization not as one technique among others but rather as a relation necessary to narrative perception and thus to narrative itself, she argues that focalization is not something a narrative can do without; for Bal, there simply are no "unfocalized passages" in narrative.[24] The difference here is that, where Genette sees focalization as a process or technique, a restriction of the narratable field that narration can manage both with and without a character's point-of-view, Bal sees focalization as a relation that exists between perceiving subjects and perceived objects within a given narrative; and, insofar as narrative *is in itself* an embodied or encoded act of perception, it must imply one or another form of focalization. Other critics have continued to explore these questions. Manfred Jahn, for instance, offers a refined opposition between "strict" and "ambient" focalization.[25] Rimmon-Kenan distinguishes between different but related "facets of focalization," perceptual, psychological, and ideological aspects of narrative perspective that "may concur but they may also belong to different, even clashing, focalizers."[26] Thinking about the nature of narrative authority has led to other debates about the politics of focalization. How should we navigate the issues of power that come up when one character is given more narrative authority than others? Is focalization only a technical issue or is it a bearer of cultural or ideological force and content?

Many of these questions about what happens when a wider narration is focalized down into one or another consciousness turn, as James Phelan and others have pointed out, on narrative's possible status as a rhetorical as opposed to an informational act; where Genette and his followers tend to restrict their view to the narrative act itself, to the information that appears as narrative discourse, others – like Phelan – look at narrative as a rhetorical or ideological act that needs to be seen as both coming from and going to somewhere or someone in particular.[27] As Harry Shaw has recently pointed out, many if not most narrative theories explicitly or implicitly assume either "information" or "rhetoric" models for defining acts of narrative communication, and which model one chooses has important consequences for seeing the position and the significance of the different addressing and receiving positions implied by any narrative. The classic communication model (which Seymour Chatman partly derived from Wayne Booth's *The Rhetoric of Fiction*) moves from the Real Author to the Implied Author to the Narrator to the Narratee to the Implied Reader, and, at last, to the Real Reader.[28] Although controversial, this model has allowed subsequent critics to ask very precise questions about the relation between the more and less visible figures assumed in any narrative act; the model helps us, for instance, to think through what is maybe hopelessly complex about something like *Jane Eyre*, a novel written by a *real author* (Charlotte Brontë), writing under the assumed, gender-neutral name of an *implied author* (Currer Bell), from the point of view of a fictional *narrator* (Jane Eyre), who, as she occasionally addresses the reader directly – "Reader, I married him." – seems to collapse into one the different positions of *narratee* (a necessarily fictional figure whom a fictional Jane can address directly), *implied reader* (the ideal reader whom it was possible to imagine reading the novel within the historical and ideological confines of British print culture in 1847), and a *real reader* (now, a person sitting and reading from a book or a screen in the twenty-first century, a reader whom Charlotte Brontë could not have imagined).

The difference between seeing this sequence in informational or rhetorical terms amounts to, first, thinking about the narrative circuit as a more or less neutral means of conveying narrative information, a model that focuses on how the circuit works as a kind of technology and, second, thinking about the narrative circuit as an event that meaningfully comes from and moves towards *someone* in particular, a model that focuses on what people think and believe about their stories and the contexts they inhabit; as Shaw puts it, the rhetorical model "serves to focus the question 'What would you have to have believed and valued to have created this work?' by constructing an anthropomorphic agent of belief, and thereby invites those who use it to employ the vast and subtle panoply of techniques, most of them unformulated and hardly conscious, that we draw upon in everyday life when we try to assess the values and intentions of others."[29] In these terms, the way a narrative relies on focalization among other techniques will read differently depending on what model – rhetorical or informational – we bring with us to the act of interpretation.

Indeed, whatever the local disputes over this or that aspect of focalization, we can see that its management can produce enormously important effects in narrative; this is certainly the case in James. For instance, late in *The Princess Casamassima*, the novel that James took in his preface to that novel as an exemplary instance of a narrative focalized through a single, intelligent consciousness, he breaks ostentatiously away from his otherwise singular reliance on the perspective of his protagonist, Hyacinth Robinson. Where, in other words, almost the whole of the novel has relied on Hyacinth's presence, his acuity, his past, and his disposition to select and organize its presentation of narrative information, James suddenly turns away from Hyacinth in order to record a conversation that goes on behind his protagonist's back at the level of both content and form, a fact that James's narrator registers explicitly: "A certain Sunday in November, more than three months after she had gone to live in Madeira Crescent, was so important an occasion for the Princess Casamassima that I must give as complete an account of it as the limits of my space will allow. Early in the afternoon a loud peal from her door-knocker came to her ear; it had a sound of resolution, almost of defiance, which made her look up from her book and listen."[30] After following Hyacinth for so long, the shift away from him to the Princess as focalizer is jarring and strange; at this late stage in the novel, it indeed produces a kind of aesthetic disorientation, one that James registers in his narrator's acknowledgement of the shift as a matter of grudging necessity: "I *must* give as complete an account of it as the limits of my space will allow." What's more, James not only shifts focalizers but also exaggerates that shift by attending so closely to the sensory experience of the Princess as *she* hears a knock, begins to interpret a knock, and alertly "looks up from her book" to anticipate what will come next.[31] The effect is strange but appropriate because, as we soon discover, the Princess's conversation with Paul Muniment, her visitor and the man who has convinced Hyacinth to become a terrorist, amounts to a conspiracy against poor Hyacinth Robinson, a conspiracy the terms of which both the Princess and the novel need to withhold from Hyacinth if the plot is to continue on towards its tragic conclusion. On the one hand, we can take

James's break away from the otherwise achieved and austere aesthetic consistency of his method as evidence of an internal generic shift, a move away from the focused realism of most of the novel to a messier, more violent, and less guarded *melodramatic* strain that Peter Brooks sees as running throughout James's work: "The desire to express all seems a fundamental characteristic of the melodramatic mode. Nothing is spared because nothing is left unsaid; the characters stand on the stage and utter the unspeakable...."[32] The end of *The Princess Casamassima* does, indeed, turn towards melodrama, giving in to the urge to see and to say *more* than a singly focalized narrative could show. James thus manages a sudden and disorienting shift from one focalizer to another as a formal response to the novel's late modal turn from the conceptual focus of realism to the unruly urges of melodrama. On the other hand, the late turn away from Hyacinth, the novel's sensitive, searching protagonist also produces an ethical effect in the novel, a queasy feeling the level of form and thus at the level of reading that mirrors the betrayal of Hyacinth that has taken place at the level of content; all at once, Hyacinth is betrayed by his friend Paul, the Princess Casamassima, the narrator, and, as it turns out, a reader who discovers that he or she *does not need* Hyacinth. This sense of narrative abandonment is made all the more poignant when we learn at last that Hyacinth has committed suicide, that he has exited the narrative before its end, something that could not have happened if the novel had remained faithful to Hyacinth as its one and only point of focalization. By turning away from Hyacinth as a focalizer, James both reveals the narrative apparatus at work and names the reader who wants to see how it all turns out as ethically complicit in the narrative abandonment of Hyacinth to his sorry fate.

Indeed, the question of point of view often extended well past technical issues for James, touching on some basic, ethical aspects of narrative and narration. After all, to select a point of view, to choose one perspective as opposed to another was in every case to make a claim about life, about who should narrate it, and about what it should or could mean to whom. Dorothy Hale makes this point in *Social Formalism*: "As [James] goes on to explain, 'life' can never actualize value because it has no point of view, no appreciative capacity; it can yield an 'interesting particle' only when something or someone in life matters *for* someone, when the objects of interest become the 'subject' of [an author's] inquiry."[33] In these terms, we need to see perspective both as what enables narrative, what gives it its shape and significance and as a limit immanent to narrative form; while a particular perspective can make life matter "for someone," it might not be able to make a life matter for everyone. The possibilities and limits of perspective begin to get to the limits of narrative in general; while this or that perspective can make events meaningful in a particular way *for* and *from* that perspective, it cannot tell us once and for all what those events could mean for everyone. That, of course, is the point of a point of view; it works because it is an enabling limit to the potentially limitless spread of narrative significance. Point of view thus turns out to be, like the *ficelle*, another type of technical irony: as opposed to reducing the novel to a single or, as Bakhtin will say, *monologic* worldview, the partial and provisional nature of any single point of view serves both to give a part of life meaning because that part is meaningful for that point of view and to call attention to the formal limits of that meaning because, after all, what's meaningful for it can't be meaningful for everyone.

Jamesian point of view thus emerges as a particular technical solution to the larger narrative problem that I've been tracking throughout: how to understand the productive imposition of form onto life, representation onto event, discourse onto story. James both cherishes the significance that narrative can bring to life and recognizes all that narrative can miss or obscure; as a result, he sees a kind of formal irony as, if not a solution, at least a way to negotiate consciously between the power and the limits of narrative. James thus foregrounds both the meaning and the unreliability that a point of view brings to life in order to dramatize the strengths and weaknesses of his own method; like the non identity of middle and center or the means-end paradox of the *ficelle*, the idea of the individual point of view allows James to instantiate a necessary and productive contradiction that I've been arguing is at the heart of narrative theory, the sense both that narrative is our best means of making sense of the past, the present, other people, and the world, and that it can only do that work well if it is made also to disclose and indeed to celebrate all that it *cannot* do. As James writes at the end of the preface to *The Portrait of a Lady*, "There is really too much to say."[34]

4.2 Starry Maps: Georg Lukács and Narrative Genre

> Consider Lukács.
>
> Jean-Paul Sartre, *Search for a Method*

Georg Lukács begins *The Theory of the Novel* with a lyrical, dense, and frankly odd description of ancient Greeks and their world:

> Happy are those ages when the starry sky is the map of all possible paths— ages whose paths are illuminated by the light of the stars. Everything in such ages is new and yet familiar, full of adventure and yet their own.

The world is wide and yet it is like a home, for the fire that burns in the soul is of the same essential nature as the stars; the world and the self, the light and the fire, are sharply distinct, yet they never become permanent strangers to one another, for fire is the soul of all light and all fire clothes itself in light. Thus each action of the soul becomes meaningful and rounded in this duality: complete in meaning—in sense—and complete for the senses; rounded because the soul rests within itself even while it acts; rounded because its action separates itself from it and, having become itself, finds a centre of its own and draws a closed circumference round itself. "Philosophy is really homesickness," says Novalis: "it is the urge to be at home everywhere."[35]

The situation he describes is perfect: it is full, rounded, happy, and *at home* in the world and with itself. More than that, it is aesthetically or *structurally* perfect, a world built on a balance or synthesis of what are for other, later cultures more or less stark antinomies: the sky reflects the earth (it is a "map of all possible paths") just as the earth responds to the sky; the new is old and the old is new; the external world (represented here by stars) is of a piece with the internal world of the soul, which burns with the same fire; everything fits with everything else because everything is made – and self-evidently made – of one and the same stuff. It is for this reason that this world and its representative aesthetic form, the epic, are also *perfectly* readable: the epic world and the epic itself are "complete in meaning – in sense – and complete for the senses." Indeed, reading as interpretation, as work, as the discovery or production of significance would be unnecessary in such a world: the *sense* or significance of a work is identical to the *sensuous* presence of the text as well as to the *sensory* impression it makes on a reader or listener. In this context, form and content, content and expression, story and discourse, part and whole are immediately and self-evidently one and the same. Indeed, as Lukács will go on to argue, the epic – and he is thinking specifically of Homeric epic – *is* perfect because it is a perfect part of this perfect world.

As a result, the epic is also a whole and perfect narrative form: Homer can balance relations between beginning, middle, and end, between form and content, between events and the narrative representation of events. We can see this formal, narrative realization in Lukács's claim that the epic and its world are both still or static because perfectly full and yet also full of adventure, activity, and movement; the mix of aesthetic stillness and the necessary mobility of adventure suggests a resolution of two aspects of narrative that we've been looking at from the beginning: the protean temporal experience – the adventure – of moving from event to event to event and the static and spatial arrangement of a whole and fully realized plot; in this way, the epic resolves in advance the generically tragic dissonance between what I referred to in Section 2.1 as the time of men and the time of the gods, of narrative experienced immanently as a sequence of discrete events and narrative experienced only after the fact as a whole aesthetic design. In a manner that goes back to and importantly back before Aristotle and the *Poetics*, Lukács looks to Homer's Greeks in order to imagine a model narrative form and the cultural conditions that could make that model form possible.

This account of ancient Greek life is, of course, a fantasy, and I'll say more about what supports and drives Lukács's fantasy in a moment; what's important for now is what Lukács does with this model. While the abstract, frankly weird opening pages of *Theory of the Novel* are dedicated to an account of the ideal and synthetic form of epic, most of the book looks at what happens after the fall, after the cultural conditions that supported epic totality are no longer possible. He moves quickly through a number of different literary forms before arriving at his proper subject, the novel and its world. The first response to the fall away from epic totality is tragedy: "The tragic hero takes over from Homer's living man, explaining and transfiguring him precisely because he has taken the almost extinguished torch from his hands and kindled it anew."[36] Where things and the meaning of things were one and the same in epic, tragedy recognizes the fragility of that system by narrativizing the relation between things and what things ultimately mean. Where, in other words, significance was immanent to everything that the epic hero said or did (we never need to ask what Achilles *means*: Achilles is Achilles and that's enough), the tragic hero makes the search after meaning into his or her whole reason for being. Oedipus is, of course, the model here, the riddle-solver, the figure who wants and needs to know more, but whose need to know ultimately destroys him. For Oedipus, the tragic meeting of the is and the ought is, in other words, both barely possible and utterly catastrophic. Put in the terms of their different narrative structures, Lukács might say that where tragedy is about suspense, about wondering what will come next, about whether or not the mystery and meaning of things will be revealed, epic is necessarily without suspense; because the meaning of an epic is everywhere present, it would make no sense to see it, as is always the case in tragedy, as unevenly distributed between beginning, middle, and end. (I'll come back to the question of Homeric suspense in Section 4.4, where I discuss Erich Auerbach's similar claim that the Greek epic is incapable of suspense as well as Meir Sternberg's argument that, on the contrary, there is Homeric suspense, but that it is not a matter of temporal delay but rather an effect of "spatial patterning" across the textual surface of epic.) Where meaning was every-where equally immanent to the epic, in tragedy it takes the place of a final and in some sense alien conclusion towards which everything else tends.

Lukács then turns to philosophy, which he takes – after Nietzsche, a powerful influence on the young Lukács – as proof of a final, Socratic fall away from the possibility of a unified and whole Greek culture: "That is why philosophy, as a form of life or as that which determines the form and supplies the content of literary creation, is always a symptom of the rift between 'inside' and 'outside,' a sign of the essential difference between the self and the world, the incongruence of soul and deed."[37] The problem with philosophy is that, where the epic managed to resolve differences between the real and the ideal in advance, and where tragedy made meaning into a structural endpoint towards one could at least strive (whatever the ultimate consequences), with the rise of Platonic philosophy, the ideal becomes separated off from the real and established as something that exists on the other side of an impassable divide. In a sense, Lukács goes over ground that we covered in Section 2.2, acknowledging and working to look past a system that relies on an insoluble Kantian divide between the real and the ideal, between thoughts about things and the things themselves: "Truly a folly to the Greeks! Kant's starry firmament now shines only in the dark night of pure cognition, it no longer lights any solitary wanderer's path (for to be a man in the new world is to be solitary). And the inner light affords evidence of security, or its illusion, only to the wanderer's next step."[38] Because philosophy idealizes meaning and thus seals it off from everyday life, it makes narrative in either its epic or its tragic forms impossible. Meaning becomes something that one can contemplate but not touch; as a result, the idea of doing things, of moving towards something, of seeking out experience or change becomes unthink-able, a fact that, for Lukács, threatens the two defining aspects of narrative form: the structuring relation between events and the meaningful representa-tion of those events as well as the motivated relation between beginning, middle, and end.

Like Hegel, whose *Aesthetics* is a clear influence on *The Theory of the Novel*, Lukács found the idea of a hard divide between life and meaning intolerable. As a result he both turns methodologically to Hegel, attempting a synthesis of what he would later refer to as "'left' ethics and 'right' epistemology," and embraces the novel as modern life's equivalent to epic; he argues that both forms are interested in the same thing, in the production of a whole narrative representation of a social totality: "The epic and the novel, these two major forms of great epic literature, differ from one another not by their authors' fundamental intentions but by the given historico-philosophical realities with which the authors were confronted. The novel is the epic of an age in which the extensive totality of life is no longer directly given, in which the immanence of meaning in life has become a problem, yet which still thinks in terms of totality."[39] The idea here is that the novel is an epic form because, like the great Homeric epics, it uses narrative form, i.e., the relation between events and the representation of events, to present a whole world. Both forms use the same tools, have the same goals, and represent a similar human urge. What separates them is not their essential design but rather the historical contexts in which they work; where Greek culture was unified and organic, the content of modern culture has become too big, too complicated, and thus too internally divided to resolve itself into any one narrative: "The circle within which the Greeks led their metaphysical life was smaller than ours: that is why we cannot, as part of our life, place ourselves inside it. Or rather, the circle whose closed nature was the transcendental essence of their life has, for us, been broken; we cannot breathe in a closed world. We have invented the productivity of the spirit: that is why the primaeval images have irrevocably lost their objective self-evidence for us, and our thinking follows the endless path of an approximation that is never fully accomplished."[40] Where Greek life was always already bound by a magic circle, where it was unified, homogenous, and small enough to allow for the whole and just representations of the Homeric epic, our world is unbound, messy, and resistant to any immediate or single significance. "Increasingly," writes Fredric Jameson, "in the late 19th century, writers became aware that the world of newly emergent capitalism was an unrepresentable totality which it was nonetheless their duty and vocation to represent."[41] Once again, although faced with the impossibility of totality, the novel seeks nonetheless to achieve totality; that, for Lukács as well as Jameson, is its essential character.

As a result, the work of the novel as modern epic is to draw the circle that culture can no longer provide on its own; it is to use narrative form – the relation between event and representation as well as the relation between beginning, middle, and end – to make an apparently insignificant life feel significant. If, however, the novel can give life meaning, it can't simply return to Greek models; the imposition of the beautiful simplicity of the Homeric epic onto modern content would do a kind of violence to the complicated and contradictory content of modern life. What Lukács instead sees in the great novel is a narrative form that both reaches after the forms of totality associated with epic and yet also recognizes and works to address its own formal limits: it "is the epic of an age in which the extensive totality of life is no longer directly given, in which the immanence of meaning in life has become a problem, yet which still thinks in terms of totality."[42]

Lukács returns to something like this idea in more accessible and extensive terms in *The Historical Novel*: "Tragedy and great epic thus both lay claim to portraying the totality of the life-process. It is obvious in both cases that this can only be a result of artistic structure, of formal concentration in the artistic reflection of the most important features of objective reality. For obviously the real, substantial, infinite and extensive totality of life can only be reproduced mentally in a relative form."[43] Lukács' account of the novel's formal response to the complexity of modern problems thus recalls both Nietzsche's sense of the tragic chorus as a magic circle drawn around the otherwise impossible content of Dionysian experience and James's claim that, because "relations stop nowhere," because life is big and complicated and unruly, it is the work of the novel to "draw a circle" around a part of life in order to give that part a temporary, a fragile but a nonetheless real wholeness. As we saw in the last section, James offered an account of the novel and, more particularly, novelistic point of view as forms that could invest some part of life with a real if ephemeral aesthetic and maybe ethical significance.

~

Before turning to the question of how Lukács imagines the novel as responding in specifically narrative terms to the character of modern life, I want to look back to the beginning and ask what encouraged Lukács to frame the question of narrative form and its uses in terms of an opposition between the imagined and certainly fantastical epic culture of ancient Greece and his own sense of the novel as the representative form of a fallen, modern age. What was it that Lukács was looking for when he looked to this idea of the epic? By the time Lukács wrote *The Theory of the Novel* he was already well-known in his native Hungary and beyond. His earlier works, the collection of essays on aesthetics, *Soul and Form,* and his monograph on modern tragic drama had already secured his reputation as a subtle theorist of literary and, in particular, narrative genres as well as a sharp, if despondent, critic of bourgeois culture. The son of a successful banker, Lukács rejected what he took to be the emptiness of middle-class life in Europe, a fact that helps to account for his turn in the *The Theory of the Novel* to the distant and frankly fabulous example of Greek culture and, later, for his difficult and lifelong commitment to Marxism.

Some of Lukács' ideas about ancient Greece as an especially "integrated" society were informed by the eighteenth-century art critic, Johann J. Winckelmann, whose *Thoughts on the Imitation of Greek Art in Painting and Sculpture* (1755) was broadly influential (on Kant, Lessing, Herder,

Goethe, Pater, and many others). For Winckelmann, Greek art and Greek culture were characterized by their simplicity, honesty, and directness; Frank Turner writes that, "in contrast to modern culture that was informed by false social values, inhibiting aesthetic rules, and ascetic Christian morality, Greece functioned [for Winckelmann] as a metaphor for a golden age inhabited, if not by prelapsarian human beings, at least by natural children who made use of their imagination to comprehend the world and their reason to restrain their passions against excess."[44] This sense of a just relation to the world, one that steered a course between unnecessary asceticism or excess, thus provided Lukács and others with a model for a truly organic culture, for a way of living that could naturally balance the demands of both ideas and things. As a result, the Greek epic in general and Homer in particular (Lukács writes that, "strictly speaking, his works alone are epics") seemed able to bring together terms that modern, alienated life had torn asunder. If, however, Lukács' ideas about the Greeks can be traced back to a larger set of cultural questions, questions that in turn animated the famous "quarrel between the ancients and the moderns," a more immediate influence was the work of several social and cultural critics with whom Lukács became acquainted while studying in Germany. The fantasy world that Lukács imagines at the beginning of *The Theory of the Novel* has, in other words, less to do with the ancient Greeks than with the ideal of an organic culture that he had encountered in thinkers like Ferdinand Tönnies, Max Weber, and Georg Simmel, an ideal, integrated community defined by its limited scope, the close and closed nature of its social relationships, and its reliance on and full immersion in a world of shared, traditional, and tested values, customs, and beliefs.

Lukács had read Tönnies' enormously influential *Community and Civil Society* (1887) and, as Martin Jay points out, in fact "knew him in Heidelberg from 1912–1917."[45] For Tönnies, modern life was characterized by a move from an organic experience of community (*Gemeinschaft*) to life in an internally riven civil society (*Gesellschaft*), a move, in other words, from a way of living based on shared rules and practices that emerge as a result of living amidst the deep traditional bonds that exist between members of an organic community to a way of living based on relations between disconnected individuals who follow the calculated, rational, and self-interested dictates of a society rooted in the market logic of capitalism; Tönnies writes that, "We have on offer two contrasting systems of collective social order. One is based essentially on concord, on the fundamental harmony of wills, and is developed and cultivated by religion and custom. The other is based on convention, on a convergence or pooling of rational desires; it is guaranteed and protected by political legislation, while its policies and their ratification are derived from public opinion."[46] This distinction, which Tönnies himself adapted from a variety of largely Romantic sources, went on to influence not only Lukács but also the two crucial figures with whom the young Lukács studied: Georg Simmel and Max Weber.

One of the most distinctive thinkers of the period, Simmel brought together Tönnies' sense of a human community on the verge of extinction with what Gillian Rose identifies as an idiosyncratic synthesis of "aspects of the philosophy of Kant, Hegel, Marx, and Nietzsche."[47] On the one hand, Simmel offered the young Lukács the beginnings of a critical method built around oppositions that seemed to call out for one or another kind of resolution: country and city, subject and object, life and form, etc. For Simmel, culture is what we call the result of the effort to impose forms or values onto the matter or facts of life; the productive tension between the two sides of this dualism became the basis for Simmel's early sociology and fed directly into the young Lukács' effort to think through the relation between literary form and content. On the other hand, Simmel also offered Lukács a way to explain the apparently tragic character of modern life, the fact that, where certain shared values had seemed more or less capable of accounting for a particular community, the accelerated and objectifying character of modernity's content had pushed those old values up to and past their limits; Jay writes that, "The resulting conflict between submission to received forms and the desire to create anew, or between the intersubjective legacy of the cultural past and the subjective need to break free from it, produced what Simmel called the tragedy of culture."[48] Simmel's focus on the breakdown between fact and value, between life and the meaning of life is both an effort to think through some of the same alienated dissonances that Marx explored in the relation between base and superstructure and a way of casting the tragic, which is to say essentially conflicted, nature of modern life in terms of the difference between events and the shared social representation of events.

Simmel cast this distance between life and value in starkly existential terms in his great essay on "The Metropolis and Mental Life": where an older style of communal life had allowed the human mind a "slower, more habitual, more smoothly flowing rhythm," the onset of metropolitan modernity rationalizes, routinizes, and abstracts an onrushing experience that would otherwise overwhelm the mind: "Thus the metropolitan type which naturally takes on a thousand individual modifications creates a protective organ for itself against the profound disruption with which the fluctuations and discontinuities of the external milieu threaten it. Instead of reacting emotionally, the metropolitan type reacts primarily in a rational manner, thus creating a mental predominance through the intensification of consciousness, which in turn is caused by it."[49] As society and technology advance, the individual develops a set of psychological and social techniques with which to manage the increased amount of fast-moving stimuli: on the one hand, these new attitudes and schemes – the increased and increasingly fungible logic of the money economy, the rationalization of meeting, travel, and living times, the development of an increasingly jaded and thus falsely "secure" urban character – help proactively to protect the mind from the shocks of modern life; on the other hand, while these techniques protect the mind in the short term, they also threaten to change and thus to destroy what made that mind human in the first place. In other words, as the mind attempts to come to terms with the content of modern life, values that once allowed people to recognize each other as members of the same community lose their force; summing up a position that Simmel and the young Lukács shared, György Márkus writes, "Within the bourgeois world, culture in the true sense of the world is impossible. It is objectively impossible: no general goal, no meaning can be discerned in the abstract and irrational necessity of the conditions created by the 'anarchy of production.'"[50] For Simmel and Lukács, the historically conditioned division between fact and value provides both the methodological basis for the analysis of different cultures at different times and the grounds for a diagnosis of what is specific and specifically tragic about modern life.

Max Weber, one of the most significant figures in the development of modern sociology, similarly understood culture as the ordering and aspirational imposition of values onto life: "The concept of culture is a value-concept. Empirical reality becomes 'culture' to us because and insofar as we relate it to value ideas. It includes those segments and only those segments which have become significant to us because of this relation to value."[51] In other words, the difference between society and culture is the difference between life understood as a certain quantity of unrelated or barely related facts and life understood as a qualitatively meaningful whole. Again, there is both a descriptive and a prescriptive aspect to this. On the one hand, the fact-value distinction is an essential part of Weber's method; it not only allows him to identify his ultimate object of study – culture, or the productive and lived relation between facts and values – but also provides him with the tools necessary to understand the relation between both the different parts and the parts and the whole of a culture. On the other hand, the idea that culture had somehow waned, that values had lost their ability to bring facts together into a meaningful relation, gives him a way to understand the history and the whole character of modern life, which he casts in terms of a progressive process of secular *disenchantment*; where things once appeared as if they were imbued with an essential and felt significance, a sense of the deep and seemingly ordained relation between things, modern life seemed to have been stripped of its immanent, organizing significance: "in principle, no mysterious and unpredictable forces play a role in that respect, but that, on the contrary, we can – in principle – dominate everything by means of calculation. And that, in its turn, means that the world has lost its magic. Unlike the savage, for whom those forces existed, we no longer need to resort to magical means in order to dominate or solicit the spirits. That can be done by technology and calculation."[52] Modern life appears disenchanted because a formerly reciprocal relation between facts and values has become frayed; and, with the decay of that relation, *culture* as opposed to *society* (the organic as opposed to the objectified) becomes less and less possible.

For the young Lukács, Weber's distinction between fact and value worked both to underwrite his own literary critical method, one that tacked back and forth between individual cases and large conceptual categories, and to give expression to the lived distance between art and life that Lukács took as a sign of the essentially alienated quality of modernity, the distance between what he referred to as soul and form or, later, life and form. As was the case for Simmel and Weber, "*Culture* was," as Márkus puts it, "the 'single' thought of Lukács life. Is culture possible today? To answer this question and at the same time to contribute, through his own activity, to the creation of realization of this possibility remained one of the central concerns of his life."[53] Culture was for Lukács a way to name the significance of or the possibility of significance in social life: "In an authentic culture, everything becomes symbolic."[54] This is partly why Lukács began his career thinking both about the decline of a shared and significant culture as an essentially tragic phenomenon and about tragedy as the literary form best suited to represent that culture in the midst of its decline; what's more important for us, he began at the same time to develop an account of literary form as an especially potent and, we might say, strategic value: J. M. Bernstein writes that, for Lukács, forms "order and evaluate; they are principles of intelligibility in the dual sense of the cognisable and the meaningful ... Life is ... in-formed by form."[55] What, in other words, Lukács adds to Simmel and Weber is his specific effort to understand how particular literary genres might be able to represent or to overcome the tragic condition of modern life; Lukács sees the specifically narrative genre of the novel as a way to capture the experience of being cut off from but nonetheless longing for wholeness and community and culture and of feeling the increasingly tenuous relation between fact and value, life and form, freedom and necessity.

~

To return now to Lukács's hope for the novel as a narrative response to modernity: for Lukács the impossibility of epic was the result of a cultural loss. As culture became more complicated and "problematic," literary forms became increasingly self-conscious and divided from and within themselves. In a sense, the move from antiquity to modernity is a move from a closed to an open culture and thus from closed aesthetic forms to open aesthetic forms, from a condition in which all the parts of a world made visible sense with one another as part of an organic community to a condition in which the parts no longer hung together, in which the meaning of either the part-as-part or the part-as-part-of-a-whole is no longer evident or immanent, a condition in which what sense an event or object might have is not given but needs rather to be found out or made. Crucially and insofar as he casts this shift as most visible in the move from Homeric epic to the modern novel, he understands this enormous cultural shift in terms of a fundamental difference between how we once and how we now make and understand particular narratives; this is because, alongside the different antinomies that Lukács associates with the fall from classical unity into modern dissonance – self and other, interior and exterior, soul and form – is the essential narrative difference between events themselves and the significant and ordered representation of events.

Where, in other words, the epic emerged as an organic response to the character of an essentially integrated civilization, modern individuals need instead to invent more and more narrative forms to keep up with the bewildering and innovative diversity of contents that come along with a wider more productive and more terrifying kind of life; he writes that, "Our world has become infinitely large and each of its corners is richer in gifts and dangers than the world of the Greeks, but such wealth cancels out the positive meaning—the totality—upon which their life was based."[56] As with Simmel and Marx before him, Lukács sees the modern expansion of the world and its productive forces with a mix of excitement and trepidation; Marx had imagined modern life not so much as a form of disenchantment as a kind of bad or wicked enchantment, writing that "modern bourgeois society, with its relations of production, of exchange and of property, a society that has conjured up such gigantic means of production and of exchange, is like the sorcerer who is no longer able to control the powers of the nether world whom he has called up by his spells."[57] For Lukács as well as for Marx, modern life has brought us the Faustian bargain of more and more possibility with less and less meaning or, at least, less and less meaning immediately available to us.

The narrative form of the novel is crucial here because, as a self-consciously fallen, late, or *ironic* response to the epic, the novel manages to register this experience of bewildering and exciting openness: "The epic and the novel, these two major forms of great epic literature, differ from one another not by their authors' fundamental intentions but by the given historico-philosophical realities with which the authors were confronted."[58] As opposed to the novel, some other forms that Lukács describes seek simply to reproduce the closed conditions of Greek art, to return via an act of misguided aesthetic will to an immanence of meaning that had been lost; for Lukács this is not only a mistake, a misrecognition of the essentially open nature of modern life, but also a kind of aesthetic or epistemological violence. To impose a closed form onto an open life is to mutilate that life; "Henceforth," he writes, "any resurrection of the Greek world is a more or less conscious hypostasy of aesthetics into metaphysics—a violence done to the essence of everything that lies outside the sphere of art, and a desire to destroy it; an attempt to forget that art is only one sphere among many, and that the very disintegration and inadequacy of the world is the precondition for the existence of art and its becoming conscious."[59] Genres that forcibly impose form on to life are, in this sense, not total but rather totalitarian; they anxiously choose the purity of form not only over the messiness of life but also at life's expense. What they cannot recognize, they cut out. Lukács is explicit: closed forms imposed onto life tell life how it "should be," and "the 'should be' kills life."[60]

As opposed to the false and violent purity of these other forms (Lukács focuses on what he considers the ersatz form of the "entertainment novel," a narrative form that sells itself as an authentic epic despite what he takes as the impossibility of any simple return to that genre), the novel is for Lukács an eminently and, in a sense, paradoxically open form.[61] His claim is that the novel is particularly and appropriately modern because it manages – or at least seeks to manage – both to reach towards a whole and thus epic account of a world and to bring the impossibility or limits of that reach into itself as both form and content. Failure is, in a strong sense, what the novel is all about. The novel is, in other words, a special form because it is able not only *partly* to represent its content but also to represent its own inability *fully* to represent that content; the novel is a self-consciously modern epic because it has found a way to encode life's openness and resistance to form within form itself: "The composition of the novel is the paradoxical fusion of heterogeneous and discrete components into an organic whole which is then abolished over and over again."[62] Put in other words, the novel is a special form because

it manages the paradoxical synthesis of the homogenous and the heterogeneous, the finished and the unfinished, the closed and the open; its totality is
not the simple totality of a given, integrated world but rather the *dialectical*
totality that results from bringing the representation of a world and the failure
to represent a world together into the same internally divided but nonetheless
whole form. That's easy enough to say; how, in fact, does the novel manage
both to represent the world and, at the same time, to represent its essential
inability to represent the world?

Unlike epic, which begins in the midst of great actions already underway,
the novel is an essentially *biographical* form that relies on the given but
contingent structure of a character's life for its formal management of beginning, middle, and end: "The outward form of the novel is essentially biographical. The fluctuation between a conceptual system which can never
completely capture life and a life complex which can never attain com-
pleteness...."[63] Biography is an appropriate formal model for the novel's
openness because the individual life doesn't obey the organic laws of beginnings and endings that governed Greek tragedy in Aristotle; for Lukács,
Aristotle could see plot in that way because Greek epics and Greek tragedies
simply began where they needed to begin, they answered the demands of their
content in a way that one can take as self-evident. Because there is no real
difference between one thing and another, one beginning or end is as good
and as authentic as any other. The modern content of the novel doesn't work
that way; because the particular value of one or another fact or event is no
longer self-evident, questions of where to begin, where to end, what to
accentuate, and what to leave out become almost hopelessly complicated.
Where a particular story once immediately suggested or, rather, demanded its
most appropriate form of discourse, authors now need to choose and to
impose their forms; they need to project a value on to facts that appear
essentially to resist that kind of shaping intention. So, rather than seeking to
find the *right* form for a given content, the novel borrows the form of the
individual life and applies it to the content of the world as a workable but only
partial solution to the modern divide between fact and value, story and
discourse.

Although where lives begin and end is obviously important to those who
live them, they are too personal, too contingent to invoke the shared social
and cultural significance of tragic or epic beginnings. When Homer writes,
"Sing, goddess, the anger of Peleus' son Achilles," he brings the poet, the
audience, the hero Achilles, and the gods themselves into a shared space and
invokes Achilles' rage not as a private emotional or pathological fact but
rather as a human emotion that has risen to the status of a shared and almost

natural event; like the wind or the rain, the rage of Achilles is there and equally there for anyone and everyone.[64] And when Sophocles begins *Oedipus Rex* with, "Oh my children . . . why are you here? Huddling at my altar, praying before me, your branches wound in wool. Our city reeks with the smoke of burning incense, rings with cries for the Healer and wailing for the dead?," he brings out two related and public aspects of the tragic form.[65] First, even though the play is about Oedipus, it does not begin with his story; it instead begins with the plague, with an event characterized precisely by its impersonal and indiscriminate quality: "the miseries numberless, grief on grief, no end— too much to bear, we are all dying o my people . . ."[66] Second, exactly because the plague is a shared event, it brings Oedipus into contact with the chorus, whose presence as the city's representative in Athenian tragedy speaks to the form's essential capacity or desire to bring an audience that would otherwise remain on the outside of a dramatic performance into its structure; indeed and as we saw, for Nietzsche, the contact between the hero and the chorus worked precisely to "smash" individuality, to undo what he takes as the illusion of the single, significant personality. In both cases, the beginning of narrative doesn't rely on the contingent significance of the individual life; it rather depends on the idea of a shared and self-evident hierarchy of values, on a poet's faith or, indeed, sure sense that everyone ought to know when it is proper to begin because such matters are the stuff of shared, communal knowledge.

As Lukács suggests, where to begin or to end is not obvious for the novel, which tends instead to rely on the wholly contingent and personal facts of individual birth, death, and sometimes marriage. We might think of the many novels that begin with a birth or something like it. *Robinson Crusoe* (1719): "I was born in the year 1632, in the city of York, of a good family, though not of that country, my father being a foreigner of Bremen, who settled first at Hull."[67] *Tristram Shandy*: "I wish either my father or my mother, or indeed both of them, as they were in duty both equally bound to it, had minded what they were about when they begot me."[68] *Great Expectations*: "My father's family name being Pirrip, and my Christian name Philip, my infant tongue could make of both names nothing longer or more explicit than Pip. So, I called myself Pip, and came to be called Pip."[69] *The Portrait of the Artist as a Young Man* (1916): "Once upon a time and a very good time it was there was a moocow coming down along the road and this moocow that was coming down along the road met a nicens little boy named baby tuckoo. . ."[70] Lukács' sense of the novel as relying incompletely on the contingent shape of the individual life once again recalls James's commitment to a character's single, motivating consciousness as a way to manage the selection, the arrangement, and order of the events that come together as discourse to produce a given narrative. Just as Lukács sees the biographical order of a life as giving the novel a borrowed form it couldn't otherwise have, so does James see the individual and embodied point of view as a way "to draw, by a geometry of his own, the circle" around relations that "really, universally ... stop nowhere."[71]

Even so, insofar as novels are always ultimately about *more* than a single life – they are about the experience of time and history, ethics, politics, and aesthetics, the inadequacy of language, the nature of commerce, and so on – the fact of the individual birth or death both allows a narrative to begin and also calls our attention to the inadequacy of that beginning. Because we can never really know either of them, birth and death are exactly and absolutely alien to the individual's narrative of his or her own life; they are the points at which apparently closed lives in fact bleed out into existential openness. As Walter Benjamin argues in an essay heavily influenced by Lukács, with the passage from one to another age, even death has lost its power to bring narrative to a meaningful conclusion: "The novel is significant, therefore, not because it presents someone else's fate to us, perhaps didactically, but because this stranger's fate by virtue of the flame which consumes it yields us the warmth which we never draw from our own fate. What draws the reader to the novel is the hope of warming his shivering life with a death he reads about."[72] As a result of embracing the real but contingent, the ultimately *slight* significance of the particular human life as a form of narrative or discursive architecture, the novel both lays claim to a real and shapely structure and reveals the limits of that structure when faced with the demand for an authentic totality. Because it models itself on the bewildering openness of a life that somehow misses both its own beginning and its own end, the novel is able to lay paradoxical claim to a dialectical and real – if ultimately melancholic – openness that eluded other forms.

The novel, says Lukács, also tends to represent characters and lives that exist in a problematic as opposed to integrated relation to the world. As I have said, the hero of classical epic was for Lukács always of a piece with his or her world: Achilles *belongs* to his world, his challenges, victories, enemies, disappointments, and, at last, his death are fully appropriate to him; and even the wily and ambitious Odysseus ultimately ends up *at home* with his wife, his son, and the world. As opposed to the hero of epic, the protagonist of the novel is always more or less at odds with the world: he or she is too full or too narrow for things as they are, he or she either harbors illusions that are too powerful to overcome or has seen so fully through the illusions that govern others' lives that he or she is no longer fit to live alongside them. (Lukács feeling for the centrality of illusion to modern life is another point at which we can trace the influence of Marx and Nietzsche.) For example, Cervantes' Don Quixote applies fantasies taken from books of adventure and romance to the everyday world, awkwardly imposing a set of romantic forms or values onto a prosy and everyday life; he is, as a result, treated as a danger, a menace, a madman and is at last unfit for life; his soul, to use Lukács' terms, is too big for his world. In Flaubert's *Sentimental Education* (1869), the protagonist Frederic Moreau had been so stripped of his illusions, of his sense that things could or ought to have any value at all, that he at last withdraws from life altogether; he rejects and encourages us to reject the idea that any narrative could somehow add up to a moral. As a result, his soul seems to shrivel and, in some sense, to fall between the world's cracks. In both cases, the lack of fit between a character and a world helps to reveal the nature of a split between story and discourse that appears not only as a formal precondition of the novel but also as an important part of its content. By focusing its attention on the problematic individual, the figure whose own life has failed to manage or to close off the relation between fact and value, story and discourse, the novel manages to import the openness of modern life into the otherwise closed space of a particular aesthetic form.

Finally, another way in which the novel is able to signal both its capacity and its necessary limits as a form is in its ability to incorporate other genres:

> This is the formal reason and the literary justification for the Romantics' demand that the novel, combining all genres within itself, should include pure lyric poetry and pure thought in its structure. The discrete nature of the outside world demands, for the sake of epic significance and sensuous valency, the inclusion of elements some of which are essentially alien to epic literature while others are alien to imaginative literature in general. The inclusion of these elements is not merely a question of lyrical atmosphere and intellectual significance being added to otherwise prosaic, isolated and inessential events. Only in these elements can the ultimate basis of the whole, the basis which holds the entire work together, become visible: the system of regulative ideas which constitutes the totality.[73]

In part, the novel's ability to bring together disparate materials into a provisional, dissolving unity is an effect of its special understanding of time as a unifying but brute force: "The unrestricted, uninterrupted flow of time is the unifying principle of the homogeneity that rubs the sharp edges off each heterogeneous fragment and establishes a relationship—albeit an irrational and inexpressible one—between them."[74] Because the novel takes place in an ordinary and yet inexorable time, it is able to accommodate without real resolution differences that would tear another genre apart. As opposed to the form-giving qualities of epic narrative or tragic drama, where beginning, middle, and end are charged with a strong and evocative significance, the novel relies on the almost entirely value-neutral fact of time's passage; represented time for Lukács is the form that comes as close as possible to insignificance while still serving as an ordering vessel for its content. It is almost but not quite meaningless that things happen and happen together in time, that everything that happened on July 16, 1984 in fact happened on July 16, 1984; for the novel, that almost-but-not-quite significance has to be enough. There is another, more significant and paradoxical aspect to the novel's representational management of heterogeneity. Because the modern world is itself heterogeneous, its representational form must also be heterogeneous; because, though, it is in the nature of form to give coherence to things and thus to become homogeneous, the novel must not only manage to incorporate heterogeneous materials into its form without reducing their difference but also to reflect on the rules that govern the incorporation of those heterogeneous materials. The novel thus treats the rules that govern its form into a content that can, in turn, be brought into its form: "For the creative individual's reflexion, the novelist's ethic vis-à-vis the content, is a double one. His reflexion consists of giving form to what happens to the idea in real life, of describing the actual nature of this process and of evaluating and considering its reality. This reflexion, however, in turn becomes an object for reflexion; it is itself only an ideal, only subjective and postulative; it, too, has a certain destiny in a reality which is alien to it; and this destiny, now purely reflexive and contained within the narrator himself, must also be given form."[75] This ability or need to reflect on its own conditions of existence and thus on its own limits is, for Lukács, the source of the novel's power, its irony, and its considerable melancholy: "by a strange and melancholy paradox, the moment of failure is the moment of value; the comprehending and experiencing of life's refusals is the source from which the fullness of life seems to flow."[76] The novel is thus unique among narrative genres because it is able to undo while maintaining the difference between its inside and outside, a fact that allows it really to achieve what would otherwise seem impossible or at least pardoxical: a closed form that represents without distorting the essential openness of life.

~

Years later, Lukács wrote a preface, in which he reflected on what worked and what didn't in *The Theory of the Novel*. In the intervening years, Lukács became a committed if sometimes controversial Marxist and so felt it necessary to identify what he took to be the overly idealistic elements of his book and to reject them "root and branch."[77] What's maybe most interesting about the preface is the degree to which he understands his earlier work as a response to the First World War; although *The Theory of the Novel* never mentions that or any other war, the elder Lukács nonetheless understood his book first and foremost as a comment on and reaction to the war:

> The immediate motive for writing was supplied by the outbreak of the First World War and the effect which its acclamation by the social-democratic parties had upon the European left. My own deeply personal attitude was one of vehement, global and, especially at the beginning, scarcely articulate rejection of the war and especially enthusiasm for the war. I recall a conversation with Frau Marianne Weber in the late autumn of 1914. She wanted to challenge my attitude by telling me of individual, concrete acts of heroism. My only reply was: "The better the worse!" When I tried at this time to put my emotional attitude into conscious terms, I arrived at more or less the following formulation: the Central Powers would probably defeat Russia; this might lead to the downfall of Tsarism; I had no objection to that. There was also some probability that the West would defeat Germany; if this led to the downfall of the Hohenzollerns and the Hapsburgs, I was once again in favor. But then the question arose: who was to save us from Western civilization?[78]

How should we understand *The Theory of the Novel* as a book about war? We need, I think, to see that Lukács saw the Romantic enthusiasm for the war evinced by some of his friends as an aesthetic as well as a political problem; for Simmel, Max and Marianne Weber, and many others, the urgency of war promised to bring order, significance, and value to a world that had lost its meaning. It offered them a way to re-enchant a life that had been made meaningless by the technological advances, the break-up of organic communities in the face of urbanization, and, above all, the rationalizing logic of capitalism. War was to close off and give form to a society that had been robbed of its immanent significance. For Lukács, this was not only war-mongering; it was also an aesthetic error, a belief that one could simply impose the military enthusiasms of Achilles and the *Iliad* onto the twentieth-century in order to make life epic once again. This was, for Lukács, the logic of neither the authentic epic nor the genuinely ironic novel; rather, the war understood in these terms followed a large-scale logic of what he had called "the entertainment novel," the genuine novel's "caricatural twin."[79] The entertainment novel is what happens when the genuine novel loses its capacity for self-reflection and irony, when it closes off and contains life, when it excuses things as they are as opposed to opening them critically up so as to imagine what they might be. In other words, insofar as Simmel and the Webers believed that the war was going to make the world epic once again, they were, in Lukács' estimation, misled by a wrongheaded understanding of the probable practical consequences of the war and of the crucially, essentially critical nature of the novel form.

As a narrative genre and as a kind of narrative theory, Lukács' version of the novel stands as a form that can both give form to experience, that can represent that experience in the ordered and significant form of a contingent but nonetheless suggestive structure. He looks to the novel as a self-reflexive and ironic epic in order to imagine the possibility of a resolution between terms that had previously seemed hopelessly opposed. As he acknowledges in his preface, this effort at imagining the novel as one important and maybe penultimate stage in a longer dialectical process, a longer effort to imagine the different parts of history and life as somehow adding up to something meaningful, represented his effort to develop an authentically Hegelian aesthetics, a way of thinking about aesthetic form and the history of aesthetic forms as part of another, ultimately significant masterplot, one that might make sense not only of the different forms taken by narrative over time but also of events as brutal and stupid as the First World War. It was also a way to see in the novel as an especially critical form of narrative not only the means necessary to understand and to reject the bad logic of the entertainment novel but also a source of significance and hope that had eluded him in his earlier works.

~

Lukács' subsequent work in both politics and aesthetics can be seen as developing and often grueling series of attempts to make good on narrative's promise. He ends *The Theory of the Novel* looking to Dostoevsky as one possible future for narrative and for humankind: "It is in the words of Dostoevsky that this new world, remote from any struggle against what actually exists, is drawn for the first time simply as a seen reality. That is why he, and the form he created, lie outside the scope of this book. Dostoevsky did not write novels, and the creative vision revealed in his works has nothing to do, either as affirmation or as rejection, with European nineteenth-century Romanticism or with the many, likewise Romantic, reactions against it. He belongs to the new world."[80] For Lukács, Dostoevsky's aesthetic achievement, his apparent solution to the problems of life and form represented a kind of ethical leap, the possibility of a sudden or intuitive or irrational or, indeed, saintly fall out of sin and into meaning. Indeed, his admiration for the great Russian writer seemed to combine an appreciation of an essential and apparently unmotivated goodness with a longing for the sudden and transformative violence of an ethical apocalypse. Indeed, the ethical pressure of this turn to Dostoevsky is in part what led to Lukács' sudden and, to his family and friends, inexplicable turn to Marxism and, more particularly, to a Bolshevist faith in the power and, indeed, the responsibility of party leaders and intellectuals to bring about proletarian class consciousness and then revolution.

In his late preface, Lukács said that *The Theory of the Novel* was characterized by its mix of "'left' ethics and 'right' epistemology." What he meant was that, while he took his sense of history's development, of the move from one form to another from Hegel and his dialectic, he maintained, in a way that was to prove incompatible, a Kantian or neo-Kantian sense of the hard divide between fact and value, experience and ideas, story and discourse. Put in different terms, the mix of left ethics and right epistemology is like the mix of the tragic and the comic that motivated both Hegel's and Marx's narratives of history. The question was still how to provide a way to imagine the comic overcoming or resolution of the tragic antinomies that still clung to the early Lukács' thinking. Indeed, his speculative turn to Dostoevsky and his real turn to Marxism were both efforts to get past was proved to be partial about this methodological mix of left and right ideas. This is why he dedicates a long section of the greatest work of his Marxist period to "the antinomies of bourgeois thought," antinomies that in later works – *History and Class Consciousness*, *The Historical Novel*, etc. – he sought, albeit in different terms, still to overcome.

4.3 To Kill Does Not Mean to Refute: Bakhtin's Narrative Theory

Like Lukács, Mikhail Bakhtin is often thought of as a theorist more of the novel than of narrative in general. Much of this has to do with the influence of *The Dialogic Imagination*, a collection of four essays on the novel that he wrote in the 1930s and 40s that did much to secure Bakhtin's reputation among English-speaking audiences. Although other of his works – *Toward a Philosophy of the Act*, *Problems of Dostoevsky's Poetics*, *Rabelais and His World*, and so on – have since appeared in translation, he is still best known for his rightly celebrated account of the novel as a genre with a unique and crucial relation to literary history, to the literary presentation of speech, and to the modern development of attitudes towards space and time, as well as for a few powerfully idiosyncratic concepts: "dialogism," "heteroglossia," "the chronotope," etc. The focus on Bakhtin's writings on the novel has however tended to obscure the wider scope of his thinking as it applies not only to philosophy and linguistics but also to narrative as well as novel theory and, even more, to what I have been calling *the comparative analysis of narrative forms*. That is not to say that we should demote the essays in *The Dialogic Imagination*; it is rather to recognize that the mix of ideas that he addresses there should be seen as part of a larger project that focuses, as I will argue, centrally on the nature of narrative and its relation to history. This project, while broadly significant, was also remarkably consistent across the several decades of Bakhtin's thinking; Tzvetan Todorov writes that, "Properly speaking, there is no development in Bakhtin's work. Bakhtin does change his focus; sometimes he alters his formulation, but, from his first to his last text, from 1922 to 1974, his thinking remains fundamentally the same."[81] (Importantly and as we will see in Section 6.1, Todorov, who coined the term "narratology," was instrumental in bringing Bakhtin into the mix of narrative theory in and around the 1960s structuralist turn in France.) Although that might be too strong a way to put it, it is nonetheless true that the novel is more a means than an end for Bakhtin, more an exemplary narrative tool with which to understand how history, form, and consciousness come together in general than an object to consider entirely and only for its own sake. As a result, we can look at Bakhtin's writings on the novel in relation to his ideas about ethics, action, and phenomenology, a fact that once again encourages us to understand narrative theory not only as a field important in its own right but also as an intellectual project that links together some of the key intellectual movements of the twentieth century. Along with Lukács, Bakhtin serves as an important hinge between emerging theories of narrative and the currents of a wider intellectual history.

Like Lukács, Bakhtin was born in and lived through turbulent times. He grew up on the cosmopolitan edge of Russia, the son (again like Lukács) of a banker. He had a classical education and was, from the first, terrifically prolific. That said, the political and logistical circumstances of the Revolution of 1917 and what followed prevented him from publishing many of his works, which were often lost or cut short or suppressed. His first major work, *Problems in Dostoevsky's Poetics*, appeared in 1929, shortly before he was accused of associating with underground Russian Orthodox religious groups. After narrowly avoiding exile and almost certain death in Siberia, Bakhtin spent six years in exile in Kazakhstan, where he taught and continued to write. The next years were spent living in a minor way in minor places to avoid periodic and terrifying Stalinist purges; his right leg was amputated in 1938. After World War Two, he came to Moscow where he presented and defended a heterodox doctoral dissertation, which later became *Rabelais and His World*. The book, while brilliant, didn't do him any favors with official culture – indeed, the book wasn't coy about its admiration for Rabelais' ability to undermine his own official culture – and he continued to work in obscurity until, as a result of Russian graduate students discovering both his Dostoevsky book and the surprising fact that he was somehow still alive, he found a late popularity, which brought him back to Moscow, where he worked to reassemble and publish lost or unfinished works until he died in 1975.

It has often been pointed out that Bakhtin's terms and methods demand direct comparison with Lukács and, in particular, with *The Theory of the Novel*. Indeed, Bakhtin came into contact with Lukács and his work on more than one occasion. In the 1920s, Bakhtin "began translating Lukács' *Theory of the Novel*, but he gave up the project upon learning though a Hungarian acquaintance that Lukács no longer liked the book."[82] The continued influence of *The Theory of the Novel* is, however, clear in the case of essays from the 1930s and 1940s like "Epic and Novel" and "From the Prehistory of Novelistic Discourse," where, as we will see, Bakhtin relies on a repurposed Lukácsian opposition between epic and novel. Later, his full turn to the novel as an object of study coincided with Lukács' own arrival in the USSR in 1929, when he began both publicly to renounce his early work on the novel and "history and class consciousness" and to deliver talks on his new and more or less orthodox theories of narrative realism; as Clark and Holquist put it, Bakhtin's work on the novel can be read as taking implicit issue "with the main points made by Lukács at a conference on the theory of the novel held at the Communist Academy in 1934–1935."[83] Although Bakhtin's ideas took a very different turn, we need nonetheless to see them in relation to Lukács' development and, most importantly, his own comparative method.

What Bakhtin most importantly shares with the early Lukács is a commitment to genre as a tool of historical analysis. As I've already said, for the early Lukács, the history of narrative forms from the epic to the novel can be understood as a coherent, progressive, and dialectical movement, as the development of narrative forms from the closed and homogenous form of the epic to the open and ironic form of the novel. *The Theory of the Novel* is thus often characterized as a Hegelian project, which is to say that Lukács sees the great narrative forms as part of a larger, progressive sequence, a process of development that can be more or less mapped on to Hegel's account of the spirit's passage from naiveté, through self-consciousness, to knowledge; for Lukács, the history of narrative genres is a passage from the happy simplicity of epic ("Happy are those ages. . ."), through the ironic and unhappy self-consciousness of the novel, to *something else*, maybe to Dostoevsky, maybe to catastrophe, maybe to revolution. The point, however, is that Lukács could see the whole history of culture in a progressive series of representative narrative genres. For the early Lukács, the history of narrative genre was thus a rich *expression* of the logics and beliefs that governed different moments in time; art and, more particularly, narrative art *represented* history as it happened. Once again, what makes this mode of analysis possible for Lukács is that he sees these different but related narrative genres as sharing a crucial and nearly universal common denominator, their status, in other words, as narratives, which is to say as representational systems built on the relation between events and the representation of events, between story and discourse; the different ways in which different moments in time understand and use that common denominator is what allows Lukács to see them as historically and culturally significant. The epic arrangement of story and discourse tells us something about the culture of ancient Greece in the same way that the novelistic arrangement of story and discourse tells us something about modernity. This is why his theory of generic history needs also to be a strong theory of narrative; for him, narrative and genre are in fact two aspects of one methodology.

Bakhtin is similarly committed to genre and, in particular, the generic management of narrative as tool of historical and cultural analysis. In other words, like Lukács, Bakhtin sees a given culture's representative genres as concentrated expressions of how a culture thinks, of what it believes, and of how it structured its relations between individuals, between social classes, and over the course of time; Gary Saul Morson and Caryl Emerson write that, "According to Bakhtin, intellectual historians often overlook the greatest discovery in the history of thought because they do not recognize genres and artistic forms *as* forms of thought."[84] And Katerina Clark and Michael Holquist write that, "He looks at genres not just in their narrow literary context but as icons that fix the world view of the ages form which they spring. Genre is to him an x-ray of a specific world view, a crystallization of the concepts particular to a given time and to a given social stratum in a specific society. A genre, therefore, embodies a historically specific idea of what it means to be human."[85] Insofar as he sees genre as an expression of a culture's way of thinking at a moment in time, Bakhtin does indeed follow Lukács. In both cases, looking at the historically specific ways in which genre encodes, shapes, and motivates the practically universal experience of narrative gives one a powerful set of diagnostic tools; understanding narrative genres is thus a powerful way of understanding the world.

That said, Bakhtin goes beyond Lukács' theory in a couple of important ways. First, Bakhtin understands different genres as not only reflecting but also playing a crucial formative role in the shaping of thought and, indeed, what it is even possible to think. Crucial to this expanded sense of genre's capacity to shape thought is Bakhtin's account of "the chronotope." For Bakhtin the term "chronotope" names – albeit vaguely – how a particular text or kind of text establishes a reader's rules and expectations about space and time as a background against which narratives can occur. The chronotope of *the gothic castle*, with its murkiness, its hidden passages, its tendency to put the past – in the form of old portraits, antiquated objects, or restless ghosts – into overlapping contact with the present, is fundamentally different from the chronotope of *the road*, which is often light and open, allowing for chance encounters in a pure and linear present as opposed to the gothic's involuted conflicts with a repressed and impacted past. In other words, when a narrative accepts the structuring spatiotemporal terms of either the gothic castle or the open road, it also accepts a whole set of rules and expectations about what life is and how it works, rules and expectations that Bakhtin takes as more generally representative of how different people think at a given moment in time. Because the chronotope thus characterizes the expectations and assumptions that underwrite a narrative work, which is to say that narrative's possible relations with other similar or dissimilar works, it is essentially generic: "The chronotope in literature," says Bakhtin, "has an intrinsic generic significance. It can even be said that it is precisely the chronotope that defines genre and generic distinctions, for in literature the primary category in the chronotope is time. The chronotope as a formally constitutive category determines to a significant degree the image of man in literature as well. The image of man is always intrinsically chronotopic."[86] Bakhtin is making what we might see as a phenomenological point here; to be human is to understand or to perceive oneself as living in time and space in a particular way.

Literature thus both reflects and shapes a period's idea of what it means to be human; and, because being human means being in time, the chronotope and thus the literature that chronotopes govern will always be fundamentally narrative: "What is the significant of all these chronotopes? What is most obvious is their meaning for narrative. They are the organizing centers for the fundamental narrative events of the novel. The chronotope is the place where the knots of narrative are tied and untied. It can be said without qualification that to them belongs the meaning that shapes narrative."[87] Chronotopes dictate the rules according to which narratives come together or fall apart, and because narratives give meaning to story by rendering it in the form of discourse, they give life what actual and potential meanings it has or can have for a particular culture: "Chronotopes are not so much visibly present in activity as they are the ground for activity. To use one of Bakhtin's favorite distinctions, they are not represented in the world, they are 'the ground essential for the ... representability of events.' They are not contained in plots, but they make typical plots possible."[88] Because, in other words, a chronotope governs the selection, the organization, and the management of events as they are turned into a meaningful repression of events, it is also a way of theorizing the relation between story and discourse.

The considerable power that Bakhtin gives over to the chronotope, genre, and narrative is partly the result of his own intellectual development. Bakhtin was heavily influenced by a strain of thinking associated with Herman Cohen and the so-called Marburg School of Neo-Kantianism; Holquist and Vadim Liapunov write that, "Bakhtin's connection with the Marburg School was relatively direct, in that his closest friend [at the time] was Matvei Isayevich Kagan," who had "taken up the study of philosophy with Cohen in Marburg."[89] Cohen, who worked and wrote at the university of Marburg at the end of the nineteenth century, was committed to understanding and advancing Kant's notion of transcendental categories of understanding, that is the organizational apparatuses that he took as innate to human consciousness and necessary to the conversion of raw, unprocessed reality into workable forms of perception. Two of Kant's most important categories were, of course, time and space, which Bakhtin saw literature as codifying in the form of the chronotope: a generically specific scheme for managing the conversion of events into a meaningful discursive form. What made Cohen's interpretation of Kant different was precisely the degree of authority that he gave to the categories; as opposed to seeing them as facilitating the organization and perception of the real world, he took it that the categories *made* the world: "Thinking itself," wrote Cohen, "produces that which is held to be."[90] What's more, Cohen sought to ground his more robust sense of the categories in terms of mathematics and logic, treating time and space not as "faculties" of a unified self, but rather as "rules," "methods," or "procedures" that, like mathematics, existed independently of the mind and made all thinking and being possible.

We can see the influence of Cohen and Cohen's most famous student, Ernst Cassirer, on Bakhtin in a couple of ways. On the one hand, it helps to account for Bakhtin's lifelong interest in models taken from math and physics and, in particular, from Einstein, on whom he draws in creative ways in the essay on the chronotope. More importantly, Bakhtin's sense of the more than merely reflective power of the chronotope and thus of narrative has its beginning in this strong account of the forming power of the categories – the rules – of space and time. After all, insofar as the chronotope is exactly a historically specific but nonetheless powerful system of rules, of methods, of procedures for making the world, it emerges after Kant, Cohen, and Cassirer as a powerful ideological and philosophical tool. Put in different terms, while many of the systems that we have considered to this point (with the exception, perhaps of Nietzsche) both treat discourse as a more or less parasitical representation of an already extant story and treat narrative in general as a way to deal with and to understand an already present if woefully complex world, Bakhtin's embrace of Cohen's strong form of Neo-Kantianism allows him to approach and to ground the more difficult notion that discourse in fact *makes* story, that our representations – or rather our instantiations of chronotopic rules that govern and limit the ability to make representations – in fact make the world; form doesn't represent or manage but rather produces the world; or to paraphrase Cohen, narrative "produces that which is held to be." (This returns us once again to the paradox of priority that I laid out in the introduction, the question of which comes first, story or discourse?)

This by itself constitutes an important break from Lukács' theory of the novel, from his account of narrative genre as an *expression* or *reflection* of things as they are in ancient Greece or the modern world or any time at all. What's even more striking about Bakhtin's idea and, indeed, what ultimately distanced him from Cohen, too, is the degree of autonomy that he gives to the historical agent over these rules; for Bakhtin, "the individual subject is conceived as similar to the artist who seeks to render brute matter, a thing that is *not* an artwork in itself (independent of the artist's activity), into commuting that is the kind of conceptual whole we can recognize as a painting or a text."[91] That is, although we are as historical beings limited by what chronotopes are available to us at a given time (the Greeks had theirs, we have ours), Bakhtin imagines that, in some cases, cases that he thinks of in terms of what's potentially great about the novel as a form and what's remarkable about certain writers (Rabelais, Goethe, Dostoevsky, etc.), some strong individuals not only can see the fact that their thinking is governed by these systems and see the degree to which the world is conditioned by historically specific configurations of time and space but also can somehow *rewrite* those rules, can intervene in the conceptual and ideological structure of the historical world at a given moment, and can, via literary form, remake the very potential of human life and human history: the significance of "this kind of artistic thinking," he writes, "extends far beyond the limits of the novel alone."[92] Dorothy Hale writes that the "imaginative engagement [of] the Bakhtinian novelist [makes him] an agent as well as a recognizer of alterity:

his participation in the juxtaposition, supplementation, contradiction, and dialogical interrelation among points of view creates, as it were, *more* alterity by establishing new ways for points of view to interrelate."[93] Because thinking makes the world and art changes (or at least *can* change) the way we think, literature and those who make it – like Dostoevsky – can *remake* the world; Hale writes that, "It could even be said that Dostoevsky created something like a new artistic model of the world, one in which many basic aspects of old artistic form were subjected to a radical restructuring."[94]

In a broad sense, Bakhtin associates this capacity to produce entirely new genres or to intervene in and, in a sense, "hack" the genres we already know with the essentially mixed form of novel as such. Rather than imagining the novel as a fixed or consistently chronotopic form, he instead treats it as essentially critical, as a *dialogic* and *heteroglossic* form that works precisely to unsettle other narrative genres once they have become calcified and begun to work in the service of official culture, which is to say in the service of those who already have power and want to keep it. He describes this quality of the novel (what he refers to as "novelness") in his 1941 essay, "Epic and Novel": "The novel comes into contact with the spontaneity of the inconclusive present; this is what keeps the genre from congealing. The novelist is drawn toward everything that is not yet completed."[95] Again, like Lukács with the authentic as opposed to the "entertainment" novel and like Nietzsche with his distinction between monumental and critical histories, Bakhtin opposes this sense of the novel as an open, incomplete form to the closed form of the epic; as opposed to opening the present up, the epic subordinates the present to the closed authority of an official past: "the epic past is absolute and complete. It is as closed as a circle; inside it everything is finished, already over. There is no place in the epic world for any openendedness, indecision, indeterminacy. There are no loopholes in it through which we glimpse the future."[96] And, just as Lukács' sense of the closed nature of the epic needs to be seen in relation to his sense of the novel's critical potential in relation to the onset of the First World War, so does Bakhtin's stark sense of the difference between the official culture of the epic and the unofficial, critical character of the novel need to be seen against the backdrop of the Stalinization of both the novel and the Russian cultural past. In the first case, Bakhtin's turn to the novel as an object of study coincided with the genre's emergence in the Soviet Union as, as Holquist puts it, "the primary focus of the government's efforts to bring Soviet intellectual institutions into line. In 1932 all authors, no matter what their style or politics, were forced to join the new union of Writers. Two years later there was a concerted effort to cap this institutional unity with a stylistic unity base on the Socialist Realist novel: one leader, one party, one aesthetic."[97] And in the second, in the interest of bringing the Russian past into line with the Soviet present, folk culture, which Bakhtin understood as essentially unofficial, ribald, and open, was retroactively streamlined to fit in with the epic logic of official Soviet culture, resulting in "a rapid Stalinization of Russian folklore: the folk artists of Palekh were commissioned to paint new enamels in their traditional style, with Lenin and Stalin appearing on the firebirds and flying steeds that had previously carried the begetters of the Russian epic."[98] For Bakhtin, in that case, the novel represented something more than a criticism of official thinking; as Jean-Michel Rabaté puts it, his "powerful and empowering insight [is] that each text is made up of conflicting voices, often opposing an 'authoritative discourse' (the discourse of official ideology which cannot stand any dissenting opinion) and an 'internally persuasive discourse' through which new evaluations can emerge until alterity be recognized as such."[99] For Bakhtin, the novel is thus a way to try actively to use genre to counter the official, ideological, state rules that governed that thinking at the level of the chronotope, which is to say that the level of the categories that made thinking possible in there first place.

Instead of seeing either the epic or the novel as stable expressions of a given culture and given time, Bakhtin in that case sees them as constitutive worldviews that he associates with the difference between having and not having power, the difference between being of the official or the unofficial parts of a society. Again, the question of genre here is fundamentally narrative; how do different classes or groups manipulate or manage the narratives that organize facts into values that work for or against the official status quo? For obvious reasons, Bakhtin is less interested in the generic stability of official narratives than he is in those narratives or anti-narratives that have the capacity to call critical attention to or in fact to disrupt official culture. On the one hand, this notion of competing narratives connects Bakhtin with contemporary and later critics of ideology like Antonio Gramsci and Ernesto Laclau; Gramsci in particular offered an account of culture built on the idea of a structuring contest or conflict between a range of ideological positions, positions that he in turn associated with the different intellectuals who would work for, with or against a given political position: "Every social group, coming into existence on the original terrain of an essential function in the world of economic production, creates together with itself, organically, one or more strata of intellectuals which give it homogeneity and an awareness of its own function not only in the economic but also in the social and political spheres."[100] Gramsci's distinction, in other words, between "organic," "hegemonic," "traditional," and "counter-hegemonic" intellectuals stands as a suggestive complement to Bakhtin's sense of a culture as a contest of narrative positions represented by different strategic approaches towards the idea and experience of the chronotope.[101]

On the other hand, Bakhtin also paves the way for later narrative theorists interested in putting pressure on the idea of narrative *as a social norm*; in other words, once narrative genres are understood as working necessarily for or against an official culture, they become available to different forms of mobilization and critique, a fact taken up by feminist, postcolonial, queer, and other theorists of the novel. In *Fictions of Authority: Women Writers and Narrative Voice*, Susan Lanser writes that, because his work helps to reveal a relation between narrative as technique and narrative as the expression of social norms, Bakhtin gives feminist critics a powerful set of tools with which to real relations between literature and power: "When these two approaches to 'voice' converge in what Mikhail Bakhtin has called a 'sociological poetics,' it becomes possible to see narrative technique not simply as a product of ideology but as ideology itself: narrative voice, situated at the juncture of 'social position and literary practice,' embodies the social, economic, and literary conditions under which it has been produced."[102] In other words, Bakhtin's sense of the profound ideological power of the chronotope allowed him to see the novel's unique capacity to intervene in our ideas of how things are and how they should or could be.

Take also for example Henry Louis Gates' influential account of "Signifyin(g)" in *The Signifying Monkey: A Theory of African American Literary Criticism*, a book that begins with epigraphs taken from both Frederick Douglas and Bakhtin. Gates draws on Bakhtin's account of parody as an especially dialogic form in order to account for the essential double-voicedness of some African American works: "Two of Bakhtin's subdivisions of [double-voiced discourse] seem appropriate categories through which to elaborate upon the theory of Signifyin(g) as a metaphor for literary history: parodic narration and the hidden, or internal, polemic. As we shall see, and as Bakhtin suggests, these two types of discourse can merge, as they do in several of our tradition's canonical texts."[103] Gates goes on to read texts by Richard Wright, Ralph Ellison, and Ishmael Reed in order to lay out patterns of repetition, reversal, and critique that govern relations among these texts, the African American tradition, and literary history more generally. More to the point, Gates develops Bakhtin's account in order to show how Reed, for instance, uses parody and hidden polemic to re-motivate conventional genres in the service of a new Signifyin(g) narrative function: "Reed employs these two voices in the manner of, and renders them through, foregrounding, to parody the two simultaneous stories of detective narration (that of the present and that of the past) in a narrative flow that moves hurriedly from cause to effect. In *Mumbo*

Jumbo, however, the narrative of the past bears an ironic relation to the narrative of the present, because it comments not only on the other narrative but on the nature of this writing itself."[104] Gates shows, in other words, how the Bakhtinian possibility of using parody, as it were, to *hack* and thus to reanimate the traditional genres of the novel has at least the potential to reveal how powerful but nonetheless constructed social categories like race can be revealed and perhaps even rewritten; because literary genres are also social forms, reworking the one has at least the potential to rework the other.[105]

Bakhtin's own main example of a writer who was able to adapt genre in such a way as to create new chronotopes and thus new possibilities both for the relation between story and discourse and thus for life itself was Dostoevsky. Bakhtin's almost immoderate hopes for Dostoevsky are, once again, something that he shares with Lukács, who ended *The Theory of the Novel* gesturing towards the great Russian writer's works as a kind of genre that might transcend the conditions of both the novel and the epic. Lukács hoped that Dostoevsky could bring together the coherence and clarity of the epic while keeping his forms open enough to accommodate not just one but all kinds of life. Similarly, Bakhtin makes large aesthetic and historical claims for Dostoevsky, seeing him as not only as a great writer but also as a sort of world-historical figure. For Bakhtin, and again this is something that the young Lukács would have appreciated, Dostoevsky's novels are *polyphonic*, which is to say they are able to admit and to represent a plurality of voices: "*A plurality of independent and unmarked voices and consciousnesses, a genuine polyphony of fully valid voices is in fact the chief characteristic of Dostoevsky's novels*. What unfolds in his works is not a multitude of characters and fates in a single objective world, illuminated by a single authorial consciousness; rather *a plurality if consciousnesses, with equal rights and each with its own world*, combine but are not merged in the unity of the event."[106] One needs to think of this claim against Bakhtin's sense of the epic and of other official genres as *monologic*; as many voices or as many views as those texts seem to represent, they are in fact governed by a single set of rules and expectations that give them their semantic and ideological center. Because they are monologic and speak with the singular voice of power, they are able to help reproduce things as they are; what the open, polyphonic work brings is not simply an ability to show and thus to reproduce things as they already are but rather an ability to capture the world's latent potential for difference and change: "In a universe of uncertainties, capacity to perform a present, specific function is not the sole value; no less important is the flexibility to adapt to the unexpected. Major genres contain that kind of flexibility, and major works exploit it."[107] For Bakhtin, Dostoevsky and writers like him have the capacity to open thinking up and to put a reader and, in fact, a whole culture in some kind of touch with the idea that things don't need to be as they are. To put this more clearly in terms of genre and narrative: Bakhtin suggests that Dostoevsky uses a particular technique (polyphony) in order to create a distinct genre (the Dostoevskian novel) that uses narrative form (the relation between discourse to story) not to limit experience, not to impose official, monologic values onto life, but instead to reveal the potential inherent to life at the level of discourse. In the hands of a Dostoevsky, discourse not only reflects but also makes or in fact alters an existing story. In other words, where some narrative genres can, as Lukács saw, limit experience, Bakhtin looks to Dostoevsky to imagine a case where discourse really could be capacious and open enough to respect the energy and heterogeneous variety of life. He calls this particular generic arrangement of story and discourse the novel.

In a set of late notes for revision of the Dostoevsky book that he prepared in 1961, Bakhtin wrote, "A completely new structure for the image of a human being—a full-blooded and fully signifying other consciousness which is not inserted into the finalizing frame of reality, which is not finalized by anything (not even death), for its meaning cannot be resolved or abolished in reality (to kill does not mean to refute)."[108] We can see that, despite exile, illness, censure, and almost absolute precarity, Bakhtin maintained a powerful if cryptic sense of both Dostoevsky's and the novel's potential. What his novels offer is not a new kind of human but rather a new structure of action and belief for humanity, a structure we should understand as a specifically narrative structure. If the human is life, fact, story, what Dostoevsky offers are forms, values, and discourses that somehow manage to give things meaning, significance, and interest while not limiting them to one or another frame; this is yet another version of the philosophical problem that Bakhtin considered throughout his life: is it possible to establish concepts that can give meaning to life without limiting life's potential? Can one maintain the creative power of the Kantian account of transcendental categories while also attending to the character of history as well as to human possibility? The stakes of Bakhtin's project are made clear in his claim that the right kind of narrative structure, the relation between story and discourse that would respect both meaning and potential could even transcend death; the human, as imagined by Dostoevsky's version of narrative (his genre), is not "finalized" by death. On the one hand, we can take this as another moment of engagement with Lukács, who saw death as having a necessary but vexed relation to the novel: in the absence of other, more organic genres, the novel relies on the biographical facts of birth and death for its form; without another, culturally shared sense of an ending, the novel has to make use of the individual death in order to bring its plots to however artificial a conclusion. The novel thus both underestimates and relies on death. Bakhtin's sense of Dostoevsky's genre as one that can see past the finality of death is thus an effort to imagine a form of the novel that could somehow return to natural and communal modes of closure. As a result, this other kind of novel might both end in a more authentic way and, insofar as it would avoid reducing death to a narrative function, could return to the individual death some kind of narrative or more than narrative dignity. On the other hand, read in the context of Bakhtin's own time, when political limits on thinking and acting, the forms that Stalinization had imposed onto life, were directly and disastrously associated with the threat and the reality of death, Bakhtin's idea of a narrative genre that could allow its characters to live lives that could be both meaningful and free, that could retain the sense-making force of the relation between story and discourse without lapsing into the totalitarian, represents a moment where an explicitly narrative theory was also an act of intellectual and literal survival.

4.4 Story's Scar: Erich Auerbach and the History of Narrative Thinking

Like Bakhtin and Lukács, Erich Auerbach was committed to the comparative analysis of narrative forms. This is true of all his work but sits at the very heart of his most famous and intimidating book, *Mimesis: The Representation of Reality in Western Literature* (1946). As its title suggests, Auerbach's book is a massive thing that, from chapter to chapter, takes on dozens of major and minor works from nearly the whole of Western literature. He tends to follow a similar method in each of the book's twenty chapters: he begins with a lengthy passage from Chrétien de Troyes, Montaigne, Rabelais, Goethe or Virginia Woolf before moving on to a close and careful reading of the passage's style – its pacing, its tone, its syntax, its use of rhetorical technique, etc. In each case, Auerbach reads these passages not only to understand them or the works from which they come but also to identify in them a representational logic or worldview that he takes as characteristic of a whole culture. For Auerbach, mimetic styles are concentrated expressions or distillations of how particular cultures imagined themselves and the world; his book is, in that case, a bravura work of literary analysis, a powerful theory of literary representation, and, maybe most ambitiously, a history of how in different places and at different times people think.

Auerbach famously wrote his book during the Second World War while living in Istanbul, where he had sought refuge from the Nazis. As the story goes, Auerbach lacked access to a full research library and so had to write his book without secondary and some primary sources, a fact that he later took as paradoxically necessary to the book's character and, in some less prominent way, to the arguments it ultimately makes: "it is quite possible that the book owes its existence to just this lack of a rich and specialized library. If it had been possible for me to acquaint myself with all the work that has been done on so many subjects, I might never have reached the point of writing."[109] Auerbach's sense of being exiled from his home in the midst of a war contributes both to the style and shape of his book – its almost causal mastery of whole literatures, its conspicuous lack of footnotes – and to its pathos; for Edward Said, one of his most sensitive readers, Auerbach "was a Jewish refugee from Nazi Europe, and he was also a European scholar in the old tradition of German Romance scholarship. Yet now in Istanbul he was hopelessly out of touch with the literary, cultural, and political bases of that formidable tradition. In writing *Mimesis*, he implies to us in a later work, he was not merely practicing his profession despite adversity: he was performing an act of cultural, even civilizational, survival of the highest importance."[110] Like almost all of the works I've looked at so far, *Mimesis* needs thus to be looked at with a kind of double vision; it needs to be seen both for what it is obviously and ambitiously about – the history of the literary representation of reality in the West – and for what it must also be obscurely but truly about: the experience of social and political trauma that came along with personal and academic exile amidst the personal, physical, and cultural devastation of the Second World War.

Auerbach's first chapter, "Odysseus' Scar," can stand as the book's statement of methodological purpose, his effort to make clear what is at stake with his approach and to articulate some of the arguments that structure the whole of his project. He begins with a scene from Homer in which Odysseus returns home after his own years of exile; although he is in disguise, his old housekeeper, Euryclea, recognizes him as a result of seeing a familiar scar on his thigh. What most interests Auerbach about the scene is its clarity of presentation at almost every level, the fact that everything relevant to the scene and to the whole of the *Odyssey* seems to be present there "on the surface": "Clearly outlined, brightly and uniformly illuminated, men and things stand out in a realm where everything is visible; and not less clear— wholly expressed, orderly even in the ardor—are the feelings and thoughts of the persons involved."[111] Auerbach then goes on to compare this scene in Homer with "an equally ancient and equally epic style from a different world of forms," the account in the Book of Genesis of Abraham's near sacrifice of his son Isaac. As opposed to the clarity and light of Odysseus' scar, the story of Abraham and Isaac is murky, confusing, and mysterious: the scene allows us to see "only so much of the phenomena as is necessary for the purpose of the narrative, all else is left in obscurity; the decisive points of the narrative alone are emphasized, what lies between is nonexistent; time and place are undefined and call for interpretation; thoughts and feelings remain unexpressed, are only suggested by the silence and the fragmentary speeches; the whole, permeated with the most unrelieved suspense and directed toward a single goal (and to that extent far more of a unity), remains mysterious and 'fraught with background.'"[112] Both examples are narratives in the technical sense that I've been working with throughout this book; although they manage the relation very differently and with different effects, they are nonetheless both representations of an event or a sequence of events.

Looking at these two scenes, Auerbach manages to lay out a broad opposition between "two kinds of style" "in order to reach a starting point for an investigation into the literary representation of reality in European culture."[113] By "style" he means not only the specific character of a passage's language but also and more crucially the particular way in which a work represents links story to discourse. Homer or the Bible's "style" is in this sense the particular way in which it understands the essential nature of events as well as the particular way in which it goes about representing those events as discourse; and because the cultures that produce these texts are entirely different, their styles will be entirely different as well:

> the two styles, in their opposition, represent basic types: on the one hand, the fully externalized description, universal illumination, uninterrupted connection, free expression, all events in the foreground, displaying unmistakable meanings, few elements of historical development and of psychological perspective; on the other hand, certain parts brought into high relief, others left obscure, abruptness, suggestive influence of the unexpressed, 'background' quality, multiplicity of meanings and the need for interpretation, universal-historical claims, development of the concept of the historically becoming, and preoccupation with the problematic.[114]

There's far too much to say about this, about the metaphors of light and dark, foreground and background applied to text, about the forms of historical consciousness contained in each style, about the suggested resonance between literature, "free expression," and "the problematic." What I want to focus on for the moment is a basic assumption of Auerbach's method, the assumption that, while these texts are in fact almost entirely opposed in style, they share an essential and possibly universal quality: they are both narratives, they can have different, historically specific styles precisely because they rely on but differently motivate the same structural relation between events and the representation of events. "Style" for Auerbach thus refers to the particular ways in which particular texts activate a more or less universal narrative relation in historically specific terms. This methodological sense of narrative as a practically universal common denominator and style as historical and thus measurable variant is part of what connects Auerbach's method to both Lukács and Bakhtin; they are all interested in what style and genre can tell us about the nature of historical particularity when that particularity is seen against the formal regularity of narrative as such.

Auerbach's analysis of narrative *suspense* in Homer and the story of Abraham's sacrifice is a case in point. Suspense, the feeling of anxious expectation about a possible future, appears in narrative partly as the effect of managed relations between events and the representation of events; how and at what pace and with what frequency events are represented or revealed are essential to the production of narrative suspense. We might think here of Alfred Hitchcock's classic account of the difference between surprise and suspense:

> There is a distinct difference between "suspense" and "surprise," and yet many pictures continually confuse the two. I'll explain what I mean. We are now having a very innocent little chat. Let's suppose that there is a bomb underneath this table between us. Nothing happens, and then all of a sudden, "Boom!" There is an explosion. The public is surprised, but prior to this surprise, it has seen an absolutely ordinary scene, of no special consequence. Now, let us take a suspense situation. The bomb is underneath the table and the public knows it, probably because they have seen the anarchist place it there. The public is aware the bomb is going to explode at one o'clock and there is a clock in the decor. The public can see that it is a quarter to one. In these conditions, the same innocuous conversation becomes fascinating because the public is participating in the scene.[115]

Hitchcock is, of course, talking about telling the same story in two different ways or, more appropriately to the cinema, of cutting the same scene in two different ways. In one case, the film wouldn't show us the bomb until it goes off; in the other, it would cut back to the bomb regularly, reminding us that it's there, and building tension via the rhythmic management of two sets of images. The story and, indeed, the raw footage are exactly the same in both cases; what's different is only but very significantly how that story is managed at the level of cinematic discourse or, in this case, the editing of that raw material. In other words, where at the level of story, we can think of events as events, as facts that need to be taken on their own discrete terms, at the level of discourse those events can be arranged, paced, revealed so as to give them different kinds of value, to make the move from one event to another obvious, mysterious, anxious, happy or, indeed, suspenseful. Suspense is especially suggestive because it allows us not only clearly to see a particular representative style at work but also to observe how specific cultures manage their ideas about time; to understand or to enjoy suspense is to hold particular beliefs about the nature and value of the future.

Along with curiosity, suspense and surprise are also key terms in Meir Sternberg's account of the experience of narrative temporality and, in fact, account for narrativity as such: "Suspense arises from the gap between what we have been told so far and what we anticipate lies ahead. Curiosity arises from the gap between what we have been told of the past and what else we might imagine might have happened. Surprises arises when a twist in the order of narrative conceals from us an even which is subsequently revealed. For Sternberg, 'the play of suspense/curiosity/surprise between represent and communicate time' defines narrativity."[116] In this sense, the presence or absence of suspense in a narrative style would be one expression of what Auerbach understands as the "world of forms" that organize a particular culture's expectations and experience; it helps to reveal what a given culture understands as more or less narratable. And, indeed, he sees Homer and the story of Abraham's sacrifice as having almost opposite relations to the idea of suspense. Despite its reliance on digressions, asides, and delays, Homer's style is, for Auerbach, almost entirely without suspense: "the element of suspense is very slight in the Homeric poems; nothing in their entire style is calculated to keep the reader or hearer breathless."[117] The point here is not only that Homer doesn't cultivate suspense but also that Homer's worldview – his "world of forms" – makes suspense almost impossible: everything in Homer "takes place in the foreground—that is in a local and temporal present which is absolute. One might think that the many interpolations, the frequent moving back and forth, would create a sort of perspective in time and place; but the Homeric style never gives any such impression."[118] Because the Homeric style and its cultural milieu assume an easy continuity between past, present, and future, they can never really produce suspense.

It should be said here that Sternberg takes issue with Auerbach's distinction between Homer and the Bible, arguing that the *Odyssey* in fact uses a complex system of *spatial* or *analogical* patterning to create effects of suspense across its temporal duration. In other words, because a later scene structurally resembles an earlier one, the outcome of the first will condition our expectations and thus heighten our suspense as we wait to see whether or not what we expect to happen – with, after all, little causal justification – will *in fact* happen; for Sternberg, Homer's use of spatial patterning – the repetition of structurally similar events or sequences – to produce temporal effects "affords an impressive illustration of the multifunctional use to which a seeming waste of expositional materials may be put, and of the variety of devices, patterns, and indirections . . . by which literary art may affect the dynamics of narrative interest, notably though the sequential manipulation and development of suprasequential ('spatial') structures."[119] As a result, Sternberg concludes by hoping that his analysis "has also demonstrated the groundlessness of such prevalent claims as Erich Auerbach's that 'the element of suspense is very slight in the Homeric poems. . . .'"[120] While I find Sternberg's analysis of the crossing of the spatial and the temporal aspects of the *Odyssey* compelling, I'm less interested here in the veracity of Auerbach's claims than in the influential methodological and historical ideas about narrative and narrative theory that underwrite those claims.

So, if for Auerbach the *Odyssey* lacks suspense, the opposite is true of the story of Abraham's sacrifice: "in the story of Abraham's sacrifice, the overwhelming suspense is present; what Schiller makes the goal of the tragic poet—to rob us of our emotional freedom, to turn our intellectual and spiritual powers. . .in one direction, to concentrate them there—is effected in this Biblical narrative. . . ."[121] In other words, rather than representing its story in Homeric fashion, as a series of equally important, equally delineated events, the story of Abraham's sacrifice so consistently draws our attention to its possible end, that it subordinates every other event to that same end. Because we can't forget the possibility that Abraham might kill Isaac, we are constantly, uncomfortably, and effectively pulled back and forth between present events and their possible future outcome. All events live, as it were, towards and for an end. This difference brings us back to Hitchcock's distinction, with the Homeric poem as a narrative of surprise (hey, a cyclops!) and the story of Abraham's sacrifice as a narrative of suspense in which we imaginatively cut again and again to the dreaded and narrowly avoided conclusion. Left there, we could see this as simply a choice between two available styles; Auerbach wants, however, to make a larger argument.

What, he suggests, separates classical Greek culture from its Judeo-Christian counterpart is exactly their different and deep senses of how history and time work. Where Greek culture saw its time all of a piece, saw its past and future as aspects of the same visible surface, the Judeo-Christian tradition depends on the idea of time as radically divided between past, present, and future; history in this tradition is a history of falls, breaks, exile, and apocalypse. It is a history of discontinuities and breaks. In *Mimesis* and in an earlier essay on "Figura," Auerbach associates Judeo-Christian thinking and thus the Judeo-Christian representation of historical reality in terms of a particular style of "figural interpretation," the effort to see past and present events in relation to a whole and divinely sanctioned narrative, a narrative that allows one to move surely and interpretatively between events and ideas that would seem otherwise to have little to do with one another. From the present's point of view this is experienced as a double knowledge, one similar to the play between *the time of men* and *the time of the gods* in Section 2.1. That is, while one can have a motivating faith that the whole history of things adds up to an internally coherent narrative, the local experience of events is often mysterious and painful. This mix of confidence and confusion is what both demands and, in a sense, defines the interpretive project for Auerbach. We engage in acts of interpretation knowing that things will mean something to someone even if they don't mean much to us. Figural interpretation thus assumes a communication between the past and the future across the threshold of a hard difference between them, a difference that, according to Auerbach, couldn't make sense to Homeric antiquity:

> This type of interpretation obviously introduces an entirely new and alien element into the antique conception of history. For example, if an occurrence like the sacrifice of Isaac is interpreted prefiguring the sacrifice of Christ, so that in the former the latter is as it were announced and promised, and the latter 'fulfills'. . .the former, then a connection is established between two events which are linked neither temporally nor casually. . ... This conception of history is magnificent in its homogeneity, but it was completely alien to the mentality classical antiquity, it annihilated that mentality down to the very structure of its language, at least of its literary language, which—with all its ingenious and nicely shaded conjunctions, its wealth of devices for syntax arrangement, its carefully elaborated system of tenses—became wholly superfluous as soon as earthy relations of place, time, and cause had ceased to matter. . ..[122]

This idea is difficult because it is double or, more properly, dialectical. The Biblical text is significant and capable of bringing different elements of the world together precisely because it accentuates the difference and disconnection between those events, it is apparent barrier between experiences that both allows and demands their interpretive synthesis: "The greater the separateness and horizontal disconnection of the stories and groups of stories in relation to one another, compared with the *Iliad* and the *Odyssey*, the stronger is their general vertical connection...."[123] Because figural interpretation assumes *both* the felt mystery and apparent disconnection between events *and* their ultimate synthesis, it leads for Auerbach to new narrative styles, styles that can treat the relation between life and form, fact and value, story and discourse in new and newly capacious ways. (We can think back to Freud's reliance on the concept of *afterwardsness*, or the psychic threshold across which relations between past and present become interpretable and thus narratable.)

This circular idea – that figural interpretation demands a divide in history so that that divide can be interpretively overcome, – might account for Auerbach's idiosyncratic choice of examples, his choice, in other words, to focus on the idea of cutting. Although he could presumably have picked any scene from either the *Odyssey* or the Old Testament in order to make his point, he chooses two that are fundamentally about cutting, about scars, about violently separating one thing from another. Odysseus' thigh was cut by a boar's horn and healed; Abraham goes to the site of the sacrifice with knife in hand, prepared to cut his son. In both cases, the idea of the cut corresponds with Auerbach's sense that figural history needs a break, it needs a threshold to cross in order to work. And although the cut is thus an important and ultimately productive part of the historical theory that Auerbach lays out, it is nonetheless painful. History, once again, is what hurts. Where the epic mentality (as defined by Lukács, Bakhtin, and now Auerbach) refuses the idea of a break or a gap between things, accepts the idea that all cuts will heal, the story of Abraham's sacrifice might be taken as an allegory for figural history itself: one needs to be willing make a sacrifice, to accept the discomfort and confusion of living in the disconnected and alien present in order to make room for and to have faith in the ultimate resolution of events in history. Abraham's own suspense is the result of falling between the dim certainly of one's own ignorance and pain and the faith that things will all make sense in the end; it is the suspense of waiting to see what will happen, to see how the parts add up to a whole, and to find out whether the whole story can account for events that seem otherwise bewildering, unmotivated or cruel. To accept the cut of history as it is lived and felt is a precondition for the experience of healing that comes along with the kind of totalizing history that Auerbach sees in the story of Abraham's sacrifice and that he hopes for a Western civilization in the midst of cutting itself to pieces.

Auerbach historical stylistics thus allows him to see and to articulate the way a culture really thinks about itself, to see how each culture understands itself as a "world of forms." A suspense culture thinks differently about itself and time than a surprise culture. As the expression of how individual groups find significance in life, style in this sense can reveal the deep structure behind cultures, their beliefs, and their practices: "For it is precisely in the intellectual and economic conditions of everyday life that those forces are revealed which underlie historical movements; these, whether military, diplomatic, or related to the inner constitution of the state, are only the product, the final result, of variations in the depths of everyday life."[124] Catherine Gallagher and Stephen Greenblatt write that, "For Auerbach, textuality—in its specificity, its local knowledge, its buried network of assumptions—is not a system distinct from lived experience but an imitation of it, and 'imitation' (that is representation) is the principle way human beings come to understand their existence and share it with others."[125] In this sense, the difference between Homeric and Old Testament styles of representation allow us to see into the fabric of the "everyday" structures of two different cultures and to begin to understand how people in those cultures lived, felt, and interacted with each other and with the very idea of history.

Insofar as Auerbach's stylistic and comparative analysis of narrative forms allows us to see into those deep structures, it also allows us to evaluate the political and ethical character of a given culture. Auerbach reads the Homeric epic as a poem of a pure present, a poem where everything relevant about the past, the future, or the feelings and ideas of both men and gods is offered up on and as the surface of things; what allows it to remain serenely on the surface is the fact that the social world that underwrites the epic is falsely constricted; that is, the world of the epic seems fully present to its readers and its characters because it obscures the presence of while relying on workers and slaves who barely rate mention in Homer: "Thus we become conscious of the fact that in the Homeric poem life is enacted only among the ruling class— others appear only in the role of servants to that class."[126] The Homeric epic can be fully present because it is a beautiful but artificial and politically violent restriction of content and style; the epic offers what *feels* like a whole form of life because it represents the experience of the few to those same few. Epic achieves its formal purity because it is the expression of a culture that recognizes only some kinds of experience as being suitable for representation; narrative form (discourse) doesn't follow the real demands of a culture's many stories; those stories are instead curtailed or managed in order to make them fit the available and official narratives. The murkiness of the Old Testament is, on the other hand, the result of what Auerbach takes as a more democratic and more honestly historical attitude of the culture that produced it. The Bible creates confusion, discordance, the experience of the mysterious and the deep precisely because it tries to fit all of life, even the parts that are embarrassing or that don't make sense, into the same frame; where the epic cuts differences out in order to cultivate the false purity of official forms, for Auerbach the Bible seeks to find a form conceptually large enough to acknowledge and to embrace the widest differences. It is a text that, once again, counsels coming to terms with the cut.

Where, in other words, the Homeric epic restricts itself to a single, homogenous, and high style, the Bible somehow permits the simultaneous presence of multiple styles at once, a fact that connects the Bible to the stylistic unruliness of the modern realist novel, which "broke with the classical rule of distinct levels of style, for according to this rule, everyday practical reality could find a place in literature only within the frame of a low or intermediate kind of style."[127] What the Bible and the modern realist novel share is a capacity not only to admit different styles within the same space but also to treat everyday individuals and lives, those that don't come from this or that ruling class, with the full representational dignity of tragedy. How a culture translates its experience and the experiences of its people into form, how, in other words, in converts or fails to convert everyday stories into narrative discourse is, for Auerbach, a sure sign of the political and ethical values that govern that culture more broadly. Elsewhere he makes a similar point, one that recalls Bakhtin's opposition between unofficial and official forms, when he distinguishes the closed and reactionary logic of *legend* with the open and progressive logic of *history*: "Even where the legendary does not immediately betray itself by elements of the miraculous, by the reputation of well-known standard motives, typical pattern and themes, through neglect of clear details of time and place, and the like, it is generally quickly recognizable by its composition. It runs far too smoothly. All cross-currents, all friction, all that is casual, secondary to the main events and themes, everything resolved, truncated, and uncertain, which confuses the clear progress of the action and the simple orientation of the actors, has disappeared. The historical event which we witness, or learn from the testimony of those who witnessed it, runs much more variously, contradictorily, and confusedly...."[128] Auerbach goes on make the case for the ethical and political superiority of the messiness of history over the polish of legend in immediate terms: "Let the reader think of the history which we are ourselves witnessing; anyone who, for example, evaluates the behavior of individual men and groups of men at the time of the rise of National Socialism in Germany, or the behavior of individual people and states before and during the last war, will feel how difficult it is to represent historical themes in general, and how unfit they are for legend...."[129] Reading this same passage, Seth Lerer writes that, "With the complexity of motives, the bluntness of propaganda, and the ambiguities of political discourse, a simple understanding of these public events becomes nearly unimaginable. No 'careful historical and philological training' can distinguish true from false...in these matters."[130] As opposed to the sleek simplicity of legend, real history is contradictory, difficult, apparently ironic. We should think once again of Lukács' opposition between "the genuine novel" and "the entertainment novel" in *The Theory of the Novel*; where the latter imposes a false and politically motivated meaning onto experience, thus distorting its sense and its future, the former – the "genuine novel – instead uses irony and formal openness to engage with reality in a manner that is, for Lukács, both critical and true. For Lukács, Bakhtin, and Auerbach, the presentation of reality as form isn't merely a matter of aesthetics; it rather represents a fundamental aspect of a culture's political and ethical sense of itself. Narrative styles, which is to say the way in which particular genres and cultures manage experience or story at the level of form or discourse, shows us something essential about the very value of those cultures, a fact that Erich Auerbach, who saw his culture and indeed the very possibility of culture as under threat, would have understood all too well.

Chapter 5

Form, Structure, Narrative

Propp, Shklovsky, Saussure, Lévi-Strauss

There are moments that are made up of too much stuff for
them to be lived at the time they occur.
John le Carré, *Tinker, Tailor, Soldier, Spy*

In the previous chapter I discussed several theorists of narrative who shared a
commitment to what I called *the comparative analysis of narrative forms*. In
other words, Lukács, Bakhtin, and Auerbach each developed a distinct critical
methodology around two implicit or explicit but nonetheless axiomatic claims.
The first is that narrative, understood as the reciprocal relation between story
and discourse, represents a more or less universal means of engaging with,
processing, and organizing the world. On the basis of ideas resulting from
Hegel's effort to think about history as a whole and significant story of
consciousness realizing itself and a Neo-Kantian effort to reimagine and to
reinvigorate Kant's sense of the reciprocal relation between conceptual categories and lived experience, Lukács, Bakhtin, and Auerbach each accept both that
living in the world requires that we narrate the world to ourselves and to others
and that the formal demands of narrative – that story needs to find expression
in discourse in order to be communicable – remain more or less stable. The
second axiomatic claim is that, although narrative itself is more or less stable,
the particular forms that it takes in different places at different moments in time
are radically different because radically historical. That is to say, while we can
treat narrative (which is to say the narrative relation between story and
discourse) as a kind of given, the history of narrative, which Lukács, Bakhtin,
and Auerbach understand as the history of narrative genres, is not at all given; it
is contingent, cultural, and subject to all manner of social and political pres-
sures. And, although they all think very differently about the mechanism that
allows for the move from one narrative genre as a culture's dominant genre
(epic, tragedy, novel, etc.), they nonetheless accept that there is a deep relation
between the character of a culture and the character of the genres that a culture
uses to describe itself to itself and to others. As a result, the comparative
analysis of narrative genres allows both for a more precise understanding of

the nature of narrative as narrative and for a rigorously historical analysis of particular cultures and their stories at particular times.

I want to turn now to two related movements that both work to synthesize much of what has preceded in my account and explicitly set the terms of narrative theory today. I will want, in other words, to treat both Russian Formalism and structuralism after Saussure as points at which a range of philosophical, methodological, and historical ideas join both to allow for the disciplinary consolidation of different ways of thinking about narrative and to make visible levels of narrative that were already at work in the philosophical, political, and literary ideas that I have addressed thus far. I want, that is, to see these schools emerging at a moment of what we might call genealogical intensity, a moment when a range of intellectual and historical influences, revisions, and family resemblances merge to make a partial history visible. In looking to genealogy as an appropriate model for the intellectual history of narrative theory, I am echoing both, as we know, Nietzsche's demand for critical as opposed to monumental history as well as a recent essay by David Herman, in which he stresses the field's productive historical complexity: "The field constitutes ... a cluster or family of related developments with intersecting lines of descent; in this context, earlier developments have a shaping but not determinative influence on later ones, and whereas some modes of analysis branch out from and feed back into a shared historical tradition, others represent theoretical innovations that have not had a larger continuing impact on this research domain."[1] I will want, in other words, to look at Russian Formalism and structuralism in a few related ways: I will want to see both in terms of their more or less uneven engagement with the different versions of the story–discourse relation that I have traced back to Hegel and beyond; I will want to look at how, in the midst of testing and developing those different versions, Russian Formalism and structuralism also depend on a set of differently inflected points of historical and methodological contact; and I will want to consider how both are characterized by their respective encounters with their own times, a fact that made them differently sensitive to the political character of the influences they draw on at whatever level of consciousness. Turning to these schools will allow us, in other words, to think about what happens when a discipline or an intellectual tradition seems suddenly and, to a degree, inexplicably to achieve disciplinary coherence.

Russian Formalism emerged out of a couple of loosely constituted intellectual endeavors that took place in Russia in the years just before the revolution of 1917, the Moscow Linguistic Circle and the Society for the Study of Poetic Language (Opojaz); the Russian Formalist interest in the ways in which literary form can and should announce itself as distinct from thematic or conceptual content led, as we will see, to one of the earliest and most explicit accounts of the story–discourse relation. Structuralism derives its most important terms and ideas from the work of the Swiss linguist Ferdinand de Saussure and spread to other figures and fields as part of "a broader structuralist revolution that sought," as Herman puts it, "to use Saussurean linguistics as a 'pilot-science' for studying cultural phenomena of all sorts."[2] Although they make different assumptions and reach different conclusions, Russian Formalism and structuralism are deeply linked. First, in the broadest of strokes the two movements represent overlapping attitudes toward the relation between the parts and the whole of a given system, overlapping sets of metaphors with which to think about linguistic, social, historical, and literary coherence. Where the idea of *form* suggests an organic unity of the kind that Aristotle had imagined, a morphological unity associated with biologically inflected assumptions about development and the necessary relation between means and ends, the idea of *structure* looks past these organic metaphors in order to consider what extrinsic as opposed to intrinsic forces, rules, or expectations are necessary to give a system its order; where structures (such as buildings) are made and governed by external ideas and forces, organic forms (such as flowers) seem somehow to make themselves from within. In these rough terms, we could perhaps think about the difference between form and structure in terms of older oppositions between the organic and the mechanic, differences that circulated in aesthetics from Aristotle, through the work of German Idealists and English Romantics, into more contemporary modes of critical and ethical thought; and, as we have seen, that same opposition took a related but distinctly social character in the reliance of early sociologists including Ferdinand Tönnies, Georg Simmel, and Max Weber. Indeed, as Herman points out, the Russian Formalists drew direct influence from a German "morphological" tradition that drew together several of the concerns that I have been working to join: Aristotelian form, Goethean morphology, Kantian and Neo-Kantian analyses of the relation between fact and value, and Hegelian assumptions about the necessary relation between historical part and whole: "In the domain of narrative poetics, the morphological method was pioneered in Germany in the early years of the twentieth century. It was then further developed by Russian Formalist theorists and subsequently by Prague structuralists who built on the Formalists' work."[3]

Indeed, in practice the distinction between form and structure tends to get blurry, as different and usually indistinct and apparently inevitable confusions about nature, intention, intuition, rules, and time tend to upset easy practical distinctions between the organic and the inorganic. Peter Rabinowitz writes that "literary form – with its shadow twin, structure – has long been a vexed topic in critical discourse."[4] As a result, assumptions about and expectations for both form and structure tend to be mixed up; we should, however, see these mix-ups not as evidence of individual intellectual failure but rather as expressions of problems or contradictions or conflicts that go deep into the stuff of human experience and, as we have seen, might help to account both for our need to narrate and also for our need to narrate our subsequent attempts to meet that other need. More concretely, there was in fact considerable exchange among figures associated with both movements. On the one hand, Saussure's ideas were important in the early Soviet Union, in part because they promised to systematize what had seemed to be the especially bourgeois field of philology: Michael Holquist writes, "The [Soviet] response to Saussure began very early when [Sergej Iosifovic] Karcevskij, who had worked with the master himself in Geneva, joined Jakobson in Moscow in 1917. But it was really only after 1923, when there appeared a flood of Russian publications explicating, attacking, or defending him that Saussure's great importance became apparent."[5] As a result, figures such as Bakhtin, Vladimir Propp, and Roman Jakobson had early on to articulate their own ideas about narrative and the literary in relation to Saussure's distinctions. Jakobson in particular did much to offer a synthesis of structuralism and Russian Formalism, using the rigor of Saussure's structuralist terminology to help to account for the hidden or unspoken bases of some Formalist ideas, including defamiliarization, literariness, and the "baring of the device"; and, as a kind of intellectual gadfly, Jakobson offered a point of social contact for many of the period's most important figures: François Dosse writes, "A veritable globetrotter of structuralism, his pivotal position and influence were the products of an itinerary that took him from Moscow to New York by way of Prague, Copenhagen, Oslo, Stockholm, and Uppsala – not to mention his very frequent trips to Paris. Retracing his steps amounts to following the international path of the nascent structuralist paradigm."[6] And, on the other hand, the work of the Russian Formalists had an early and lasting influence on some of the figures who later worked to extend Saussure's structural linguistics to a broader set of concerns; associates of the *Tel Quel* group in particular (Julia Kristeva and Tzvetan Todorov) introduced Russian Formalist techniques into French intellectual life alongside the rise of structuralism in anthropology, political theory, psychoanalysis, and literary theory. All of this is to say that, as we move into this section, it is important both to recognize the implicit and explicit differences between Russian Formalism and Saussure's structuralism and to acknowledge the different ways in which these two approaches must be and in fact were thought about together.

5.1 The Hero Leaves Home: Vladimir Propp and Narrative Morphology

Vladimir Propp's *Morphology of the Folktale* appeared first in Russian in 1928; although it remained more or less obscure for decades, its appearance in English in 1958 and in other languages soon after marked an important turning point for the analysis of narrative. David Bordwell writes that "anthropologists and folklorists were quick to praise, criticize, test, and revise his claims. A. J. Greimas, Tzvetan Todorov, Claude Bremond, and Roland Barthes made the *Morphology* one point of departure for structuralist narratology, and homage is still plain in the poststructuralist era."[7] It is, in a sense, easy to see why the book made the impression that it did when it did. As I will describe in Section 6.1, Propp's book was one of several sources taken up by Bremond, Greimas, Barthes, and others as part of an effort to make the study of literature and narrative in France more systematic, more rigorous in its attention to style, more aware of the ways in which literature as literature functioned in relation to itself and other discourses. Because Propp was able methodologically to restrict the folktale's rich aesthetic and cultural complexity to a few moving parts without losing and perhaps even increasing the form's essential quality or strangeness, his book offered an exciting and practical model to apply to the study of narratives in general. It offered, in that case, a model of methodological *reduction*, one that, as I will argue over the next several sections, also characterizes the Russian Formalists' literary analyses, Ferdinand de Saussure's structural linguistics, Claude Lévi-Strauss's structuralist anthropology, and the first generation of narratological analyses; I am using *reduction* in the mathematical sense of a "conversion ... to a simpler or more basic form" (OED). What Propp's *Morphology* shares with these later works is, in other words, a sense that the first step toward knowing what to study when thinking about a particular phenomenon is to identify all the topics that one *should not* study; this methodological asceticism – of giving up *some* in order ultimately to get *more* in return – is, as I will argue, at the heart of the narratological project: the effort to see and to understand what is essentially narrative about narrative.

Indeed, much of Propp's continuing appeal results from exactly this combination of methodological modesty and intellectual ambition. Propp is clear in the *Morphology* about the limits of his project; although some have looked to his work as a sort of key to any and all narratives, he maintains throughout that his observations about narrative structure are in fact limited to the fairy tale and only to the fairy tale: "This work is dedicated to the study of fairy tales," "a special class" of narrative.[8] Although his claims about the relation among narrative functions, characters, and plots taken as a whole have definite consequences for other types of narrative (myths in general, short stories, novels, films, etc.), Propp himself makes no suggestions about ways in which his work should be extended beyond the specific form of the fairy tale. Indeed, although the *Morphology* has had its greatest impact in the wider world of narrative analysis and narrative theory, its systematic analysis of a collection of tales is most legible as a late and focused contribution to thinking about folklore going back to Johann Gottfried von Herder, the Brothers Grimm, and others, eighteenth- and nineteenth-century efforts to identify, collect, and analyze what seemed to an emerging nationalist imagination to be evidence of a culture's authentic self. (We might, in this case, see Propp alongside the narrative turn that I associated with Hegel in Section 2.1, the effort to understand other people's beliefs, ideologies, and narratives in the response to events such as the French Revolution and its after-effects.) Indeed, although he is often grouped together with the Russian Formalists, his work is in closer conversation with other folklorists, scholars such as the Grimms, the Finnish folklorist Antti Aarne, as well as with contemporary Russian scholars in ethnopoetics who were looking for ways to differentiate among different folk cultures as well as to see what characteristics or qualities might finally link them.[9] That said, the *Morphology* and its method are indeed enormously ambitious: Propp aims in the *Morphology* not only to supplant almost all previous commentary on the fairy tale but also to isolate and to account for what is *essential* to its structure.

Propp writes early on in the *Morphology* that other well-intentioned scholars had failed to account for the true nature of the fairy tale for a number of related reasons: because they begin with and falsely impose abstract classification schemes on individual tales; because they mistake merely incidental themes, particular objects, or character types as essential to the form; because they establish systems of measure that cannot keep one type of tale distinct from others: "Such a classification always distorts the essence of the material under examination. To this is added an inconsistency in the basic principle of division, i.e., one more elementary rule of logic is violated."[10] Propp's question in that case is how to identify what is *essential* to the tale, what is present in every particular instance of the genre, and what can stand as a minimum unit both of definition and of analysis. As the book's title suggests, Propp looks to the natural sciences as a model: he writes that "the word 'morphology' means the study of forms. In botany, the term 'morphology' means the study of the component parts of a plant, of their relationship to each other and to the whole – in other words, the study of a plant's structure."[11] In a way that will now seem familiar to us, the morphology of the folktale, which is to say the morphology of a particular narrative genre, is an attempt to identify the tale's parts, the relation among those parts, and the relation between those parts and the tale taken as a narrative whole. Propp's procedure, as limited and arcane as it seems, thus emerges as another attempt to reckon with and to update the terms of Aristotle's account of tragedy as both an ordered narrative representation of events as well as the joining of discrete parts into an organic whole, which he, in turn, compares with an animal neither too large nor too small. It is because folk narratives have a particular morphology that they may similarly "be compared in many respects to that of organic formation in nature."[12] More immediately, as David Herman has recently pointed out, Propp's book draws on a range of roughly contemporary German work on the formal analysis of language and poetry (Otmar Schissel von Fleschenberg, Bernard Seuffert, Wilhelm Dibelius), work that built on Goethe's earlier and Aristotelian sense of the organic nature of both art and nature: "Explicitly associating his approach with Goethean morphology, Propp distinguished between variable and invariant components of higher-order narrative structures."[13] In his introduction to a recent edition of Goethe's *The Metamorphosis of Plants* (1790), Gordon Miller writes that it was "Goethe [who] coined the term and founded the fertile field of 'morphology,' a science of organic forms and formative forces aimed at discovering underlying unity in the vast diversity of plants and animals."[14] (It might be worth noting here that Bakhtin also writes beautifully about Goethe's observations about natural forms and morphology in his late essay "The *Bildungsroman* and Its Significance in the History of Realism.")[15] Insofar as Propp merges a theory of literary structure with self-consciously normative assumptions about what culture is and what it can be, he is an appropriate successor to the several figures I have been talking about, thinkers and writers concerned with understanding narratives and the relation among narrative genres as ways to link a discrete part of life with life as a meaningful whole.

Where, however, Propp distinguishes himself is in his particular understanding of what in fact constitutes a recognizable narrative "part": as opposed to taking character or theme or, really, any kind of represented content as an identifiable part of folk narratives, he looks self-consciously to what he claims is the smallest identifiable unit of specifically narrative form, a base narrative element of the tale that he calls a *function*: "Function is understood as an act of a character, defined from the point of view of its significance for the course of the action."[16] The functions of the fairy tale are particular kinds of action (lacking, seeking, testing, being tested, fighting, marrying, etc.) associated with particular types of character (the hero, the villain, the donor, etc.) that are essential to the forward movement of a folktale's plot; they make up the necessary DNA of a fairy tale as fairy tale. Without them, plot in Propp's generically specific sense would be impossible: the villain *needs* to steal the princess in order for a plot to begin; the hero then *needs* to seek her out if the plot is to continue; and he finally *needs*, after some difficulty, to get her back if the plot is to conclude and thus, in a sense, to *become* itself. If a necessary function is either left out or put in the wrong place, the tale as a whole will not make sense. A function is thus an action necessary to the order and sense of the tale as a whole; it is the point or hinge at which part and part or part and whole join in a significant unity.

Propp goes on in the *Morphology* to catalogue what he understands as the necessary components of the fairy tale; he "isolates thirty-one core functions that constitute the fundamental components common to every fairy tale."[17] The functions include plot segments such as "an interdiction is addressed to the hero," "the hero reacts to the actions of a future donor," or "the villain is punished." He goes on to identify the seven character roles that accompany his thirty-one functions: hero, villain, donor, helper, dispatcher, sought-for person, and false hero. In addition to his identification of the component parts of the fairy tale, he identifies some stable rules that allow for their selection and combination in particular cases. For instance, while every function does not need to appear in every tale, the appearance of some will require the appearance of others; for instance, you cannot have the princess stolen without eventually seeing her returned if you are to have a whole plot; in cases like these, one function necessarily closes off and resolves what had been opened by another. Although particular character roles are associated with particular functions, it is possible for a single character to play more than one role (the princess can, for example, function both as a donor and as the sought-for person in a given tale). And, most controversially, Propp argues that, while a tale does not need to exhibit all thirty-one functions, the functions that do appear always need to appear in the same order; put differently, for Propp the order of events at the level of both story and discourse is fixed in the fairy tale, a fact that, as we have seen, differentiates the tale from other forms of narrative, which rely both on the fixed causal order of story and on the relative chronological malleability of narrative discourse. Propp sums up his argument this way: "Fairy tales exhibit thirty-one functions, not all of which may be found in any one fairy tale; however, the absence of certain functions does not interfere with the order of appearance of the others. Their aggregate constitutes one system, one composition.

This system has proved to be extremely stable and widespread."[18] Propp identifies, in that case, what he takes as the two essential aspects of the fairy tale, the parts or the units the make them up and the rules that govern the selection and arrangement of those parts or units. That is all you need; everything else is incidental.

~

There are, as I have begun to suggest, different reasons why Propp's brilliant and idiosyncratic system might have caught on when it did, some three decades after its first appearance in Russian. On the one hand, the *Morphology* offers a powerful method by which narratives more complicated than the relatively stable fairy tale might be analyzed; the strength in this case was not one or another particular function or rule, but rather the clarity with which he modeled the need for and the results of his methodological reduction. On the other hand, there was and is something deeply seductive about the idea that all narratives could in the end be reduced to a handful of functions, a small set of modular components that would, when properly identified, allow us to understand all narratives. I will address both different but related forms of appeal in what follows.

To begin with method: as I have already said, part of what is so powerful about Propp's system is its founding methodological reduction, the fact that it recognizes the need to restrict its focus, to hone in on a single, specific, empirically testable object of study before proceeding on to more general claims. At the heart of Propp's project is thus a straightforward desire to identify what makes a fairy tale a fairy tale as opposed to one or another genre; as Bordwell puts it, "Propp's functional scheme aims not to describe every possible or existing [fairy tale] but only to identify those minimal conditions that distinguish this genre from its neighbors."[19] There are two sides to this reduction. The first, as his most successful followers saw, was the identification of a *specific* part–whole relationship at the heart of the fairy tale. While, in other words, we might export the idea of function as such to other kinds of narrative, what is crucial to Propp is how his particular functions join in a particular way to form the fairy tale. Although it is the more beguiling aspect of the theory, the fact that there are thirty-one functions is actually less important than the way in which the individual function relates to the narrative whole in the fairy tale as fairy tale. That is, if the fairy tale is in fact a distinct genre, what makes it so is the way in which its functions link story to discourse in a generically specific manner. That is, while we could imagine functions such as "the villain is punished" appearing in almost any kind of narrative, the fact that that function must appear in one and only one position in the fairy tale is unique. That is, the fact that the order of functions is identical at the level of both story and discourse is a distinct and, for Propp, historically and culturally specific version of a more or less universal narrative relation.

Propp thus relies on the two axioms of the comparative analysis of narrative forms that I identified in the previous section: (1) that the narrative relation between story and discourse seems to be more or less universal and (2) that a particular relation between story and discourse that characterizes one as opposed to another genre is, on the contrary, entirely specific and historical. Insofar as he implicitly relies on a theory of all narratives (the function marks the point at which part and part; beginning, middle, and end; and story and discourse merge in an organic and significant whole), he does so in order to make a historical argument about one and only one narrative genre: the fairy tale. Although we could speculate on the cultural reasons for the shape that this genre takes (an aspirational alignment of natural and human rhythms, an association with styles that seem to eschew style as such, etc.), the important point is that a fairy tale is a fairy tale because it relies on a stylistically specific relation between story and discourse, a style that "chooses" more or less to map the otherwise variable temporality of discourse directly onto the necessary temporality of story. It would be interesting in these terms to put Propp's account of the fairy tale alongside Lukács's history of narrative genres in *Theory of the Novel*; that is, if we take it with Lukács that it is the creative or ironic alienation of discourse from story that distances the novel from the epic, the unnecessarily or meaninglessly identical order of events at the levels of story and discourse in the fairy tale might give it the status of what we might call a residual or, rather, a transitional genre. Not epic, the fairy tale might rather be seen as a particular society's shared wish fulfillment, its implicit cultural effort to act *as if* we lived still beneath the "starry skies" of epic.

So, instead of seeing Propp's thirty-one functions as a one-size-fits-all solution to the problems of narrative, his best readers took on and developed the methodological rigor of his analysis, his sense that it is the way in which story and discourse together make the fairy tale generically and thus culturally distinct, as the basis for their own works. As we will see in Section 6.2, the role of the function as a generically specific hinge between story and discourse is an important part of Roland Barthes's foundational "An Introduction to the Structural Analysis of Narrative"; indeed, Barthes's abstraction and expansion of Propp's system into a more general account of the narrative field is one of narratology's founding moments. The most committed developments of the Proppian system occur, perhaps, in the work of Claude Bremond and A. J. Greimas. Where, for instance, Bremond accepts Propp's general sense of the function as a given unit of action associated with a particular type of agent, he introduces a greater level of modular flexibility into his system; as Rimmon–Kenan describes it, for Bremond, "every three functions combine to form a sequence in which they punctuate three logical stages: possibility (or potentiality), process, and outcome. Rather than automatically leading to the next function, as in Propp, each function opens two alternatives, two directions the story can subsequently take."[20] Similarly, Greimas took Propp's analysis of narrative morphology as part of a wider turn toward the identification and analysis of the surface and deep structures that govern the organization of stories:

> In the first instance, a comparison of the results from various independent research activities – those of Vladimir Propp on folklore, Claude Lévi-Strauss on the structure of myth, Etienne Souriau on theater – has allowed us to confirm the existence of an autonomous field of study. New methodological refinements – those by which Claude Bremond interprets narrative from the perspective of decisional logic, or by which Alain Dundes focuses on giving a narrative grammar form to the organization of story – have subsequently provided us with a diversity of theoretical approaches. Our own concern during this period has been to extend as much as possible the area of application of the analysis of narrative and to formalize to an ever greater extent the partial models produced in the course of this research.[21]

As a result of this synthesis, Greimas was able to develop his influential "actantial model," a play of six essential and relational roles (Subject, Object, Sender, Receiver, Helper, and Opponent) that together form a "deep structure" that makes narrative and the relation between narrative levels possible.[22]

Propp's work has also proved useful in contexts that transcend the more strictly morphological concerns of structuralist narratology. For instance, Sharon Marcus has recently drawn on Propp's model in order to reveal limits to ways of reading Victorian fiction "that focus solely on the heterosexual dynamics of marriage plots."[23] Because modern critics have assumed that lesbian desire was as "unspeakable" in the nineteenth century as it seemed sometimes to be in the twentieth, they were unable to account for or even to see the essential and *functional* role that affectionate and erotic relationships between women played in the structuring of the conventional marriage plot.[24] Marcus writes in *Between Women: Friendship, Desire, and Marriage in Victorian England*:

> Like the donor and helper in Vladimir Propp's analysis of the folktale, the female friend is not a static or dispensable secondary character but one with a crucial role to play in achieving the marriage plot's ends. As Propp notes, even in the fairy tale "a helper at times may perform those

functions which are specific for the hero," and in complex novels one finds both the heroine and the female friend taking actions that conclude the marriage plot. The female friend is not simply an auxiliary, brought onstage as matchmaker, then whisked off after fulfilling the secondary function to which she would therefore be reduced. She is a mate, an ally, and a critic, the repository of confidences, a bestower of wisdom, a conspirator, nurse or patient, teacher or pupil, a source of physical contact and pleasure, an object of admiration, a link to the past and a bridge to the future.[25]

For Marcus, an analysis of the female friend as a figure *functionally* necessary to the novel not only helps to highlight "what [Victorian] texts present on their surface but critics have failed to notice" (an act of highlighting she calls "just reading") but also reveals the degree to which "the currents of desire and affiliation" activated by the female friend understood as what Greimas would call an *actant* necessary to the morphology of the marriage plot contributes to the *narrative matrices* that give that a plot its shape: "Female friendship is thus best described as what I will call a 'narrative matrix,' a relationship that generates plot but is not its primary agent, subject, or object. The relative stability of a narrative matrix endows it with power and endurance; it is a contributing cause that maintains its identity and presence even after achieving its end."[26] Seen, then, in relation to the Victorian novel and its frank structural reliance on forms of desire that exceed the "heterosexual dynamics of marriage plots," Propp's tools are revealed as capable not only of laying bare the deep formal structures of Victorian plots but also of making clear the degree to which those formal structures help in turn to organize, direct, and distribute sexual desire at a particular historical moment. Marcus helps us once again to see how Propp's morphology relies on the two axioms of the comparative analysis of narrative forms, on, in other words, the relation between the generality of narrative form and the specificity of historical content.

~

Another, arguably less helpful source of Propp's appeal is the idea that he reduced not only the fairy tale but also any and all narratives to a few discrete functions. It is this overreliance on the Proppian functions in and of themselves that animated David Bordwell's attack on Proppian film criticism in the late eighties: "For many critics, Propp has become the Aristotle of film narratology; yet his influence has come at the cost of serious misunderstandings ... film scholars have taken Propp out of context and recast him almost out of recognition. There are good reasons to regard the 'Proppian' approach to film narrative as a dead end."[27] It is ironic, in other words, that his specification of thirty-one functions has given his work an unintentionally mystical quality, the suggestion that he had somehow divined the "secret" of the fairy tale or narrative as such. Although this sense of having found out a secret is, I think, antithetical to the modesty and clarity of his work, it nonetheless connects his project to a number of other efforts to identify the ultimate number of possible plots. The interest to identify the few essential plots goes back at least to the eighteenth-century Italian playwright Carlo Gozzi, who, as Goethe said to Eckermann, "maintained that there can be but thirty-six dramatic situations."[28] Since then there have been many more and less serious attempts to enumerate *all* of the plots: there is Rudyard Kipling's claim that "there are nine and sixty ways of constructing tribal lays / And every single one of them is right!"; Georges Polti's attempt to identify *The Thirty-Six Dramatic Situations* (1916); Etienne Souriau's more serious effort to reduce all dramatic situations to the interplay of six archetypal functions: the Lion, Mars, the Sun, the Earth, the Balance, and the Moon; Christopher Booker's promise to introduce aspiring writers to *The Seven Basic Plots* (2004); and Ronald Tobias's equally pragmatic offer to reveal the secrets of *20 Master Plots and How to Build Them* (2012). More recently and with broader and more complicated methodological significance, Matthew Jockers has developed a digital program, which he has dubbed "the Syuzhet Package," and which is "designed to extract sentiment and plot information from prose," "in order to reveal six common, perhaps archetypal, plot shapes."[29] Whether or not it is in fact possible to identify five, ten, or twenty essential narrative functions, it should be clear that the effort to do so ultimately runs against the grain of what seems most important about Propp's work. Indeed, instead of looking for a more or less stable key to all narratives, Propp did encourage some and should encourage us rather to look with methodological rigor at the indefinitely large number of ways in which story and discourse can be related to produce different, historically specific effects. Indeed, it is not the universality but rather the historical specificity of Propp's *Morphology* that gives it its pride of place in the development of narrative theory.

5.2 Knight's Move: Viktor Shklovsky and Russian Formalism

At about the same time that Vladimir Propp was developing the terms of his *Morphology*, a dispersed but like-minded group of Russian intellectuals, artists, and critics began to ask similar questions about the nature of literary form, the relation between literature and culture, and the structure of narrative. Russian Formalism emerges from the work of a couple of loosely constituted groups formed in Russia in the years just before the 1917 revolution: the Moscow Linguistic Circle and the Society for the Study of Poetic Language (Opojaz). The critics – Roman Jakobson, Boris Eichenbaum, Boris Tomashevsky, Viktor Shklovsky, and others – who came to be associated with Russian Formalism made their name via a number of brilliant and iconoclastic articles on poetic language, the analysis of plot, and studies of particular literary works. Their success was, however, short-lived. By the late 1920s, the Formalists found themselves on the outside of official Soviet culture. This was in part an effect of Leon Trotsky's influential attack on "The Formalist School" in his *Literature and Revolution* (1924) as well as of a number of well-placed articles that pointed to the perceived "decadence" of the movement, the idea that its attention to literary form amounted to a reactionary celebration of art for art's sake.[30] Despite efforts on the part of its main figures – especially Shklovsky and Eichenbaum – to manage some kind of compromise between Formalist principles and official commitments to historical or social approaches to literature and literary study, their influence waned.

The later resurgence of Russian Formalism took two related paths. First, with the success of British and American varieties of New Criticism, there appeared an opening for a new appreciation of the Formalists' attention both to literature as a more or less autonomous type of language and to the analysis of poetic technique for its own sake. This meeting between the two methods was most visible in René Wellek and Austin Warren's influential *Theory of Literature* (1948), which introduced Russian Formalism to a new audience (Wellek had himself been a member of the Prague Linguistic Circle, the group formed by Jakobson after he left Moscow in 1920); in this context, the Formalists were understood most centrally as theorists of poetic language and poetic technique. Aligning their work with other new methods originating in France, Germany, and Britain, Wellek and Warren pointed particularly to "the brilliant movement of the Russian formalists and their Czech and Polish followers [which had] brought new stimuli to the study of the literary work, which we are only beginning to see properly and analyze adequately."[31] They go on in their chapter "The Nature and Modes of Narrative Fiction" to draw on the Russian Formalists both for their sense of the motif or "motive" as the basic unit of narrative structure and for *fabula* and *sjuzhet*, their version of the story–discourse relation: "The Russian formalists distinguish the 'fable,' the temporal–causal sequence which, however it may be told, is the 'story' or story-stuff, from the 'sujet,' [sic] which we might translate as 'narrative structure.' The 'fable' is the sum of all the motifs, while the 'sujet' is the artistically ordered presentation of the motifs (often quite different)."[32] Second, and perhaps more central to our story, Russian Formalism appeared, as I will describe in Section 6.1, in France when the Bulgarian expatriate and member of the *Tel Quel* group Tzvetan Todorov translated and assembled his 1966 collection of Russian Formalist essays. As I will describe, the rediscovered Russian Formalists made an enormous impression in France for a few related reasons: first, they offered such critics as Barthes, Genette, and others a rigorous, apparently technical, and specifically literary methodology, a method that they marshaled against what they took as an overly impressionist academic orthodoxy. Second, the exotic political provenance of the Formalists' work allowed left-wing thinkers made uneasy by Soviet aggression to imagine a different, less compromised relation with the East; François Dosse writes that "the French were interested in and responsive to the Russian formalist texts that Todorov was publishing, and in the political and literary events unfolding in Eastern Europe at a time when East-West relations were thawing."[33] Finally, French critics found that the Formalists' work on narrative and plot resonated with their other, already current methodological obsession: the structuralism of Saussure, Lévi-Strauss, and others. In other words, critics such as Barthes and Genette synthesized the Russian Formalist writing about the relation between story and discourse–what they referred to as *fabula* and *sjuzhet*–with aspects of Saussurean structuralist linguistics in order to create what would soon come to be known as narratology. I will go into more detail about the international reception of Russian Formalists later; for now, I want to turn back to the development of their own ideas about literary technique and narrative structure, ideas that remain central to narrative theory.

~

Like Propp, the Russian Formalists begin with an act of methodological reduction, with the effort to identify what was specifically *literary* about literature and then to restrict literary analysis to that specifically literary fact: "The driving force behind Formalist theorizing was," writes Victor Erlich, "the desire to bring to an end the methodological confusion prevailing in traditional literary studies and systematize literary scholarship as a distinct and integrated field of intellectual endeavor."[34] The Formalists, in other words, argued that other influential Russian critics (especially Symbolists such as Andrey Bely and Alexander Blok) had made essential category errors when it came to the objects and methods of literary study, mixing up social, cultural, psychological, or metaphysical questions that, while interesting in themselves, were not defensible within a coherent course of study; as Boris Eichenbaum suggested in an essay that reflects on the history and goals of the Formalist movement: "Before the appearance of the Formalists, academic research, quite ignorant of theoretical problems, made use of antiquated aesthetic, psychological, and historical 'axioms' and had so lost sight of its proper subject that its very existence as a science had become illusory."[35] As a result Shklovsky, Jakobson, Eichenbaum, and others worked in different ways to try to isolate and define the "literariness" of literature, a quality of a given linguistic performance that would allow one to differentiate it from other, nonliterary linguistic performances; Fredric Jameson writes of the Formalists that "the initial task of the theory is the isolation of the specifically literary fact itself."[36] Although, as I will argue, their account of literariness has an interesting ethical dimension, their initial differentiation between the literary and the nonliterary avoided evaluation in favor of straight analysis; they tried, in other words, to restrict their consideration of the literary to what was methodologically essential to the identification and description of literary works. Eichenbaum writes, "In principle the question for the Formalist is not how to study literature, but what the subject matter of literary study actually is."[37] As opposed to thinking about the particular qualities or, rather, the *quality* of particular literary texts, which can and should be understood in sociological, anthropological, linguistic, ideological, or broadly historical terms, the Russian Formalists restricted themselves to thinking about *the literariness of literature*.

The earliest and most forceful proponent of literariness as an object of study was Viktor Shklovsky, one of the founding members of Opojaz. Shklovsky was an intellectual gadfly and provocateur who wrote forcefully, erratically, brilliantly. His many books – *Knight's Move*, *Theory of Prose* (1925), *A Hunt for Optimism* (1931), *Mayakovsky and His Circle* (1941), *Bowstring: On the Dissimilarity of the Similar* (1970), *Energy of Delusion: A Book on Plot* (1981), and others – shift suddenly among different styles, tones, and disciplinary registers, joining critical analysis, aesthetic appreciation, memoir, anecdote, and political commentary. In "Art as Technique," one of Russian Formalism's founding texts, Shklovsky begins to define *literariness* by once again identifying what it was not, by identifying what he takes as others' misguided attempts to define literary art. He points initially to Russian academic critics such as Alexander Potebnya, who claimed that "art is thinking in images," which is to say that art is valuable because it somehow contains images that it can later conjure in the mind of a reader. Under this definition, the words on a page – language *as* language – must be seen as secondary to their effects, to the images and ideas that they transmit to the mind of the reader; the best art is, in these terms, art that allows a reader to get most efficiently past the words to the ideas behind the words. Shklovsky relates this view of the literary as a mere material means to ideational ends to Herbert Spencer's "law of the economy of creative effort," which stated similarly that the best literary style is the style that presents "ideas that they may be apprehended with the least possible mental effort."[38] Like Potebnya's, Spencer's definition of literary style subordinates the material fact of language – its form – to the ideas that that language is meant to convey – its content; indeed, given the zero-sum terms in which Spencer imagines a reader's fixed amount of cognitive power, *any* attention consumed by language will be attention taken away from the ideas that that language is meant to convey: "A reader or listener has at each moment but a limited amount of mental power available. . . . Hence, the more time and attention it takes to receive and understand each sentence, the less time and attention can be given to the contained idea; and the less vividly will that idea be conceived."[39] In these terms, the best literary style would be the style that reduces the felt presence, the "friction" of words, to a minimum and thus allows us to perceive the idea as immediately as possible. Both Spencer and Potebnya argue that, insofar as art is about its effects, the matter of art should do its best to get out of the way and make the appearance of images or ideas immediate, transparent, and easy; and, in both cases, these critics rely on methods taken from fields other than literary studies (psychology, sociology, biology, metaphysics, etc.) in order to define literature.

Shklovsky's goal in "Art as Technique" is to return our attention to the literary object as literary, as, that is, a materially present organization of words on a page. As Eichenbaum later said, "The Formalists, when they abandoned Potebnya's point of view, also freed themselves from the traditional correlation of 'form and content' and from the traditional idea of form as an envelope, a vessel into which one pours a liquid (the content)."[40] What, for both Shklovsky and Eichenbaum, makes literature *literary* is that, instead of reducing language's presence, it rather forces us to confront language as a material fact; it prevents us from moving too efficiently from word to idea or from form to content and instead gets us pleasurably stuck at the level of language itself, allowing us to feel the work that words do while they are doing it: "Poetic language," writes Eichenbaum, "is distinguished from practical language by the perception of its structure. The acoustical, articulatory, or semantic aspects of poetic language may be felt."[41] And because literary language makes us feel language at work, it prevents us from falling into an unthinking or automatic relationship with either form or content. As Shklovsky characterizes it, "The purpose of art is to impart the sensation of things as they are perceived and not as they are known. The technique of art is to make objects 'unfamiliar,' to make forms difficult, to increase the difficulty and length of perception because the process of perception is an aesthetic end in itself and must be prolonged."[42] Literature is literary because it makes the perception of language into an aesthetic end in itself.

This is the famous Russian Formalist principle of *defamiliarization*, the idea that art can or should "estrange," or make unfamiliar and thus newly perceptible, beliefs, practices, or objects to which we have become unthinkingly habituated. Indeed, Shklovsky casts the concept in terms of a more general theory of habit:

> Habitualization devours works, clothes, furniture, one's wife, and the fear of war. . . . And art exists that one may recover the sensation of life; it exists to make one feel things, to make the stone stony. The purpose of art is to impart the sensation of things as they are perceived and not as they are known. The technique of art is to make objects "'unfamiliar,'" to make forms difficult, to increase the difficulty and length of perception because the process of perception is an aesthetic end in itself and must be prolonged. Art is a way of experiencing the artfulness of an object; the object is not important.[43]

Shklovsky conflates two different but related arguments here. On the one hand, he makes a conceptual and even ethical argument about the nature of habit and its tendency to deaden us to the passage and consequence of our own lives. Art, in this sense, can and should tear down the veil of habit and force the reader to see past expectation, convention, or ideology to things as they really are. Art thus has the capacity to let us see past what Bakhtin would in a similar sense think of as *official* ways of seeing, ways of seeing that merely reproduce an already available idea about the world as opposed to allowing us to think authentically or critically. This is an important argument and I will return to it. This potentially ethical point stands, however, somewhat to the side of Shklovsky's main case in the essay: that what is most important about literature as literariness is not that it defamiliarizes the world but rather that *it defamiliarizes itself*, that it reveals itself as artful, that it uses what he calls technique or "the device" to draw the reader's attention to what others would reduce to the means as opposed to the end of art: the perceptible forms that language takes when it becomes specifically literary language. What makes literature literary is thus its ability to foreground and thus to defamiliarize its own status as formed language. Literary art makes language and thinking difficult – as it should be: "A crooked road," writes Shklovsky, "a road in which the foot feels acutely the stones beneath it, a road that turns back on itself – this is the road of art."[44]

The Formalist attention to technique or to "the device" thus registers the particular ways in which literature slows a reader, calls attention to the fact of language, creates difficulty, reminds the reader that he or she is not receiving images easily or directly but is rather engaged in a kind of work. The most obvious examples of devices that call attention to language at work appear in poetry, where different forms of linguistic patterning – meter, rhyme, alliteration, assonance, and so on – put us in a position to feel the design of a line at work; with each of these patterns, a conceptual or semantic logic of resemblance or association that we have, at least since Romanticism, taken as essential to the imagination is projected onto the syntactical flow of the sentence itself. What is important is not (or not only) how literary images point to something else (the rose's metaphorical capacity to suggest love), but rather how literary language points to formal relations between one word or sound and another within the same line, sentence, stanza, or poem. When Alice, falling down the rabbit hole, wonders "in a dreamy sort of way, 'Do cats eat bats? Do cats eat bats?' and sometimes, 'Do bats eat cats?'" she is letting the sound of the words, which is to say the words *as* words, overtake their content; she can reverse their order because, at that moment, it is not the content but rather the form of the words that matters. While a cat does not suggest a bat at the level of content (one would be a poor metaphor for the other), the word "cat" does indeed sound and look like the word "bat" (or "mat" or "hat") at the level of its material form. Alice's surrender to form over content forces us to attend not to what the words mean but rather to what they materially are. Indeed, the whole of *Alice's Adventures in Wonderland* (1865) is given over to moments when the sound of words seems more important than what they mean; this is part of the book's larger critical effect, its tendency to reveal for and from a child's point of view the degree to which adult rituals and social conventions are artificial and, indeed, absurd. The literary word play in Alice is, in other words, part of an effort to defamiliarize a condition that might define habituation as an ideological process: the socialized life of the "well-adjusted" adult.

In the important 1960 essay "Linguistics and Poetics," Roman Jakobson formalized this aspect of language – its literariness or its capacity to point to itself materially at work – as one of six communicative functions that he saw as operative in any and all language: the referential, the poetic, the emotive, the conative, the phatic, and the metalingual. Jakobson argues that while *the poetic function* – language's particular capacity to call attention to itself as language – is most visible in literary language, it is in fact present to one degree or another in all language: in poetry, "the poetic function is not the sole function of verbal art but only its dominant, determining function, whereas in all other verbal activities it acts as a subsidiary, accessory constituent. This function, by promoting the palpability of signs, deepens the fundamental dichotomy of signs and objects. Hence, when dealing with the poetic function, linguistics cannot limit itself to the field of poetry."[45] Although all language will call attention to itself to one degree or another, literary langauge fore-grounds this aspect as "dominant and determining" in order to force the reader to reflect on the words at hand and, maybe, to think differently about how words work elsewhere as well. We need in that case to understand poetic or literary technique in two ways: first, it is, when it is the "dominant, determining function," that which allows us to differentiate between literature and other kinds of verbal activity; second, because it is present to a greater or lesser degree in all verbal activity, its operation can help us to see and understand a material, literary residue at work in all language.

Fair enough. But, if the poetic function is most visible in the form of techniques specific to the individual sentence or the poetic line, then what about prose, where the form of a single line tends to be lost? What about short stories or novels (particularly novels associated with one or another kind of realism), where instances of rhyme, meter, or alliteration are relatively rare? What is the prose and, indeed, the narrative equivalent of the poetic tech-niques that reveal language as language and thus make language into verbal art? What, if anything, makes narrative literary in this technical sense? Shklovsky makes a number of suggestions across his work and, in particular, in his great essay on *Tristram Shandy;* he points, for instance, to Laurence Sterne's famously odd and entirely brilliant efforts to expose narrative con-ventions – his playful use of epigraphs, chapter breaks, and so on – *as* conventions (what Shklovsky refers to as "laying bare the device"), to use elaborately euphemistic language to produce effects of "erotic defamiliariza-tion," and to manage, order, and reorder events so as to slow the experience of the novel: "Slowing the action of a novel is not accomplished by introducing rivals, for example, but by simply transposing parts. In so doing the artist makes us aware of the aesthetic laws which underlie both the transposition and the slowing down of the action."[46] In each of these cases, narrative becomes art when it draws attention to itself as narrative. In a recent essay on modes of narrative organization that exceed or undermine traditional views of plot, Brian Richardson writes that Shklovsky

> identified a number of formal arrangements of narrative materials, including repetition, parallelism, antithesis, and triadic patterns, and pointed out that much of the *Chanson de Roland* is composed around dual and triple repetitions of the same scenes and events. In fact, many of these actions are present *only* because they complete the formal pattern that animates the rest of the text, in contravention of other compositional principles like causal connection, verisimilitude, or rhetorical efficacy.[47]

These devices – deceleration, double-plotting, stepped construction, and the general "baring of the device" – are thus prose and plotted equivalents of the different forms of verbal patterning – rhyme, meter, alliteration, etc. – that we associate with the poetic line. In a sense, we can see Shklovsky as developing Propp's account of the *function* in fairy tales; where, however, Propp insisted that the order of events at the level of discourse had to follow the order of events at the level of story, Shklovsky sees the difference between story and discourse and, indeed, discourse's characteristic "relative autonomy" (to repurpose a phrase I used in relation to Marx's thinking about base and superstructure) from the order of story as an opportunity to create different kinds of patterning, repetition, inversion, etc. Indeed, although he makes only a brief gesture toward the terms at his essay's end, narrative patterning relies on the relation between story and discourse or, rather, between what Shklovsky and other Russian Formalists referred to as *fabula* and *sjuzhet*. Erlich writes,

> In what was clearly an application to the problems of narrative fiction of the dynamic dichotomy between "device" and "materials" the Formalists differentiated between "fable" (*fabula*) and "plot" (*sjuzhet*). In Opojaz parlance the "fable" stood for the basic story stuff, the sum-total of events to be related in the work of fiction, in a word, the "material for narrative construction." Conversely, "plot" meant the story as actually told or the way in which the events are linked together.[48]

As Shklovsky saw it in his essay on *Tristram Shandy*, it was the difference between story and discourse that gave the literary artist the greatest opportunity to create the kinds of patterns repetitions, effects of pacing and displacement that transform a narrative into narrative art.

In his essay on plot, Boris Tomashevsky – another important Formalist – expands on the equivalence between the poetic line and the literary plot similarly understood as "a wholly artistic creation."[49] He begins, again following Propp, by identifying the "motif" as a plot's minimum unit of narrative significance: "After reducing a work to its thematic elements, we come to parts that are irreducible, the smallest particles of thematic material: 'evening comes,' 'Raskolnikov kills the old woman,' 'the hero dies,' 'the letter is received,' and so on. The theme of an irreducible part of a work is called the motif."[50] A motif is, in other words, to plot what the individual word is to the poetic line; where the individual line is made up of words related to one another in terms of both sound and sense (*cat* and *bat*), a plot is made up of motifs that share other but similar kinds of relation. In Mary Shelley's *Frankenstein* (1818), we might, for instance, take "discovery" as a motif. We could then see Walton's arctic exploration ("What may not be expected in a country of eternal light?"), Victor's creation of the monster ("It was already one in the morning ... when, by the glimmer of the half-extinguished light, I saw the dull yellow eye of the creature open"), the monster's first awakening of consciousness ("By degrees, I remember a stronger light pressed upon my nerves, so that I was obliged to shut my eyes"), and even Shelley's own account of her work's origin in her 1831 introduction ("Swift as light and as cheering was the idea that broke in upon me") as moments where the "discovery" motif appears and reappears. Seen as a discursive line, the plot could then be read in relation to the more or less rhythmic repetition of that motif; seen thematically, its repetition encourages us to evaluate and to compare different, similarly positioned enterprises: exploring, creating, seeing, reading, and writing. We would notice that the motif, seen in relation to narrative structure, not only falls at regular intervals across the line of the novel's discourse but also serves as a thematic and formal link creating echoes among the novel's several diegetic frames: Walton's letter to his sister, the tale that Victor tells Walton, the story that the creature tells Victor, and so on. Reading *Frankenstein* as a system of repeating and ramifying motifs allows us all to read it at once for its plot, for its discursive form, and for its thematic and narrational structures; seeing a motif as it works across the line of a narrative allows us to begin to approach it as a complex and multifaceted aestethic whole.

Tomashevsky goes on to differentiate among different kinds of motifs: where, for instance, "bound" motifs are essential to the causal coherence of a given plot, "free" motifs are inessential; they are events that might add to but are not necessary to a given plot. (As we will see, Barthes and Seymour Chatman adapt this pairing to their own works; where Barthes differentiates between a *nucleus* and a *catalysis*, Chatman opposes *kernels* to *satellites*.) And, where a "static" motif names a steady state, a "dynamic" motif is an event or a change of state. Because motifs thus both represent different contents and take different forms, their arrangement into different plots can produce an indefinitely large variety of patterns, relations of near-identity, antitheses drawn, alternating or lopsided alternations between static and dynamic, free and bound. Plot, in other words, appears at the level of its form as an enormously complicated and rich opportunity for palpable aesthetic patterning, a fact that reduces the distinction between poetry and prose or, rather, that makes the difference into one of scale and not kind. To see the relation between the motifs that make up a particular plot is thus to begin to see the ordering patterns that give that plot its coherence and aesthetic significance.

Because Tomashevsky and Shklovsky understand narrative effects as the result of motifs merging into a textured and significant whole, they represent another, by-now-familiar effort to update Aristotle's sense of plot as the presentation of discrete events as a beginning, middle, and end that, in turn, join into a higher and significant unity; their word for the significant relation between part and part and part and whole is *motivation*:

> The system of motifs comprising the theme of a given work must show some kind of artistic unity. If the individual motifs, or a complex of motifs, are not sufficiently suited to the work, if the reader feels that the relationship between certain complexes of motifs and the work itself is obscure, then that complex is said to be superfluous. If all the parts of the work are badly suited to one another, the work is *incoherent*. That is why the introduction of each separate motif of complex of motifs must be *motivated*. The network of devices justifying the introduction of individual motifs or groups of motifs is called *motivation*.[51]

For Tomashevsky, in other words, *motivation* refers to the immanent and distinct logics that govern a particular plot and thus allow for the writer and the reader to make decisions about what is appropriate or inappropriate to that plot. He describes three kinds of motivation: *compositional, realistic*, and *artistic* motivation.

Compositional motivation refers to the general demand that all of the motifs that appear in a given plot have one or another reason for being there, that a plot not deploy motifs wastefully: nothing "may remain unused in the telling, and no episode may be without influence on the situation."[52] Tomashevsky goes on to invoke Chekhov's insistence that "if one speaks about a nail beaten into a wall at the beginning of a narrative, then at the end the hero must hang himself on that nail."[53] This is, once again, a way of maintaining that the relation between part and whole in narrative is a necessary relation. We can think here of a number of other figures who described the compositional or conceptual work that went into producing a particular plot or narrative as internally coherent and meaningful: we can think of the early Lukács's sense of the novel's self-conscious reliance on the biographical structure of a life to give the random stuff of modern existence some kind of provisional or ironic order; or we can think of Henry James's sense of using a single point of view as a means of an author's drawing, "by a geometry of his own, the circle within which" otherwise disparate things could appear as part of the same internally coherent and significant world.[54] For Tomashevsky, to motivate a particular narrative compositionally is to give it its apparently immanent meaning, to lend it the particular rules that govern what belongs and does not belong in a given plot. Put in different terms, to motivate a plot is to identify or, rather, to posit the rules that govern a particular relation between *fabula* and *sjuzhet*; it is to see that which governs the aesthetic arrangement of events – or story – at the level of narrative discourse.

Tomashevsky goes on to discuss *realistic motivation*, which refers to the idea that events, characters, and objects need to be believable within the terms of world or plot in which they exist: "We demand an element of 'illusion' in any work. No matter how convention-filled and artistic it is, our perception of it must be accompanied by a feeling that what happens in it is 'real.'"[55] Fair enough: but what does it mean that Tomashevsky links the apparently opposed terms "real" and "illusion"? His point is that narrative believability is not a matter of testing a given event or image against our ideas and expectations about the "real world" but rather a matter of seeing it in relation to the particular rules that exist internal to a particular plot, the particular rules that *motivate* or make sense of the characters, objects, and events that make up that plot. For instance, while we know that rubbing an old lamp three, thirty, or three hundred times in the real world will produce no effect (except for maybe a sore arm and a very clean lamp), it is self-evident that in some fairy tales rubbing an old lamp three and exactly three times will release the genie that lives inside. What is more, we also understand that rubbing the lamp two or four times will not work and that those seemingly arbitrary differences take on the status of a natural law in a fairy tale. For instance, in Melville's "Bartleby, the Scrivener" (1853), the lawyer-narrator finds that he needs to call Bartleby three times before he will appear: "Like a very ghost, agreeably to the laws of magical invocation, at the third summons, he appeared at the entrance of his hermitage." Why at the third summons? Because in the topsy-turvy world Bartleby's appearance has brought into being, events just work that way. Particular plots and particular genres thus depend on the tacit presence of rules and norms that allow a reader to differentiate between what is believable and unbelievable within and only within the world of that particular plot or genre.

We might think here of Samuel Taylor Coleridge's famous account of the "willing suspension of disbelief," which we can understand as the willingness to suspend everyday beliefs while in effect doubling down on the beliefs that structure a particular plot; we might also think of Tzvetan Todorov's account of the several meanings of *verisimilitude*, which can refer to a simple "relation with reality," to a more complicated "relation of the specific text to another, more generalized text which is called 'common opinion,'" and to a relation that exists not between the text and the natural or the social world but rather between the parts of a text and the immanent and generically specific rules that govern the appearance of those parts: "Comedy has its own verisimilitude, different from tragedy's; there are as many verisimilitudes as there are genres, and the two notions tend to meld into each other."[56] Gérard Genette writes that

> a *vraisemblable* narrative is thus a narrative where the actions answer, as so many applications of particular cases, to a body of maxims accepted as true by the public to which the narrative is addressed; but these maxims, due to the very fact that they are accepted, most often remain implicit. The relation between the *vraisemblable* narrative and the system of *vraisemblance* to which it is attached is thus essentially silent: generic conventions function as a system of natural forces and constraints, which the narrative follows as if without perceiving and, *a fortiori*, without naming.[57]

The rules immanent to every plot thus allow us to say what does and does not belong or what is and is not allowed within that plot; this is, then, another form of motivation.

We might also think of *realistic motivation* in terms of recent work that links narrative theory to *possible-worlds theory*, a notion imported from philosophy. As Marie-Laure Ryan describes it, possible-worlds theory was developed "by a group of philosophers including David Lewis, Saul Kripke, and Jaako Hintikka to solve problems in formal semantics, such as the truth value of counterfactuals, the meaning of modal operators of necessity and possibility, and the distinction between intension and extension (or sense and reference)."[58] She goes on to define possible-worlds theory as "the set-theoretical idea that reality – the sum total of the imaginable – is a universe composed of a plurality of distinct elements, or worlds, and that it is hierarchically structured by the opposition of one well-designated element, which functions as the center of the system, to all the other members of the set. The central element is commonly interpreted as 'the actual world' and the satellites as merely possible worlds."[59] The value of possible-worlds theory is that it allows us to map out what is required for those of us who inhabit "the actual world" to negotiate both the different interpretations that individuals have of the same world (you believe in magic lamps and I do not), different interpretations that thus produce a plurality of actual worlds and, more to the point, the different kinds of *nonactual possible worlds* that we encounter in literary or cinematic narratives, worlds that we can imagine but also recognize as outside or other than what we call the real world. Part of what immersing ourselves in different nonactual possible worlds demands is navigating the relative distance of different worlds from the rules that govern our actual world: "If we interpret possible worlds as textual worlds, the model predicts that for most readers the world of the realist novel is closer to reality than the world of the fairy tale, because its actualization does not require a modification of physical laws."[60] In other words, the degree to which we need as readers to suspend disbelief can be measured in terms of the distance between the actual and a particular fictional possible world. Ryan goes on to suggest that the move "into" a nonfactual possible world requires a kind of imaginative "recentering": "Insofar as fictional worlds are, objectively speaking, nonfactual possible worlds, it takes reentering to experience them as actual – an experience that forms the basic condition for immersive reading."[61] For Lubomir Dolezel, possible-worlds theory also offers a useful methodological test with which to distinguish among different kinds of narrative:

> The relationships between possible worlds, their similarities and differences, are determined by comparing or contrasting their macromorphologies. Relocating the problem of fiction and history from the level of discourse to the level of world means asking whether the possible worlds of history and fiction are homomorphous or whether they show some marked macrostructural differences.[62]

David Herman, drawing instead on methods taken from cognitive science, offers a different but related account of how narrative *storyworlds* motivate relations among *existents, events, actions,* and *states*: "I use *storyworld* to suggest something of the world-creating power of narrative, its ability to transport interpreters from the here and now of face-to-face interaction, or the space-time coordinates of an encounter with a printed text or a cinematic narrative, to the here and now that constitute the deictic center of the world being told about."[63] Put back in the less precise but no less compelling terms of Tomashevsky's scheme, to read a plot depends on our accepting that particular form of motivation, which is to say the particular set of implicit and explicit rules that governs the association of part to part and part to whole; it is, in other words, temporarily to accept rules that govern another nonfactual but possible reality.

Tomashevsky's third form of motivation is maybe the most complicated because most historical: *artistic motivation*, which refers to the historically specific codes and conventions that govern the production of plots at a given moment in time; it refers in other words to the history of literary style, a history of changing rules or fashions that govern what is or is not *appropriate* to a particular plot or genre at a particular moment in time: "Usually quarrels between new and old literary groups arise over artistic motivation. The old, tradition-oriented group generally denies the artistry of the new literary form.

This is shown, for example, in poetic diction, where the use of individual words must be in accord with firmly established literary traditions."[64] Tomashevsky's sense of literary history as an ongoing sequence of changing motivations adds an important level of complexity to the Formalist method. That is, where it can seem that Shklovsky and the others were solely committed to the play of forms within a given text, the presence of an extrinsic logic of historical change within or amid the intrinsic rules that govern the selection and arrangement of parts into a plot not only imagines a real and dialectical point of contact between the text and the world but also imagines history as a particularly mobile plot of its own.

Years later, Shklovsky reiterated the point: "The concept of the whole is historical and it changes."[65] Fredric Jameson writes that, with the notion of artistic motivation, Russian Formalism

> permits a new concept of literary history: not that of some profound
> continuity of tradition characteristic of idealistic history, but one of
> history as a series of abrupt discontinuities, of ruptures with the past,
> where each new literary present is seen as a break with the dominant
> artistic canons of the generation immediately preceding . . . the
> Formalists saw this perpetual change, this artistic permanent revolution,
> as being inherent in the nature of artistic form itself, which, once
> striking and fresh, grows stale and must be replaced by the new in
> unforeseen and unforeseeable manners.[66]

We might think, for example, of the rise and fall of the epistolary style as a series of moments that put pressure on and revealed the movement of artistic motivation. Where for much of the eighteenth century in France and England, novels routinely and successfully took the form of letters sent between characters (*Pamela* and *Clarissa*, *Les Liaisons dangereuses*, and *The Sorrows of Young Werther*) that form seemed to have reached a point of exhaustion at about the time that Jane Austen began to write her great novels. An early draft of *Pride and Prejudice* (1813), called "First Impressions," in fact took an epistolary form, and traces of that older style are still apparent in the finished novel, in its reliance on the timed arrival of letters for its plot as well as in the "quoted" appearance of a few key letters within the novel itself. There is, for instance, the lengthy scene in which Elizabeth and Miss Bingley look on as Mr. Darcy writes a letter: "How delighted Miss Darcy will be to receive such a letter!"[67] It is a letter from Miss Bingley to Jane that temporarily dashes the latter's hopes of happiness with the former lady's brother. And, most importantly, it is as a result of reading a long letter from Mr. Darcy that Elizabeth at last changes her mind – loses her prejudices – about him and, really, about everything: "She could only think of her letter."[68] Seen in relation to Toma-shevsky's concept of artistic motivation, Austen's use of the letter both gestures back to a literary style that had become antiquated and makes clear the difference and relation between her new devices – omniscient narration, free indirect style, etc. – and the old. Indeed, thinking back to my discussion of Marx, the more or less undigested appearance of epistolary matter within a novel self-consciously committed to newer, more sophisticated techniques creates the effect of a conflict among what Raymond Williams called the residual, the dominant, and the emergent, the three different temporal rela-tions that cultural productions can take in relation to history as such. This, of course, makes sense within *Pride and Prejudice*, a novel that is about the idea of a new and more modern conception of love and courtship coming into soft conflict with older, more "prejudiced" models.

We might also consider the move from the novel of letters to the omnisci-ently narrated novel in the light of Susan Lanser's recent feminist and queer analysis of the difference between forms of *homodiegetic* and *heterodiegetic* narration as it opens or closes the possibility of representing intimacy between women. Lanser takes her terms from Genette, who differentiates, as we will see in the next chapter, between *heterodiegetic* narrators, who do *not* belong to the situations they recount, and *homodiegetic* narrators – such as Jane Eyre or Nick Carraway – who are or were characters in the situations they describe. The move from an epistolary form – where narrative was the result of women writing and speaking to one another on the same diegetic level – to later forms of narrative – where narrator and narratee exist on opposite sides of a formal divide – makes impossible or difficult an older kind of narrative intimacy between women. On the one hand, as Austen moves away from the epistolary form and its letters between women, she moves toward a model that places a heterodiegetic narrator on the "safe" side of an existential divide; on the other hand, "what in light of the novel's history amounts to the wary withholding of female intimacy on the level of narration becomes all but completed in a novel like *Jane Eyre*, in which the confidante is an anonymous and voiceless reader and Jane's beloved friend Helen Burns has been killed off."[69] (This work expands on Lanser's earlier effort in *Fictions of Authority* to replace Genette's simple opposition between heterodiegetic and homodiegetic narration with a more socially nuanced account of narration's possible relations to what is narrated: "authorial voice," "personal voice," and "communal voice.") For Lanser, in other words, the Russian Formalist sense of *artistic motivation*, precisely because it straddles a line between history and form, might provide another lens through which to consider the necessary and necessarily political mixing of narrative form and narrative content: "I will suggest that the intersections of narrative theory with the history of sexuality make the case for both a more consciously historicized narratology and a more consciously narratological history of sexuality."[70]

Insofar as Austen uses the device of the letter in a self-aware and innovative way, she calls attention to its appropriate place within her whole plot (*compositional motivation*); she underscores the special, even magical force of the letter within her novel's world (*realistic motivation*); and, because she *lays bare the device* and its difference from earlier styles, she makes an audacious claim for its propriety in relation to a new set of rules (*artistic motivation*). If, in other words, we understand *motivation* as the rules that govern the selection and arrangement of appropriate motifs within a given plot, then we need to draw together the related demands of form, genre, and style in order to have a full sense of what should and should not appear. It is also against this tripartite sense of motivation that we can understand the different ways in which especially great artists can identify, diverge from, and sometimes remake those rules. I have talked about Austen as one such innovator and, as we have seen, Shklovsky looked to Laurence Sterne as another; we might also think about Bakhtin's sense of Dostoevsky as someone who did something new with character or the late Lukács's admiration for Tolstoy and Balzac as writers who made the novel see the real, which is to say history, more clearly than anyone had before. In each case, artistic achievement is understood as a reconfiguration of the historically specific rules that govern both the production of narratives, which is to say the arrangement of story into discourse, and, implicitly, our ability to engage with and to see the world.

~

I mentioned earlier that there was a sort of implicit division in Shklovsky's thinking about the relationship among art, narrative, and the device. First, the idea of *literariness*, of literature as an activity that calls attention to its own motivations and to the rules that govern its structures and that allow for its coherence, allows us to understand literary art as always engaged in its own defamiliarization. That is, because the literary work points to its own material existence, to the words and forms that exist independently of any particular content, it allows neither form nor content to take on the status of the natural, the habitual, or the self-evident. This leads to a second aspect of Shklovsky's thinking, the fact that, despite his claim to have limited his attention to literature as literature and nothing else, he nonetheless believes that the artwork's defamiliarization of itself opens the door to a wider-ranging defamiliarization of the world; because the artwork denies us the comfort of remaining numb to the world, it serves – regardless of its particular content – as an evergreen reminder of what the world really is. This allows us to see Russian Formalism as an especially corrosive because especially restless form of ideology critique: as Jameson puts it, "The effect of habituation is to make us believe in the eternity of the present, to strengthen us in the feeling that the things and events among which we live are somehow 'natural,' which is to say permanent."[71] Because *literariness* calls attention to both the artificiality and the historicity of convention and conventional beliefs, it allows or rather forces us to move endlessly forward, to discard ideas as soon as they begin to shade into habit or dogma. The Russian Formalists tended to see this aesthetic truth telling not merely as a kind of criticism but rather as a way to confront the essential and sometimes overwhelming difficulty of things; as Jameson suggests, "Art is in this context a way of restoring conscious experience, of breaking through deadening and mechanical habits of conduct … and allowing us to be reborn to the world in its existential freshness and horror."[72] As I suggested in the Introduction, Shklovsky's own experience was significantly but not unusually dire; after participating in an attempted and failed anti-Bolshevik coup, Shklovsky chose exile before ultimately returning to the Soviet Union, where he experienced hunger, loss, disavowal; where he saw friends die; and where he was forced, as we have seen, to betray or to at least suppress his beliefs about both art and life. Even so, he chose to see these conditions not only as an impediment or a failure but also as a particularly horrible but productive set of aesthetic constraints, limits that forced him into modes of thinking and expression that would have been unnecessary otherwise. These are what he referred to as his *knight's moves*, ways across the board that combine a necessary recognition of the given historical limits with an oblique and strategic sense of indirection or play. There is not space here to go into the mix of intelligence, compromise, hunger, exile, death, and disaster that served as the real backdrop for what can feel like airless debates about the relation between form and content in literary narrative. Suffice it to say that Shklovsky and the Russian Formalists give us yet another opportunity to reflect on the seemingly necessary relation among uncertainty, danger, and the most powerful forms of narrative theory.

5.3 Differences without Positive Terms: Ferdinand de Saussure and the Structuralist Turn

Although Ferdinand de Saussure never published some of his most important ideas about the nature and object of linguistics, his students took careful notes over the course of his three series of lectures in 1907, 1908–1909, and 1910–1911. In 1916, three years after Saussure's death, two of those students – Charles Bally and Albert Sechehaye – assembled, edited, and published the notes as the famous *Course in General Linguistics*. Bally and Sechehaye write in their preface to the first edition that, "all those who had the privilege of participating in his richly rewarding instruction regretted that no book had resulted from it. After his death, we hoped to find in his manuscripts, obligingly made available to us by Mme. de Saussure, a faithful or at least an adequate outline of his inspiring lectures. At first we thought that we might simply collate F. de Saussure's personal notes and the notes of his students. We were grossly misled. ... We had to fall back on the notes collected by students during the course of his three series of lectures."[73]

Reassembled from those notes, Saussure's *Course* is built around a single, simple but powerful methodological claim: that the nineteenth-century study of language faltered because it had failed properly to identify and to delineate its object of study. This was, to a certain extent, understandable. Something as pervasive, as essential, as really universal as language will not and should not be reduced to a single definition. Language is a *historical* fact, having been at the center of every recorded human experience; it is a *social* fact, providing the basis for most if not all exchanges among human beings; it is a *material* fact, taking, as it does, the various forms of sound waves traveling through the air, words written on the page, or symbols transmitted pictorially or physically from one person to another; one could continue this list indefinitely. With so many aspects to language, it made sense that researchers who had sought to understand its nature and use might have become confused, mixing up aspects, and looking in one place where the answers to their questions would be found in another.[74] So, in the same way that Propp and the Russian Formalists began by limiting their focus to what made the fairy tale a fairy tale or to what was essentially *literary* about literature, Saussure begins by attempting to define his object of study, to identify, in other words, what can be considered exclusively or technically *linguistic* about language. And, like those other figures, Saussure seemed to take this reduction as an almost ethical responsibility; in an 1894 letter, he writes that "the utter inadequacy of current terminology, the need to reform it and, in order to do that, to demonstrate what sort of object language is, continually spoil my pleasure in philology, though I have no dearer wish than not to be made to think about the nature of language in general."[75] For Saussure, thinking about language *as* language was something he apparently felt he had to do.

Saussure's answer was not to reduce language to one or another of its aspects but rather to limit his methodological attention to what language did as it was passed significantly between an addresser and an addressee in a given communicative situation: "In order to separate from the whole of speech the part that belongs to language, we must examine the individual act from which the speaking-circuit can be reconstructed."[76] As a result of restricting his attention to the "speaking-circuit," Saussure was able to reduce language as an object of study to the way in which sounds were associated with concepts, and vice versa, the way in which one's private ideas could find more or less communicable and thus public expression in words. This was the question: how, if language were reduced to the scene of two people speaking, of two people making private thoughts public, could we understand what made language possible? "Among all the individuals that are linked together by speech, some sort of average will be set up: all will reproduce – not exactly of course, but approximately – the same signs united with the same concepts."[77] What mechanism makes this more or less faithful mode of communication possible? What allowed a speaker to associate a sound with an idea, to send that sound across a room, and to know that a listener would be able to associate the sound with the same or something at least like the same concept? How, in other words, does language allow the private contents of one person's mind to take public form before becoming the private property of another person's mind? The process is, after all, both simple and miraculous; it sees what is ultimately unknowable – what goes on in the heart or mind of another – become at least partly knowable. For Saussure, the recognition of this everyday magic led to two areas of inquiry. First, what are the shared conditions that allow members of a community to communicate with one another? If we can understand one another, it must be because we are operating according to some shared set of rules, some tacit framework that would govern the shared association of words and ideas. Second, what is the nature of the linguistic sign, the thing that is in fact passed back and forth among speakers when they communicate? If communication is an act of moving back and forth between thoughts and words, how does that process work? What is the stuff of language? In order to address these related levels of his inquiry, Saussure identifies two pairs of terms that he derives from the linguistic situation and that provide the basis for structuralist linguistics and for the fields that were subsequently inspired by Saussure's thinking; they are *langue* and *parole*, on the one hand, and *signifier* and *signified*, on the other.

~

First, *langue* and *parole*: for Saussure *langue* refers to all of the materials and moves available to language users in a particular language community at a particular moment in time and space; it is the totality of rules and units that are *potentially* available to speakers of the same language at the same time:

> If we could embrace the sum of word-images stored in the minds of all individuals, we could identify the social bond that constitutes *langue*. It is a storehouse filled by the members of a given community through their active use of speaking, a grammatical system that has a potential existence in each brain, or, more specifically, in the brains of a group of individuals. For language is not complete in any speaker; it exists perfectly only within a collectivity.[78]

The classic analogy here is a game of chess. When one sits down to a game of chess, one assumes a shared access to and understanding of the units that make up the game – the pieces, the board, etc. – and the rules that govern the way those units can be used. If one knows how to play chess, one thus has the *potential* to play an indefinitely large number of different games even if one only ever plays a few or one or none at all. Language works in the same way: if one knows the rules and the units of a language, one *can* make an indefinitely large number of meaningful statements even if one never does. Knowing a language is to be able to say all the things one has said and will say along with all the things one never said but could have said; *langue* is, in a sense, a potential waiting to be realized.

We can, in other words, think of *langue* as the shared set of rules, conventions, and assumptions that govern the production and reception of speech, as the conceptual backdrop against which communication between individuals within a community occurs at a particular moment in time. Although language of course has a history, linguistics is concerned not with how it changes over time but rather with how it is structured at one hypothetical moment in time. This is once again a form of methodological reduction; although Saussure recognizes language as profoundly historical, he argues that the study of language needs to proceed *as if* it were possible to freeze language, to see how all of its rules and parts work together at a given moment in time: "Each state of a language of course carries over the bulk of its content from the state that preceded it. But as a system, each state is new, and what determines its fundamental nature is not inherited, but 'what exists at a given moment.'"[79] Think again of chess: when one sits down to a game, the history of its rules does not matter; knowing the long and rich history of the game is fascinating, but it will not help you to win or even tell you how to play. What matters is that you know the rules in the more or less same way an opponent knows them *at the same moment* that he or she knows them. This focus on how language stands – on what it is – at a moment in time as opposed to over the course of its history is the basis of Saussure's famous distinction between *synchronic* and *diachronic* modes of analysis. (I mentioned this distinction in relation to Hegel's theory of tragic conflict in Section 2.2.) To look at a system *diachronically* is to measure its changes over time and, perhaps, to compare its later to its earlier states; this was the method that characterized much thinking about language before Saussure. To look at a system *synchronically* is rather to act *as if* it could be frozen in time so that one could analyze the relation between the parts that constitute it at a particular moment. Jonathan Culler writes that "because the language is a wholly historical entity, always open to change, one must focus on the relations which exist in a particular synchronic state if one is to define its elements."[80] Saussure, of course, understood that the idea that one could stop time to look at a structure as a structure was a fiction; however, like Max Weber's "ideal types" it was a necessary, self-conscious, and immensely productive fiction: "Saussure's concept of *langue* needs to be seen as an idealization which is needed in order to define the boundaries of a new scientific endeavor. Similarly, for him the opposition between synchrony and diachrony likewise represents a necessary scientific distinction."[81]

If *langue* thus refers to the shared "sum of word-images," to the linguistic potential that defines a linguistic community at a given moment in time and thus serves as the rules against which individual acts of communication take place, then *parole* refers to speaking as it, in fact, happens; to individual acts of communication; to the concrete ways in which individuals put words and ideas together, drawing from that "storehouse" and relying on those shared rules. Barthes writes, "In contrast to [*langue*], which is both institution and system, speech [or *parole*] is essentially an individual act of selection and actualization; it is made in the first place of the 'combination thanks to which the speaking subject can use the code of the language with a view of expressing his personal thought. . ., and secondly by the 'psycho-physical mechanisms which allow him to exteriorize these combinations.'"[82] If, in other words, *langue* names all of the things that one could say at a given time in a given place, *parole* refers to what individuals do in fact say to one another. We might think here of the linguist Noam Chomsky's distinction between *linguistic competence* and *linguistic performance*; for Chomsky, linguistics is the study of the reciprocal relation between what we understand to be a speaker's full capacity or competence under ideal circumstances and the particular forms that linguistic performances take:

> Linguistic theory is concerned primarily with an ideal speaker-listener, in a completely homogeneous speech-community, who

knows its (the speech community's) language perfectly and is
unaffected by such grammatically irrelevant conditions as memory
limitations, distractions, shifts of attention and interest, and errors
(random or characteristic) in applying his knowledge of this language
in actual performance.[83]

As Chomsky understands it, once restricted in the terms that Saussure
proposes, linguistics emerges as the study of the relation between the things
that people could say and what in fact they actually say; or, as Barthes suggests
in *Elements of Semiology*, "Language and speech: each of these two terms of
course achieves its full definition only in the dialectical process which unites
one to the other: there is no language without speech, and no speech outside
language."[84] Once again, we need to keep in mind that, although the two
terms are used methodologically as if they named different substances, they
are in fact reciprocally implicated aspects of one and the same thing.

The other key relation in Saussure's linguistics is between the two things
that linguistic competence allows speakers to put together in order to produce
speech: the sound pattern and the concept or, to use the more technical terms,
signifier and *signified*. If, in other words, *langue* allows speakers to speak, to
produce realized instances of *parole*, that is because it is the shared set of rules
that governs the association of sounds and concepts, signifiers and signifieds;
and because linguistics is committed to the study not of one or the other term
alone but rather of their relation to one another, Saussure introduces a third,
synthetic term, *sign*: "The linguistic sign unites, not a thing and a name, but a
concept [or signified] and a sound-image [or signifier]."[85] In these terms,
"signified" names the private matter or content of an individual's thoughts;
"signifier" names the form that that conceptual content takes when it is put
into words and transmitted from one individual to another; and "sign" names
the constitutive relation between the first two terms: "The sign," writes
Barthes, "is therefore a compound of a signifier and a signified. The plane
of the signifiers constitute the *plane of expression* and that of the signified the
plane of content."[86] Much of Saussure's thinking and influence turns on the
complex nature of that relationship. It is important to note here that, as he
focuses on the conceptual relation between signifier and signified, Saussure
needs methodologically to bracket the question of the *referent*, "the object," as
Fredric Jameson says, "in the reality outside the mind, where its merely
mental image is registered."[87] Signification is not, in other words, about the
relation between words and objects; it is, for Saussure and from the point of
view of his methodological reduction, restricted to the strictly conceptual
relation between words and ideas.

What characterizes the relation between signifier and signified? First, Saussure says that it is an *arbitrary* relationship. Where some theories of language had assumed a natural and necessary relationship between particular words and things and suggested that a particular word could somehow be more or less naturally suited to the thing that it named, Saussure argues that the association between signifiers and signifieds is purely arbitrary, conventional, and, thus, historically specific; Culler writes that the fact that the sign is arbitrary means in part that "there is no natural or inevitable link between the signifier and the signified. Since I speak English I may use the signifier represented by *dog* to talk about an animal of a particular species, but this sequence of sounds is no better suited to that purpose than another sequence. *Lod, tet,* or *bloop* would serve equally well if it were accepted but members of my speech community."[88] The sign, in that case, is not only the carrier of meaning from one person to another but also evidence of the complicated, culturally specific, and communal rules that govern the possibility of producing signs in a particular way at a particular time; the sign is, in other words, the hinge that connects *langue* and *parole*, the rules that allow for all the combinations between signifier and signified that one could make at a given moment and all the combinations that one in fact makes. And because for Saussure linguistics is the study of *langue*, which is to say the rules that allow for the association of signifiers and signifieds as they find expression in linguistic communication, then the methodological unit of linguistic study is, at last, the sign, that figure for the possibility and the reality of the practical, which is to say social, association of signifier and signified.

While the arbitrary and thus social nature of the signifiers (the sound patterns or words) is easy to see, Saussure also insists on the arbitrary and thus social nature of the signifieds (the private ideas that find public expression in the signifieds). This is a harder idea that we need to consider once again in relation to Saussure's methodological reduction. A psychologist or a philosopher might speculate on the nature of the raw contents of the mind, the brain, the soul, of whatever; from, however, the point of view of *linguistics*, which for Saussure is and only is the analysis of the relation between signifiers and signifieds as they are associated according to the rules of *langue* at a given moment in time in order to produce *parole*, thoughts (signifieds) only meaningfully exist insofar as they can find expression in words (signifiers). In these terms, linguistics assumes that language not only reflects but also to some degree conditions or shapes our thoughts; Saussure states, "The signified associated with a signifier can take any form; there is no essential core of meaning that it must retain in order to count as the proper signified for that signifier."[89]

His point is that, although we might think of our ideas as a stable and prior stuff that finds later expression in the form of speech or writing, signifieds take on their specific meaning at a given time as a later result of the process that links them linguistically to one or another signifier; it is, in other words, the case that just as the presence of a signified within a linguistic community leads to one set of possible signifiers, so does the ultimate choice of one or another signifier remake or condition the meaning of the signified. Just as an idea makes me search for a particular word, so does a particular word limit and condition what ideas I can have. This leads us to another version of the which-came-first question that I first raised in the Introduction; as with the case of story and discourse, it is maybe impossible finally to say which aspect of the sign precedes the other, signifier or signified. This difficult aspect of Saussure's system is central to some later efforts to think about the more or less coercive relation between the social world and the individual, efforts associated with such figures as Jacques Lacan, Louis Althusser, and Michel Foucault; in each case, these writers took inspiration from Saussure in order to understand how the social world not only represents but also *produces* the individuals who constitute it. The social rules we inherit upon joining a particular signifying community are, in other words, at least partly responsible for what it is possible not only to say but also to think.

Because he understands both signifiers and signifieds as arbitrary, Saussure also understands them as "negative and differential," which is to say as meaningful only in relation to one another.[90] Because, in other words, language is a system of units and rules and because no unit carries an essential meaning (no sound or concept is simply what it is), what gives words and ideas their meaning is their position within a system of other relative values. We cannot understand cold without hot, black without white, up without down, the middle without a beginning and an end, etc. It is important to see here that these differences are not the isolated differences between one word or idea and another but the larger difference between any particular word or idea and the whole set of other words or ideas that make up the whole of a given structure, which is to say the particular combination of units and rules that govern the production of individual utterances; "Everything," says Saussure,

> that has been said up to this point boils down to this: in language there are only differences. Even more important: a difference generally implies positive terms between which the difference is set up; but in language there are only differences without positive terms. Whether we take the signified or the signifier, language has neither ideas nor sounds that existed before the linguistic system, but only conceptual and phonic differences that have issued from the system.[91]

The point here is that structuralism demands that we see the individual part not only in relation to the whole but also as meaningful only because it exists as a part among other parts within that whole; the play between rules and units that governs the association of signifiers and signifieds and thus the production of signs is in and of itself the source of what Saussure would call value and what we would call meaning or significance.

In these terms, we can see one reason why Saussure's particular insights found such a wide variety of intellectual homes, influencing anthropology, psychoanalysis, as well as political, literary, and – most importantly for us – narrative theory. Indeed, his work provided the basis for the so-called structuralist turn; François Dosse writes, "The descriptive approach, the prevalence of the idea of system, the concern for going from constructed and explicit procedures back to elementary units, Saussure's new orientation offered all of this and would become the lowest common denominator for the entire structuralist movement."[92] As I have already said, the question of how to think about the relation between fact and value is one that occupied many of the figures I have considered. How is it possible to move from the level of empirical experience to an account of things as connected and meaningful? How, in other words, can we see the isolated facts of experience as adding up to make values? What, to use a word important to both the Russian Formalists and Saussure, *motivates* the relation between part and part and part and whole? With that in mind, we can see where Saussure's account of the structural rules that govern the association of signifiers and signifieds, which, in turn, he understands as necessary to the production of linguistic and conceptual value, would appeal to so many figures; if one wants to know whether and how we can move back and forth between fact and value, Saussure's detailed account of signification as a process helps to give a close and technical analytical force to those questions. His system, in other words, helps to make practical the analysis of value in general. In what follows I will look more closely at how particular theorists – Lévi-Strauss, Barthes, and Genette, among others – used these different terms *langue* and *parole*, *signifier* and *signified* in order to develop their own systems. I want, though, both to anticipate and to reminisce for a moment so as to hint at the wider applicability of Saussure's terms.

In terms of *language* and *parole*: several of the figures I have considered were committed to what I called *the comparative analysis of narrative forms*, to, in other words, understanding how a particular culture's narratives helped to reveal something essential about how those cultures felt and thought. We can formalize that thinking in terms of Saussure; if a particular narrative is an instance of *parole*, it is possible only because it emerges as a performance out of a larger and shared competence, a *langue* that has its own historically and culturally specific character. As we saw with Lukács, Propp, and especially Bakhtin, genre similarly comes to name a way in which a historically specific cultural competence can take form as a textual performance. Even more, Tomashevsky's third form of motivation – *artistic motivation* – assumed that each artist or artistic movement enters into, either supporting or disrupting, a synchronic field of values, conventions, and more or less set aesthetic relations; it is thus in the nature of aesthetic innovation diachronically to upset the terms of one seemingly finished set of synchronic values while beginning to articulate another set, which will in time be upset again. Saussure thus gives a rigorous justification to the notion that just as we need "to know" the rules of narrative in order to understand particular narratives, so should we look at particular narratives in order to understand something fundamental about the logics that organize how a culture thinks; he gives us, in other words, a set of terms within which to relate texts to genres and genres to cultures and cultures to history. And, because what we look at when we look at the embodiment of competence in the form of *parole* is the relation between signifier and signified, the system also helps to give systematic force to the distinction that I have relied on throughout, the distinction between story and discourse. If a sign is what happens either when the stuff of thinking (signifieds) takes shape in the form of organized patterns of sound (signifiers) or when the form of a word or sentence (signifiers) helps to produce or at least to shape a thought (signifieds), then we can see how these relations could coincide with our three terms: story as signified, discourse as signifier, and narrative as sign or, rather, the whole reciprocal relation between the first two.

Attentive readers will have noticed that this alignment of signified and signifier with story and discourse leaves no room for what I previously called *the referent*, the "really real" stuff to which signs somehow refer. We can think about the status of that third term in a few ways. First, as we have seen, many narrative theorists are happy indeed to leave the referent out of the equation and instead to treat the story–discourse relation as a closed conceptual circuit; these would include figures who see story as an imaginative back-formation produced as a result of a discourse that in fact occurs first. Second, there are those who more or less consciously assume a point of contact between signifier and referent, figures who would maintain a relation between the stuff of story and the stuff of history or the world; this can take the form of an assumed or untested convergence between signified and referent (for instance, Jameson writes that "Shklovsky himself always implied a kind of convergence between signified and referent") or, as we will see with Lévi-Strauss and

Griemas, *deep structures* that, while at last remaining within the signifying circuit, seem nonetheless to approach the condition of the really real.[93]

What we see, in that case, is that Saussure's system takes us back to the paradox with which we began, the fact that the order of terms in narrative theory – story and discourse or discourse and story – must remain a problem. The point here is perhaps that, as Saussure understood, we need to see signifier and signified, discourse and story not as things different in kind but rather as related aspects of the same much larger human system, a fundamentally *problematic* system that he proposes to organize under the terms of a general science of semiology; he writes:

> A science that studies the life of signs within society is conceivable; it would be a part of social psychology and consequently of general psychology; I shall call it semiology (from the Greek semeion "sign"). Semiology would show what constitutes signs, what laws govern them. Since the science does not yet exist, no one can say what it would be; but it has a right to existence, a place staked out in advance.[94]

The point here is that several of the figures to whom I will now turn accepted Saussure's challenge and, alongside similar work in anthropology, psychoanalysis, political theory, and so on, felt that narrative could and should also be understood as part of that "science that studies the life of signs." In the case of narrative and narrative theory, work that seeks to understand the character and the function of narrative in these terms is often referred to as narratology, which provides the basis for much contemporary narrative theory.

5.4 The Elementary Structures of Story and Discourse: Claude Lévi-Strauss and the Narrative Analysis of Myth

The next major figure to take up Saussure's terms and to apply them to a semiotic system other than language proper was the anthropologist Claude Lévi-Strauss. Lévi-Strauss first turned to Saussure and structuralism in the 1940s when he met Roman Jakobson – as we know, another figure crucial to the development of narrative theory – while both were European exiles seeking refuge in New York City. Lévi-Strauss and the elder Jakobson became friends and interlocutors and began to attend each other's lectures: "Jakobson's on phonetics and Lévi-Strauss's on kinship."[95] Jakobson's work, which, as I have said, had already begun to synthesize Saussure's thinking about structure and signification with the Russian Formalists' interlocking interest in defamiliarization and literary history, provided Lévi-Strauss with a necessary way to step back from the sheer amount of empirical data that resulted from anthropological field work; Patrick Wilcken writes that "the symbiosis of their respective research gave birth to structural anthropology."[96] When Claude Lévi-Strauss returned to Paris in 1945, French intellectual life was organized around a few central figures (most centrally Jean-Paul Sartre) as well as around varieties of phenomenology that had emerged from Jean Hyppolite's and Alexandre Kojève's celebrated lectures on Hegel, on the one hand, and from the French encounter with Husserl and Heidegger, on the other. As Wilcken indicates, Lévi-Strauss's very different investments entered the French scene at an oblique and, as it turned out, seductive angle: "Lévi-Strauss's experiences had been very different. Through Jakobson, he had been exposed to Saussure and the Prague and Vienna linguistic schools – a genealogy that had largely bypassed France, where linguistics was still relatively backward."[97] As a result, then, of the publication of several works – *The Elementary Structures of Kinship* (1949), *The Savage Mind* (1962), and *Tristes Tropiques* (1955) – Lévi-Strauss would come to have more and more of an influence, giving Saussure and Jakobson a new critical prominence and directly influencing a number of the most important postwar figures: Barthes, Michel Foucault, Jacques Derrida, Jacques Lacan, and so on. "The fingerprints of Lévi-Strauss were all over these diverse projects. At different points, Lacan, Barthes, Foucault and Braudel openly acknowledged his impact on their thinking."[98] In addition to his embrace of linguistics, the analogic turn of Lévi-Strauss's mind helped to reveal new and newly adaptable versions of Marx and Freud, a fact that encouraged subsequent thinkers not only to look forward and back but also to see large areas of overlap among methods that had once seemed more or less mutually exclusive. One can see this analogic imagination at work in the concluding chapters of *The Elementary Structures of Kinship*, where the Marxian money form of the commodity, the Freudian Oedipal subject, the Maussian gift, and the structuralist relation between *langue* and *parole* appear in a beautiful and deeply ambitious synthesis: "Experimental study of the facts can join with the philosophers' presentiments, not only in attesting that this is what happened, but in describing, or beginning to describe, how things happened."[99] As a result, then, of Lévi-Strauss's increasing centrality, a rapprochement between Saussure and structural linguistics, on the one hand, and Marx, Nietzsche, and Freud, on the other, became more and more of a shared cultural project, one that both complemented and supplemented the primary influences of the previous generation. As Vincent Descombes characterizes it, "In the recent evolution of philosophy in France we can trace the passage from the generation known after 1945 as that of the 'three H's' [Hegel, Husserl, and Heidegger] to the generation known inside 1960 as that of the three 'masters of suspicion' Marx, Nietzsche, and Freud."[100]

Just as the Formalists sought to restrict literary analysis to literariness and just as Saussure was committed to identifying what was properly linguistic about language, so was Lévi-Strauss able to use structuralist methods to cut through the noise of data and disciplinary confusion in order to identify the patterns and rules that seemed in fact to govern human kinship:

> As Lévi-Strauss continued his course on kinship, the fit seemed uncanny. Kinship was, after all, a relational system par excellence. Kin diagrams naturally lent themselves to simple oppositions: male/female; in marriage/out marriage; opposing moieties, clans and grades. Running underneath the drama of human relations were unspoken rules, unconsciously observed, which allowed groups of people to communicate with almost mathematical efficiency down the generations. Although the array of bizarre marriage rules seemed baffling in isolation, taken as a set—as contrasting strategies within an overall system – Lévi-Strauss could begin to see the outlines of a grand scheme.[101]

Just as Saussure sought to redirect the linguist's attention from the whole human fact of language to a handful of binary relations that appeared to govern the production of signs and thus meaning (*langue* and *parole*, signifier and signified, synchronic and diachronic), so did Lévi-Strauss begin to perceive a few shared and structuring rules (the incest taboo, reciprocity, the traffic in women) behind the otherwise bewildering fact of human relations; and like Saussure, he looked for and seemed to find the *langue* behind the *parole*, the shared rules and relations that allowed different cultures to express themselves in their own particular ways: "Lévi-Strauss made a reduction, in the mathematical sense of the term, by defining a limited number of possibilities as elementary kinship structures."[102] More to the point, Jakobson's influence allowed Lévi-Strauss to imagine and execute an intellectual compromise between the rigor of structural linguistics and the work of his two other great influences, Marx and Freud, a fact that makes him especially important to subsequent theorists – and theorists of narrative – who sought similarly to join these figures together. As with both Saussure and Propp, Lévi-Strauss's methodological reduction allowed him to isolate certain synchronic aspects of human behavior not in order to distance them from history and politics but rather to understand their historical and ideological character in more rigorous terms.

As his work developed, Lévi-Strauss turned from kinship in and of itself to some of the narratives that both underwrite and express what he took as the deep structure of kinship: myth. Take, for example, his classic essay, "The

Structural Study of Myth" (1955). Like Saussure and the Russian Formalists, Lévi-Strauss begins his essay by identifying what he takes as a condition of disciplinary confusion that has interfered with our ability to understand the nature and the structure of myth:

> From a theoretical point of view the situation remains very much the same as it was fifty years ago, namely, chaotic. Myths are still widely interpreted in conflicting ways: as collective dreams, as the outcome of a kind of esthetic play, or as the basis of ritual. Mythological figures are considered as personified abstractions, divinized heroes, or fallen gods. Whatever the hypothesis, the choice amounts to reducing mythology either to idle play or to a crude kind of philosophic speculation.[103]

As a result of this chaotic situation, Lévi-Strauss goes on to propose a solution, a scheme that would allow researchers to study what was essentially mythic about myth while leaving other aspects – the social, the historical, the psychological, etc. – to workers in other fields. In order to identify that essentially mythic quality of myth, Lévi-Strauss coordinates two observations: first, that individual myths seem entirely contingent, entirely and radically particular; and, second, that this radical particularity seems undermined by "the astounding similarity between myths collected in widely different regions."[104] The apparently contradictory copresence of radical particularity and wide generality in myth leads him to associate the structure of myth with the structure of a linguistic system that is similarly divided between the particularity of individual speech performances and the shared and general rules that govern and limit the production of those individual speech performances. The question, then, becomes how to reconstruct the shared and implicit rules that govern those performances from the performances themselves: "For language itself can be analyzed into things which are at the same time similar and different. This is precisely what is expressed in Saussure's distinction between *langue* and *parole*, one being the structural side of language, the other the statistical aspect of it, *langue* belonging to a reversible time, *parole* being non-reversible."[105] On the one hand, Lévi-Strauss uses the apparently contradictory copresence of the similar and the different in language as a way to understand that same characteristic of myth; in both cases, the systems are, in a sense, motivated by an immanent and necessary conflict between the particular and the general, a fact that recalls the structuring tension between what I referred to as the *time of men* and the *time of the gods* in Aristotle and classical Greek tragedy. On the other hand, he uses what he takes to be the timelessness of *langue* and the timeliness of *parole* as a way to organize the analysis of myth. In other words, if we want to relate the temporal unfolding of a particular myth to the timeless rules that govern its unfolding, then we need to release the shared, conceptual aspects of myth in general from their position in a particular version of that myth. The work of the structural analysis of myth will unpack the ideas and relations and governing rules that have been put into the misleading because merely temporal arrangement of a particular plot; in order to understand myth as a whole, we need, in a way that prefigures Gérard Genette's characterization of his own work in *Narrative Discourse*, to find the general within the particular, to see that "the general is at the heart of the particular, and therefore (contrary to the common perception) the knowable is at the heart of the mysterious."[106] The analysis of myth reveals precisely the fact that the general, abstract, timeless, and deep structures that govern systems of belief exist not over and above but rather *within* the particular myths that in turn rely on exactly those structures.

Lévi-Strauss's great example is the Oedipus myth. Taking many versions of that myth, he lays out what he takes to be the most common expression of the plot in terms of a sequence of *mythemes,* or what he calls "the gross constituent units" of a myth, which is something like what Propp calls *functions* and what Tomashevsky called *motifs.* "In the method outlined by Lévi-Strauss, structural analysis of a myth required segmenting the text into *mythemes* and then grouping those constituent units into paradigmatic classes, whose members may in fact be dispersed at various points along the syntagmatic chain of the discourse."[107] Laid out in their plotted order, the sequence of "gross constituent units" could look like this: A–B–C–D–E–F–G–H, with A standing for an event such as "Oedipus kills his father" or B standing for "Oedipus marries his mother." In these terms, we could take the whole sequence of those units as the story of the myth, a story that finds individual discursive expressions in its different iterations, as they select, arrange, emphasize, and present different – in some cases wildly different – versions of what Lévi-Strauss imagines as one and the same sequence of mythic events. Once he has identified the "gross constituent units," Lévi-Strauss goes on to think of them in terms of not only their causal or temporal relations but also their thematic relations in order to discover a pattern behind the pattern, a play of conceptual relations and oppositions that gives events a significance that exceeds their position not only in one or another particular discursive arrangement but also in the shared story that itself underwrites all of those discursive arrangements. Thinking of the deep sequence in these terms, he ends up with four thematically organized columns that rearrange the order of the units into something like this: {AF}{BG}{CD}{EH}, with {AF} standing for something like events that indicate the "overrating of blood relations" or events that indicate the "underrating of blood relations."

Decoding the myth in this way reveals a kind of general or deep plot behind the particular surface plot, or rather a general order at work within the story that finds expression in the indefinitely large number of Oedipus variations; it is the deep structure that finds expression in a story that, in turn, is expressed in myriad discursive particulars. Stated in Saussure's terms, the process of freeing the deep and shared cultural themes from the particulars of a given plot allows one to identify how a mythic *langue* stands behind every individual version of a myth, which we can call mythic *parole*; and, because we can now see the mythic *langue* beneath the *parole* we can say something true about the rules that govern the culture or cultures that produced that myth. It is important to see here that Lévi-Strauss is not proposing to have discovered the *origin* of the Oedipus myth, to have found its first or founding form. Indeed, on the contrary, he denies that the versions of a myth can refer to some original, fundamental myth; that they are in some sense copies of an ideal and prior myth. What instead functions as *langue* in his account is something more like culture itself or rather the rules that organize or make possible a culture's thinking.

As Lévi-Strauss himself understood, this sense of culture as a set of implicit and structuring rules is close to a Marxian theory of ideology, a fact that he acknowledges when he admits, as we have already seen, that he "rarely broached a new sociological problem without first stimulating my thought by rereading a few pages of *The 18th Brumaire of Louis Bonaparte*."[108] Behind the myth stands a set of relations that make lived historical significance possible. Once again, this recalls something like what I have called *the comparative analysis of narrative forms*, a narrative theoretical method that I have associated with Lukács, Bakhtin, and others; it helps, in other words, to reveal the logic that governs particular cultures at different times. To identify the scheme of relations that stands as the condition of semantic possibility for a given culture is to see something like a genre in Bakhtin's sense, a categorical arrangement of ideas about time, space, causality, etc., that set the limits of what can be thought or said at a given moment in time. One level of the mythic narrative follows a necessary structure, a deep and irreversible structure; the other is both the transmissible form that that deep structure takes and subject to all manner of transformations as particular versions of the myth are told, retold, and reworked. In this, we can see where Greimas, whom I discussed in Section 5.1, developed his sense of "deep structures" via an engagement with both Propp and Lévi-Strauss; for Greimas and Lévi-Strauss, the analysis of discourse down to story leads to the next question: what deeper, cultural structure is there that allows us to put story into order? We might think, too, of Nietzsche's sense that there was, even beyond the apparent immediacy of the Dionysian, a level of experience that both made representation possible and ultimately resisted representation.

What, though, does Lévi-Strauss in fact learn about the Oedipus myth? He argues that the structure behind the story that underwrites different discursive representations of the Oedipus myth reveals a basic contradiction:

> The myth has to do with the inability, for a culture which holds the belief that mankind is autochthonous ... to find a satisfactory transition between this theory and the knowledge that human beings are actually born from the union of man and woman. Although the problem obviously cannot be solved, the Oedipus myth provides a kind of logical tool which, to phrase it coarsely, replaces the original problem: born from one or born from two? born from different or born from the same?[109]

Lévi-Strauss suggests, in other words, that all versions of the Oedipus story are attempts to come to some kind of terms with an irresolvable mystery: where do people originate? How is it that I can feel that I am from nowhere, that I am "my own person," and yet also know that I am from a mother and a father and, in fact, a whole human history? What does it mean, to state it in terms closer to this project, to feel that I am my own, autonomous narrative; my own beginning, middle, and end; and yet to know without feeling it that I am in fact just one part of a much larger narrative? This is part of what motivates the Sphinx's riddle; when asked, "What walks on four legs in the morning, two in the afternoon, and three in the evening," Oedipus answers, "Man." As I argued in Section 2.1, his answer is, in a sense, a narrative theoretical answer insofar as he manages to join the three necessary parts of an Aristotelian plot into a single, unifying thing; in the context of *Oedipus Rex*, though, it is also a moment of hubris, a moment when Oedipus, because he asserts his narrative autonomy as a man, denies his necessary place in a larger narrative, one that includes, as he comes with horror to learn, a mother and father whom he had tried but fails to escape. It is as a result of learning that he is not "man" (autonomous, general, free, an event in and of himself) but rather only "Oedipus" (a particular man who was born into and named within a narrative already well under way) that Oedipus experiences his tragic fall; his fall is, in other words, a perspectival shift from seeing his part of the world as a whole to seeing it as part of a longer and more complicated story, one that must reduce his sense and the reality of his freedom. The tension between autochthonous birth and sexual reproduction is another version of the tragic conflict between the time of men and the time of the gods, two related but seemingly opposed temporalities that, I argued, Aristotle formalizes as the necessary relation between the event as a discrete part and the event as it merges with other events to form a whole, plotted representation of events. In other words, Lévi-Strauss's narrative analysis of the Oedipus myth leads him to identify as essential a structuring contradiction that is in fact also the founding insight of narrative theory: that story and discourse are aspects of the same narrative whole.

This begins, appropriately enough, to take us full circle insofar as Lévi-Strauss's approach turns out not only to draw on Saussure but also to invoke terms and relations that go back to the very beginning of this book. His sense that the Oedipus myth is, after all, a figure for contradiction or conflict in general marks him as an ancestor of Aristotle, who, as Hegel helped us to see, not only understood the content of tragedy to be conflict but also tacitly understood its structure – the relation between actions and whole representations of actions – as a formal analogue to that other, deeper relation (turtles all the way down). And, if he seems in this way to be the inheritor of Aristotle, Hegel, and, as I have already mentioned, Marx and Freud, his more troubling, resistant sense of narrative as a three-tiered system, where story and discourse and *langue* and *parole* are themselves belated versions of some more fundamentally resistant thing, connects him maybe most powerfully to Nietzsche, whose theory of the torque between Dionysian and Apollonian models was, in the end, a front for a necessarily partial engagement with a force or an idea that would at last and always resist an attempt at representation. To paraphrase Fredric Jameson, behind myth is the history that hurts. That is to say, in both his effort to articulate myth as a narrative response to conflict and his ultimate sense that narrative must fail in the face of that conflict's most radical expressions, Lévi-Strauss reveals ways in which we might see the structural analysis of myth and narrative as a fuller and more rigorous engagement with the whole tradition that I have been working to describe. In other words, rather than seeing his version of structuralism as a break from or culmination of efforts to think about the relation between story and discourse as it recalls other relations (experience and ideas, fact and value, the is and the ought, etc.), we should see the complexity of Lévi-Strauss's narrative analysis as a living engagement with all of the figures I have tried to describe so far. And, just as Lévi-Strauss stands as a kind of synthesis of these several threads of thinking about the relation among experience, meaning, and narrative (who walks with Marx in the morning, Saussure in the afternoon, and Nietzsche at night?), so does his influence have a varied but determinate effect on the next major moment in the development of narrative theory: structuralist and poststructuralist narratology.

Chapter 6

Narratology and Narrative Theory

Kristeva, Barthes, and Genette

Eternity is in love with the productions of time.
William Blake, *The Marriage of Heaven and Hell*

As we begin at last to approach our end, we end up, as it were, back at the beginning of what is usually understood as narrative theory. While I have, in other words, been looking closely at some of the movements, individuals, and ideas that together form what I have been calling a prehistory of narrative theory, our turn now to Julia Kristeva, Roland Barthes, Gérard Genette, and the consolidation of these ideas in the form of structuralist narratology takes us to the point where most accounts of narrative theory rightly begin. Indeed, as I said in the Introduction, although the story–discourse relation is one that we can trace conceptually from Aristotle to the Russian Formalists and beyond, the terms derive their current disciplinary force from a moment in the late 1960s and early 1970s when a combination of intellectual and political conditions – particularly in France – made not only possible but also seemingly necessary a narrative theory that could draw at once on structuralist linguistics, Russian Formalist poetics, and critical theories derived from Marx, Nietzsche, and Freud. As I will suggest, it is with the appearance of Kristeva's, Barthes's, and Genette's major works (along with a number of others that I will mention along the way) that narrative theory begins to take its current institutional shape and to be defined in terms of controversies, problems, questions, and developments internal to it as a discipline.

Where, however, their place as founders of contemporary narrative theory is obvious and secure, what is less visible is their own vital and contested relation to the messy and exciting intellectual context I have been working to sketch out over the course of this book. Although works such as *S/Z: An Essay* (1970) and *Narrative Discourse: An Essay in Method* (1970) can seem to have come from nowhere, they are in fact situated responses to the long tradition of thinking about representation and narrative, story and discourse that I have been trying to map out, a tradition that moves from Aristotelian theories of tragedy to the appearance of the Hegelian dialectic; from the post-Hegelian critical theories of Marx, Nietzsche, and Freud to the literary critical politics of Lukács, Bakhtin, and the Russian Formalists; from the structural linguistics of Saussure to Lévi-Strauss and the structural analysis of myth. More immediate was the effect of the literary journal *Tel Quel* and the writing of Julia Kristeva; where Kristeva's work offered opportunities both to imagine a synthesis among a number of different intellectual traditions (especially those of Hegel, Marx, Freud, Bakhtin, and Saussure) and, even more importantly, to rethink the status of writing *as* writing, *Tel Quel*'s varied aesthetic and political trajectory provides a complicated backdrop for both Genette and Barthes. This is, here at the near-end of our story, to take them as the methodological and self-conscious and contested culmination of a longer and larger intellectual history.

My point here is that, while Genette and Barthes are rightly read as the start of a narratological project that has unfolded in particular ways over the last several decades, it is important to see where narrative theory begins, how it responded to its own moment in time, and what these contexts might have to tell us about necessary if obscure aspects of narrative theory as a whole. That is to say, seen in relation to the rest of their work, their influence, and their historical moment, Kristeva's, Barthes's, and Genette's narratologies appear not only as moments of methodological consolidation, moments when the different threads of stylistics, aesthetics, formalism, and structuralism meet in a potent and self-conscious form of narrative analysis but also as reflections of the larger political and historical problems that run through the whole tradition that I have been working to lay out. Seen – as they must be – in relation to this intellectual history, these works are powerful if tacit efforts at political, cultural, and historical critique as well as some of our most fully elaborated theories of the manifold ways in which story and discourse can be aligned, misaligned, put to work for the status quo, or imagined as an alternative to life as it is. In what follows, I want to look at some of the shared contexts in which Kristeva, Barthes, and Genette worked before moving on to a look at their most influential works of narrative theory, works that, as we will see, do much to set the terms and establish the limits of subsequent theories of narrative.

6.1 It Is What It Isn't: Julia Kristeva and *Tel Quel*

The journal *Tel Quel* was launched in 1960 by Philippe Sollers and subsequently published works by Barthes, Genette, Todorov, Jacques Derrida, Michel Foucault, Julia Kristeva, and many others. The journal took its name from a line of Nietzsche's, which appeared on its masthead: "I want the world and I want it *as it is* [*tel quel*], and I want it again, eternally; I cry insatiably: again! – not just for myself alone, but for the entire play and the entire spectacle; not for the spectacle alone, but fundamentally for me, since I require the spectacle – for it requires me – and because I make it necessary."[1] The journal changed aesthetic and political tack frequently and radically over its more than twenty years of operation, shifting from an aesthetic embrace of Alain Robbe-Grillet and the *nouveau roman* to structuralism and poststructuralism while also making more overtly political moves, which included its tense alliance with the French Communist Party (PCF) in 1967, its reaction to the student protests and strikes of May 1968, and finally its break with the PCF and turn to Maoism in 1971, which culminated in an "ill-advised expedition to the People's Republic of China" in 1974. Despite these several shifts, the journal remained at the center of French intellectual life, helping to launch and to sustain a number of figures crucial to twentieth-century intellectual history.[2] Most importantly for us, the journal helped within this shifting political and intellectual context to further the intellectual synthesis of Marx and Freud with the works of the Russian Formalists and Saussure, an intellectual act that led very directly to the specifically narrative questions that motivated Kristeva, Todorov, Barthes, Genette, and others as they turned their attention more and more to the different types of literary and historical narrative. As I will suggest, it was Kristeva's particular synthesis of political and aesthetic questions along with her systematic and syncretic engagement with Saussure, Levi-Strauss, Marx, Freud, the Russian Formalists, and Bakhtin that set the intellectual stage for some subsequent and very influential works of narrative theory.

Part of *Tel Quel*'s project was archival, an effort to look back and to recover writers and thinkers who had fallen out or to the side of official academic culture. The journal was especially interested in recovering what it saw as the revolutionary quality of some of the nineteenth-century writing that we have already considered, especially writing by Hegel, Marx, Nietzsche, and Freud. Alongside its new and differently engaged interpretations of these figures, the journal also helped to reintroduce a number of more or less outré characters such as Sade, Roussel, Lautréamont, Artaud, Joyce, and Bataille. What is more, the journal was – through the particular efforts of Kristeva and Todorov – directly responsible for the appearance of both Russian Formalism and Bakhtin on the French scene; especially important here was Todorov's 1965 anthology of Russian Formalist essays, which he translated and published as part of the Collection *Tel Quel*; Danielle Marx-Scouras writes that "the publication of the *Théorie de la littérature* was viewed as nothing less than a major event, and it gave *Tel Quel* a new 'scientific' status ... on the

French cultural scene, at a time when the structural analysis of literary texts had become the new intellectual trend."[3] The sudden success of Russian Formalism in France was the result of at least two factors: first, it introduced a rigorous method of poetic analysis into a critical tradition that had more or less lacked a stylistics. According to Marx-Scouras, official "university criticism was suspicious of any critical approach that dared to use conceptual tools tied to linguistics, that dared to return to what Paul Valéry, the French formalist precursor, had called 'the verbal condition of literature.'"[4] Jean-Michel Rabaté writes, "By the mid-1960s *Tel Quel* could be seen as a serious, committed, and unrivaled magazine aiming at disseminating the theory and practice of a literary structuralism which looked very much like a revised version of Russian Formalism."[5] Second, the appearance of Todorov's translations was politically timely as well; where the French intellectual Left had in the past tended to follow the French Communist Party in its opposition to Formalism, the decline of the party over the course of the 1950s and 1960s opened the door to a reassessment of Russian Formalism as a different representative of the communist East, one that could see its way past the aesthetic limits of party-approved socialist realism, on the one hand, and Sartrean "engagement," on the other.

This story is complicated by *Tel Quel*'s alliance with the PCF in the late 1960s. The journal's fraught relationship with the party took several forms: colloquiums held on the relation between Marxism and the new theoretical methods held at Cluny in 1968 and 1970; a partnership between the journal and the party's own monthly publication, *La Nouvelle Critique;* and the establishment of a weekly seminar that, writes Dosse, "identified its objective as putting together an overall Marxist-Structuralist theory. The group included Barthes, Derrida, Klossowski, and many others."[6] These different efforts to relate the journal's work on language and textuality to Marxism and, more, to the particular work of the French Communist Party now seem strange, backward, and, perhaps, simply opportunistic given, first, the party's continued support for the Soviet orthodoxy in the wake of both the suppression of the Hungarian Revolution in 1956 and the invasion of Czechoslovakia in 1968 and, second, the PCF's lack of support for and understanding of the events of May 1968. As the editors of the British *New Left Review* expressed it in a special issue responding to the event in the winter of that year, "The French Communist Party went to great lengths actually to prevent the union of the revolutionary forces."[7] As a result of these and other difficulties, the relationship between *Tel Quel* and the PCF was strained from the start and led in time both to the journal's rejection of the party and to its embrace of a Maoist as opposed to Soviet version of Marxism: "Rejection of the

Communist Party signaled for *Tel Quel* the beginning of a period of considerable interest in, occasionally verging on enthusiasm for, Mao Zedong's version of communism; this lasted until the Chinese leader's death in 1976."[8] More directly relevant for us is the wedge that the developing politicization of *Tel Quel* drove between the journal, on the one hand, and Todorov and Genette (Genette had already left the party in 1956 in the wake of Soviet intervention in Hungary) on the other: "Todorov and Genette would part company with *Tel Quel* circa 1968, as the journal embarked on its phase of 'theoretical terrorism' – the ill-fated alliance with PCF Stalinism – in order to found the more scholarly *Poétique*."[9] As we turn from *Tel Quel* to Kristeva, Barthes, and Genette, it will be important to keep in mind the specificity of this cultural and political moment, its possibilities, and its conceptual limits; it was a moment when different figures were forced to make choices and declare allegiances that cut across levels of politics, political history, literary history, theory, and, at last, assumptions and expectations about the power and potential of narrative forms to reflect, respond to, or, indeed, rewrite the social world. To what degree can or should we see Kristeva's or Barthes's or Genette's narrative theories in relation to the events of May '68 or the differently perceived failure of the French Communist Party to react to those events? Does it make sense to read an apparently apolitical book such as *Narrative Discourse* as having something to say about not only story and discourse but also the unfolding political history of the twentieth century?

Julia Kristeva was one of the most important figures associated with *Tel Quel*, the thinker who turned the journal's attention fully to *writing* as its primary object of analysis and its chief value. Indeed, Kristeva's appearance on the scene in 1965 marked a turning point in Parisian intellectual life: "When the twenty-four-year-old Julia Kristeva arrived in Paris in a snowstorm just before Christmas 1965 with only five dollars in her pocket, this young Bulgarian woman never imagined that she would become the Egeria of structuralism. Indeed, the structuralist period was, along with everything else, an encounter between a daring cultural adventure and a talented woman."[10] Kristeva's influence resulted in large part from her ability to synthesize and to motivate Marx, Hegel, Freud, Saussure, and, later, Bakhtin; and, at the same time that Kristeva was drawing these different figures together, she was also working to make methodologically clear what it meant to see language *as* language, what it meant, in other words, to see language's possibilities and limits alongside and against the insights of other, more or less related fields. In other words, like Propp and Saussure and Lévi–Strauss and the Russian Formalists before her, Kristeva was engaged in an act of methodological reduction, an attempt to identify what was essentially poetic about poetic language. As opposed, in that case, to looking to who wrote it, what it represented, or where it originated, Kristeva was interested in *the writing itself*, in how it worked and in what roles writing and poetic language might have to play in the midst of the enormously significant political events and debates of the day. Kristeva would, of course, go on after the early period I discuss to produce important and controversial works that develop her ideas about writing in the related contexts of psychoanalysis, feminism, and nationalism; given the limits of this project, we will have to focus on what her initial critical synthesis made possible for the specific development and consolidation of narrative theory.

First, from Saussure and Lévi-Strauss she took and advanced the idea that all language exists in the space between the general and the particular, between *langue*, seen as a socially shared system of rules that govern an individual's expression within a linguistic community, and *parole*, the particular forms that language takes as it finds embodied expression in speech and writing. Where, however, all language depends upon this relation between the particular and the general as an implicit structural precondition, specifically poetic language "realizes," embodies, and makes explicit the relation itself, thus calling attention to what other types of language tend to erase:

> Only in poetic language is found the practical realization of the "totality" (though we prefer the term "infinity") of the codes at man's disposition. From this perspective, literary practice is revealed to be the discovery and the exploration the possibilities of language; an activity that frees man from certain linguistic (psychical, social) networks; a dynamism that breaks the inertia of language-habits and offers the linguist a unique opportunity to study the becoming of the signification of signs.[11]

Poetic language shows *langue* – the codes – at work in *parole*; as we saw with Lévi-Strauss and the deep structure of myth, poetic language reveals the otherwise hidden presence of the general at the heart of the particular; and because these codes represent the limits of what is sayable and thinkable at a given moment in time, Kristeva's sense of *writing* as an activity that can reveal the presence and influence of the codes takes on an intensely critical and even political aspect; it calls our attention to the fact that expression is never merely natural, never without its historical or ideological causes and effects.

In this way, Kristeva adapts both Shklovsky's concept of *defamiliarization* and Jakobson's analysis of the "poetic function"; as with both of those models, poetic language appears as language that calls attention not only to its own material form but also to the whole psychosocial apparatus that makes communication between and thus life with other people possible in a particular way at a particular place and time. Kristeva's understanding of *writing* as a form of historical or ideological analysis thus also recalls Bakhtin's understanding of the "chronotope"; she would, in fact, go on to translate Bakhtin's book on Dostoevsky into French in 1973. Susan Stanford Friedman writes that "Kristeva's earliest essays pose a critique of the static analysis of structuralism and call for an identification of textual process. Invoking Bakhtin, Kristeva identifies this process as fundamentally dialogic and intertextual—at the level of word, sentence, and story."[12] Finally, she turns this sense of *writing* into a portable critical method, into a way of drawing an openness out of texts that would otherwise seem committed to closing things down:

> The *book* ... situated within the infinity of poetic language,
> is *finite*: it is not open, but closed, constituted once and for all;
> it has become a principle, *one*, a law, but it is readable as such within a possible opening onto the infinite. This readability of the closed opening onto the infinite is only *completely* accessible to the one who writes, that is, from the point of view of that reflexive productivity which is writing.[13]

Because, as opposed to *writing* as such, the finished book seems to close matters, to imagine the finished collapse of *langue* into *parole*, it is the job of critical reading to reopen the book, to show how all language is always a play between particular expression and a shared set of social and thus ideological rules. It is, in other words, the work of criticism to take the *book*, which is to say language that presents itself as natural, as closed, as monologic, as finished, and to reveal it as *writing*, which is to say as language that knows itself as opening up onto the infinite. (In some of her later work, the opposition between writing and the book will be recast as the opposition between what she calls the *genotext* and the *phenotext*, with the former standing in for a poetic or ironic embodiment of "language's underlying foundation" and the latter denoting language that "obeys rules of communication and presupposes a subject of enunciation and an addressee"; the phenotext is thus what Bakhtin might refer to as an official or monologic text.)[14]

Her take on what she identifies as the *arbitrary* nature of the book or what she elsewhere refers to as *the bounded text* recalls arguments that we saw at work in both James and Lukács:

> All ideological activity appears in the form of utterances compositionally completed. This completion is to be distinguished from the structural finitude to which only a few philosophical systems (Hegel) as well as religions have aspired. The structural finitude characterizes, as a

fundamental trait, the object that our culture consumes as a finished product (effect, impression) while refusing to read the process of its productivity: "literature" – within which the novel occupies a privileged position. The notion of literature coincides with the notion of the novel, as much on account of chronological origins as of structural bounding. Explicit completion is often lacking, ambiguous, or assumed in the text of the novel. This incompletion nevertheless underlies the text's structural finitude.[15]

Kristeva's argument here is that the novel occupies a privileged position in relation to narrative and ideology because of the way it reveals a relation between two apparently opposed ideas. On the one hand, the novel does in fact rely on arbitrary forms of competition or closure, forced biographical or sentimental ends that seem designed to create an effect of finitude and thus ideological closure. On the other hand, precisely because this work is arbitrary, because a novel cannot pretend to achieve the levels of synthesis associated with Hegel's system or with religion, it calls ironic attention to the failure of finitude at exactly the same moment that it attempts – however halfheartedly – to produce finitude as an aesthetic effect: "Nothing in speech can put an end – except arbitrarily – to the infinite concatenation of loops."[16] This play between the effect of finitude and closure and an ironic acknowledgment that finitude is not for us is a version of what we saw both in James when he admitted that the novelist's art consists in drawing a provisional aesthetic circle around relations that "really, universally ... stop nowhere," and in Lukács when he identified the novel with the fact that we moderns want but know that we cannot have totality: the novel, for Lukács, "is the epic of an age in which the extensive totality of life is no longer directly given, in which the immanence of meaning in life has become a problem, yet which still thinks in terms of totality."[17] Kristeva characterizes what Lukács would call irony as a text's *productivity*: "The text is therefore a productivity, and this means: first, that its relationship to the language in which it is situated is redistributive (destructive-constructive), and hence can be better approached through logical categories rather than linguistic ones; and second, that it is a permutation of texts, an intertextuality: in the space of a given text, several utterances, taken from other texts, intersect and neutralize one another."[18] In another context she makes the critical force of a text's productivity – its materiality, its irony, to use the Russian Formalist phrase, its literariness – more apparent: "this thinking points to a truth, namely, that the kind of activity encouraged and privileged by (capitalist) society represses the *process* pervading the body and the subject, and that we must therefore break out of our interpersonal and interracial experience if we are to gain access to what is repressed in the social mechanism: the generating of significance." Stated differently, Kristeva takes literature's self-conscious attention to its own matter and rules as a semiotic (which is to say as a self-consciously and immanently *in-process*) basis for a frankly revolutionary way of thinking about the body, about desire, about gender, and about possibility insofar as these have been limited by but continue nonetheless to exceed the symbolic structures (Bakhtin might again have called them chronotopes) that define an individual's relation to a social world at a given moment in time.

As both a methodological advance and as an intellectual consolidation, Kristeva's work is enormously important to the history of narrative theory. Although, like other figures we have looked at (and most immediately Bakhtin), she tends to focus her attention on particular narrative genres, Kristeva's large and rigorous synthesis of Russian Formalism, structuralism, psychoanalysis, and Marxism form an important backdrop for methodological assumptions necessary to the subsequent development of narrative theory (this is especially so for Barthes, whose sense of the readerly and the writerly is, as we shall see, taken directly from Kristeva). We need, however, also to see the enormous political hopes that Kristeva and others had for this theoretical synthesis as well as for the kind of attention she and others at *Tel Quel* paid to language in general and to literary language in particular. This is to return to how thinking about narrative in relation to Saussure's semiology or about the novel as bound or unbound is related to *Tel Quel*'s fraught political backdrop, its encounters with Marxism, the PCF, and, later, Maoism. What does the study of narrative and the novel have to do with revolution? In a 1971 essay on Barthes's work, Kristeva makes big claims for the role that literature and literary analysis have to play in world history:

> How does literature achieve this positive subversion of the old universe?
> How does there emerge, through its practical experience, a negativity
> germane to the subject as well as to history, capable of clearing away
> ideologies and even "natural" languages in order to formulate new
> signifying devices? How does it condense the shattering of the subject, as
> well as that of society, into a new apportionment of relationships
> between the symbolic and the real, the subjective and the objective?[19]

Although cast as a series of questions, Kristeva's passage makes clear that writing is or ought to be a revolutionary activity, one that might finish or at least further the practical or imaginative efforts of, for instance, a party mired in old orthodoxies or a student movement that went far but not far enough. She goes on to associate the radical work of literature with a version of Hegel: "At the same time, it is clear that it is the Hegelian dialectic (whose transcendence veils the objective progress it has achieved since Descartes, Kant, and the Enlightenment) that first pointed to the masterly lines of this interplay between limit and infinity, rationale and objectivity – a stumbling block for contemporary sciences. It succeeded in this by imposing at its foundations the *knots*, invisible without it where the opposites – *subject* and *history* – are interwoven."[20] This is a complicated passage, too complicated to explicate fully here. A few points: first, we will want for now simply to notice that Kristeva identifies what is important about her and Barthes's methods with Hegel, a fact that creates yet another link among the beginning, middle, and end of our story. I will turn to Barthes's Hegelian inheritance shortly. Second, what Kristeva identifies as the essence of the dialectic is its ability to reveal the "knots" that seem to structure antinomies on which our culture and beliefs are based, antinomies or oppositions between subject and object, limit and infinity, fact and value, particular and general, etc. In other words, the work of the dialectic is not to overcome oppositions but to reveal the degree to which seemingly necessary and structuring antinomies always carry within them their own logical and existential limits. Literature – thanks to its irony, its productivity, its self-consciousness or its dialogism – reveals those knots; it shows how systems of belief that seem *only natural* always in fact rely on historical contradictions that can be exposed and thus – potentially – undone.

And third, as we turn now to Barthes and Genette, we can see that Kristeva's particular interest – in narrative, in the novel, in narrative genres that try and fail spectacularly to draw a circle around relations that really stop nowhere – depends on ideas and techniques that depend on what I have already identified as the antinomy at the heart of narrative theory: the story–discourse relation. As we will see, both Barthes and Genette draw on and tactically back away from one of the hopes that seemed to emerge from Kristeva's synthesis: the hope that the structuring opposition between story and discourse (she might call it a *thetic* opposition, which is to say an opposition or event that makes subsequent acts of socially recognized signification possible), the opposition, in other words, upon which narrative depends, might be overcome, and that overcoming that opposition might result in something like the revolutionary pulsation on which much of her work with *Tel Quel* seemed to depend. As I will suggest, Barthes and Genette both emerge from the same political scene, from the same encounters with the PCF, with the promise of Maoism, with the unexpected, unimagined events of May '68; instead, however, of working or, rather, continuing to work to imagine a radical or antimimetic form of narrative that could overcome the story–discourse relation, both Barthes and Genette turn in the late sixties and early seventies back to classic forms to narrative, to works that would seem from one perspective to offer a conservative (a younger Barthes would say *readerly*) alternative to the revolutionary potential that Kristeva and others associated with *Tel Quel* saw in experimental narratives, in *Finnegan's Wake*, in the aleatory logic of Raymond Roussel, in the "new novels" of Robbe-Grillet, and elsewhere. What is more, these works – *S/Z* and *Narrative Discourse* in particular – form one basis for much of what we continue to understand as narrative theory. The question then becomes, what would it mean to see Barthes and Genette as not only writing about narrative but also writing about narrative at a moment when narrative and the possibility of its political and historical end were tied up with the sharpest political hopes and enthusiasms? What did it mean, after the new novel, *Tel Quel*, and May '68, to turn back to familiar or narrative forms, to "classic" versions of the story-discourse relation?

It is in this context, in the mix of intellectual synthesis, political contingency, and cultural risk that we should read Barthes and Genette, two writers who were associated with *Tel Quel*, who also worked to further the compromise between structuralism and Russian Formalism, and who might be said to take the relation between story and discourse to one of its logical conclusions. It is, of course, no surprise to see Genette and Barthes as central to the development of narrative theory as we understand it today; *S/Z* and *Narrative Discourse* appeared within a year of one another and remain two of the most powerful examples of narrative theory at work. They also share another quality: while both works are justly celebrated for their ability to articulate methods and rules that could apply to almost any narrative, they both do so in the context of extremely detailed readings of single texts. Barthes reads Balzac's short story "Sarrasine," and Genette reads Proust. So, in addition to isolating some of the salient aspects of this founding moment of narratology and structuralist narrative theory, I will want both to anticipate some important developments in the field and, more importantly, to show how a look at its relation to the whole complicated history that I have been working to lay out helps to make clear the assumptions, hopes, and limits of narrative theory at one of its high points.

6.2 Parisian Gold: Roland Barthes and the Analysis of Narrative

A few years before *S/Z: An Essay*, the book on which I will focus here, Roland Barthes published "An Introduction to the Structural Analysis of Narratives," a powerfully compressed and foundational work of narrative theory. The essay first appeared in a 1966 special issue of the journal *Communications* that included a number of now-classic narratological essays: essays by Greimas, Bremond, Todorov, Genette, Umberto Eco, Christian Metz, and others. Barthes begins his essay, the most influential in that very influential issue, with the observation that "the narratives of the world are numberless"; he then lists a few of many, many narrative types: "myth, legend, fable, tale, novella, epic, history, tragedy, drama, comedy, mime, painting (think of Carpaccio's *Saint Ursula*), stained glass windows, cinema, comics, news items, conversation."[21] Barthes begins by arguing that, because the sheer number of narratives makes an empirical, inductive method impossible, the analysis of narrative instead requires a "theory," a single model or method that could account more or less for a phenomenon that is "international, transhistorical, transcultural" and yet nonetheless expressed in the sublimely particular form of "millions" of particular narratives.[22] Barthes goes on to invoke Saussure, Jakobson, and Lévi-Strauss, while also engaging contemporary efforts by Todorov, Bremond, Benveniste, Greimas, and others who had already begun to imagine the application of Saussure's analytical tools to specifically narrative forms in the wake of the recent French synthesis of structuralist linguistics and Russian Formalism. At once crisply synthetic and utterly original, Barthes's work occupies a central place in the emerging field that Todorov would soon name *narratology*.[23]

By the time he wrote his "Introduction," Barthes was already well-known. In 1953 he published *Writing Degree Zero*, a text that worked to nominate and thus potentially to surpass what he took as the historical and political limits of literary writing in France; because, following Saussure, Barthes understood that writing (as a form of *parole*) relies on language and that language (*langue*) is an expression of a society as it stands at a given moment in time, he argued that "literary writing carries at the same time the alienation of History and the dream of History; as a Necessity, it testifies to the division of languages which is inseparable from the division of classes; as Freedom, it is the consciousness of this division and the very effort which seeks to surmount it."[24] Literary writing thus both reflected and, to a degree, supported a particular political situation and seemed, however dimly, to allow readers and writers to imagine the utopian or revolutionary possibility of something else. A few years later, his *Mythologies* (1957), a collection of short essays on different aspects of everyday life and culture in France that had appeared as columns in *Les Lettres nouvelles* from 1954 to 1956, drew explicitly on Lévi-Strauss's model of myth analysis and a mode of semiological analysis adapted from Saussure's account of the relation between signifier and signified, an account that he later worked to codify and present in a short volume of 1964, *Elements of Semiology*: "The *Elements* here presented have as their sole aim the extraction from linguistics of analytical concepts which we think a priori to be sufficiently general to start semiological research on its way."[25] Barthes had also published works on Michelet (1954) and Racine (1963), the latter of which created a scandal when the Sorbonne's Raymond Picard attacked Barthes in "the evocatively entitled work, *New Criticism or New Imposture?*" which "denounced the tendency toward generalization, toward taking a single, concrete example for a category of universals in a critical game that confuses everything."[26] The subsequent Barthes–Picard debate (including Barthes's response, *Criticism and Truth*) marked an important moment in the rise of structuralism in France.

In "An Introduction to the Structural Analysis of Narratives," Barthes applies these different ideas directly to the study of narrative, which he understands once again in terms of the structuralist play between *langue* and *parole*, the shared and general rules that govern the production of individual stories and those individual stories themselves, as well as the play between signifier and signified, the matter or content of a given story and the particular verbal form that the story takes. Put in other words, Barthes understands a structural analysis as one that focuses not on one or another aspect of narrative but rather on a *relation* that articulates different aspects of a structure into a more or less meaningful whole: "From the outset, linguistics furnishes the structural analysis of narrative with a concept which is decisive in that, making explicit immediately what is essential in every system of meaning, namely its organization, it allows us both to show how a narrative is not a simple sum of propositions and to classify the enormous mass of elements which go to make up a narrative. This concept is that of *levels of description*."[27] By levels of description, Barthes means our now-familiar relation between story and discourse, which he expands here into a three-tiered system of *functions*, *actions*, and *discourse*. The idea of *narrative levels* is important to Barthes because it demands at least two modes of interpretation. On the one hand, one needs to read across the *syntax* of a particular level, to see how one event follows or occurs before another at the level of story or how word follows or precedes word at the level of discourse. This reading along the contiguous or combinatory line of story or discourse is what Roman Jakobson, following Saussure, would call a *syntagmatic* mode of reading. On the other hand, one needs also to read across or between levels, to treat the *relation* among levels as itself a significant aspect of a narrative's whole structure. This other kind of interpretation, one that occurs not along but across different levels of narrative, is what Jakobson would refer to as a *paradigmatic* or metaphoric mode of reading, a mode that "jumps" vertically among choices made at those related levels of story and discourse.[28]

Barthes calls the minimal unit of narrative a *function*, an explicit reference to Propp, who, as we saw, reduced all possible iterations of the folktale into a nonreversible sequence of thirty-one functions: lacking, seeking, testing, being tested, fighting, marrying, etc. Barthes, however, takes the term in a more flexible sense (something closer to Tomashevsky's *motif*), using it to account for whatever elements count as irreducible within the context of a particular narrative structure. In other words, Barthes's account of the relation between a given narrative and its functions seeks, in a self-consciously Aristotelian vein, to account for the reciprocal relation between parts and whole. As opposed, that is, to cataloging narrative functions in the abstract, Barthes posits a specific and generative relation between each narrative whole and the parts that compose it; once again, we can look to the Russian Formalist notion of *motivation*, the sense that all parts of a whole narrative structure will or should be motivated in relation to another as well as to that whole. Barthes is, in other words, interested in structure at several related levels: there is, at the top, the structural relation between all the rules that govern the production of narratives in general and all the individual narratives; there is, at a lower level, the structural relation that orders the relation between the parts and whole of a particular narrative, the rules of combination, substitution, and order on which a narrative relies (those rules would, for instance, be different for a detective and a romance novel); and then, at an even lower level, there is the structural relation between the signifiers and signifieds that together make up the various signifying elements that are those parts. Herman and Vervaeck write that, Barthes "starts from minimal components such as functions and indexes, proceeds to create minimal relationships between these components (arbitrariness, implication, mutual implication), and so arrives at larger units in the story such as sequences and their combinations."[29] What, in that case, makes a "structural analysis" powerful is the fact that it identifies a single structural *relation* (loosely, the relation between part and part and the relation between part and whole) that works in the same way at several levels of abstraction and analysis. Because Barthes understands a narrative as a nested set of structures or, rather, a structure of structures, every part of that structure must by definition have a significant role to play: "The essence of a function is, so to speak, the seed that it sows in the narrative, planting an element that will come to fruition later – either on the same level or elsewhere, on another level."[30] Every function, which is to say every part of a particular narrative structure no matter how apparently trivial or random, will turn out to have a *meaningful* relation with the other parts and thus the structure as a whole. Indeed, even when an object or event appears meaningless, that meaninglessness can and in fact must become its own kind of meaning: "Even were a detail to appear irretrievably insignificant, resistant to all functionality, it would nonetheless end up with precisely the meaning of absurdity or uselessness: everything has a meaning, or nothing has."[31] (Barthes later pursues this argument – that even insignificance is a form of significance in classic narratives – in his great essay on "The Reality Effect.")[32] Meaning is in this context equivalent to Saussure's understanding of *value*, the significant quality that individual units take on as a result only of being part of a whole and internally differentiated structure; and Saussure's value is in turn related to the ideal of value that Simmel, Weber, and Lukács sought to derive from or to locate in the mass of otherwise inert social facts, a connection that Lévi-Strauss made when he saw that the abstract rules of structuralism, rules that help us to see how individual linguistic facts emerge *in context* as values, could be used to understand how the most important kinds of significance, the deeply human stuff of myth, kinship, and culture, could in the end be understood as and only as a significant, value-producing structural play between units and rules.

Barthes then goes on to develop a number of important and influential oppositions. First, he distinguishes between *functions*, which initiate, sustain, or conclude narrative activities and thus stitch together earlier and later moments, and *indices*, which add significance, color, and sense to a narrative without necessarily affecting, initiating, or concluding events. When, on the one hand, Queequeg climbs into bed with Ishmael, it is a *function* if only because *climbing in* seems to necessitate a later *climbing out*; the fact, on the other hand, that Queequeg is covered with tattoos when he climbs in is an *index*: it is a meaningful detail; it adds significance or color (in this case "a dark, purplish, yellow color") to the narrative without opening, sustaining, or closing off an action. Barthes then further divides his *functions* into two categories, those that are necessary to a narrative and those that are not; he refers to the first as *nuclei* and the second as *catalysers*. *Nuclei*, which he also refers to as cardinal functions, are events that "open (or continue, or close) an alternative that is of direct consequence for the subsequent development of the story"; they are events that "inaugurate or conclude an uncertainty."[33] Catalysers, on the other hand, "merely 'fill in' the narrative space separating the hinge functions." (In *Story and Discourse*, Seymour Chatman adapts Barthes's distinction, renaming these differently necessary narrative functions *kernels* and *satellites*.) Once we have a better sense of their parts, narratives become visible as a rhythmic and harmonic sequence of these different elements, with more and less necessary functions marking time while indices give tone and emphasis to what unfolds.

We could think here of *Wuthering Heights* (1847). When Heathcliff runs away, when Cathy marries Edgar Linton, when Lockwood decides to make a second trip to visit Heathcliff: all of these are *nuclei* (or kernels) because, without them, the narrative as a whole could not proceed in the way that it does; the narrative structure as a whole needs these events to happen, needs them in order to make its way from beginning to end. When, on the other hand, Hindley shows Isabella his knife-gun or when Lockwood mistakes a pile of dead rabbits for a bundle of cute kittens, these are *catalysers* (or satellites). Although they are actions or events with beginnings and ends (showing and mistaking), they are not strictly necessary to the progress of the plot; but, while they are not necessary, they nonetheless contribute at this other level to the whole meaning and sense of the narrative. Lockwood's inability to distinguish between dead rabbits and living cats helps us to understand and to anticipate his more necessary role as a surrogate for the reader first coming to terms with the alien and violent nature of life in and around Heathcliff; the *catalyser*, "mistaking dead rabbits for cats," resonates with and deepens the more necessary *nucleus*, "working to understand the mysteries of Wuthering Heights." What is more, narrative *indices* such as the gothic murkiness of the interior of Heathcliff's house, its speaking difference from the lightness of Thrushcross Grange, Joseph's heavily marked regional dialect, or the number as opposed to the brute fact of Heathcliff's dogs provide a static but significant symbolic and atmospheric network against which to see the events and characters of the novel. Indeed, we can say that the novel as narrative is and only is the play among nucleus, catalyzer, and index, and part of its particular aesthetic effect, its music, as it were, emerges from the experience of feeling the tempo with which different orders of signification and structural necessity take each other's place.

Barthes goes on in the essay to identify several other aspects of narrative as such, which is to say the model of narrative that he proposes to use in order potentially to analyze any and all individual narratives, which is, in turn, to say the narrative *langue* against which he can measure narrative *parole*. He writes about *actions*, which he associates with a narrative's character system and the way it distributes the ownership and effects of functions across what he understands as a narrative's grammatical subjects and objects. Characters stand as the grammatical nodes against and around which functions occur. He writes about *narrative communication*, the implied position from which a narrative as a communicative act makes its way to an implied receiver. That position – the narrative *I* of enunciation – can, he suggests, take several forms: the author as "real" person outside the narrative, the impersonal narrator as tacit and immanent guarantor of the narrative, and, finally, the "narrator

[who] must limit his narrative to what the characters can observe or know, everything proceeding as if each of the characters in turn were the sender of the narrative." In his account of the productive limits of the *I* of enunciation, Barthes draws on the linguist Émile Benveniste's essay "The Nature of Pronouns": "*I* is 'the individual who utters the present instance of discourse containing the linguistic instance *I*.'"[34] Just as the *I* limits and situates the source and possible scope of discourse, so does it draw an implicit circle around a narrative world, functioning grammatically like biography in Lukács or point of view in James. Barthes also writes about the narrative discourse itself, that level at which the functions of a particular story find textual expression and undergo a whole series of distortions as the narrative reverses, slows, or collapses the chronological order of events: "This generalized distortion is what gives the language of narrative its special character. A purely logical phenomenon, since founded on an often distant relation and mobilizing a sort of confidence in intellective memory, it ceaselessly substitutes meaning for the straightforward copy of the events recounted."[35] As we will see, it is this last aspect of narrative structure that will occupy Gérard Genette in his *Narrative Discourse.*

As we have seen, it is the play between the events as they exist at the level of *story* and the events as they are represented at the level of *discourse* that gives a narrative its particular capacity for meaning; with this, Barthes draws out a paradox that was already implicit in Aristotle, the fact that although narratives will always take the form of a mimetic representation of real or imagined events, they derive neither all of their interest nor all of their meaning from those events. It is rather *the relation between* the event and its representation, the relation itself that constitutes the real and, again, paradoxical matter and force of narrative:

> It may be that men ceaselessly re-inject into narrative what they have known, what they have experienced; but if they do, at least it is in a form which has vanquished repetition and instituted the model of a process of becoming. Narrative does not show, does not imitate; the passion which may excite us in reading a novel is not that of a "vision" (in actual fact, we do not "see" anything). Rather it is that of meaning, that of a higher order of relation which also has its emotions, its hopes, its dangers, its triumphs.[36]

The founding gesture of the structural analysis of narratives is, in other words, an act of nomination, of naming *the relation* among narrative levels – as opposed to the levels themselves – as that which is essential to narrative and to the study of narrative. As with Freud and the work that goes on between the manifest and latent content of a dream; or with Lukács and his commitment to irony, which is to say the experience of narrative form as form; or with Kristeva and her sense of *writing* as a form of critical thinking that foregrounds the relation between verbal expression and historically specific social code, Barthes sees literary narrative as effective because it thematizes its own form, because it forces us to confront the idea of *the relation among levels within a structure* as essential to the production of narrative significance.

As I said before, it is important to see Barthes's narratology not only as a methodological effort or experiment but also within the context of the social and political shifts that made his particular synthesis of Freud, Marx, Saussure, and Shklovsky possible. Although, as we will see, this meeting of the political and the aesthetic is more obvious in *S/Z*, it is also a real if quiet aspect of "An Introduction to the Structural Analysis of Narratives." One trace of that connection is Barthes's odd choice of examples throughout the essay. Although, in the nature of things, he could have chosen anything, he relies in his essay on examples from Ian Fleming's *Goldfinger*, a James Bond novel that first appeared in 1959 and that was then made into a movie in 1964. From one point of view, we can see the purely methodological appeal of the novel for Barthes. The novel is technically achieved without being high art, it is an avowed work of genre fiction that works and, indeed, excels as a familiar form without trying to exceed the rules of the form; it is, as Herman and Vervaeck point out, simply a book in which "many things happen." Also, because it had already been made into a film, its presence in the essay makes a tacit argument for the portability of plot from one to another narrative medium, for the fact that something about *Goldfinger* can make its way from one medium to another, a fact relevant to Barthes's claim for the generality of narrative as such, for its ability to cross divides between novel and film, painting and conversation.[37]

The novel also, it could be said, allegorizes two different assumptions about narrative that stand behind Barthes's whole project and that will be especially important to his thinking in *S/Z*. *Goldfinger* is, perhaps, an appropriate example not only because it offers instances of what Barthes will later refer to as the *readerly* and the *writerly* but also because it presents that distinction in terms that resonate within the Cold War historical context of Barthes's writing and narratology's emergence. On the one hand, Bond is the man of action, someone who excels because training and disposition have reduced the space between thought and deed to something close to zero. Jeremey Black writes that "Bond can be seen ... as a central figure in the paranoid culture of the Cold War. The novels and early films chartered a period when Britain was making adjustments to her world status in uneasy alliance with the United

States against Communism, and, increasingly, offering skill, brains and professionalism, instead of mere might."[38] In this way, Bond stands as a figure for a naturalized, motivated view of narrative, the ideological notion that narrative *discourse* could or should be reduced to a single practical or "professional" significance; and, in the context of the Cold War, that certainty, that lack of ambiguity or nuance jibes with a view of politics and society that reduced the possibility of meaning or nuance in the name of a false political or ideological certainty. Bond is thus a *readerly* hero, someone who succeeds precisely because he treats a situation as a more or less stable code to be cracked, broken, or shot. And, on the other: although the character appears in the movie and not the book, one is tempted to see Barthes's critic as something closer to Q, the scientist–artist figure who attends productively if eccentrically to the gadgets and doodads of the spy trade and who counts on the fact that even the most innocuous of devices can conceal – in broad daylight, if for your eyes only – all manner of overlapping and counter-intuitive significance. This is to see the narratologist or critic as the effective and only apparently distracted purveyor of exploding pens and cameras secreted within cigarette lighters, seemingly homely but really sophisticated terms that hold out the possibility, one embraced by Shklovsky, Jakobson, Kristeva, and others, that literary narrative works precisely because it forces us to look for the hidden or unexpected uses of what habit would otherwise reduce to the everyday. (Catalyzer! Function! Motif! Please return them in one piece, Mr. Bond.) We might extend this reading, seeing Goldfinger's ultimate goal – to steal all the gold in Fort Knox – in relation to some of the larger questions about the nature of value that I have been asking throughout; to what degree does gold stand in (1) as a value in and of itself, (2) as a signifier for a value that in fact resides elsewhere, or (3) as what any reader of fairy tales would recognize as an almost pure narrative *motif*, an ultimately empty object of desire – Hitchcock called them MacGuffins – that serves in this context to motivate plot and little else. Indeed, despite or maybe because of his defining love of the stuff, Auric Goldfinger characterizes it best: "No, no, gentlemen. Fort Knox is a myth like other myths."[39] Indeed, Goldfinger wants to steal (or in the film to irradiate) all the gold in Fort Knox, a scheme that would make him rich while also destabilizing the United States and related economies. As Colonel Smithers, a Bank of England security expert and, as Fleming puts it, a man who "looked exactly like someone who would be called Colonel Smithers," explains to Bond, "gold and currencies backed by gold are the foundation of our international credit. We can only tell what the true strength of the pound is, and other countries can only tell it, by knowing the amount of valuta we have behind our currency." Seen in these terms, gold is not only a value; rather, under the terms of the 1944 Bretton Woods Agreement, the relative and exchangeable value of different currencies was tied to and thus regulated by the value of gold, which was in turn pegged to the value of the U.S. dollar. Gold was thus a value that made other values possible, insofar as it brought different monetary systems together into a strategic, regulated, uneven, and, one might say, an internally motivated system. It is, in other words, a nice figure for a narrative structure, for which, as Barthes says, "everything has a meaning, or nothing has." Gold was, in other words, what allowed individual values within the contested and internally riven structure of the Cold War economic system to have what meaning they did; this became clear in the early seventies when Richard Nixon at last severed the tie between gold and the dollar and let the currency float free (it took Nixon to do, in other words, what Goldfinger could not). Fleming thus casts gold as a very particular historical fact, one tied to the last gasp of a particular postwar economic arrangement as well as to Britain's own late imperial anxiety about the shifting bases of social and cultural values that were very much on the wane. Bond's presence as *the* example in "An Introduction to the Structural Analysis of Narratives" raises a hint – a bare hint but a hint nonetheless – of another layer to the essay, of a political meaning that Barthes sought to register as connotation, as opposed to denotation, because, as we will see, the difference between those two modes of signifying was for him indeed a crucial political difference.

~

Barthes's next major work of narrative theory – indeed, one of *the* major works of narrative theory – is *S/Z: An Essay*, a book that makes explicit the relations that exist among narrative, ideology, and history. In *S/Z* Barthes offers a long, sustained, and incredibly – one might say manically – detailed reading of Honoré de Balzac's novella *Sarrasine* (1830), a reading presented as a "starred" analysis of 561 *lexias*, Barthes's term for what, following Propp, Tomashevsky, and his own work in the "Introduction," he takes as his minimal unit of analysis: "The lexia will include sometimes a few words, sometimes several sentences; it will be a matter of convenience: it will suffice that the lexia be the best possible space in which we can observe meanings; its dimension, empirically determined, estimated, will depend on the density of connotations, variable according to the moments of the text."[40] In addition to his numbered analysis of the lexias, Barthes offers ninety-three short essays that address questions of method, broader interpretive possibilities, his sense of the limits and possibilities of writing. Because the book is divided in this way, because it divides – indeed shatters – its source text into pieces, it is both functionally unreadable and exquisitely beautiful, a practical mix of the virtues and limits of the *readerly* and the *writerly*, the two styles of writing that he takes as his larger subject in *S/Z*. It is thus one of only a few books – we might think also of Mallarmé, maybe Beckett, maybe the late Flaubert – to make its own unreadability into a productive and moving part of its design. *S/Z* is not only a theory of the writerly; it is a practical instantiation of it:

> The writerly text is a perpetual present, upon which no consequent language (which would inevitably make it past) can be superimposed; the writerly text is *ourselves writing*, before the infinite play of the world (the world as function) is traversed, intersected, stopped, plasticized by some singular system (Ideology, Genus, Criticism) which reduces the plurality of entrances, the opening of networks, the infinity of languages.[41]

Barthes's account of both the *writerly* and the *readerly* owes a clear debt to Kristeva; as I said earlier, Kristeva identified *poetic language* as language that foregrounds and thus makes problematic the open relation between the particular text or utterance and the world of codes on which that text or utterance draws. As a result, the poetic or the *writerly* calls critical attention to its own preconditions; and, as was the case with Lukács's sense of novelistic irony and Bakhtin's sense of the dialogic, this ability to confront a form with both its limits and conditions of possibility results ideally in a text that is open, critical, productively self-conscious. The *readerly*, on the other hand, is like what Kristeva called "the book," an utterance or text that naturalizes or obscures its rules and limits.

Although he reiterates the preference for the writerly that he laid out in *Writing Degree Zero*, Barthes acknowledges in *S/Z* that his chosen object *Sarrasine* is indeed a "classic" and thus apparently readerly text; but, just as Kristeva saw a certain kind of critical reading as capable of opening the closed book, of giving it something like the status of poetic or revolutionary language, so does Barthes see his "step-by-step" method as one that opens a story by revealing and problematizing, by defamiliarizing the universe of codes upon which it relies. As D. A. Miller writes, one of *S/Z's* tasks was "by evincing the artifice of signifying procedures at work throughout the classic realist text, to render what one may have been used to considering their natural operation as fully weird as anything that one may have been prepared to call *un*natural."[42] This shift from the innate literariness of the object to the applied literariness of reading is one that Barthes enacts via a set of procedures adapted from the Russian Formalists:

> For the step-by-step method, through its very slowness and dispersion, avoids penetrating, reversing the tutor text, giving an internal image of

it: it is never anything but a decomposition (in the cinematographic sense) of the work of reading: a slow motion, so to speak, neither wholly image nor wholly analysis; it is, finally, in the very writing of the commentary, a systematic use of digression ... and thereby a way of observing the reversibility of the structures from which the text is woven.[43]

Barthes, in other words, takes technical aspects of what Shklovsky and others saw at work in the poetic text itself – digression, slowness, inversion, etc. – and turns them into a style of interpretation; as opposed, then, to seeing some texts as essentially more poetic than others, Barthes invites the reader to see any text as possibly writerly, which is to say as a text that can be made to reveal its relation to historically specific ideological codes. Read rightly, every text can be writerly because every text owes a structural debt to ideology that can in turn be disclosed.

Barthes casts the relation between the text and its ideological context in terms of what he calls the code: "The code is a perspective of quotations, a mirage of structures; we know only its departures and returns ... they are so many fragments of something that has always been *already* read, seen, done, experienced; the code is the wake of that *already*."[44] The code is, in other words, a version of what Saussure called *langue*, the shared, social, and historically specific rules that established the limits of what it was possible to think or to say at one or another time; and, just as *langue* stands behind any particular utterance (*parole*), so does the code stand behind any particular textual performance. Barthes goes on to identify five particular codes, five related but different sets of rules that govern the production and reception of any given text (we might instead think of them as five aspects of *the* code). The work of the critic is, in that case, to reveal the several codes at work, to show how a text that would seem reducible to one or another meaning is in fact characterized by the plurality of its significance. Barthes calls this work *interpretation*: "This new operation is *interpretation* (in the Nietzschean sense of the word). To interpret a text is not to give it a (more or less justified, more or less free) meaning, but on the contrary to appreciate what plural constitutes it."[45] Although the codes form the practical basis of Barthes's mode of interpretation and allow him to parse Balzac's tale out into a series of differently significant fragments, they are less a real fact of narrative structure than a heuristic device, a way to reveal the significant relations – both *paradigmatic* and *syntagmatic* – that exist among the different parts of a given narrative: "We are, in fact concerned not to manifest a structure but to produce a structuration."[46] Once again, the analysis of the codes allows Barthes to reveal and to deal with the ideologically motivated relation among different aspects of the whole structure that is a narrative.

The five codes run as follows: (1) *The hermeneutic code* involves "all the units whose function it is to articulate in various ways a question, its response, and the variety of chance events which can either formulate the question or delay its answer; or even, constitute an enigma and lead to its solution."[47] The hermeneutic is the code of question and answer, tension and release, mystery and revelation, the initiation and the cessation of suspense; and, along with the proairetic code, it is the most "narrative" of the five: because an answer to a question needs always to follow a question, the hermeneutic code unfolds in time and is irreversible. (2) *The proairetic code* is the code of action: actions "can fall into various sequences which should be indicated merely by listing them."[48] For Barthes, actions (*stroll, murder, rendezvous*) are events that involve some kind of movement or change and that must in that case open and close; they are in this sense equivalent to what he had identified in his earlier essay as functions as opposed to indices. Like the hermeneutic code, the proairetic code is irreversible. (3) *The semic code* is the code of "meanings," the level at which significances, suggestions, senses, themes gather "like motes of dust" on the surface of the narrative; the *semes* are thus atemporal and related to what Barthes referred to as *indices* in "An Introduction to the Structuralist Analysis of Narrative." That a given character is "old" or "musical" or "feminine" might or might not matter to the plot, but it will "tell" us something about the values contained in or evoked by a whole narrative; Barthes will go on, in fact, to suggest that literary characters are always more or less reducible to a number of *semes* grouped around or organized under a proper name. (4) *The symbolic code* is the code of mostly antithetical relations that underwrite and organize and highlight the cultural significance of events and things in a narrative: good and bad, light and dark, male and female. *The symbolic code* is close to the base network of relations that Lévi-Strauss saw running among different versions of a myth in his "The Structural Study of Myth" or to what Greimas refers to as the *deep structure* of narrative systems; the symbolic code is, in other words, made up of positions and limits that "define the fundamental mode of existence of an individual or a society, and subsequently the conditions of existence of semiotic objects."[49] (5) *The cultural code* activates "references to a science or body of knowledge; in drawing attention to [the cultural code], we merely indicate the type of knowledge (physical, physiological, medical, psychological, literary, historical, etc.) referred to, without going so far as to construct (or reconstruct) the culture they express."[50] The cultural code is the code of allusion, the code that links the discourse of a particular narrative to other discourses. Taken together, the five codes give Barthes a way, however provisional, to begin to name both the relation among parts of a narrative and that narrative's relation to the social rules that more or less make it possible.

Barthes goes on to cast the difference between the text seen as having a single significance and the text as having a "parsimoniously plural" set of more or less apparent meanings in terms of the difference, taken from linguistics, between *denotation* and *connotation*. Where *denotation* refers to a single or at least dominant meaning of a given text or utterance, *connotation* is "a correlation immanent in the text, in the texts; or again, one may say that it is an association made by the text-as-subject within its own system."[51] Connotations are, in other words, an utterance's or an image's or a text's secondary meanings, the levels or layers of significance that are present in a text even if they seem somehow unnecessary to it. To state this in Saussure's terms, where a given signifier (word, sentence, text) appears to point more firmly toward one or another signified (the concept), that signifier will also suggest at some other, more or less proximate distance, a indefinite number of other, less dominant concepts. Where, for instance, "dog" would seem to denote a four-legged domesticated mammal, it might, depending on the context, also connote loyalty, good humor, hunger, danger, luxury, poverty, envy, love, and so on. And, because they can *seem* unnecessary, connotations are typically understood as minor, as merely associative, or by-the-way, as meanings that might add to or distort a signifier's primary sense without getting to the heart of the matter (they are the *indices* as opposed to the *functions* of textual interpretation). Denotations, on the other hand, seem to stand as the *ground* of a text's meaning, as that which guarantees thought and allows patterns or plots or ideas to be taken to a narrative or ideological close: "It is to return to the closure of Western discourse (scientific, critical, or philosophical), to its centralized organization, to arrange all the meanings of a text in a circle around the hearth of denotation (the hearth: center, guardian, refuge, light of truth)."[52] Where denotation stops reading and allows us to feel that we have figured out what a particular text at last means, connotation serves to open up the text, pointing to the layered plurality of its significance.

S/Z is, in part, an effort to revalue the relation between denotation and connotation, releasing the latter from its position as merely secondary or minor; more than a minor distraction, "connotation is the way into the polysemy of the classic text, to that limited plural on which the classic text is based."[53] That is not to say that Barthes attends to connotation at the expense of denotation, that he sees the text as a pure or frictionless play of secondary as opposed to primary significances; it is, rather, to see the classic text as a kind of compromise between the singularity of denotation and the pure play of connotation; it is, in other words to see the text as a "parsimonious plural," as a signifier that means more than one thing, that means a lot of things, but that does not mean anything or everything. This revalued sense of connotation and denotation is especially important in *S/Z* because it allows Barthes not only to think about the indefinite but not infinite play of the signifier but also and more particularly to reimagine the relation between story (as signified) and discourse (as signifier). As opposed, in other words, to seeing narrative *either* as a simple, direct, or denotative relation between one story – one sequence of events – and one discursive representation of those events *or* as an ideally or infinitely plural text, a purely and impossibly connotative writing whose discourse refers to anything or everything or nothing, Barthes reveals Balzac's classic narrative as itself "a parsimonious plural," a text in which the overlapping and even contradictory play of codes does not deny the possibility of representation but rather underscores the degree to which any narrative representation is an encounter between a complex discursive totality and a life or world that must exceed or, at least, strain narrative discourse. *S/Z*, in other words, attempts – after Lukács – to imagine classic narrative as that which would not reduce but rather show respect for the essential complexity of life. The point here is not to suggest that discourse *really* represents a world; it is rather to see that the particular relation between story and discourse that Barthes associates with the classic narrative is itself a representation or, rather, a textual embodiment of complexity.

Of course, some readers have taken Barthes as suggesting that narrative is indeed reducible to its discourse, to a play of signifiers floating freely without reference to this or any world; as suggesting that, because it does not mean any one thing, narrative can in fact mean anything. This, though, is to miss the point of Barthes's argument. Rather than arguing for the pure and free play of the text, Barthes suggests that the writerly text (or a readerly text read in a writerly way) is what allows discourse to come to terms with the full and productive richness of story, with the real complexity of a life and a history that must exceed any one interpretation and yet nonetheless really exist; it is to imagine a form of narrative that would really represent history or life without reducing either to one and only one idea. This takes us back to some earlier figures including Nietzsche, Lukács, Bakhtin, James, and others who understood successful narrative in terms of its more or less successful urge toward an open relation between form or discourse, on the one hand, and life or history as imagined in story on the other. While narrative form can sometimes give real meaning to the events, it can also distort those facts, can reduce our ability to understand or to engage with life, it complexities, and thus its connotations. In these terms, we need to see Barthes's style of reading in both analytical and ethical terms. While he is indeed interested in articulating a method that might be able technically to address the parsimoniously plural nature of narrative signification, he is also interested in a critical mode that would be able not only to respect the real and essential richness of history's meaning but also to counter ideological efforts to limit history to one or another ideologically motivated meaning. More than a work of literary criticism, *S/Z* is a demand that we acknowledge both the reality and the bewildering complexity of life, that we reconcile ourselves to the imperative to confront a world the totality of which must exceed our best efforts at representation.

Indeed, we need to see Barthes's method, his interest in seeing what a writerly narrative can really say about the complexity of life, in relation to some of *S/Z*'s key concerns: money, to which I will turn in a moment, and sex. How, for instance, should we understand what *S/Z* has to say about the narrative representation of sexual desire and sexual difference? Balzac's story of the male sculptor Sarassine's passionate and doomed love for the castrato La Zambinella allows Barthes to explore ways in which the truth of sexual desire can be left unsaid; can be made to say one and only one thing; or can be allowed simply to drift over the surface of the text and its connotations. Is Balzac's story "about" the sculptor's mistake, his seeing the castrated man as a woman? Is it "about" a man's real love for a boy in drag? Is it "about" the ways in which sexual difference is itself always a kind of connotation, a secondary expression of a prior and inexplicable cut? Is it "about" all of these things at once or none of them at all? We might look here to D. A. Miller's *Bringing Out Roland Barthes*, which seeks to explain and overcome what he takes as a homophobic silence around Barthes's own homosexuality and the complex, often unacknowledged role that it plays in *S/Z*: "To refuse to bring Barthes out consents to a homophobic reception of his work."[54] Miller argues not only that a homosexual significance is at the heart of both Balzac's and Barthes's texts but also that readings of Barthes that exaggerate either the text's denotative singularity or its discursive, connotative plurality can work to screen or to repress that significance. On the one hand, to reduce the text denotatively to one or another meaning is a way to suppress the possible consequence of Sarrasine's real desire for La Zambinella: "It was *only*," one might say, "a mistake, an infatuation, a symbol, a convention, a joke, etc." On the other hand, to leave Sarrasine's real and passionate love for a "boy in drag" as one connotation among an indefinite number of others and thus as evidence of the text's immanent capacity for play and polysemy is similarly to reduce its consequence. Seen from this perspective "Barthes's general problematic of the text contours La Zambinella as nothing more or less than an instance of a classificatory disturbance, the local habitation and name of that hemorrhaging of meaning which tends to occur – to the great scandal of the *bien-pensant* guardians of the readerly, to the overwhelming delight of the avant-garde prolocutors of the writerly – when a binary opposition breaks down."[55] In other words, treating Barthes's analysis either simply as this or that thing or simply as a celebration of plurality or ambivalence or play for its own sake is not only a form of denial but also an interpretative or methodological error; it is to miss that homosexual desire is a real part of the plural that Balzac's story is and that Barthes's method counts on a real and reciprocal relation between that story and the discourse of *Sarrasine*. Sarrasine's love for La Zambinella is both a fact really to be represented as part of the text's "parsimonious plural" and a fact that resists representation because it is, as it were, a *living* fact; as we know from Nietzsche, Lukács, and Bakhtin, living facts are complex facts. Life both demands and resists representation. To fail, in that case, "to bring out Roland Barthes" is thus not only to participate in a homophobic disavowal of what *Sarrasine* and *S/Z* are all about but also to miss the critical force of Barthes's method, which is, above all, a demand that we try to see, to engage with, and to respect life, history, sex, and desire as they really and complicatedly are.

~

Sex and money: the initiating mystery of *S/Z*, the mystery that opens the hermeneutic code and thus provides the tale with its narrative frame and much of its motivation – where did the de Lanty family get its enormous wealth? This question is at the heart of Balzac's whole project; a historian of the passage from the French Revolution to the Bourbon Restoration and beyond, Balzac follows the money to origins that always reveal themselves as compromised, scandalous, or bloody. For the de Lantys, whose wealth is gained from their elderly castrato uncle, it is indeed all three. We might think of *Père Goriot*, which derives much of its own tragic energy from the desire of Goriot's daughters to distance themselves from the source of his and thus their wealth; a former pasta maker, Goriot acquired his money hoarding and selling grain at an enormous profit during the revolution. For Barthes, this Balzacian split between the synchronic appearance and the diachronic history of money provides an opportunity to reflect on the larger logic of value as its drifts analogically between Balzac's reflections on the history of money and his own thinking about semiotic value, on the difference between wealth as an index of a particular history and money as an ideological fantasy that works precisely to deny the past. "Parisian Gold," Barthes's name for a value that works in spite of being based on nothing, thus links his own thinking about the bourgeois instability of the sign to a quietly Marxian critique of the money form as a value that is paradoxically both full and empty. Barthes writes that

> Parisian indifference to the origin of money equates symbolically with the non-origin of money; a money that has no smell is money withdrawn from the basic order of the index, from the consecration of origin: this money is as empty as being-castrated: for Parisian Gold, what corresponds to the physiological impossibility of procreating is the impossibility of having an origin, a moral heredity: the signs (monetary, sexual) are wild because, contrary to the indices (the meaningful regime of the old society), they are to based on an original, irreducible, incorruptible, immovable otherness of their component parts: in the index, what is indicated (nobility) is of a different nature from what indicates (wealth): there is no possible mingling; in the sign, which establishes an order of representation (and no longer of determination, of creation, as does the index), the two elements interchange, signified and signifier revolving in an endless process: what is bought can be sold, the signified can become signifier, and so on. Replacing the feudal index, the bourgeois sign is a metonymic confusion.[56]

Barthes argues that Balzac uses the story of the de Lantys' fabulous and fabulously obscure wealth to track a broader historical shift from one kind of value to another. Where an earlier system was based on the relatively fixed form of the *index*, bourgeois capitalism is based on a logic of pure exchange that Barthes associates both with money and with the *sign*; and, as the de Lantys' efforts to hide their history demonstrate, that logic of pure exchange is one that the bourgeoisie both enjoy and need to conceal. This is why the de Lantys hide their uncle.

We can see Barthes returning here to an argument he had made in *Mythologies*; if, he argued, the move from feudalism to capitalism is a move from the clarity of the index to the mystery of the sign, it also corresponds with the invention of the bourgeois myth, a figural representation that neutralizes the arbitrariness and, thus, the connotations of the sign, allowing it to take on the look if not the actuality of denotative truth: "What the world supplies to myth is a historical reality, defined, even if this goes back quite a while, by the way in which men have produced or used it; and what myth gives in return is a *natural* image of this reality ... myth is constituted by the loss of the historical quality of things: in it, things lose the memory that they once were made."[57] Parisian Gold aligns an economic history that moves from that stability of wealth to the instability of money to *the myth of money as wealth* (the de Lantys or the Goriots) with a semiotic history that moves from index to sign to myth, from value as achieved in use, to value set free in the process of exchange, to value transformed into a static and mystified representation of itself. To quote Auric Goldfinger once again: "Fort Knox is a myth like other myths." In *S/Z*, this twinned analysis takes a particularly narrative form, with Barthes looking to a changing relation between story and discourse in order to track the ways in which narrative follows money, moving from an imagined sacred or archaic narrative stability (where discourse simply denotes story) to narrative instability (where discourse and story exist in a parsimoniously plural relation), to the myth of instability as stability (where the market encourages us to read books, no matter how complex, once and only once; to treat them, in other words, as commodities to consume and then throw away). Lukács would cast this progression as a move from the simplicity of *epic* to the self-conscious irony of the novel to the crassly ideological myth making of the *entertainment novel*, a last turn that both exaggerates and obscures the ubiquity of the writerly in the classic readerly text. It is, in that case, the work of the critic to reveal the degree to which narrative presents itself both as the denial and as the culmination of economic or, rather, a revolutionary logic that Barthes and Kristeva identify with writing as such.

Barthes characterizes this kind of reading, a reading that can reveal the ambiguity and thus the history behind the readerly narrative, as *rereading* in the strongest possible sense:

> Rereading, an operation contrary to the commercial and ideological habits of our society, which would have us "throw away" the story once it has been consumed ("devoured"), so that we can then move on to another story, buy another book, and which is tolerated only in certain marginal categories of readers (children, old people, and professors), rereading is here suggested at the outset, for it alone saves the text from repetition (those who fail to reread are obliged to read the same story everywhere), multiplies in its variety and its plurality: rereading draws the text out of its internal chronology ("this happens before or after that") and recaptures a mythic time (without before or after); it contests the claim which would have us believe that the first reading is a primary, naive, phenomenal reading which will only, afterwards, have to "explicate," to intellectualize. . .; rereading is no longer consumption but play (that play which is the return of the different).[58]

Barthes thus understands rereading not only as necessary to the kind of close and seemingly exhaustive analysis he applied to Balzac's tale but also as a tactical response to a capitalist culture that treats books – and, we are to take it, nearly everything else – as disposable, as consumable, as easy. (We should remember here the difference between the Lord and the Bondsman in Hegel's story; where the Lord simply consumes things and throws them away, the Bondsman *works* them over, learns about them, and thus develops a more and more active, which is to say dialectical, relation to the world.) Rereading emerges for Barthes as a way to work against the dehumanizing logic of life under capitalism precisely because it refuses to see narrative discourse as a simple representation of an event or series of events. This resistance to the logic of disposability and the single reading mirrors Barthes's interest in moving past *denotation* as the sole logic of reading, the reduction of a narrative to one and only one meaning, toward the parsimonious plurality of *connotation*, to a style of reading capable of engaging with the richness, the resistance, and – seen from an "entrepreneurial" or "bourgeois" point of view – the revolutionary waste of the literary work.

Barthes's commitment to readers as opposed to writers represents an important adjustment to the radical project that began with *Writing Degree Zero*. Where that book imagined a kind of writing – namely, the writing of avant-garde figures such as Robbe-Grillet – as carrying a directly revolutionary potential, as possibly leading to a real shift in thinking and thus in life, his effort in *S/Z* represents a kind of compromise between his hopes for revolution and his acceptance of the world as it was. It is, after all, a book that appears *after Tel Quel*'s misguided alliance with the PCF, *after* Todorov and Genette's break away from the journal, *after* the events of May '68, after, in other words, a brief and exciting but ultimately inconclusive period of revolutionary possibility. As Lukács had thirty years before, Barthes comes to terms in *S/Z* with the tenacity of capitalism, with Parisian Gold, with the persistence of what he understands as an inauthentic mode of life; for Lukács, this took the form of a Hegelian "reconciliation with reality" that "made possible an understanding of the connection between logical categories and the structural forms of bourgeois society. By rejecting the utopian ought and focusing philosophy on the understanding of the present, grasped dialectically, Hegel had pointed to the only way of knowing that which was alone knowable about the future – the tendencies in the present that impel history forward."[59] Where, in that case, revolution had come to seem unlikely or impossible, Barthes turns – again as Lukács did in his reading of Hegel – to moments or flashes of dialectical possibility in the midst of everyday life, to see how even the greatest and most conservative of readerly texts can contain or can be seen as immanently alternative, as always already expressive of possibilities that exceed the status quo; and, also like Lukács, Barthes sees that possibility as woven through narrative, as reflected in the polysemic drift of the five codes that took the place of story as well as in the narrative spots where, as Barthes understands it, the difference between signifier and signified, between story and discourse dissolves. As with the later Lukács and the Russian Formalists, Nietzsche, and Bakhtin, Barthes turns to reading narrative in an effort to see the *ought* at the heart of the *is*, as, in other words, a way to maintain radical possibility in the face of the flexible durability of a late and indefinitely persistent capitalism.

Barthes was explicit about what he took as the historically penultimate status of modern narrative, as its particular position between bourgeois culture as it was and had been and a possibility that he had seen at work in avant-garde writing and began to look for in a particularly rigorous style of reading informed by structuralist narratology. In a short piece on Genette, Barthes writes in terms that he could have applied to his own work:

> Now, a theory of "skidding" is necessary *precisely today*. Why? Because we are in that historical moment of our culture when narrative cannot yet abandon a certain readability, a certain conformity to narrative pseudo-logic which culture has instilled in us and in which, consequently, the only possible novations consist not in destroying the story, the anecdote, but in *deviating* it: making the code skid while seeming to respect it. It is this very fragile state of the narrative, at once conforming and deviant, that Genette has been able to see and to make us see in Proust's work. His work is at once structural and historical because he specifics the conditions on which narrative novation is possible without being suicidal.[60]

His point is that Genette's style of narrative analysis works because it accepts the culture's social and political need for the coherence of narratives, for the order of the classically readerly, for narrative ends that help us to understand or rather to believe in the logic of beginnings and middles while showing how those stories work against or in spite of themselves and thus reveal what's excessive or dialectical in even the most conservative of narratives. So, while his analysis is committed to showing how the narrative antithesis between story and discourse works, it is also and ultimately concerned with revealing the very idea of antithesis as a historically specific and ideologically potent myth: "The several hundred figures propounded by the art of rhetoric down through the centuries constitute a labor of classification intended to name, to lay the foundations for, the world. Among all these figures, one of the most stable is the Antithesis; its apparent function is to consecrate (and domesticate) by a name, by a metalinguistic object, the division between opposites and the very irreducibility of this division."[61] As with Bakhtin's chronotopes, Lévi-Strauss's structural analyses of myth, Greimas's deep structures, or Barthes's own account of the ideological motivation of signifier and signified in *Mythologies*, antithesis is the most powerful of many figures that structure and limit our apprehension of the world in historically and ideologically specific terms.

In one way, this recognition of the historically specific nature of antithesis links *S/Z* to *History and Class Consciousness* (1923), where Lukács revealed what he called the "antinomies of bourgeois thought," oppositions between subject and object, idea and experience, noumena and phenomena that shape our philosophical view of history and the world, while deriving their own form and force from a set of specific socioeconomic conditions. Barthes's interest in demonstrating the need to see, to understand, but ultimately to think past the antitheses that structure our social world offers him a way to push narrative theory to and potentially past its own immanent limits. That is, if, as I have been saying, the project of narrative theory depends on an antithesis between story and discourse, the overall logic of *S/Z* can be read as the effort to think past those terms, to make the case that what seem to be two different substances are, in fact, two aspects of one and the same substance. Barthes's "parsimonious plurality," his confrontation with the real but bewilderingly complex nature of events thus takes us back to the paradox of the story–discourse relation. Where other critics ask which occurs first, story or discourse, Barthes's method recognizes that they rather represent two aspects of the same effort, the effort to come to terms with the political imperative really to represent a life, the complexity of which must and will resist efforts at representation. Seen in this light, the story–discourse relation does not name an opposition or an antithesis; it rather names two aspects of a single problem, the problem that accompanies our need to find forms in which to represent a life that will resist exactly those forms. Or, as Lukács might put it, story and discourse are necessary and coterminous aspects of "an age in which the extensive totality of life is no longer directly given, in which the immanence of meaning in life has become a problem, yet which still thinks in terms of totality."[62]

In *S/Z*, Barthes offers an account of readerly narrative – which is to say an apparently or ideologically single or natural relation between story and discourse – that recognizes its power, its appeal, and, most importantly, its necessary relation to a particular historical moment, a moment characterized by the logic of capitalist exchange, on the one hand, and by the heteronormative logic of bourgeois sexuality on the other. At the same time, using structuralist methods to delineate the operational terms of that logic – the logic of the narrative antithesis between story and discourse – he offers the reader a glimpse of an alternative way of thinking about and ordering experience, a way that he characterizes as *writerly* and that he imagines as the revelation of antitheses not as fundamental to all understanding but rather as characteristic of how a particular historical moment thinks; and, just as Hegel saw history as the dialectical overcoming of opposition, so does Barthes use *S/Z* to imagine conditions under which antithesis would no longer be the governing logic of life and thus conditions under which narrative could no longer be understood in relation to an opposition between story and discourse, events and the representation of events. It was with something like this in mind that Kristeva made the relation between Barthes and Hegel explicit: "It is clear that it is the Hegelian dialectic ... that first pointed to the masterly lines of this interplay between limit and infinity, rationale and objectivity.... It succeeded in this by imposing at its first foundations the knots, invisible without it, where the opposites – subject and history – are interwoven. They are indeed the ones that we encounter at the crossroads of the Barthian reflection."[63] Barthes's work in and beyond *S/Z* represents one culmination and, perhaps, one conclusion to narrative theory as such. Imagining conditions under which the two could become one, conditions under which story and discourse would be at least revealed as different aspects of one and the same thing as opposed to two things different in kind, Barthes offers *S/Z* both as one of the most sophisticated versions of narrative theory and as suggestion that, along with the other antitheses of modern life, the antithesis that governs the analysis of narrative – the antithesis of story and discourse – might someday be overcome. In the meantime, while "we are in that historical moment of our culture when narrative cannot yet abandon a certain readability," the analysis of narrative must rather reveal *knots* within the antithetical logic of that historical moment that suggest at least the possibility of *something else*. In a short 1974 note, "Utopia," Barthes writes, "But it is the elements, the inflections, the obscurer nooks and crannies of the utopian system that reappear in our world as flashes of desire, as thrilling possibilities. If we were more receptive to them, they would prevent Politics from congealing into a totalitarian, bureaucratic, moralistic system."[64] The idea here is that, where we can no longer imagine an end to a capitalist world system based in the alienating antinomies of bourgeois thought, we need to look to local moments where that system and the antinomies that underwrite it slip or skid, where dialectical possibility remains immanent to a system that would seem otherwise unchangeable. In narrative, where that system takes the form of a readerly, which is to say totalizing, story–discourse relation ("these novels crop up in a system that hasn't ceased to be capitalist"), we need, as he does in *S/Z*, to look to moments of writerly excess, moments when the limits of the apparently "natural" operations of narrative are – however fleetingly – revealed.[65] In *S/Z*, Barthes suggests at the beginning of narrative theory that the utopian and thus the impossible end of narrative theory must always have been to make any narrative theory unnecessary.

6.3 The Knowable Is at the Heart of the Mysterious: Genette's Narrative Poetics

Alongside Barthes's *S/Z: An Essay*, Gérard Genette's *Narrative Discourse: An Essay in Method* represents a key moment in the development of narrative theory. It is almost certainly the one text that allowed a subsequent generation of narrative theorists to develop and to consolidate a field. In a recent piece on the history of narrative theory from "structuralism to the present," Monika Fludernik writes that "most prominent [in that history] is, obviously, the paradigm instituted by Gérard Genette in *Narrative Discourse*, whose international influence was cemented by its early translation into English and by its adoption on the part of prominent American, European, and Israeli scholars."[66] *Narrative Discourse*'s appeal is partly the result of what Genette refers to with half-joking exasperation as "all this technology," the frankly daunting number of terms that he invents and then divides and subdivides in order to account for how real or fictive events at the level of story find more or less coherent form at the level of discourse.[67] Indeed, the book has been both appreciated for and sometimes misunderstood as a result of its spiral of arcane but instantly useful terms of art: *prolepsis, analepsis,* the *iterative,* the *pseudo-iterative, focalization, paralipsis,* and so on. While some of these terms have not caught on, others have become broadly indispensable to the analysis of narrative and literature in general: "Genette's term for a flashback, *analepsis,* has become a household word in literary criticism, and – especially in work dealing with postmodern fiction – the term *metalepsis,* which refers to a transgression of narrative levels, occurs again and again."[68] Because he names and thus sharpens our sense of some of the most important aspects, movements, and paradoxes of narrative form, *Narrative Discourse* represents a moment at which several of the ideas, problems, questions, and terms that I have been looking at throughout are at last joined into a whole, robust, and more or less self-contained system; for many critics, the classical period of narrative theory at least begins and maybe begins already to end with Genette. I, for one, could not have written this book without Genette and *Narrative Discourse*; I already discussed some of his key terms in the Introduction both because they were necessary to my provisional definition of narrative as the relation between story and discourse and because the clarity of his work and his distinctions helped us to see different anticipations of the story–discourse relation in concepts that might otherwise seem remote from the mainstream of narrative theory: base and superstructure, latent and manifest, soul and form, fact and value.

What is more, as much as Genette's system can seem to stand alone, it not only motivates but also draws more or less explicitly on the whole complicated history that I have laid out here. Genette's double role in this project – he helps us to see an intellectual history that made it possible for him to help us see that intellectual history – produces an interesting narrative problem of its own: insofar as Genette is both one of my last subjects and a thinker whose articulation of the story–discourse relation enabled the historical view I take, he sits both at the beginning and at the end of my story. As he might say, his appearance in the Introduction and elsewhere amounts to an intellectual *prolepsis* of an *analepsis*, the early anticipation and, indeed, *assumption* of a later critical position that allows us to look meaningfully back. Genette thus stands as an Aristotelian end to a newly visible beginning and middle of narrative theory; he does this partly because his book *defamiliarizes* narrative, because it lays bare narrative techniques, devices, patterns, and relations that would otherwise have remained invisible. For instance, Genette makes explicit use of the Russian Formalist vocabulary when he writes, "The role of the analyst is not to be satisfied with the rationalizations, nor to be ignorant of them, but rather, having 'laid bare' the technique, to see how the motivation that had been invoked functions in the work as aesthetic medium."[69] To "lay bare" the device or the technique was, as we saw in Section 5.2, at the heart of the Russian Formalist project. Genette goes on in the next sentence to refer explicitly to Shklovsky, and, indeed, it was Genette who encouraged Todorov to produce *Théorie de la littérature* (1965), his enormously influential translation of Russian Formalist writings. In terms that also echo the Russian Formalist practice of *making strange*, Jonathan Culler writes that Genette "achieves something that most interpreters do not: he leads us to experience the strangeness of the text."[70] Similarly, Roland Barthes asserts, "Genette *names* what his classification finds: he argues against received acceptations, he creates neologisms, he vivifies old names, he constructs a terminology, i.e., a network of subtle and distinct verbal objects."[71] As I will go on to describe, we should see Genette's method in relation not only to the Formalists and Barthes but also to several other figures whom we have considered thus far: Saussure, Propp, Lévi-Strauss, and Aristotle, to be sure, but also less expected figures such as Marx, Freud, James, and even Hegel. Seen in this light, Genette represents an important culmination of the intellectual sequence that I have been tracing; he offers one possible end to a long, digressive, and sometimes shaggy story.

There is yet another aspect of Genette's writing in *Narrative Discourse* that I would like to consider, a quality that exceeds the book's deserved reputation for clarity, methodological austerity, and analytical efficacy. There is, in other words, a kind of critical intensity or even pathos at work in Genette's treatment of both narrative in general and its particular instantiation in Proust's *À la recherche du temps perdu*; this aspect of Genette's book is harder to talk about and tends as a result to go missing in most accounts of Genette's work. In addition to being an indispensable guide to narrative technique, *Narrative Discourse* is an oddly funny, sometimes moving, and deeply strange book; like Proust's own great work, it is its own self-consciously futile effort to capture time's passage, to try and to fail to develop *enough* terms, *enough* schemes, *enough* paradoxes somehow to get hold of what will not remain still: the protean experience of life lived in and through time.

Read in this light, it seems that, instead of simply offering a reading of Proust, Genette is following Proust's conceptual path in his own way; as Malcolm Bowie suggests, Proust's representation of time

> ordains that past, present and future are composites rather than simples; that recapitulations of the past are projections into the future too; that synchronicity comprises, and maybe broken down into, myriad diachronic sequences; that certain time-effects are intelligible only if spatially extended; that parallel universes may be conflated tiny a single newly conceived space-time continuum; and that any temporally extended system of differences may collapse into an undifferentiated flux. This is the time of human desire, and the time that Proust's book inhabits sentence by sentence.[72]

This description of Proust could apply just as well to *Narrative Discourse*, a book that is, after all, committed to what it acknowledges as the impossible task of naming and thus capturing narrative time. In addition, then, to offering a systematic account of narrative discourse, Genette's book lends itself to a number of distinctly Proustian meditations: how can we make sense of the past in the present while anticipating the future? What will the present look like once it has become the past in what will be the future? What allows the temporally distinct events of a story to become something more than the sum of their parts? Despite its reputation for dryness, these big, messy, emotional questions are, to my mind, what *Narrative Discourse* is all about. I want, in other words, to read *Narrative Discourse* against the usual grain, to see it as a book about narrative *as* narrative but also as a book about something *more*, as a book that seems quietly committed to recognizing and then slipping self-consciously past the methodological limits of a narrative theory that it more or less invents.

Genette makes this point in his preface, when he acknowledges that the book might seem to some readers to fall between the poles of what he calls *criticism* and *theory*:

> I confess my reluctance – or my inability – to choose between these two apparently incompatible systems of defense. It seems to me impossible to treat the *Recherche du temps perdu* as a mere example of what is supposedly narrative in general, or novelistic narrative, or narrative in autobiographical form, or narrative of God knows what other class, species, or variety. The specificity of Proustian narrative taken as a whole is *irreducible*, and any extrapolation would be a mistake in method; the *Recherche* illustrates only itself. But, on the other hand, that specificity is not *undecomposable*, and each of its analyzable features lends itself to some connection, comparison, or putting into perspective. Like every work, like every organism, the *Recherche* is made up of elements that are universal, or at least transindividual, which it assembles into a specific synthesis, into a particular totality. To analyze it is to go not from the general to the particular, but indeed from the particular to the general: from that incomparable being that is the *Recherche* to those extremely ordinary elements, figures, and techniques of general use and common currency that I call anachronies, the iterative, focalizations, paralipses, and so on.[73]

Genette thus understands his work not only as negotiating between criticism and theory and thus the particular and the general but also as moving toward a dialectical synthesis of the two positions:

> This is the paradox of every poetics, and doubtless of every other activity of knowledge as well: always torn between those two unavoidable commonplaces – that there are no objects expect particular ones and no science except of the general – but always finding comfort and something like attraction in this other, slightly less widespread truth, that the general is at the heart of the particular, and therefore (contrary to the common preconception) the knowable is at the heart of the mysterious.[74]

Genette's claim to see "the knowable at the heart of the mysterious" connects him with other figures we have examined. Genette is – like Propp, Saussure, Lévi-Strauss, Greimas, Kristeva, Barthes, and others – interested in isolating a set of shared basic and deep rules and structures that underwrite some or all narratives, that would stand as a historically specific way of organizing experience into something more or less meaningful; to see "the knowable at the heart of the mysterious" is, in other words, to look for a culture's shared patterns or deep structures that govern the arrangement of story and discourse at particular moments in time. And, indeed, because he chooses Proust's great novel, a text that represents both the culmination of and the limits immanent to a particular narrative genre, Genette is able to place his arguments about narrative form in relation to the historical specificity and the historical limits of narrative genres.

Genette is indeed explicit about the historical consequence of his project, calling it a contribution to "the (as yet unborn) *history of literature*."[75] His interest in the specific generic conditions that govern the arrangement of story and discourse in Proust connects him to other figures whom I identified with *the comparative analysis of narrative forms*: Lukács, Bakhtin, Propp, and so on. To see the shared rules that make individual utterances possible is to see the knowable in the mysterious, the general in the particular. (With this I take up Monika Fludernik's suggestion that someone look at the relation between narratology and history in Genette.)[76] That said, Genette also remains committed to the idea that that real and constitutive generality, that real relation to the shared rules that make narratives possible at a given time, will not account fully for what is particular and, indeed, strange about narrative discourse: "Here the code, like the message, has its gaps and its surprises."[77] This is what Genette sees in Proust and what, importantly, he models in *Narrative Discourse*: a practical, dialectical, and felt confrontation between the particular and the general. We can, in other words, see in Genette what Theodor Adorno also saw in Proust: "Just as the temperament of his work challenges customary notions about the general and the particular and gives aesthetic force to the dictum from Hegel's *Logic* that the particular is the general and vice versa, with each mediated through the other, so the whole, resistant to abstract outlines, crystallizes out of the intertwines individual presentations."[78] For Genette, the work of narrative theory is to trace out how narrative can stand as a practical embodiment of that Hegelian principle, how it can synthesize without reducing or subordinating either the general or the particular, either the knowable or the mysterious.

I will begin by laying out some of the most obviously useful and influential distinctions that Genette offers in *Narrative Discourse*, terms that have become more or less necessary to the classical and postclassical analysis of narrative. There is not space to cover everything, so I will rely on a few representative examples and gesture toward their relation to the whole of his system. I will turn then to Genette's initially bewildering decision to focus not on moments of "normal" narrative functioning in Proust but rather on moments when narrative form breaks down, when the relation between story and discourse ceases to make sense, when, from a certain perspective, narra- tive *fails*; Jonathan Culler writes that "it might be the case that Genette's work is testimony to the power of the marginal, the supplementary, the exception."[79] I will, in that case, look to some special uses of the exceptional in *Narrative Discourse*. Finally, I will try to situate Genette's book both within its historical context and in relation to other figures with whom I have already dealt. I will consider both Genette's relation to the intellectual context of *Tel Quel* and Paris in the 1960s as well as his reliance on the longer critical tradition that I have been laying out. Once again, I will want to suggest that beneath the exoteric surface of Genette's justly indispensable theory of narrative is an esoteric reflection on narratology as a way to manage the politics of everyday life.

~

Genette makes clear at the outset that his is a study not of objects but rather of relationships: "As we will see, analysis of narrative discourse as I understand it constantly implies a study of relationships: on the one hand the relationship between a discourse and the events that it recounts. . ., on the other hand the relationship between the same discourse and the act that produces it."[80] As with several of the figures we have looked at – Marx on the relation between base and superstructure, Freud on the relation between latent and manifest contents, Saussure on the relation between signifier and signified, etc. – Genette looks not simply at one or another part of the system, either story or discourse, but rather at the relations that characterize narrative as a whole and significant system. Genette thus identifies three aspects of narrative: *story*, or the real or fictive represented events; *narrative discourse*, or the discursive representation of those events; and *narrating*, or "the producing narrative action and, by extension, the whole of the real or fictional situation in which that action takes place."[81] He then turns to the relations that exist among those different aspects of narrative, using a scheme adapted from Tzvetan Todorov's work on the morphological equivalence between narratives and the grammatical structure of sentences; for Todorov, "To combine a noun and a verb is to take the first step towards narrative."[82] Genette writes,

> This perhaps authorizes us to organize, or at any rate to formulate, the problems of analyzing narrative discourse according to categories borrowed from the grammar of verbs, categories that I will reduce here to three basic classes of determinations: those dealing with temporal relations between narrative [discourse] and story, which I will arrange under the heading of *tense*; these dealing with modalities (forms and degrees) of narrative "representation," and thus with the *mood* of the narrative; and, finally, those dealing with the way in which the narrating itself is implicated in the narrative, the narrative situation or instance,

and along with that its two protagonists: the narrator and his audience real or implied ... this term is *voice*.[83]

Genette then divides the category of *tense*, which names the different temporal relations between story and discourse, into three subcategories – *order*, *duration*, and *frequency* – while leaving *mood* and *voice* to stand on their own. In each of the chapters that follow, Genette takes up one of these grammatical or, rather, pseudogrammatical categories or subcategories and offers terms and tools with which to make the particular relations that govern narrative visible, to understand the ways in which they work, and to see where they inevitably reach their limits. (Recent narratological work by Monika Fludernik, Marie Laure-Ryan, David Herman, and others has sought to show the limits of exclusively grammatical models, turning instead to approaches taken from discourse analysis, possible-worlds theory, and cognitive science.)

For instance, in the case of "Order," Genette looks at what we have seen again and again as the two different temporalities of story and discourse: "To study the temporal order of a narrative is to compare the order in which events or temporal sections are arranged in the narrative discourse with the order of succession these same events or temporal segments have in the story, to the extent that story order is explicitly indicated by the narrative itself or inferable from one or another indirect clue."[84] Genette suggests a couple of points here: first, as we have seen time and again, while it might seem self-evident that story needs to occur ontologically *before* discourse, that events need to happen *before* any representation of those events, narrative can in fact offer us a paradox whereby the story not only does not precede discourse but also allows us to imagine or to reconstruct events only *after* the fact of their discursive representation; which happens first, the event that makes representation possible or the representation that allows us to perceive or to imagine the event? As I said in the Introduction, Jonathan Culler and others have offered this as a paradox essential to narrative theory, a possibility that both animates detective stories (it is the sleuth's power to make story out of discursive clues after the fact) and, according to Culler, is thematized in the venerable *Oedipus Rex*:

> Oedipus becomes the murderer of his father not by a violent act that is brought to light but by bowing to the demands of narrative coherence and deeming the act to have taken place. Moreover, it is essential to the force of the play that Oedipus take this leap, that he accede to the demands of narrative coherence and deem himself guilty. If he were to resist the logic of signification, arguing that "the fact that he's my father doesn't mean that I killed him," demanding more evidence about the past event, Oedipus would not acquire the necessary tragic stature. In

this respect the force of the narrative relies on the contrary logic, in which event is not a cause but an effect of theme. To describe this logic is not to quibble over details but to investigate tragic power.[85]

In some cases and for different reasons (thematic, formal, cognitive), ontological priority within narrative seems to drift between story and discourse, and Genette builds exactly this paradox as paradox into his account.

More importantly, Genette expands on the idea that where temporal sequencing at the level of story needs to follow a set of "natural" rules more or less particular to a particular text or a narrative genre, discourse is free to arrange and rearrange the order of events (although, as we saw with Propp, some genres such as the folktale or myth can be characterized exactly by their unwillingness to do so). Herman writes that

> the sequence ABC can be told chronologically as ABC, the sequence of the telling exactly matching the order of the events being recounted. Through analepsis (flashback), the same sequence can be narrated BCA. Through prolepsis (flashforward), it can be told as CAB. Genette calls such departures from chronological sequence "anachronies"; these departures from linear narration not only have a "reach" that bears them more or less far from the present into the past or the future, but also a wider or narrower "extent" insofar as they can cover a duration of the story that is more or less long.[86]

Where, in other words, events need to appear in one and only one order at the level of story (A–B–C–D–E) those events can be rearranged in any number of ways at the level of discourse. Some narratives more or less match discourse to story, beginning with the beginning and ending at the end. In others, for instance, *Citizen Kane* (1941) or *The Lorax* (1971), we begin at the end and then flash back to the beginning in order to see what how we got from A to E (E–A–B–C–D–E): "What was the Lorax? / And why was it there? / And why was it lifted and taken somewhere / from the far end of town where the Grickle-grass grows? / The old Once-ler still lives here. / Ask him. *He* knows."[87] Other types of narrative – such as detective stories – might repeat the same sequence of events from two or more perspectives: if we take A and B as the events leading up to the crime, and C as the crime itself, D as the arrival of the detective and his or her investigation, and E as the crime's ultimate solution, we might see something like this: C–D–A–B–C–A–B–C–A–B–C–A–B–C–E. Each of the A–B–C sequences would refer to moments when the detective returns to and rehearses the events leading up to and including the crime from the perspective of each of the story's suspects and with the addition of newly discovered clues; we might, in that case, want to bracket each of those sequences in order to represent them as nested narrative acts within the larger narrative (Genette, as we will see, might call them "internal homodiegetic analepses"): C–D–[A–B–C]–[A–B–C]–[A–B–C]–[A–B–C]–E. This pattern is common in whodunits such as *Murder on the Orient Express* (1934) or in television series such as *Columbo* or *Murder, She Wrote*, where the internal (often metadiegetic) analeptic narration of events from different perspectives (flashbacks) will make up much of a given narrative. (As we can already see and as Genette acknowledges, while each of his chapters is devoted to a different single aspect of narrative discourse, in practice questions related to one category will always imply or invoke another; we often cannot talk about *order* without also talking about *frequency, mood,* or *voice.* This is another way in which Genette's narrative theory is first and last a study of relationships.)

In order to account for the indefinitely large number of moves forward and back that narrative discourse can make in relation to story, Genette identifies two basic varieties of what he calls *anachronies,* or "types of discordance between the two orderings of story and narrative [discourse]": *prolepses* and *analepses.*[88] *Analepses,* the more common of the two, are evocations "after the fact of an event that took place earlier than the point in the story where we are at any given moment."[89] *Analepses* are, in other words, flashbacks, and there are several varieties of them.[90] *External* analepses are flashbacks that both begin and end in a past prior to the proper beginning of a narrative; *internal* analepses are flashbacks that begin and end after the proper beginning of a narrative; Genette also describes *mixed* analepses, which begin before the proper beginning of the narrative but "catch up" and overlap with what has already been narrated. We might think here about the fifteenth chapter of George Eliot's *Middlemarch*, where the narrator reveals an "interesting" passage in the romantic history of Tertius Lydgate, an account of his love affair with the murderous French actress Laure. Although important to us as a way of understanding Lydgate's character, the passage remains unknown to any of the novel's other characters: "At present I have to make the new settler Lydgate better known to any one interested in him than he could possibly be even to those who had seen the most of him since his arrival in Middlemarch."[91] The analepsis remains external because it stands both before and outside anything else in the narrative; it began and ended before the start of the novel's main events. If, however, Lydgate had met and had an affair with Laure while on vacation in Paris after first arriving in Middlemarch or, perhaps, if Laure had reappeared in the novel, directly linking his earlier time in Paris with his present in Middlemarch, an external analepsis would then become either an internal or a mixed analepsis. Genette also differentiates *heterodiegetic* analepses, which are introduced from *outside* the main line of the narrative in order to explain or to shed light on events, from *homodiegetic* analepses, which refer to events that happened earlier within the main line of a narrative but that were for one or another reason left unnarrated the first time around. These can either *complete* a narrative, filling in necessary information that somehow has been "skipped over," sidestepped, or elided (as we will see, he uses the terms *ellipsis* and *paralipsis* to name two ways in which story information goes missing in narrative discourse) or *repeat* a narrative, retracing steps and re-presenting events and information that we have have seen before, albeit in a different discursive form: "in these the narrative openly, sometimes explicitly, retraces its own path."[92]

Genette then goes on to discuss *prolepses*, moments when narrative discourse flashes forward instead of back; he breaks down the kinds of prolepsis into a similarly precise set of kinds, which I will not lay out in detail here.[93] Suffice it to say that different types of narrative use prolepses to produce suspense, to give readers real or false "advance notice" of what events mean or what is to come, and to evoke the sense or feeling of a narrative in progress as a nonetheless coherent whole (this last function is especially important in Proust, where all *anachronies* are "obviously connected to the retrospectively synthetic character of the Proustian narrative, which is totally present in the narrator's mind at every moment").[94] As I have already said, because Genette's account of narrative discourse is a system, attending to one of its categories often if not always requires that we turn to others at the same time; in order to talk about an instance of analepsis, we need often also to talk about *ellipses*, about how a given narration is *focalized*, about whether the remembered event took place only once or whether it was something that happened more often (the *singulative* or the *iterative*). Rather than go through each chapter of *Narrative Discourse*, I want now to turn to an example in order to touch on several of Genette's other terms and, more importantly, to show how, in practice, they need often if not always to be thought of together. In order, in other words, to look at how *Narrative Discourse* is, in fact, a study of relationships, I will turn briefly to Jacques Tourneur's 1947 film noir, *Out of the Past*.

Like Proust's great novel, *Out of the Past* announces its interest in time and the presentation of fractured narrative temporalities with its title, one that evokes a traumatic version of time in which the past will not stay put; it is not only that events emerge *out of the past* to haunt us in the present but also that the past has somehow been put *out* of its usual place, has been knocked, as the man says, "out of joint." And as with Proust, it is the job of narrative and its surrogate hero to put matters back into order. The film opens with Jeff Bailey (Robert Mitchum), an ex-private detective, formerly known as Jeff Markham, who has escaped his troubled past and taken on the role of a small-town mechanic; after being discovered by Whit Sterling (Kirk Douglas), a powerful "operator" whom he had double-crossed, stealing (and then also losing) the girl he had been hired to find, Jeff decides to stop running and to confront Whit directly. He then proceeds over the course of a long drive to share his story with and to seek forgiveness from his trusting new sweetheart, Ann Miller (Virginia Huston). He describes how had been hired in New York by Whit to find Kathie Moffat (Jane Greer) and take her back; he tracked her down to Acapulco and instead fell in love with her; she betrayed him and he was forced to go on the run and to hide out in Ann's small town, which draws us out of the past and into the film's present. Like many classic noirs, *Out of the Past* makes extensive use of voice-over during this sequence, a fact that periodically returns us to the level of the film's soundtrack from the represented past to the implied narrative present of Jeff as he tells Ann his tale. After finishing both their drive and what amounts to his confession, we arrive more or less where we started, ready now to move into the film's future, to the rigged assignment that Whit gives to Jeff in order to "square things"; to his second encounter with Kathie; and, at last, to Jeff's final and fatal meeting with Whit and Kathie; they all manage to kill each other and the film ends with Jeff's funeral, which confers hard-won closure on both Ann and the narrative as a whole. The past, which had encroached on the present in terms of its ethical and practical consequence as well as of its formal presence as the unruly stuff of narrative, returns to where it apparently belongs.

At the level of *story* we can represent *Out of the Past* like this: A (Jeff's first meeting with Whit, who hires him to find Kathie); B (Jeff meets and falls in love with Kathie in Mexico; they make their way to San Francisco; she double-crosses him and makes off with Whit's money); C (Jeff hides out in the Sierras as a small-town mechanic and is discovered by one of Whit's henchmen); D (he confesses to Ann while driving to Whit's Lake Tahoe home, taking us back into the past); E (he is offered and warily pursues Whit's second case and reconnects with Kathie in San Francisco); F (he encounters Whit and Kathie for the last time, a meeting that leads to all of their deaths); G (we witness his funeral and the film's end). If, in that case, the story must proceed "naturally" from beginning to end – A–B–C–D–E–F–G – it takes a far more complicated form at the level of narrative discourse: something loosely like C–D–A–D1–B–D_1–C–D_1–E–F–G (I have changed D to D_1 where the position appears in the form of Jeff's voice-over narration of B). The film thus depends heavily both on *analepsis* (much of its narrated material is dragged "out of the past" in the form of Jeff's narration) and, in a way, also on *prolepsis*; although, from the perspective of the film as a whole, much of what is told has *already* happened, from the perspective of Jeff's present narration of his past (it is a framed narrative-within-a-narrative, or what Genette would call the *metadiegetic* narrative), he is able as narrator to anticipate and to gesture toward what as a narrated character he could not have known: the nature and consequence of Kathie's duplicity when revealed in the future. As a narrated narrator, Jeff is thus able proleptically to signal the future outcomes of past events as they were experienced in their present. The displaced temporal position of the voice-over (it is the present narrating a past for which it is the future) in fact represents something like an *analeptic prolepsis*, a figure that draws out temporal complications essential to this film and to the noir genre as a whole. *Out of the Past* represents this complexity in visual terms as Jeff's narration and his subsequent trip to San Francisco take him from the wide and light open spaces of the Sierras into the dark, claustrophobic, high-contrast urban interiors of noir.

Out of the Past indeed forces at least three different kinds of narrative order into one highly impacted form: from the perspective of Jeff as narrator, the film follows a flashback structure, moving analeptically from the narrating present D to the narrated past A–B–C; from the perspective of the film's representation (and thus its narration) of Jeff's own automotive narration, it follows that same sequence A–B–C but adds a zigzag rhythm that pings from past to present to future as it returns us again and again to the voice-over's temporal point of origin D; and from the perspective of the film as a whole, which includes both Jeff as *narrator* of a *metadiegetic* narrative and Jeff as *narrated* by the unmarked but organizing point of view implied by the film as a whole (Jeff is both a narrator and the subject of another, higher-level narration, what Genette might call an instance of *zero focalization*), the film follows a more straightforward narrative pattern beginning in the present C, moving through D and E and F, and ending, as narratives often do, with the death of a protagonist – G.[95] With this in mind, Jeff's narrative should perhaps be represented as a single event "containing" other events – Jeff's narration of his past. We might from that perspective represent the narrative discourse of *Out of the Past* like this: C–D–[A–D_1–B–D_1–C–D_1]–E–F–G.

It makes a certain structural as well as thematic sense that D/D_1, Jeff's confession, takes place in a moving car; the close, isolated, but nonetheless mobile space of the car thematically underscores both its nested separateness from the rest of the film's narrative and the way in which it is threaded through and punctuates the representation of events A–B–C as a kind of temporal counterpoint. We might think here of the car trip as an example of what Bakhtin would call a *chronotope*, with the space of the moving car representing a space in which it might be possible to tell the awful truth about the past; in this way, the car is the narrative equivalent of what Michel Foucault once referred to as *heterotopias of crisis*, "privileged or sacred or forbidden places, reserved for individuals who are, in relation to society and to the human environment in which they live, in a state of crisis."[96] Jeff's confession is itself a narrative representation of time and, as it takes place over a long drive, it is an act that both falls out of fully or richly narratable time of events and yet also takes its own kind of time; it is a discursive representation of a sequence of events that includes as an event someone's making a discursive representation of another event or sequence of events. It is not only a present representation of past events but also a present representation that takes place while Ann and especially Jeff literally *move* on toward an inexorable future. In this way, the setting and the form of Jeff's narration oddly plot a difference between two ideas about narration and what, in the chapter "Voice," Genette calls "the time of the narrating."[97]

On the one hand, we know that, like everything else, telling a story takes time; that Jeff will need to speak to Ann for ten, twenty, or ninety minutes in order to tell the story of his past; on the other hand, it is unusual for fictions to dwell on the time of narration – on how long it actually takes to tell the tale – as opposed to the time of narrative: "Nevertheless – and this is finally very odd – the fictive narrating of ... almost all the novels in the world ... is considered to have no duration; or, more exactly, everything takes place as if the question of its duration had no relevance."[98] In other words, as much as we attend – sometimes obsessively – to the time of a story, we tend paradoxically to assume the essential timelessness of certain kinds of narration. While, for instance, we track Pip's growth from child to man with some care in *Great Expectations*, we never wonder what happens to the already-grown, narrating Pip while he narrates; in other words, although it must have taken the imagined Pip (as opposed to Charles Dickens) some time to arrange and deliver his narrative, we act rather as if the narrative arrives all at once from some instantaneous future present. Where the narrated Pip is entirely a creature of time, the grown, narrating Pip exists somehow *out* of time – *out*, as it were, of the past. Joseph Conrad makes a dry-as-dust joke about this strange kind of narratorial no-time in the "Author's Note" to *Lord Jim* when he reflects that Marlow *could* have spoken the whole of his long part of the narrative if, perhaps, he had had "a glass of mineral water of some sort to help" him on; the joke is that it makes no sense to imagine the timeless abstraction that is narration drinking *anything*.[99] In the case of Jeff's own indeterminately long metadiegetic narration in *Out of the Past*, the film tries, it seems, to have it both ways: we are given one sense of how long the narrating act takes because it takes place over the course of a drive from eastern California to Whit's place on the Nevada side of Lake Tahoe; because, however, we cannot know exactly how long the drive takes or where Jeff's voice-over in fact fits in with the duration of the drive, it is an especially elastic marker. More to the point, the eventless, merely instrumental driving that Jeff does is at last an almost empty kind of time, a time that, as anyone who commutes to work knows, lacks *narrativity* and seems to approach without quite becoming the abstract no-time of classical narration. The film uses the space of the car ride to navigate what might otherwise seem uncomfortable about Jeff's dual role as narrator and character.

As I have already said, any analysis of narrative will require that we move beyond any single one of Genette's categories. In order to account for the *order* of *Out of the Past*, we had to consider how its different narratives and narrators are situated in relation to one another, an issue that Genette takes up in the chapter "Voice," where he lays out his influential account of narrative levels: the relation, in other words, that exists between a narrator and the discursive world that he, she, or it narrates: "We will define this difference in level by saying that *any event a narrative recounts is at a diegetic level immediately higher than the level at which the narrating act producing this narrative is placed.*"[100] He goes on to distinguish among *extradiegetic, intradiegetic,* and *metadiegetic* events: *extradiegetic* objects and events stand outside the narrated world produced by a narrator's discursive act and thus include the narrator as narrator. As Jeff narrates his past, he and Ann stand *outside* the frame of that discursively rendered narrative; they thus exist in an *extradiegetic* relation to his representation of the past; when Marlow and Pip narrate their past experiences, *as narrators* they too exist in an extradiegetic relation to the worlds they narrate; the unnamed, abstract, "omniscient" narrator of *Pride and Prejudice* is also an extradiegetic narrator, a figure that exists "outside" of narrative discourse because it is the source of that narrative discourse. Events take place at the same level as other events within a given narrative world exist in an *intradiegetic* (sometimes simply *diegetic*) relation to one another. As Jeff and Ann sit together in a car in the film's narrative present, they exist at the same narrative level, a level immediately "below" the cinematic act that is the whole of *Out of the Past* and immediately "above" the material that makes up the story that Jeff tells Ann about the past; because they exist at the same discursive level, because they exist in the same relation to the narrative act that is the film, they exist in a diegetic relation to one another. When, however, Jeff the diegetic character begins to narrate his past, his discursive act produces what Genette refers to as a *metadiegetic* narrative; as he tells the story of his past self, of a character who lived in New York, met Kathie in Mexico, etc., he thus produces a second-degree discursive world within a world that stands in a *metadiegetic* relation to the film as a whole. An image might help to clarify the relation among these different levels: in the image, A represents an extradiegetic narrator producing a narrative in which an (intra)diegetic character B is also an (intra)diegetic narrator of another narrative in which a metadiegetic character C could in turn become a metadiegetic narrator of a narrative in which we might learn about character D, and so on. Put in terms of *Out of the Past*, A would stand in for an extradiegetic act of cinematic representation that includes Jeff as one of its (intra)diegetic characters; and because Jeff goes on to tell his story to Ann, he becomes an (intra)diegetic narrator (B) of the metadiegetic narrative of his time with Kathy (C); if, within *that* narrative, the metadiegetic character Kathy told Jeff a story about *her* past, then metadiegtic Kathy would become a metadiegetic narrator C; and so on.[101]

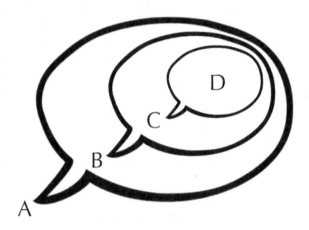

Genette goes on to describe both the "normal" state of these different relations and some transgressive instances when events seem paradoxically to cross between narrative levels: "The transition from one narrative level to another can in principle be achieved only by the narrating, the act that consists precisely of introducing into one situation, by means of a discourse, the knowledge of another situation. Any other form of transit is, if not always impossible, at any rate always transgressive."[102] *Metalepses*, moments when the line between one and another level is "impossibly" crossed, are common in different kinds of postmodern or experimental fiction, where narrators often exert undue influence on or appear in the midst of what they narrate or where the events of a story told within a story seem somehow to bleed out into that higher level; we might think of fictions that rely on metalepses by

Sterne or Diderot or Cortázar or Borges; of a novel like Muriel Spark's *The Comforters* (1957); or of a film like *Stranger than Fiction* (2006), in which Harold Crick (Will Ferrell) manages somehow to *overhear* the extradiegetic voice narrating his intradiegetic life. Although less spectacular, *Out of the Past* has, as I suggested previously, its own relation to metalepsis insofar as the film's represented past seems to exist not only as a story to tell but also as a force or a fate that, in the nature of noir, exceeds its position as metadiegetic content to exert an almost occult influence on the present. More than simply a past cause that produces present effects, the past rather seems to be a living, disturbing, and traumatic *presence* in *Out of the Past*, a fact that encourages us perhaps to think of noir as perhaps an essentially metaleptic genre. (See Section 3.2 for a discussion of metalepsis in relation to Nietzsche's account of the chorus in Greek tragedy.)

We could also look to the chapter on "Duration" in order to ask how Tourneur manages the relation in what Genette offers as the four classical ways of representing the passage of story-time at the level of discourse-time: *scene*, in which there is a rough equivalence between the time taken by story and the time taken by discourse; *summary*, in which more story-time is squeezed into less discourse-time; *pause*, in which a narrator "stops" events in order to speak at the level of discourse about ideas or events that *do not* occur at the level of story, a limit case in which there is discourse without story; and *ellipsis*, in which events occur either explicitly ("two years passed") or implicitly without being represented in discourse, another limit case in which there is story without discourse. While most of the film would seem to exist as *scene*, its highly edited use of retrospective narration in the form of voice-over allows the film to play with the relation among *summary*, *pause*, and *ellipsis*, as Jeff moves quickly over the details of his life with Kathie while they are on the run (summary), as he stops to reflect ironically on the nature of life and fate (pause), and as he obviously but tacitly passes over less important or uncomfortable aspects of his past so as not to wound Ann (ellipsis).

We might think here of the film's famous love scene. Jeff narrates (to Ann) returning to Kathie's little Mexican bungalow after getting caught out in the rain: "It was a nice little joint with bamboo furniture and Mexican gimcracks. One little lamp burned. It was all right." They fall onto a couch and, as they begin to kiss, Jeff throws a towel, knocking the "one little lamp" over and out. At this point, the camera pans coyly away from the couple, across the apartment, and out into the wind- and rain-swept courtyard, where it pauses for a moment accompanied by a swell of romantic music. We then return to the bungalow and the scene resumes. Seasoned filmgoers would of course know what they *were not* seeing; in the classic Hollywood vernacular, panning to a rain-swept window almost always means sex. Taken *within* the level of Jeff's metadiegetic narrative, the turn to the window is a form of *paralipsis*, a turn to a parallel event that allows one to sidestep but still to signal the presence of another, less narratable event. Seen in relation to Jeff's intent, the matter is more complicated. Insofar as what we see is a record of what Jeff is *saying* to Ann as they drive along, it is impossible to know what he has actually said to "produce" this image. Did he say something more or less tactful like "We went back to her place and you know the rest"? Did he, in fact, say, "We had sex," making the pan away from the event to the courtyard more a matter of the film's care for the viewer than of Jeff's care for Ann? (In this case, we would need to consider the relation not only between two narratives but also between two narrators, between what we cannot hear but what Jeff must nonetheless be saying to Ann and what the film as narrative "decides" to show us of or instead of what Jeff narrates.) Or, both more and less plausibly, did Jeff in fact begin, when he arrived at the sex, to describe wind blowing and rain dripping off palm trees, hoping that Ann would understand his strange euphemistic effort to handle the embarrassing details of the encounter in the sanitized terms of symbol? That none of these explanations really works points to one of the limits of the voice-over as a form of metadiegetic cinematic narration and thus to the inevitability of transgression; what is more, because the turn away marks a moment when what Jeff implicitly says and what we explicitly see are clearly distinct, it is impossible to say whether we are dealing with scene, summary, ellipsis, or pause precisely because it represents a moment when story and discourse fall into an insolubly indeterminate relation.[103]

Similarly, we could look to Genette's section "Mood" in order to ask how the film is *focalized*, or rather how focalization works differently at the level of the film as a whole (I have already referred to Genette's controversial category, *zero focalization*) and at the level of Jeff's metadiegetic narrative (which is more clearly because necessarily focalized from Jeff's perspective). We could consider the previous discussion – who sees and says what in and about the bungalow – also in terms of focalization. (See Section 4.1 for a longer discussion of these issues.) Or, finally, we could consider Genette's discussion of narrative "frequency," in which he introduces the difference among the *singulative*, the *iterative*, and what he calls *repeating narratives*. The *singulative* occurs when a single event at the level of story is represented once and only once at the level of discourse: on Sunday, March 20, I went to the park. The *iterative* occurs when an event that has occurred in the same or different ways many times is narrated only once: on Sundays, I would go to the park. *Repeating narrative* – " I went to the park, I went to the park, I went to the park" – are less common in classical narratives, but are a feature of some experimental fictions and time-travel narratives including *Groundhog Day* or *Edge of Tomorrow*, a film with the tagline "Live. Die. Repeat." Again, although one might think that a film such as *Out of the Past* would rely almost solely on the singulative – it represents once what happened once and only once – the film in fact makes occasional and surprising uses of the iterative mode. For instance, after arriving in Mexico, Jeff counts on the fact, because Kathie is on the run, that she will have to catch a boat in Acapulco; as a result, he sets up shop in a cafe and waits:

> You say to yourself, "How hot can it get?" Then, in Acapulco, you find out. I knew she had to wind up here because if you want to go south, here's where you get the boat. All I had to do was wait. Near the plaza was a little cafe, called La Mar Azul next to a movie house. I sat there in the afternoons and drank beer. I used to sit there half-asleep with the beer and the darkness. Only that music from the movie next door kept jarring me awake.

This, obviously, is an instance of the iterative, the representation of several related but not identical afternoons at the bar represented in a single act of narration: "I used to sit there." The move is particularly effective insofar as the form of the iterative manages to join aspects of the scene – its heat, languor, and boredom – not only to imply some of the more mundane qualities of life as a working private detective but also to establish those slow afternoons at La Mar Azul as a kind of narrative calm before the storm, a period of nearly nonnarratable quiet before Jeff falls in love with Kathie, an event that puts his story into a different and more frantic kind of motion, one less suited to the pseudotemporality of the iterative mode.

~

I have rushed through these categories for a few reasons. First, the precision with which Genette himself lays these out in *Narrative Discourse* means that anything like a full presentation of his terms would amount to telling the whole story over again, an effort that would be undoubtedly worthwhile, but for which we do not have time. I will thus encourage the reader to look both at *Narrative Discourse* and at some of the works that take up, develop, and challenge Genette's terms. Second, while Genette's "technology" is, as I hope I have begun to suggest, immensely powerful as a set of descriptive, analytical tools, it is only one aspect of the larger work that Genette takes on in

Narrative Discourse. That is, while he indeed provides tools that might be used to account for almost any narrative, he does so in the context of an act not only of analysis but also of interpretation; he, in other words, offers a critical evaluation of Proust's *Recherche*, a text that in his account not only exhibits many if not all of the narrative techniques that he describes but also regularly exceeds, undermines, or undoes them:

> It has no doubt become evident, in this comparison of Proustian narrative with the general system of narrative possibilities, that the analyst's curiosity and predilection went regularly to the most deviant aspects of Proustian narrative, the specific transgressions or beginning of a future development. This systematic valuing of originality and innovation is perhaps somewhat unsophisticated and altogether romantic as well, but today no one can entirely escape it.[104]

If, in other words, *Narrative Discourse* has a subject, it is not (or at least not only) narrative in general but rather the particular ways in which narrative discourse does and, indeed, must fail in Proust. Barthes writes that "what [Genette] discerns in Proust, with predilection (as he himself underlines), are narrative deviances (by which the Proustian narrative counters our possible notion of a simple, linear, 'logical' narrative). Now, deviances (from a code, a grammar, a norm) are always manifestations of writing: where the rule is transgressed, there writing appears as excess, since it takes on a language *which was not foreseen.*"[105] This is a large part of Genette's project that sometimes goes missing in accounts that move more directly to the contested normative value of one or another of his terms. Why, after all, dedicate the book *Narrative Discourse* to a text that seems defined by the beautiful failure of its narrative discourse? Why begin such a project with a novel that seems to move classical narrative close to its finish? In what follows, I want to look at a few of the more spectacular moments of transgression that Genette picks out as especially vital in Proust before going on to suggest *why* his narrative theory, which is, after all, the most immediately influential of them all, must appear first and foremost as a theory of narrative failure. I will want to suggest that Genette's love of failure points to the strange and radical politics of *Narrative Discourse.*

In the section "Order," Genette offers an extreme example of *analeptic paralipsis,* his term for the introduction of material into the present of the narrative not only from another and earlier point but also from the outside of the story; a paralipsis is, as we saw with the rain-swept window in *Out of the Past,* an event not narrated in its given place but also not simply "skipped over" as in the case of a straightforward ellipsis. A paralipsis does not skip over but, Genette says, rather *sidesteps* an event that can thus be introduced into the narrative at another point. He offers this as an especially complicated example:

> But the most remarkable case – although it is rarely picked up by critics, perhaps because they refuse to take it seriously – is the mysterious "girl-cousin" about whom we learn, when Marcel gives Aunt Leonie's sofa to a go-between, that with her on this same sofa he experienced "for the first time the sweets of love"; and this happened no where else but at Combray, and at a fairly early date, since he makes clear that the scene of the "initiation" took place "one hour when my Aunt Leonie had gotten up," and we know in another connection that in her final years Leonie no longer left her room. Let us set aside the probable thematic value of this belated confidence, and let us even admit that the omission of the event from the narrative of *Combray* is a purely temporal ellipsis: the omission of the *character* from the family tableau perhaps for that reason comes even closer to being censorship. This little cousin on the sofa will thus be for us—to each age its own pleasures – analepsis on paralipsis.[106]

There are a couple of features that make this example "remarkable." First and most importantly, it is one of many moments in Proust when the tools of narrative discourse appear turned more or less against themselves; instead of clarifying or explaining Marcel's youth and his initiation into sexual life, the unexpected introduction of the "girl-cousin" produces an unwonted and yet trivial sense of mystery, a potential but also apparently insignificant error in the chronology of Marcel's time at his aunt's house in Combray. Where, in other words, we might imagine so important an event to be firmly situated, sharply delineated within the history of his youth, it is instead introduced almost haphazardly from a past that seems not only to have been almost forgotten but also to have run disconnectedly parallel alongside the main currents of Marcel's narratable life. What makes this all the more notable is the fact that the "girl-cousin" herself is a sort of oddly familiar stranger in Proust's narrative, a pseudocharacter whose relation to the time of the *Recherche* is both decidedly oblique and taken oddly for granted despite the importance she could have had in another version of the story. On the one hand, this feels, as Genette suggests, something like the result of misplaced or, in the nature of paralipsis, a *misplacing* tact, an implied feeling on Marcel's part that one should handle such an event with delicacy. On the other hand, despite the low-key awkwardness of its presentation, the moment has, as Genette suggests, higher stakes at the level of narrative form; it seems, in other words, to threaten the internal coherence of Proust's story-world. As it seems, it is nonetheless a moment when narrative almost ceases to function; and because it almost ceases to function, it threatens to call the rest of Proust's represented world into question as well; it is a moment that reveals "narrative [discourse]'s capacity for *temporal autonomy*," which is to say its finally *antinarrative* freedom from story.[107] By itself, this points, as many of Genette's examples do, to places where ordinary narrative functions are stretched to the point where they threaten the whole logic of Proust's narrative, where, for different reasons, narrative form seems to have been turned against itself.

Left at the level of form, it is one of many instructive moments when we can see the nature of the narrative norms better when they are compared to the exceptions; thought of rather as a point where form and a particular content join, it suggests something more about Proust's method, a pointed way in which the local failure of narrative form has a role to play in relation to the *meaning* of the *Recherche*. It is, in other words, significant that this particular exception appears at a moment of sexual initiation, a fact that suggests a deeper relation among sexual knowledge, sexual desire, and the limits of narrative representation. In other words, in a manner that is characteristic of the *Recherche*, the strangely managed scene of the "girl-cousin" implies that narrative *failure* might at last be better suited than narrative *success* when it comes to the representation of sexual pleasure and sexual desire. This possibility is, I think, highlighted in the winking manner in which Genette handles the transgression's appearance. Instead of simply naming it, he indulges in a couple of uncharacteristic jokes. First, his slightly resigned and dry acknowledgment that each age has "its own pleasures" opens up his commentary in a couple of directions. On the one hand, it is an ironic nod to what is slightly ridiculous about the pleasure of the critic; compared to Marcel's experience of first, illicit love on his aunt's couch, the critic's truffle hunting after abstruse narrative figures must appear a little empty, a little belated, a little beside the point. On the other hand, the comparison also works in another direction, suggesting that there might be more of an erotic pull to the act of interpretation than the wider world could perhaps know, that the play of narrative form, the movement of one narrative level over another might indeed be understood not only as the object of a technician's gaze but also as something at least like erotic pleasure. Indeed, Genette lets himself become slightly carried away here, allowing himself what must surely be *Narrative Discourse*'s only dirty joke: "This little cousin on the sofa will thus be for us ... analepsis on paralipsis." The odd, implied, and, I think, intended spatial analogy between the cousin on the couch (and, of course, Marcel on the cousin or the cousin on Marcel) and an "analepsis on paralipsis" stands as an oddly funny because absurd moment of bawdy humor. More, though, than a bit of fun, the association of sexual desire and narrative transgression points to a deeper significance to Genette's categories in *Narrative Discourse*. As we know from Freud, sexual desire often emerges into discourse in the barely disguised form of both the slip and the joke, a fact that Genette wryly acknowledges by turning a narrative slip in Proust into his own mildly dirty joke. Although there is a lot more to say here, I will just observe that the unexpected eruption of desire in the second-degree form of jokes in Genette about slips in Proust not only points to the possible existence of a narratological unconscious but also makes a tacit point on which Proust and Genette would agree: that the truth of sex and sexual desire sometimes shows itself where narrative stops.

In a sense, Genette's distinction between the erotic possibilities of success and failure anticipates a distinction between textual *pleasure* and textual *bliss* that Barthes will subsequently make in *The Pleasure of the Text* (1973):

> Text of pleasure: the text that contents, fills, grants euphoria; the text that comes from culture and does not break with it, is linked to a comfortable practice of reading. Text of bliss: the text that imposes a state of loss, the text that discomforts (perhaps to the point of a certain boredom), unsettles the reader's historical, cultural, psychological assumptions, the consistency of his tastes, values, memories, brings to a crisis his relation with language.[108]

Barthes's point, familiar to us from *S/Z*, is that where some texts or some ways of reading merely reinforce the code – which is to say that some texts support and reproduce the rules that govern the limits of the sayable or the narratable at a given moment in time – other texts and other ways of reading show the cracks in that system and point, however tentatively, to the possibility of something *beyond the code* (the old distinction between the *is* and the *ought*). This is also the distinction between the *readerly* and the *writerly* that we looked at in the previous section and traced back to Julia Kristeva's distinction between *the book* and *writing*. In the early Barthes of *Writing Degree Zero*, this distinction named two different kinds of writing, *bourgeois* and *revolutionary* writing; it was in this period that Sollers, Barthes, and others associated with *Tel Quel* began to celebrate the narrative experiments of Alain Robbe-Grillet, "the doyen of the nouveau roman."[109] "Robbe-Grillet's innovative approach, in which nineteenth-century conventions such as plot and character counted for little, meshed seamlessly with *Tel Quel*'s formalist preoccupations, as well as its distaste for realism."[110] If his sense of the writerly initially focused on the act of writing itself, in *S/Z* the responsibility for seeing through or even undoing the codes that organize saying and thinking in everyday life moves from the author or the text on to the reader, a reader who *works* to see moments of revolutionary or writerly possibility within an otherwise readerly bourgeois text; as we saw in the last section, Barthes associates his particular work of reading with the socially subversive act of *rereading*: "Rereading draws the text out of its internal chronology ('this happens *before* or *after* that') and recaptures a mythic time (without *before* or *after*)."[111] Rereading, because it suspends the experience and the idea of chronology and thus undoes the meaning of the story–discourse relation, can thus reveal what is already or immanently writerly about even the most classic text. *Writerliness*, in other words, comes to name a reader's relation to what is read as opposed to a quality of the writing itself: "the work of the commentary, once it is separated from any ideology of totality, consists precisely in *manhandling* the text, *interrupting* it."[112]

It makes sense, in that case, that Barthes's shift of attention from the text to the reader would correspond with a shift in examples, a move away from the more obviously experimental work of a Robbe-Grillet back to a "classic" such as Balzac's; the point for Barthes is that, rather than distinguishing between readerly and writerly texts or between texts of mere pleasure and texts of bliss, the critic should turn to apparently bourgeois models in order to find moments of writerly bliss *within* the readerly, to see traces of something other than the code *within* the code itself. To reread is to see the multiple ways in which every text – and especially the great ones – is tacitly, immanently, necessarily plural and thus already writerly. As I suggested in the previous section, we can also see Barthes's methodological shift as part of a political move that follows the path of Lukács's earlier "reconciliation with reality," his coming to terms with the fact that, because authentic proletarian revolution did not appear *imminent*, one had to look at what was *immanent* to a tenacious culture of bourgeois capitalism in order to see and appreciate the revolutionary potential within it. In other words, just as Lukács began to look for moments of dialectical and thus revolutionary possibility within "conservative" novelists such as Sir Walter Scott, so does Barthes turn to Balzac and the working of moments of writerliness within the readerly text.

This search for the writerly *within* the readerly, for moments of suggestive transgression within an otherwise working code, is also at the avowed heart of Genette's project, a point he makes explicit in *Narrative Discourse Revisited*. After once again acknowledging what might seem overly "romantic" about his focus on the "innovative or 'subversive' aspects of" Proust, he writes that giving up its "romanticism" would be difficult because

> I still feel very close . . . to the Barthesian valuing of the "writerly," which
> I invoked at that time. Today I would simply give it a slightly different
> meaning, one that obviously commits no one but myself. I would
> contrast the "writerly" with the "readerly" no longer as the modern to
> the classical or the deviant to the canonical but, rather, as the potential
> to the real, as a possibility not yet produced, the theoretical approach to
> which has the power to indicate its place (the famous empty slot) and its
> nature.[113]

He goes on to say:

> What is certain is that poetics in general, and narratology in particular,
> must not limit itself to *accounting for* existing forms or themes. It must
> also explore the field of what is possible or even impossible without
> pausing too long at that frontier, the mapping out of which is not its job.
> Until now, critics have done no more than interpret literature.
> Transforming it is now the task at hand. That is certainly not the
> business of theoreticians alone; their role is no doubt negligible. Still,
> what would theory be worth if it were not also good for *inventing
> practice?*[114]

Genette is in part making an argument about his literary critical methodology,
about how and why he values the exception over the rule, the transgression
over the norm. The point is not just that one can learn a lot about a system by
looking to its occasional and exceptional lapses; it is rather that the transgres-
sions that he tracks in Proust are points where possibility reveals itself in the
midst of the everyday; they are places where something essentially resistant to
narrative and the novel manages to break through the surface of one of the
greatest representatives of narrative and the novel, where one of the most
perfect and fullest expressions of a particular cultural logic is at one and the
same time one proof of the internal limits of that cultural logic. Because
Genette follows many of the figures we have looked at – Lukács, Bakhtin, the
Russian Formalists, Saussure, Lévi-Strauss, Barthes, etc. – as seeing particular
narratives as both conditioned and limited by the generic or linguistic or
social rules that govern experience at a particular moment in time, he sees the
writerly or transgressive or antinarrative moments in Proust, the moments of
what Barthes would call textual *bliss*, as expressions of radical literary possibility emerging in the midst of literary tradition.

There is also a more explicitly political or historical argument or response
at work here. A few years before *Narrative Discourse*, Genette wrote the essay
"Frontiers of Narrative"; in it, he followed Barthes and others in looking to

Robbe-Grillet, Philippe Sollers, and others associated with the *nouveau roman* as offering an imminent and revolutionary alternative to the narrative genre of the bourgeois novel and the culture that it represented:

> It is as if literature had exhausted or overflowed the resources of its representative mode, and wanted to fold back into the indefinite murmur of its own discourse. Perhaps the novel, after poetry, is about to emerge definitively from the age of representations. Perhaps narrative, in the negative singularity that we have just attributed to it, is already for us, as art was for Hegel, *a thing of the past*, which we must hurry to consider as it retreats, before it has completely disappeared from our horizon.[115]

In 1966 Genette seemed to think and maybe to hope that a form of narrative best represented by the classic bourgeois novel, a form of narrative that he associated most strongly with the story–discourse relation, would pass away; this is, as we saw, something he shares with the early Barthes and *Tel Quel*, which held on to the hope that, as Jean-Michel Rabaté puts it, "by showing the codes, cogs, and wheels of literary language, the production of a new poetic and political truth would…shatter the dominant repressive ideology."[116] By 1968, however, Genette had separated himself from *Tel Quel* and its more extreme claims about history, the novel, and theory partly because of the journal's belated alliance with the French Communist Party, which Genette had left in 1956 in the wake of the Soviet suppression of the Hungarian Revolution (a revolution in which Lukács, the subject of Section 4.2, was himself an ill-fated participant).[117] He then formed, along with Todorov and Hélène Cixous, the journal *Poetique*, a more academic and strictly literary alternative to *Tel Quel*: "As academics, Todorov and Genette were a minority at *Tel Quel*, and it is not surprising that they would leave *Tel Quel* as it embarked on its ('terrorist') avant-garde course…in order to found a theoretical, university journal, *Poetique*, with Cixous in 1968. *Poetique* would be everything *Tel Quel* had struggled not to be."[118] And, as he moved away from *Tel Quel*, he moved *back* from the experiments of Robbe-Grillet and Sollers to Proust and the *Recherche*, a novel that represents the greatest hopes for and achievements of the novel form; and, also like Barthes, he did not see this return to the classics as form of reaction. It was, as he says, rather an effort to see the *possible* or the *potential* within the real, to look *within* as opposed to *beyond* the present and the everyday, the code and the norm for intimations of how things might or ought to be. It is significant that, with his attention to the significant failures of narrative in Proust, Genette reproduces an observation that Lukács made in *The Theory of the Novel*, the observation that "by a strange and melancholy paradox, the moment of failure is the moment of value; the comprehending and experiencing of life's refusals is the source from which the fullness of life seems to flow."[119] This is, perhaps, why he finds the relation between eros, between sexual desire, between bliss and narrative failure worth highlighting. Barthes, you'll remember, calls what Genette looks for "places where the story '*skids*'" and makes the stakes of that 'skidding' clear:

> Now, a theory of "skidding" is necessary *precisely today*. Why? Because we are in that historical moment of our culture when narrative cannot yet abandon a certain readability, a certain conformity to narrative pseudo-logic which culture has instilled in us and in which, consequently, the only possible novations consist not in destroying the story, the anecdote, but in *deviating* it: making the code skid while seeming to respect it. It is this very fragile state of the narrative, at once conforming and deviant, that Genette has been able to see and to make us see in Proust's work. His work is at once structural and historical because he specifics the conditions on which narrative novation is possible without being suicidal.[120]

Faced with the tenacity of late capitalism and its official culture, Genette looks not away from but rather deep within the classic bourgeois text in order to catch a glimpse of something different; and, like the early Lukács, he glimpses that something different in spaces between the "normal" operations of narrative, in the places where narrative *as* narrative fails but where *something else*, whatever that might be, might be said to succeed. This is, perhaps, also to suggest that, contrary to some accounts, Genette and Barthes effectively anticipate more recent efforts to highlight differences between "natural" and "unnatural" narratives; instead, though, of taking this difference as a difference in kind, they understand that the tension between operative and paradoxical forms of narrative is rather evidence of the political and social contradictions that characterize our moment in history.[121] They reveal, in other words, the apparent difference between *natural* and *unnatural* narrative as a historical problem; this is why "a theory of 'skidding' is necessary *precisely today*."

Later in *Narrative Discourse*, Genette points to another moment of transgression, one he associates with *completing analepses*, instances when discourse reaches back to an earlier moment in the main line of the story in such a way that the end of a particular analepsis would normally meet back up with the present. He opposes completing analepses to *partial analepses*, self-contained narratives of past events that both begin and end at a point prior to the narrative present. Because completing analepses need to meet up with the present, they offer particular opportunities for the kinds of narrative transgression that he associates with Proust: "This junction could hardly be without some degree of overlapping and thus an appearance of awkwardness, unless the narrator has the skill to extract from this awkwardness a sort of playful charm."[122] Where some writers – Genette points to Balzac – have a variety of more or less successful ways of acknowledging the resumption of present narration after a detour into the past, Proust often attempts instead to "elude" the juncture between the analeptic narrative and the point where the present resumes: "The typical behavior of Proustian narrative seems to consist, quite to the contrary, of *eluding* the juncture, either by dissimulating the end of the analepsis in the sort of temporal dispersion that iterative narrative procures ... or else by pretending to be unaware that the point in the story where the analepsis closes had already been reached by the narrative."[123] Genette goes on to describe a number of moments at which the Proustian narrative seems to paper over, to ignore, or to finesse the point at which narrative past and present meet again; these moments of short-circuited temporality tend to coincide with moments of confusion or, in fact, the breakdown of the narrative system.

Genette then describes what he takes as Proust's "boldest" move in this regard, an instance of temporal confusion or dissonance associated with one of the most important events in the novel – the death of Marcel's beloved grandmother:

> the boldest avoidance (even if the boldness is pure negligence) consists of forgetting the analeptic character of a section of narrative and prolonging that section more or less indefinitely on its own account, paying no attention to the point where it rejoins the first narrative. That is what happens in the episode – famous for other reasons – of the grandmother's death. It opens with an obviously analeptic beginning: "I went upstairs, and found my grandmother not so well. For some time past, without knowing exactly what was wrong, she had been complaining of her health." Then the narrative that has been opened in the retrospective mood continues uninterruptedly on up to the death, without ever acknowledging and signaling the moment (although indeed necessarily come to and passed beyond) when Marcel, returning from Mme. de Villeparisis's, had found his grandmother "not so well." We can never, therefore, either locate the grandmother's death exactly in relation to the Villeparisis matinee, or decide where the analepsis ends and the first narrative resumes.[124]

Although Proust opens the sequence as what appears to be a completing analepsis, the narrative never returns to and in fact overshoots the moment of his going upstairs to find the grandmother "not so well." It is as if a memory that was meant to mark out and to delineate a past event *as* past instead overflows and swallows up the present, as if it were an instance when the past was simply too much for the present or for the memory that would try to bind or to contain it. What is more, because it sets the moment of her death chronologically adrift, that death threatens to overwhelm the novel itself; that which cannot be tied to a particular place could be anywhere or, indeed, everywhere. There are two points to make. The first is the immediate and formal observation that, although Genette takes care to lay out the different types of temporal relations that can exist between story and discourse, his system is in the end more heuristic than descriptive; his categories are thus something like Max Weber's ideal types, models that are not found in practice but are nonetheless methodologically necessary. That is, as much as the whole of *Narrative Discourse* betrays something like a mania for categorization, for piling distinctions on distinctions, in practice the apparent conceptual purity of Genette's system comes again and again to grief. This is not a shortcoming of Genette's system; as I have already said, he owns his primary commitment to the local failure not only of narrative but also of his own system on a number of occasions. So, a moment like this, a moment when it becomes impossible to pinpoint when the past ends and the present resumes, reveals something essential about Proust's and Genette's method; it reveals, in other words, Genette's interest in both developing a truly robust narrative theory and exploring the very real limits of that system, in ironically folding what a system cannot do into the same space of all the things it can do. In this way, we might once again associate Genette's method with the early Lukács. That is, just as the early Lukács saw the novel as a powerful form because it was able to synthesize its urge toward totality with its immanent knowledge that totality is *not for us*, so does Genette's paradoxical interest in the rule and the exception, the general and the particular, the description and the inevitable failure of description point to what is immediate and necessarily critical about his project.

The second point is related to Genette's particular example of a transgressive or an incomplete completing analepsis. Although he mentions other examples, his main case is the death of Marcel's grandmother, an event of enormous importance to Marcel, to Proust, and to the reader of the *Recherche*. Genette returns to the temporally oblique death scene later in his chapter "Duration," where he talks about the fact that Marcel's period of mourning is more or less passed over in silence (an ellipsis), that it is, in other words, an event whose absence is not in any way marked and so has to be inferred:

This ellipsis is perfectly mute: we left the grandmother on her deathbed, most likely at the beginning of the summer; the narrative takes up again in these terms: "Albeit it was simply a Sunday in autumn...." The ellipsis is apparently definite, thanks to this indication of date, but it is very imprecisely so, and will soon become rather confused. Above all it is not characterized, and it will remain not characterized: we will never, even retrospectively, know anything of what the hero's life has been during these few months. This is perhaps the most opaque silence in the entire *Recherche*, and, if we remember that the death of the grandmother is to a great extent a transposition of the death of the author's mother, this reticence is undoubtedly not devoid of significance.[125]

There are different ways to think about this. We might simply say, and so it seems, that thinking about the aftermath of his grandmother's/mother's death was simply too painful to manage and that Marcel/Proust preferred, whatever the aesthetic cost, not to "remember"; we might also say, with Malcolm Bowie, that the character of the grandmother's death somehow falls outside while remaining at the center of the Proustian system: "The scenes devoted to the final illness and death of the narrator's grandmother seem often to belong to a world apart, in which the ironic imperative that governs so much of Proust's writing is by sheer force of grief suspended."[126] In these terms, the chronological "skidding" that takes place around the scene might be read as cutting across the difference between form and content, a phenomenon that we saw at work for different reasons in the case of Marcel's paraliptic sexual encounter with the "girl-cousin."

If, however, the process of recovery is unnarrated, the resulting absence is significant for its own sake. That is, although silence about an experience of loss and subsequent recovery is technically unreadable (because it escapes representation as discourse), we know from psychoanalysis that the absence of a word or act can be just as symptomatic and, thus, just as significant as its presence. In the terms of psychoanalysis as well as narrative discourse, silence speaks. It, in other words, shares the status of similar slips, gaps, stutters, or omissions that significantly punctuate Freud's case studies; indeed, Freud's method turns on measuring the strains, tensions, omissions, and exaggerations that appear in the manifest expression of latent psychic content. We could in similar terms take it that Genette's method might stand as the narratological equivalent of a psychoanalysis that works not because it decodes the latent content of the unconscious but rather because it is capable of motivating and thus making significant the structuring relation between psychic events and the representation of those events, the psychoanalytic equivalent of story and discourse. This is one way to begin to understand

Genette's commitment to the mistake or transgression or failure, a commitment that he shares with Freud. In the same way that the mistake stands not only as proof of a relation on which psychic life depends, so does it stand in Genette's method as that which animates narrative as such. The exception, the deviance, the mistake: these are proof of what brings narrative to life.

I want to make a final argument here, one less about how Proust may or may not register loss in the story-world of the *Recherche* at the level of discourse (although that is undoubtedly important) and more about ways in which Genette's method might respond to some of what he understands and appreciates about Proust. There is, in other words, a sense at this point in *Narrative Discourse* that the whole and variegated apparatus that Genette has developed, his seemingly endless spiral of terms, distinctions, and caveats, might stand as a beautiful and deeply and self-consciously inadequate response to what appears to have gone missing in Proust: the act of mourning. Freud writes that, faced with the loss of a beloved object, the mind initially denies the reality of the loss:

> This opposition can be so intense that a turning away from reality takes place and a clinging to the object through the medium of a hallucinatory wishful psychosis. Normally, respect for reality gains the day.
> Nevertheless its orders cannot be obeyed at once. They are carried out bit by bit, at great expense of time and cathectic energy, and in the meantime the existence of the lost object is psychically prolonged. Each single one of the memories and expectations in which the libido is bound to the object is brought up and hyper-cathected, and detachment of the libido is accomplished in respect of it.[127]

Freud's point is that the fact of mourning, the fact of confronting the lost object, leads to a work that involves rebuilding a system around that lost object, of building or rebuilding a coherent world around or in spite of the absence in question. I do not want to say that Genette is engaged in some unconscious act of mourning; what I rather want to say is that where his system – his theory – has real and dialectical contact with the particularity of the Proustian text is in the way that he weaves a series of ruminations on death and loss throughout *Narrative Discourse*. Indeed, once you start to look for them, references to the death of particular characters, comments on the relation between represented deaths and particular narrative techniques, and brief but immensely suggestive comments on the nature of death appear everywhere in *Narrative Discourse*; this is another way in which Genette's book not only reads but also oddly *lives* through Proust. In each of these cases, the idea of death as that which drives the Proustian text, which pushes it on from volume to volume toward more events, more writing, more plots but that also must in the end exceed or undermine even the fullest faith in narrative as a means of mastering time, suggests a different kind of investment in narrative, one that connects Genette to other figures we have considered who understand narrative partly as a way more or less to give value or significance or shape to the otherwise discrete events that make up a life. In other words, one can, I think, make the case that, although they use very different tools, both Genette and Proust are dedicated to understanding the potential and the real limits to narrative as a means of making life meaningful in the face of death, decay, and the passage of time.

~

I have been arguing that these great works of narrative theory, *S/Z* and *Narrative Discourse*, are not only two of our most thorough practical analyses of narrative at work but also quiet responses to a more and less recent critical history. In the short term, both works represent a moment in intellectual history when a series of revolutionary missteps, misunderstandings, and disappointments had forced a confrontation with the very idea of historical possibility. What could it mean in the second half of the twentieth century (after two world wars, the apparent collapse of the communist project, and a series of more local but no less dispiriting failures) to hold out hope still for the new: for a New Novel, a new kind of writing, a new way to work, a new way to live? I argued that for both Barthes and Genette, this crisis of the new resulted in a practical turn back toward classic, readerly texts, to Balzac and Proust. Rather, though, than seeing these turns as some kind of depressed or conservative reaction, I suggested that we should see them in light of what Lukács, following Hegel, called a "reconciliation with reality"; we should, in other words, see them as a recognition that, rather than reaching, as so many had hoped, any kind of decisive end, the dispiriting plot of modern life had revealed itself as more or less open-ended. It was a recognition that, for instance, capitalism had simply become late capitalism (to use the phrase that Fredric Jameson takes from the Marxist economist Ernst Mandel) and that to hope for *something else* requires that we look not to the end of stories but rather to the possibilities that they might manage dialectically to hold within. This is one way to understand Lukács's earlier turn in *The Historical Novel* to the politically conservative novels of Sir Walter Scott. It is precisely because the Tory Scott tries to find a specifically narrative form for the resolution of oppositions that had characterized and threatened social life in Britain that he manages to capture the dialectical and thus radical potential within the real and everyday experience of history as it happens: "Scott then becomes a great poet of history because he has a deeper, more genuine and differentiated sense of historical necessity than any writer before him."[128] At the level of narrative technique, Scott's critical project relies on what Lukács, following Goethe and Hegel, calls *necessary anachronisms*, the insertion of the heterogeneous and thus disruptive story-material of the present into discursive representations of the historical past; the *necessary anachronism* "can emerge organically from historical material, if the past portrayed is clearly recognized and experienced by contemporary writers as the *necessary prehistory* of the present."[129] In other words, these anachronisms are moments when a seemingly bad or ironic fit between story and discourse reveals narrative form at work and thus turns the novel into a kind of embodied criticism, into an opportunity to see and to reflect on the ideological schemes we use to organize our experience and understanding of past and present. To use the language of the Russian Formalists, the *necessary anachronism* is a formal device that defamiliarizes the narrative relation between story and discourse, revealing it as a form of historical and thus political criticism.

Like Lukács thirty years before, Barthes and Genette develop a critical method that looks not to the end of narrative but rather to technical moments of dialectical and even utopian possibility contained within narrative, to moments when the otherwise "natural" logic of story and discourse seems to break down. As a result, then, of lingering with these mistakes, these "knots," these "necessary anachronisms," these moments of what recent narrative theorists call "unnatural narrative," Barthes and Genette use narrative theory to reveal transient, immanent, and real moments of aesthetic and political paradox and thus possibility at work within classic instances of the story–discourse relation. This is one way to understand the paradox with which we began, the fact that it is, as Jonathan Culler suggests, difficult if not impossible to know whether the events of story occur *before* their representation as discourse or whether the events are rather a conceptual backformation that occur *after* narrative discourse establishes its necessary imaginative blueprint. Put differently, once we acknowledge that the story–discourse relation is both an enormously useful heuristic tool and an apparently intractable conceptual problem, we can begin to see why narrative theory is powerful not only as an account of "natural" narratives but also as a critical theory. Narrative theory is based on and alerts us to the presence of paradox and allows us to locate some of the sources of and critical energy behind narrative theory as an important and influential part of intellectual history. Because, in other words, narrative theory is based in and helps to reveal the presence of paradox, of antinomy, of contradiction in the midst of "normal" or "natural" narrative representation, it can help too to reveal the presence of the ought in the midst of the is, the general in the midst of the particular, value in the midst of fact, freedom in the midst of necessity. As imagined by both Barthes and Genette, narrative theory is, in that case, a practical extension of a critical project that goes back, as I have tried to show, to Hegel.

In the longer term, then, we can see Barthes's and Genette's attention to moments when the story–discourse relation is pushed to and past its structural limits as a late and refined response to several of the figures we have considered. They recall Aristotle's account of tragedy as a genre that turns the perspectival conflict between the "time of men" and the "time of the gods" into a kind of plot; Hegel's dialectical sense that conflict and contradiction motivate history and force us to imagine perspectives from which those contradictions might be resolved; Marx's understanding of the generic, which is to say, discursive difference (tragedy and farce!) among historical events understood in relation to class struggle; James's case that the novel reveals its sense not in its content but rather in its form, in the discursive circle it draws around events in order to give those events significance; Lukács's sense of the novel's ironic relation to its own formal limits as a way to confront a modern crisis of fact and value; Bakhtin's suggestion that narrative *chronotopes* not only represent but also produce the ideological conditions that give life its meaning in history; the Russian Formalists' effort to use form to defamiliarize narrative, to reveal the story–discourse relation at work; Levi-Strauss's effort to reveal the deep and deeper narrative structures at work behind myth; Kristeva's opposition between the ideological closure of *the book* and the critical open-endedness of *writing*; and so on. In each case, the figures I have considered turn to narrative genres in order both to reflect on the variable nature of the story–discourse relation and, more or less explicitly, to reveal that structural relation as part of a larger historical network of ideas, expectations, and beliefs about history, value, ethics, aesthetics, and politics. Stated differently, by developing narrative theory into a method that allows one to see places where the story–discourse relation breaks down, Barthes and Genette fulfill the promise of a much longer critical endeavor: the attempt to identify, describe, and analyze the forms, structures, assumptions, and ideas that allow us to see our lives and the lives of others as meaningful. And, insofar as they associate this critical project and its object with a specific set of social conditions, with, in other words, a social world that accepts complexity, insignificance, and disenchantment as *its* problems, they help us to see the historical stakes of narrative theory understood as a critical theory. Taken together, the figures I have looked at help us to see some of the intellectual sources of narrative theory, to understand why it seems self-evident that in order to know the world we need to know narrative, and to trace out limits and possibilities that attend the larger effort to understand why ours is an experience best captured somewhere between story and discourse. Put differently, the figures I have examined develop a narrative theory not only in order to reveal narrative as a problem but also in order to show why narrative has been and, indeed, why it remains *our* problem.

Bibliography

Abbott, H. Porter. *The Cambridge Introduction to Narrative*. 2nd ed. New York: Cambridge University Press, 2008.

"Story, Plot, and Narration," in *The Cambridge Companion to Narrative*. Ed. David Herman. New York: Cambridge University Press, 2007.

Abrams, M. H. *Natural Supernaturalism: Tradition and Revolution in Romantic Literature*. New York: Norton, 1971.

Adorno, Theodor W. *Notes to Literature*. Trans. Shierry Weber Nicholsen. New York: Columbia University Press, 1991.

Alber, Jan. "Hypothetical Intentionalism: Cinematic Narration Reconsidered," in *Postclassical Narratology: Approaches and Analyses*. Ed. Jan Alber and Monika Fludernik. Columbus: Ohio State University Press, 2010.

Alber, Jan, and Monika Fludernik. "Introduction," in *Postclassical Narratology: Approaches and Analyses*. Ed. Jan Alber and Monika Fludernik. Columbus: Ohio State University Press, 2010, 1–34.

Althusser, Louis. *Lenin and Philosophy and Other Essays*. Trans. Ben Brewster. New York: Monthly Review Press, 1971.

Altman, Matthew C., ed. *The Palgrave Handbook of German Idealism*. New York: Palgrave, 2014.

Anderson, Benedict. *Imagined Communities: Reflections on the Origin and Spread of Nationalism*. New York: Verso, 2006.

Arendt, Hannah. *Between Past and Future*. London: Penguin Classics, 2006.

Aristotle. *Poetics*, in *The Complete Works of Aristotle: The Revised Oxford Translation*. Ed. Jonathan Barnes. 2 vols. Princeton, NJ: Princeton University Press, 1984.

On Poetry and Style. Trans. G. M. A. Grube. Indianapolis: Hackett, 1989.

Topics, in *The Complete Works of Aristotle: The Revised Oxford Translation*. Ed. Jonathan Barnes. 2 vols. Princeton, NJ: Princeton University Press, 1984.

Auerbach, Erich. *Mimesis: The Representation of Reality in Western Literature*. Trans. Willard R. Trask. Princeton, NJ: Princeton University Press, 2003.

Augustine, Saint Bishop of Hippo. *The Confessions*. Trans. Henry Chadwick. Oxford: Oxford University Press, 1998.

Austen, Jane. *Pride and Prejudice*. New York: Modern Library, 2005.

Bakhtin, M. M. *Art and Answerability: Early Philosophical Essays*. Trans. Vadim Liapunov. Austin: University of Texas Press, 1990.

The Dialogic Imagination: Four Essays. Trans. Caryl Emerson and Michael Holquist. Austin: University of Texas Press, 1981.

Problems of Dostoevsky's Poetics. Trans. Caryl Emerson. Minneapolis: University of Minnesota Press, 1984.

Rabelais and His World. Trans. Helene Iswolsky. Bloomington: Indiana University Press, 1984.

Speech Genres and Other Late Essays. Trans. Vern W. McGee. Austin: University of Texas Press, 1986.

Bal, Mieke. "The Laughing Mice, or On Focalization." *Poetics Today* 2.2: 203–214.

Narratology: Introduction to the Theory of Narrative. 2nd ed. Toronto: University of Toronto Press, 1997.

Baldick, Chris, ed. *The Oxford Dictionary of Literary Terms*. 3rd ed. New York: Oxford University Press, 2008.

Barthes, Roland. *Elements of Semiology*. Trans. Annette Lavers and Colin Smith. New York: Hill & Wang, 1973.

Image, Music, Text. Trans. Stephen Heath. New York: Hill & Wang, 1977.

Mythologies. Trans. Annette Lavers. New York: Hill & Wang, 1972.

The Pleasure of the Text. Trans. Richard Miller. New York: Hill & Wang, 1975.

The Preparation of the Novel. Trans. Kate Briggs. New York: Columbia University Press, 2011.

The Rustle of Language. Trans. Richard Howard. Berkeley: University of California Press, 1989.

S/Z: An Essay. Trans. Richard Howard. New York: Hill & Wang, 1974.

"Utopia," in *"The 'Scandal' of Marxism" and Other Writings on Politics*. Trans. Chris Turner. London: Seagull Books, 2015.

Beiser, Frederick. *Hegel*. New York: Routledge, 2005.

Benveniste, Émile. *Problems in Linguistics*. Trans. Mary Elizabeth Meek. Coral Gables, FL: University of Miami Press, 1971.

Benjamin, Walter. "The Storyteller," in *Selected Writings. Vol. 3. 1935–1938*. Eds. Howard Eiland and Michael W. Jennings. Cambridge, MA: Harvard University Press, 2006.

Bernstein, J. M. *The Philosophy of the Novel: Lukács, Marxism and the Dialectics of Form*. Brighton, UK: Harvester Press, 1984.

Bill, Valentine Tschebotarioff. *Chekhov: The Silent Voice of Freedom*. New York: Philosophical Library: Distributed by Alpha Book Distributors, 1987.

Black, Jeremey. *The Politics of James Bond: From Fleming's Novels to the Big Screen*. Lincoln: University of Nebraska Press, 2000.

Booth, Wayne. "The Poetics for a Practical Critic," in *Essays on Aristotle's Poetics*. Ed. Amélie Oksenberg Rorty. Princeton, NJ: Princeton University Press, 1992.

The Rhetoric of Fiction. Chicago: University of Chicago Press, 1961.

Bordwell, David. "ApProppriations and ImProprieties: Problems in the Morphology of Film Narrative," *Cinema Journal* 27.3 (Spring 1988): 5–20.

Bowie, Malcolm. *Proust Among the Stars.* New York: Columbia University Press, 1998.

Boyd, Brian. *On the Origin of Stories: Evolution, Cognition, and Fiction.* Cambridge, MA: Belknap Press of Harvard University Press, 2009.

Boym, Svetlana. "Poetics and Politics of Estrangement: Victor Shklovsky and Hannah Arendt," *Poetics Today* 26.4 (Winter 2005): 581–611.

Bradley, A. C. *Oxford Lectures on Poetry.* London: Macmillan, 1909.

Shakespearean Tragedy. London: Penguin Books, 1991.

Brod, Max. *Franz Kafka: A Biography.* New York: Da Capo Press, 1995.

Brontë, Charlotte. *Jane Eyre.* London: Penguin Classics, 2006.

Brooks, Peter. *The Melodramatic Imagination: Balzac, Henry James, Melodrama, and the Mode of Excess.* New Haven, CT: Yale University Press, 1995.

Reading for the Plot: Design and Intention in Narrative. Cambridge, MA: Harvard University Press, 1992.

Bruner, Jerome. "The Narrative Construction of Reality." *Critical Inquiry* 18 (Autumn 1991): 1–21.

Bruun, Hans Henrik, and Sam Whimster, eds. *Max Weber: Collected Methodological Writings.* New York: Routledge, 2012.

Buck-Morss, Susan. *Hegel, Haiti and Universal History.* Pittsburgh: University of Pittsburgh Press, 2009.

Burian, Peter. "Myth into Muthos: The Shaping of Tragic Plot," in *The Cambridge Companion to Greek Tragedy.* Ed. P. E. Easterling. Cambridge: Cambridge University Press, 1997.

Bushnell, Rebecca W, ed. *A Companion to Tragedy.* Malden, MA: Blackwell, 2005.

Tragedy: A Short Introduction. Malden, MA: Blackwell, 2008.

Butler, Judith. *Antigone's Claim: Kinship between Life and Death.* New York: Columbia University Press, 2002.

Subjects of Desire: Hegelian Reflections in Twentieth-Century France. New York: Columbia University Press, 1999.

Carlyle, Thomas. "Characteristics," in *A Carlyle Reader: Selections from the Writings of Thomas Carlyle.* Ed. G. B. Tennyson. New York: Cambridge University Press, 1984.

Caston, Victor. "Aristotle and the Problem of Intentionality." *Philosophy and Phenomenological Research* 58 (1998): 249–98.

Chatman, Seymour. "New Directions in Voice-Narrated Cinema," in *Narratologies: New Perspectives on Narrative Analysis.* Ed. David Herman. Columbus: Ohio State University Press, 1999.

Story and Discourse: Narrative Structure in Fiction and Film. Ithaca, NY: Cornell University Press, 1978.

Chomsky, Noam. *Aspects of the Theory of Syntax.* Cambridge, MA: MIT Press, 1965.

Clark, Katerina and Michael Holquist. *Mikhail Bakhtin.* Cambridge, MA: Belknap Press of Harvard University Press, 1984.

Cohen, Margaret. *The Sentimental Education of the Novel.* Princeton, NJ: Princeton University Press, 1999.

Cole, Andrew. *The Birth of Theory*. Chicago: The University of Chicago Press, 2014.

Colley, Linda. *Britons: Forging the Nation, 1707–1837*. 3rd revised ed. New Haven, CT: Yale University Press, 2009.

Comay, Rebecca. *Mourning Sickness: Hegel and the French Revolution*. Stanford, CA: Stanford University Press, 2011.

Congdon, Lee. *Exile and Social Thought: Hungarian Intellectuals in Germany and Austria, 1919–1933*. Princeton, NJ: Princeton University Press, 1991.

The Young Lukács. Chapel Hill: University of North Carolina Press, 1983.

Conrad, Joseph. *Lord Jim*. Ed. Thomas C. Moser. New York: W. W. Norton, 1996.

Culler, Jonathan. *Barthes: A Very Short Introduction*. Rev. ed. Oxford: Oxford University Press, 2002.

Ferdinand De Saussure. Ithaca, NY: Cornell University Press, 1986.

The Pursuit of Signs: Semiotics, Literature, Deconstruction. Ithaca, NY: Cornell University Press, 2002.

Structuralist Poetics: Structuralism, Linguistics, and the Study of Literature. London: Routledge, 2002.

Defoe, Daniel. *Robinson Crusoe*. Ed. John Richetti. New York: Penguin, 2001.

De Quincey, Thomas. *Essays in Ancient History and Antiquities*. New York: Hurd and Houghton, 1878.

Derrida, Jacques. *Negotiations: Interventions and Interviews, 1971–2001*. Stanford, CA: Stanford University Press, 2002.

Writing and Difference. Trans. Alan Bass. New York: Routledge, 1995.

Descombes, Vincent. *Modern French Philosophy*. Trans. L. Scott-Fox, and J. M. Harding. New York: Cambridge University Press, 1980.

Dickens, Charles. *Great Expectations*. Ed. Charlotte Mitchell. New York: Penguin, 1996.

Didion, Joan. *The White Album*. New York: Noonday, 1990.

Dolezel, Lubomir. "Fictional and Historical Narrative: Meeting the Postmodernist Challenge," in *Narratologies: New Perspectives on Narrative Analysis*. Ed. David Herman, Columbus: Ohio State University Press, 1999.

Dosse, François. *History of Structuralism: The Rising Sign, 1945–1966*. Trans. Deborah Glassman. Minneapolis: University of Minnesota Press, 1997.

History of Structuralism: The Sign Sets, 1967-Present. Trans. Deborah Glassman. Minneapolis: University of Minnesota Press, 1997.

Dostoevsky, Fyodor. *Notes from Underground*. Trans. Richard Pevear and Larissa Volokhonsky. New York: Vintage Books, 1994.

Duncan, Ian. *Scott's Shadow: The Novel in Romantic Edinburgh*. Princeton, NJ: Princeton University Press, 2007.

Eagleton, Terry. *Ideology: An Introduction*. London: Verso Books, 1991.

The Ideology of the Aesthetic. Cambridge: Basil Blackwell, 1990.

Literary Theory: An Introduction. Anniversary ed. Minneapolis: University of Minnesota Press, 2008.

Marxism and Literary Criticism. Berkeley: University of California Press, 1976.

Easterling, P. E. *The Cambridge Companion to Greek Tragedy.* New York: Cambridge University Press, 1997.

Edelman, Lee. *No Future: Queer Theory and the Death Drive.* Durham, NC: Duke University Press, 2004.

Eichenbaum, Boris. "The Theory of the 'Formal Method'," in *Russian Formalist Criticism: Four Essays.* Ed. Lee T. Lemon and Marion J. Reis. Lincoln: University of Nebraska Press, 1965.

Eliot, George. *Middlemarch.* Ed. Bert G. Hornback. New York: Norton, 2000.

Erlich, Victor. *Russian Formalism: History, Doctrine.* The Hague: Mouton, 1955.

Favret, Mary. *War at a Distance: Romanticism and the Making of Modern Wartime.* Princeton, NJ: Princeton University Press, 2009.

Felman, Shoshana. *Literature and Psychoanalysis: The Question of Reading: Otherwise.* Baltimore: Johns Hopkins University Press, 1982.

ffrench, Patrick and Roland-François Lack, eds. *The Tel Quel Reader.* New York: Routledge, 1998.

Finlayson, J. G. "Conflict and Reconciliation in Hegel's Theory of the Tragic," *Journal of the History of Philosophy* 37.3 (1999): 493–520.

Fleming, Ian. *Goldfinger.* Las Vegas, NV: Thomas & Mercer, 2012.

Flesch, William. *Comeuppance: Costly Signaling, Altruistic Punishment, and Other Biological Components of Fiction.* Cambridge, MA: Harvard University Press, 2007.

Fludernik, Monika. "Mediacy, Mediation, and Focalization," in *Postclassical Narratology: Approaches and Analyses.* Eds. Jan Alber and Monika Fludernik. Columbus: Ohio State University Press, 2010.

——— "Structuralist Narratology: The Rage for Binary Opposition, Categorization, and Typology," in *A Companion to Narrative Theory.* Eds. James Phelan and Peter J. Rabinowitz. Malden, MA: Blackwell, 2005.

——— *Towards a 'Natural' Narratology.* New York: Routledge, 1996.

Forster, E. M. *Aspects of the Novel.* New York: Harcourt Brace & World, 1955.

Foucault, Michel. "Nietzsche, Genealogy, and History," in *The Foucault Reader.* Ed. Paul Rabinow. New York: Pantheon Books, 1984.

——— "Of Other Spaces." Trans. Jay Miskowiec. *Diacritics* 16.1 (Spring 1986): 22–27.

Freeland, Cynthia A. "Plot Imitates Action: Aesthetic Evaluation and Moral Realism in Aristotle's Poetics," in *Essays on Aristotle's Poetics.* Ed. Amélie Oksenberg Rorty. Princeton, NJ: Princeton University Press, 1992.

Friedman, Susan Stanford. "Spatialization: A Strategy for Reading Narrative," in *Narrative Dynamics: Essays on Time, Plot, Closure, and Frames.* Ed. Brian Richardson. Columbus: Ohio State University Press, 2002.

Freud, Sigmund. "An Autobiographical Study," in *The Standard Edition of the Complete Psychological Works of Sigmund Freud.* Vol. 20. Translated under the general editorship of James Strachey. London: Hogarth Press, 1953–1974.

——— "Analysis Terminable and Interminable," in *The Standard Edition of the Complete Psychological Works of Sigmund Freud.* Vol. 23. Translated under the general editorship of James Strachey. London: Hogarth Press, 1953–1974.

Civilization and its Discontents, in *The Standard Edition of the Complete Psychological Works of Sigmund Freud.* Vol. 21. Translated under the general editorship of James Strachey. London: Hogarth Press, 1953–1974.

The Interpretation of Dreams, in *The Standard Edition of the Complete Psychological Works of Sigmund Freud.* Vol. 4. Translated under the general editorship of James Strachey. London: Hogarth Press, 1953–1974.

"Mourning and Melancholia," in *The Standard Edition of the Complete Psychological Works of Sigmund Freud.* Vol. 14. Translated under the general editorship of James Strachey. London: Hogarth Press, 1953–1974.

"On Narcissism," in *The Standard Edition of the Complete Psychological Works of Sigmund Freud.* Vol. 14. Translated under the general editorship of James Strachey. London: Hogarth Press, 1953–1974.

"Repression," in *The Standard Edition of the Complete Psychological Works of Sigmund Freud.* Vol. 14. Translated under the general editorship of James Strachey. London: Hogarth Press, 1953–1974.

Three Essays on the Theory of Sexuality, in *The Standard Edition of the Complete Psychological Works of Sigmund Freud.* Vol. 7. Translated under the general editorship of James Strachey. London: Hogarth Press, 1953–1974.

Fritzsche, Peter. *Stranded in the Present: Modern Time and the Melancholy of History.* Cambridge, MA: Harvard University Press, 2004.

Gallagher, Catherine and Stephen Greenblatt. *Practicing New Historicism.* Chicago: University of Chicago Press, 2000.

Gates, Henry Louis, Jr. *The Signifying Monkey: A Theory of Afro-American Literary Criticism.* New York: Oxford University Press, 2014.

Genette, Gérard. "Frontiers of Narrative," in *Figures of Literary Discourse.* Trans. Alan Sheridan. New York: Columbia University Press, 1982.

Narrative Discourse: An Essay in Method. Trans. Jane E. Lewin. Ithaca, NY: Cornell University Press, 1980.

Narrative Discourse Revisited. Trans. Jane E. Lewin. Ithaca, NY: Cornell University Press, 1988.

"Vraisemblance and Motivation." Trans. David Gorman, *Narrative* 9.3 (October 2001): 239–258.

Gigante, Denise. *Life: Organic Form and Romanticism.* Stanford, CA: Stanford University Press, 2009.

Goethe, Johann Wolfgang. *The Metamorphosis of Plants.* Cambridge, MA: MIT Press, 2009.

Goward, Barbara. *Telling Tragedy: Narrative Technique in Aeschylus, Sophocles and Euripides.* London: Duckworth, 1999.

Gramsci, Antonio. *Selections from the Prison Notebooks of Antonio Gramsci.* Trans. Quintin Hoare and Geoffrey Nowell Smith. London: Lawrence & Wishart, 1971.

Greimas, Algirdas Julien. *On Meaning: Selected Writings in Semiotic Theory.* Trans. Paul J. Perron and Frank H. Collins. Minneapolis: University of Minnesota Press, 1987.

Hale, Dorothy J. *Social Formalism: The Novel in Theory from Henry James to the Present.* Stanford, CA: Stanford University Press, 1998.

Halliwell, Stephen. *Aristotle's Poetics.* Chicago: University of Chicago Press, 1998.

Hardy, Thomas. *The Return of the Native.* New York: Oxford University Press, 2005.

Hartman, Geoffrey H. "Romanticism and Anti-Self Consciousness," in *Beyond Formalism; Literary Essays, 1958–1970.* New Haven, CT: Yale University Press, 1970.

Hegel, Georg Wilhelm Friedrich. *Hegel on Tragedy.* Eds. Anne Paolucci and Henry Paolucci. Westport, CT: Greenwood Press, 1978.

Phenomenology of Spirit. Trans. A. V. Miller. Oxford: Oxford University Press, 1977.

Heller, Agnes, ed. *Lukács Reappraised.* New York: Columbia University Press, 1983.

Herman, David, Manfred Jahn, and Marie-Laure Ryan, eds. *Routledge Encyclopedia of Narrative Theory.* New York: Routledge, 2005.

Herman, David. "Action Theory," in *Routledge Encyclopedia of Narrative Theory.* Ed. David Herman, Manfred Jahn, and Marie-Laure Ryan, New York: Routledge, 2005.

"Glossary," in *The Cambridge Companion to Narrative.* Ed. David Herman. New York: Cambridge University Press, 2007.

"Histories of Narrative Theory (I): A Genealogy of Early Developments" in *A Companion to Narrative Theory.* Ed. James Phelan and Peter J. Rabinowitz. Malden, MA: Blackwell, 2005.

"Introduction: Narratologies," in *Narratologies: New Perspectives on Narrative Analysis.* Ed. David Herman, Columbus: Ohio State University Press, 1999, 1–33.

Story Logic: Problems and Possibilities of Narrative. Lincoln: University of Nebraska Press, 2002.

"Structuralist Narratology," in *Routledge Encyclopedia of Narrative Theory.* Ed. David Herman, Manfred Jahn, and Marie-Laure Ryan, New York: Routledge, 2005.

Herman, Luc, and Bart Vervaeck. *Handbook of Narrative Analysis.* Lincoln: University of Nebraska Press, 2005.

Hobsbawm, Eric and Terence Ranger, eds. *The Invention of Tradition.* Cambridge, MA: Canto Classics, 2012.

Holquist, Michael. *Dialogism: Bakhtin and His World.* 2nd ed. New York: Routledge, 2002.

Homer. *Iliad.* Trans. Richard Lattimore. Chicago: University of Chicago Press, 1961.

Honig, Bonnie. "Antigone's Laments, Creon's Grief: Mourning, Membership, and the Politics of Exception." *Political Theory* 37.1 (February 2009): 5–43.

Horne, Philip. *Henry James: A Life in Letters.* New York: Viking, 1999.

Huizinga, Johan. *Homo Ludens: A Study of the Play-Element in Culture,* Boston: The Beacon Press, 1955.

Hyvärinen, Matti. "Towards a Conceptual History of Narrative," in *The Traveling Concepts of Narrative.* Eds. Mari Hatavara, Lars-Christer Hydén and Matti Hyvärinen. Helsinki: Helsinki Collegium for Advanced Studies, University of Helsinki, 2006, 20–41.

"Introduction to Special Issue on France May 1968," *New Left Review* I.52 (November-December 1968): 1–8.

Jahn, Manfred. "The Mechanics of Focalization: Extending the Narratological Toolbox," *GRAAT* 21: 85–110.

Jakobson, Roman. *Language in Literature.* Ed. Krystyna Pomorska and Stephen Rudy. Cambridge, MA: Belknap Press of Harvard University Press, 1987.

James, Henry. *The Art of the Novel: Critical Prefaces.* New York: Scribner's, 1937.

Henry James: A Life in Letters. Ed. Philip Horne. New York: Viking, 1999.

The Princess Casamassima. Ed. Derek Brewer. New York: Penguin, 1987.

Jameson, Fredric. "In Hyperspace." *London Review of Books* 37.17 (September 2015).

Marxism and Form: Twentieth-Century Dialectical Theories of Literature. Princeton, NJ: Princeton University Press, 1974.

The Prison-House of Language: A Critical Account of Structuralism and Russian Formalism. Princeton, NJ: Princeton University Press, 1972.

The Political Unconscious: Narrative as a Socially Symbolic Act. Ithaca, NY: Cornell University Press, 1981.

JanMohamed, Abdul R. *The Death-Bound-Subject: Richard Wright's Archaeology of Death.* Durham, NC: Duke University Press, 2005.

Jay, Martin. *Marxism and Totality: The Adventures of a Concept from Lukács to Habermas.* Berkeley: University of California Press, 1984.

Jockers, Matthew L. blog. http://www.matthewjockers.net/2015/02/02/syuzhet/

Johnson, Barbara. "The Critical Difference: BartheS/BalZac" in *The Critical Difference.* Baltimore: Johns Hopkins University Press, 1985.

Joseph, John E. *Saussure.* New York: Oxford University Press, 2012.

Joyce, James. *A Portrait of the Artist as a Young Man.* Ed. John Paul Riquelme. New York: Norton, 2007.

Kafalenos, Emma. "Not (Yet) Knowing: Epistemological Effects of Deferred and Suppressed Information in Narrative," in *Narratologies.* Ed. David Herman. Columbus: Ohio State University Press, 1999.

Kafka, Franz. *The Blue Octavo Notebooks.* Ed. Max Brod. Cambridge: Exact Change, 1991.

Kant, Immanuel. *Critique of Pure Reason.* Translated and eds. Paul Guyer and Allen W. Wood. New York: Cambridge University Press, 1998.

Kaufmann, Walter. *Hegel: Reinterpretation, Texts, and Commentary.* Garden City, NY: Doubleday, 1965.

Keen, Suzanne. *Narrative Form.* Revised and expanded 2nd ed. London: Palgrave, 2015.

Kermode, Frank. *The Sense of an Ending: Studies in the Theory of Fiction.* New York: Oxford University Press, 2000.

Kofman, Sarah. *Nietzsche and Metaphor.* Stanford, CA: Stanford University Press, 1993.

Kojève, Alexandre. *Introduction to the Reading of Hegel.* Trans. James H. Nichols, Jr. Ithaca, NY: Cornell University Press, 1980.

Kosman, Aryeh. *Virtues of Thought: Essays on Plato and Aristotle.* Cambridge, MA: Harvard University Press, 2014.

Kreiswirth, Martin. "Trusting the Tale: The Narrativist Turn in the Human Sciences." *New Literary History* 23 (1992): 629–657.

Krieger, Murray. *A Reopening of Closure.* New York: Columbia University Press, 1989.

Kristeva, Julia. *Revolution in Poetic Language.* Trans. Margaret Waller. New York: Columbia University Press, 1984.

"Toward a Semiology of Paragrams," in *The Tel Quel Reader.* Ed. Patrick ffrench and Roland-François Lack. New York: Routledge, 1998.

Lacan, Jacques. *The Ethics of Psychoanalysis: 1959–1960.* New York: W. W. Norton, 1992.

Lanser, Susan S. "Sapphic Dialogics: Historical Narratology and the Sexuality of Form," in *Postclassical Narratology: Approaches and Analyses.* Ed. Jan Alber and Monika Fludernik. Columbus: Ohio State University Press, 2010.

"Toward a Feminist Narratology," *Style* 20.3 (Fall 1986): 341–363.

Lerer, Seth. *Error and the Academic Self.* New York: Columbia University Press, 2002.

Lévi-Strauss, Claude. *The Elementary Structures of Kinship.* Trans. James Harle Bell, John Richard Von Sturmer, and Rodney Needham. Boston: Beacon Press, 1969.

Structural Anthropology. Trans. Claire Jacobson and Brooke Grundfest Schoepf. New York: Basic Books, 1963.

Tristes Tropiques. Trans. Doreen and John Weightman. Harmondsworth: Penguin, 1976.

Laplanche, Jean. *Life and Death in Psychoanalysis.* Trans. Jeffrey Mehlman. Baltimore: Johns Hopkins University Press, 1976.

Lemon, Lee T., and Marion J. Reis, eds. *Russian Formalist Criticism: Four Essays.* Lincoln: University of Nebraska Press, 1965.

Lubbock, Percy. *The Craft of Fiction.* New York: Charles Scribner's Sons, 1921.

Lukács, Georg. *Goethe and His Age.* Trans. Robert Anchor. London: Merlin Press, 1968.

The Historical Novel. Trans. Hannah Mitchell and Stanley Mitchell. Lincoln: University of Nebraska Press, 1983.

History and Class Consciousness: Studies in Marxist Dialectics. Trans. Rodney Livingstone. Cambridge, MA: MIT Press, 1971.

The Theory of the Novel: a Historico-Philosophical Essay on the Forms of Great Epic Literature. Trans. Anna Bostock. Cambridge, MA: MIT Press, 1971.

Lupton, Julia Reinhard. "Tragedy and Psychoanalysis: Freud and Lacan," in *A Companion to Tragedy*. Ed. Rebecca Bushnell. Oxford: Blackwell, 2005, 88–106.

Mannheim, Karl. *Collected Works of Karl Mannheim*. Vol. 1. *Ideology and Utopia*. New York: Routledge, 2002.

Marcus, Sharon. *Between Women: Friendship, Desire, and Marriage in Victorian England*. Princeton, NJ: Princeton University Press, 2007.

Márkus, György. "Life and Soul: the Young Lukács and the Problem of Culture," in *Lukács Reappraised*. Ed. Agnes Heller. New York: Columbia University Press, 1983.

Marx, Karl. "Economic and Philosophic Manuscripts of 1844," in *Early Writings*. Trans. Rodney Livingstone and Gregor Benton. London: Penguin/New Left Review, 1992.

Marx: Later Political Writings. Trans. Terrell Carver. New York: Cambridge University Press, 1996.

"Preface to A Contribution to the Critique of Political Economy," in *Karl Marx: Selected Writings*. Ed. Lawrence H. Simon. New York: Hackett, 1994.

Marx, Karl, and Friedrich Engels. Collected Works. *Vol. 6: 1845–1848*. London: Lawrence & Wishart, 1975.

The Marx-Engels Reader. Ed. Robert C. Tucker. 2nd ed. New York: Norton, 1978.

"Preface to the Second Edition of 'The Eighteenth Brumaire of Louis Bonaparte'," in Collected Works. *Vol. 21. 1867–1870*. New York: International, 1976.

Marx-Scouras, Danielle. *The Cultural Politics of Tel Quel: Literature and the Left in the Wake of Engagement*. University Park: Pennsylvania State University Press, 1996.

McQuillan, Martin, ed. *The Narrative Reader*. London: Routledge, 2000.

Melzer, Arthur M. *Philosophy Between the Lines: The Lost History of Esoteric Writing*. Chicago: University of Chicago Press, 2014.

Miller, D. A. *Bringing Out Roland Barthes*. Berkeley: University of California Press, 1992.

Narrative and Its Discontents: Problems of Closure in the Traditional Novel. Princeton, NJ: Princeton University Press, 1989.

Miller, J. Hillis. "Henry James and 'Focalization,' or Why James Loves Gyp," in *A Companion to Narrative Theory*. Ed. James Phelan and Peter J. Rabinowitz. Malden, MA: Blackwell, 2005.

Moretti, Franco. *The Way of the World: The Bildungsroman in European Culture*. Trans. Albert Sbragia. New York: Verso, 2000.

Morson, Gary Saul and Caryl Emerson. *Mikhail Bakhtin: Creation of a Prosaics*. Stanford, CA: Stanford University Press, 1990.

Mosse, Calude. "How a Political Myth Takes Shape: Solon, 'Founding Father' of the Athenian Democracy," in *Athenian Democracy*. Ed. P. J. Rhodes. Oxford: Oxford University Press, 2004, 242–259.

Nairn, Tom. *The Break-Up of Britain: Crisis and Neo-Nationalism.* 2nd ed. London: NLB, 1981.

Nehamas, Alexander. *Nietzsche: Life as Literature.* Cambridge, MA: Harvard University Press, 1985.

Nelles, William. "Function (Propp)," in *Routledge Encyclopedia of Narrative Theory.* Eds. Herman, David, Manfred Jahn, and Marie-Laure Ryan. New York: Routledge, 2005.

Nietzsche, Friedrich Wilhelm. *The Birth of Tragedy and Other Writings.* Ed. Raymon Geuss and Ronald Speirs. Trans. Ronald Spiers. Cambridge: Cambridge University Press, 1999.

The Complete Works of Friedrich Nietzsche. Vol. 2. Unfashionable Observations. Trans. Richard T. Gray. Stanford, CA: Stanford University Press, 1995.

The Gay Science. Trans. Josefine Nauckhoff. Cambridge: Cambridge University Press, 2001.

Normand, Claudine. "System, Arbitrariness, Value," in *Cambridge Companion to Saussure.* Ed. Carol Sanders. Cambridge: Cambridge University Press, 2004.

Phelan, James. "Rhetoric/Ethics," in *The Cambridge Companion to Narrative.* Ed. David Herman. New York: Cambridge University Press, 2007.

Phelan, James, and Peter J. Rabinowitz, eds. *A Companion to Narrative Theory.* Malden, MA: Blackwell, 2005.

Pinkard, Terry. *Hegel's Naturalism: Mind, Nature, and the Final Ends of Life.* Oxford: Oxford University Press, 2012.

Plato. *Phaedrus.* In *Complete Works.* Ed. John M. Cooper. Indianapolis: Hackett, 1997.

Plato. *Republic.* In *Complete Works.* Ed. John M. Cooper. Indianapolis: Hackett, 1997.

Poe, Edgar Allen. "The Philosophy of Composition," in *Literary Theory and Criticism.* Ed. Lenoard Cassuto. Meneola, NY: Dover, 1999.

Polti, Georges. *The Thirty-Six Dramatic Situations.* Trans. Lucile Ray. Franklin: J. K. Reeve, 1921.

Porter, James I. *The Invention of Dionysus: An Essay on the Birth of Tragedy.* Stanford, CA: Stanford University Press, 2000.

"Nietzsche and Tragedy," in *A Companion to Tragedy.* Ed. Rebecca Bushnell. Oxford: Blackwell, 2005.

Prince, Gerald. *A Dictionary of Narratology.* Revised ed. Lincoln: University of Nebraska Press, 2003.

"Narrativity," in *Routledge Encyclopedia of Narrative Theory.* Ed. David Herman, Manfred Jahn, and Marie-Laure Ryan. London: Routledge, 2005.

"Narratology," in *The Cambridge History of Literary Criticism. Vol. VIII. From Formalism to Poststructuralism.* Ed. Raman Selden. Cambridge: Cambridge University Press, 1995.

Narratology: The Form and Functioning of Narrative. Berlin: Mouton, 1982.

"Revisiting Narrativity," in *Grenzüberschreitungen: Narratologie Im Kontext.* Eds. Walter Grünzweig und Andreas Solbach. Tübingen: Gunter Narr Verlag, 1999.

Propp, Vladimir. "Fairy-Tale Transformations," in *Narrative Dynamics: Essays on Time, Plot, Closure, and Frames.* Ed. Brian Richardson. Columbus: Ohio State University Press, 2002.

Morphology of the Folktale. Trans. Laurence Scott. 2nd ed. Austin: University of Texas Press, 2003.

Pyrhonen, Heta. "Genre," in *The Cambridge Companion to Narrative.* Ed. David Herman. New York: Cambridge University Press, 2007.

Rée, Jonathan. *Philosophical Tales: An Essay on Philosophy and Literature.* New York: Methuen, 1987.

Rabaté, Jean-Michel. *The Future of Theory.* Hoboken, NJ: Wiley-Blackwell, 2002.

Rabinowitz, Peter J. *Before Reading: Narrative Conventions and the Politics of Interpretation.* Ithaca, NY: Cornell University Press, 1987.

"Path and Counterpoint in *The Long Goodbye*," in *A Companion to Narrative Theory.* Eds. James Phelan and Peter J. Rabinowitz. Malden, MA: Blackwell, 2005.

Renger, Almut-Barbara. *Oedipus and the Sphinx: The Threshold Myth from Sophocles through Freud to Cocteau.* Trans. Alexander Smart and David Rice, with John T. Hamilton. Chicago: University of Chicago Press, 2013.

Rhodes, P. J., ed. *Athenian Democracy.* New York: Oxford University Press, 2004.

Richardson, Brian. "Anti-Narrative," in *Routledge Encyclopedia of Narrative Theory.* Ed. David Herman, Manfred Jahn, and Marie-Laure Ryan, New York: Routledge, 2005.

"Beyond the Poetics of Plot," in *A Companion to Narrative Theory*, ed. James Phelan and Peter J. Rabinowitz. Malden, MA: Blackwell, 2005.

"Beyond Story and Discourse: Narrative Time in Postmodern and Nonmimetic Fiction," in *Narrative Dynamics: Essays on Time, Plot, Closure, and Frames.* Ed. Brian Richardson. Columbus: Ohio State University Press, 2002.

Unnatural Narrative: Theory, History, and Practice. Columbus: The Ohio State University Press, 2015.

Unnatural Voices: Extreme Narration in Modern and Contemporary Fiction. Columbus: Ohio State University Press, 2006.

Ricoeur, Paul. *Freud and Philosophy: An Essay on Interpretation.* Trans. Denis Savage. New Haven, CT: Yale University Press, 1970.

Time and Narrative. Vol. 2. Trans. Kathleen McLaughlin and David Pellauer. Chicago: University of Chicago Press, 1984.

Time and Narrative. Vol. 3. Trans. Kathleen Blamey and David Pellauer. Chicago: University of Chicago Press, 1988.

Rimmon-Kenan, Shlomith. *Narrative Fiction: Contemporary Poetics.* London: Routledge, 2002.

Robbe-Grillet, Alain. *For a New Novel: Essays on Fiction.* Trans. Richard Howard. Evanston, IL: Northwestern University Press 1989.

Roberts, Deborah H. "Outside the Drama: The Limits of Tragedy in Aristotle's Poetics," in *Essays on Aristotle's Poetics*. Ed. Amélie Oksenberg Rorty. Princeton, NJ: Princeton University Press, 1992.

Rockmore, Tom. *Before and after Hegel: A Historical Introduction to Hegel's Thought*. Berkeley: University of California Press, 1992.

——— *Marx after Marxism: The Philosophy of Karl Marx*. Oxford: Blackwell, 2002.

Rorty, Amélie, ed. *Essays on Aristotle's Poetics*. Princeton, NJ: Princeton University Press, 1992.

Rose, Gillian. *Hegel Contra Sociology*. London: Humanities Press, 1981.

——— *The Melancholy Science: An Introduction to the Thought of Theodor W Adorno*. London: Macmillan, 1978.

Roudiez, Leon S. "Introduction," in Julia Kristeva, *Desire in Language: A Semiotic Approach to Literature and Art*. New York: Columbia University Press, 1980.

Ryan, Marie-Laure. *Narrative as Virtual Reality 2: Revisiting Immersion and Interactivity in Literature and Electronic Media*. Baltimore: Johns Hopkins University Press, 2015.

——— "Toward a Definition of Narrative," in *The Cambridge Companion to Narrative Theory*. Ed. David Herman. Cambridge: Cambridge University Press, 2007.

Safranski, Rüdiger. *Nietzsche: A Philosophical Biography*. Trans. Shelley Frisch. New York: W. W. Norton, 2002.

Said, Edward W. *Humanism and Democratic Criticism*. New York: Columbia University Press, 2004.

——— *The World, the Text, and the Critic*. Cambridge, MA: Harvard University Press, 1983.

Saussure, Ferdinand de. *Course in General Linguistics*. Trans. Wade Baskin. New York: Columbia University Press, 2011.

Scholes, Robert, James Phelan, and Robert Kellogg. *The Nature of Narrative*. 40th anniversary ed. New York: Oxford University Press, 2006.

Schmidt, Dennis J. *On Germans and Other Greeks: Tragedy and Ethical Life*. Bloomington: Indiana University Press, 2001.

Schmidt, James. "Cabbage Heads and Gulps of Water: Hegel on the Terror." *Political Theory* 26.1 (Feb. 1998): 4–32.

Schwartzberg, Melissa. "Athenian Democracy and Legal Change," *The American Political Science Review* 98.2 (May 2004): 311–325.

Selden, Raman, ed. *The Cambridge History of Literary Criticism. Vol. 8. From Formalism to Poststructuralism*. New York: Cambridge University Press, 1995.

Shaw, Harry E. "Why Don't Our Terms Stay Put? The Narrative Communication Diagram Scrutinized and Historicized," in *A Companion to Narrative Theory*. Eds. James Phelan and Peter J. Rabinowitz. Malden, MA: Blackwell, 2005, 299–312.

Shell, Marc. *The End of Kinship: "Measure for Measure," Incest, and the Ideal of Universal Siblinghood*. Stanford, CA: Stanford University Press, 1988.

Shklovsky, Viktor. *Bowstring: On the Dissimilarity of the Similar*. Trans. Shushan Avagyan. Champaign, IL: Dalkey Archive Press, 2011.

Knight's Move. Trans. Richard Sheldon. Normal, IL: Dalkey Archive Press, 2005.

Theory of Prose. Trans. Benjamin Sher. Elmwood Park, IL: Dalkey Archive Press, 1990.

Third Factory. Trans. Richard Sheldon. Ann Arbor, MI: Ardis, 1977.

Silk, M. S., and J. P. Stern. *Nietzsche on Tragedy*. New York: Cambridge University Press, 1981.

Simmel, Georg. *On Individuality and Social Forms: Selected Writings*, ed. Donald N. Levine. Chicago: University of Chicago Press, 1971.

Sophocles. *Oedipus Rex* in *The Three Theban Plays*. Trans. Robert Fagles. New York: Penguin, 1982.

Spencer, Herbert. "The Philosophy of Style." *The Westminster Review* Oct. 1852.

Spitzer, Leo. "Development of a Method," in *Leo Spitzer: Representative Essays*. Eds. Alban K. Forcione, Herbert Lindenberger, and Madeline Sutherland. Stanford, CA: Stanford University Press, 1988.

Steiner, George. *After Babel: Aspects of Language and Translation*. 3rd ed. New York: Oxford University Press, 1998.

Sternberg, Meir. *Expositional Modes and Temporal Ordering in Fiction*. Bloomington: Indiana University Press, 1978.

"Telling in Time (II): Chronology, Teleology, Narrativity," *Poetics Today* 13.3 (Autumn 1992): 463–541.

Sterne, Laurence. *The Life and Opinions of Tristram Shandy, Gentleman*. Ed. Ian Campbell Ross. Oxford: Oxford World's Classics, 2009.

Stewart, Garrett. *Death Sentences: Styles of Dying in British Fiction*. Cambridge, MA: Harvard University Press, 1984.

Strauss, Leo. "On a Forgotten Kind of Writing," *Chicago Review* 8.1 (Winter-Spring 1954): 64–75.

Sussman, Henry. *The Hegelian Aftermath: Readings in Hegel, Kierkegaard, Freud, Proust, and James*. Baltimore: Johns Hopkins University Press, 1982.

Taylor, Charles. *Hegel*. New York: Cambridge University Press, 1975.

Thucydides. *The Landmark Thucydides: A Comprehensive Guide to the Peloponnesian War*. Ed. Robert B. Strassler. New York: Free Press, 1996.

Tifft, Stephen. "Drôle de Guerre: Renoir, Farce, and the Fall of France," *Representations* 38 (Spring, 1992): 131–165.

Todorov, Tzvetan. *Grammaire du Décaméron*. The Hague: Mouton, 1969.

Mikhail Bakhtin: The Dialogical Principle. Trans. Wlad Godzich. Minneapolis: University of Minnesota Press, 1984.

The Poetics of Prose. Trans. Richard Howard. Ithaca, NY: Cornell University Press, 1977.

Tomashevsky, Boris. "Story, Plot, and Motivation," in *Narrative Dynamics: Essays on Time, Plot, Closure, and Frames*. Ed. Brian Richardson. Columbus: Ohio State University Press, 2002.

"Thematics," in *Russian Formalist Criticism: Four Essays*. Eds. Lee T. Lemon and Marion J. Reis. Lincoln: University of Nebraska Press, 1965.

Tönnies, Ferdinand. *Community and Civil Society*. Trans. Jose Harris. New York: Cambridge University Press, 2001.

Trotsky, Leon. *Literature and Revolution*. Trans. Rose Strunsky. Chicago: Haymarket Books, 2005.

Truffaut, François. *Hitchcock*. With Helen G. Scott. New York: Simon & Schuster, 1984.

Turner, Frank M. *The Greek Heritage in Victorian Britain*. New Haven, CT: Yale University Press, 1981.

Turner, James. *Philology: The Forgotten Origins of the Modern Humanities*. Princeton, NJ: Princeton University Press, 2014.

Vermeule, Blakey. *Why Do We Care about Literary Characters?* Baltimore: The Johns Hopkins University Press, 2010.

Vernant, Jean-Pierre. "Myth and Tragedy," in *Essays on Aristotle's Poetics*. Ed. Amélie Oksenberg Rorty. Princeton, NJ: Princeton University Press, 1992.

Vernant, Jean-Pierre and Pierre Vidal-Naquet. *Myth and Tragedy in Ancient Greece*. Trans. Janet Lloyd. Cambridge, MA: Zone Books distributed by MIT Press, 1988.

Walsh, Richard. *The Rhetoric of Fictionality: Narrative Theory and the Idea of Fiction*. Columbus: Ohio State University Press, 2007.

Warhol, Robyn R. *Having a Good Cry: Effeminate Feelings and Pop-Culture Forms*. Columbus: Ohio State University Press, 2003.

Warhol, Robyn and Susan S. Lanser, eds. *Narrative Theory Unbound: Queer and Feminist Interventions*. Columbus: Ohio State University Press, 2015.

Weber, Max. "Science as a Profession and a Vocation," *Max Weber: Collected Methodological Writings*. Ed. Hans Henrik Bruun and Sam Whimster. London: Routledge, 2012, 335–355.

Wellek, Rene, and Austin Warren, *Theory of Literature*. New York: Harcourt, Brace, 1949.

White, Hayden V. *Metahistory: The Historical Imagination in Nineteenth-Century Europe*. New ed. Baltimore: Johns Hopkins University Press, 2014.

"The Problem of Style in Realistic Representation: Marx and Flaubert," in *The Fiction of Narrative: Essays on History, Literature, and Theory, 1957–2007*. Ed. Robert Doran. Baltimore: Johns Hopkins University Press, 2010.

Wilcken, Patrick. *Claude Lévi-Strauss: The Poet in the Laboratory*. New York: Penguin Press, 2010.

Williams, Raymond. *Marxism and Literature*. Oxford: Oxford University Press, 1978.

Modern Tragedy. Ed. Pamela McCollum. Peterborough: Broadview Press, 2006.

Winnett, Susan. "Coming Unstrung: Women, Men, Narrative, and Principles of Pleasure," in *Narrative Dynamics: Essays on Time, Plot, Closure, and Frames*. Ed. Brian Richardson. Columbus: Ohio State University Press, 2002.

Wittenberg, David. *Time Travel: The Popular Philosophy of Narrative*. New York: Fordham University Press, 2013.

Wolff, Michael. "The Importance of 'Controlling the Narrative,'" *USA Today*, December 29, 2013.

Wolin, Richard. *The Wind from the East: French Intellectuals, the Cultural Revolution, and the Legacy of the 1960s*. Princeton, NJ: Princeton University Press, 2010.

Woloch, Alex. *The One vs the Many: Minor Characters and the Space of the Protagonist in the Novel*. Princeton, NJ: Princeton University Press, 2003.

Woodruff, Paul. "Aristotle on Mimesis," in *Essays on Aristotle's Poetics*. Ed. Amélie Oksenberg Rorty. Princeton, NJ: Princeton University Press, 1992.

Young, Julian. *The Philosophy of Tragedy: From Plato to Žižek*. New York: Cambridge University Press, 2013.

Notes

Chapter 1

1 For more on the story linking classical and postclassical narratologies, see David Herman's "Introduction: Narratologies," in *Narratologies: New Perspectives on Narrative Analysis*, ed. David Herman (Columbus: Ohio State University Press, 1999). 1–33. Also see Alber and Fludernik, who update Herman by breaking postclassical narratology into four different but related camps: (1) the attempt to revise or to supplement classical models from within; (2) the importation of *methodological* models taken from adjacent fields (psychoanalysis, speech act theory, deconstruction); (3) *thematic* extensions of narratology, which include "feminists, queer, ethnic or minority related, and postcolonial approaches to narrative"; and (4) *intermedial* approaches that extend analysis to texts beyond the novel. "Introduction," in *Postclassical Narratology: Approaches and Analyses* (Columbus: Ohio State University Press, 2010), 3.

2 Here is a necessarily partial list: *A Companion to Narrative Theory*, eds. James Phelan and Peter J. Rabinowitz (Oxford: Blackwell, 2005); *Routledge Encyclopedia of Narrative Theory*, eds. David Herman, Manfred Jahn, and Marie-Laure-Ryan (London: Routledge, 2005); H. Porter Abbott, *The Cambridge Introduction to Narrative* (New York: Cambridge University Press, 2008); Seymour Chatman, *Story and Discourse: Narrative Structure in Fiction and Film* (Ithaca, NY: Cornell University Press, 1978); Mieke Bal, *Narratology: Introduction to the Theory of Narrative* (Toronto: University of Toronto Press, 1997); Shlomith Rimmon-Kenan, *Narrative Fiction: Contemporary Poetics* (London: Routledge, 2003); *Postclassical Narratology: Approaches and Analyses*, eds. Jan Alber and Monika Fludernik (Columbus: Ohio University Press, 2010); *Narrative Dynamics: Essays on Time, Plot, Closure, and Frames*, ed. Brian Richardson (Columbus: Ohio University Press, 2002); *Narratologies: New Perspectives on Narrative Analysis*, ed. David Herman (Columbus: Ohio State University Press, 1999); Gerald Prince, *A Dictionary of Narratology* (Lincoln: University of Nebraska Press, 2003).

3 Martin Kreiswirth, "Narrative Turn in the Humanities," in *Routledge Encyclopedia of Narrative Theory*, eds. David Herman, Manfred Jahn, and Marie-Laure Ryan (London: Routledge, 2005), 378. For more on the "narrative turn," see also Jerome Bruner, "The Narrative Construction of Reality," *Critical Inquiry* 18 (Autumn 1991), 1–21; Kreiswirth, "Trusting the Tale: The Narrativist Turn in the Human Sciences," *New Literary History* 23 (1992), 629–657; and Matti Hyvärinen, "Towards a Conceptual History of Narrative," in *The Traveling Concepts of Narrative*, eds. Mari Hatavara, Lars-Christer Hydén, and Matti Hyvärinen (Helsinki: Helsinki Collegium for Advanced Studies, University of Helsinki), 20–41.

4 David Herman, "Histories of Narrative Theory (I): A Genealogy of Early Developments," in Phelan and Rabinowitz, *A Companion*, 20.

5 H. Porter Abbott, *Cambridge Introduction*, 13; for an overview of and an alternative to standard definitions of "narrative," see Marie-Laure Ryan, "Toward a Definition of Narrative," in *The Cambridge Companion to Narrative Theory*, ed. David Herman (Cambridge: Cambridge University Press, 2007).

6 Abbott, *Introduction to Narrative*, 15.

7 See, for instance, Brian Richardson, *Unnatural Narrative: Theory, History, and Practice* (Columbus: Ohio State University Press, 2015).

8 Genette, "Frontiers of Narrative," in *Figures of Literary Discourse*, trans. Alan Sheridan (New York: Columbia University Press, 1982), 127.

9 Ryan, "Toward a Definition of Narrative," 24.

10 Jonathan Culler, *The Pursuit of Signs: Semiotics, Literature, Deconstruction* (Ithaca, NY: Cornell University Press, 2002), 169–170.

11 Monika Fludernik, *Towards a "Natural" Narratology* (London: Routledge, 1996), 333.

12 Suzanne Keen, *Narrative Form*, revised. and expanded 2nd ed. (New York: Springer, 2015), 4.

13 Abbott, "Story, Plot, and Narration," in Herman, *Cambridge Companion*.

14 David Wittenberg, *Time Travel: The Popular Philosophy of Narrative* (New York: Fordham University Press, 2013), 120.

15 Shlomith Rimmon-Kenan, *Narrative Fiction: Contemporary Poetics* (London: Routledge, 2003).

16 Abbott, *Introduction to Narrative*, 15.

17 Richardson, *Unnatural Narrative*, 4.

18 Fyodor Dostoevsky, *Notes from Underground*, trans. Richard Pevear and Larissa Volokhonsky (New York: Vintage, 1994), 4.

19 James Phelan, "Rhetoric/Ethics," in Herman, *Cambridge Companion*; see also, Phelan and Martin, "The Lessons of 'Weymouth,'" in Herman, *Narratologies*, 93–96.

20 Brian Richardson, "Beyond Story and Discourse: Narrative Time in Postmodern and Nonmimetic Fiction," in Richardson, *Narrative Dynamics*, 47.

21 Wittenberg, *Time Travel*, 7.
22 Ibid., 48.
23 William Shakespeare, *King Lear* III.ii.91–92.
24 *King Lear* III.ii.95.
25 Luc Herman and Bart Vervaeck, *Handbook of Narrative Analysis* (Lincoln: University of Nebraska Press, 2005), 45.
26 Emma Kafalenos, "Not (Yet) Knowing: Epistemological Effects of Deferred and Suppressed Information in Narrative," in Herman, *Narratologies*, 37.
27 Monika Fludernik, "Mediacy, Mediation, and Focalization," in Alber and Fludernik, *Postclassical Narratology*, 109. See also an exchange to which Fludernik refers between Barbara Herrnstein Smith and Seymour Chatman in *On Narrative*, ed. W. J. T. Mitchell, (Chicago: University of Chicago Press, 1981), 209–233; 258–267. Among other things, Smith and Chatman spar over the possible "Platonism" of the story–discourse relation, the idea that story would represent some ideal and thus transhistorical version of any given discursive representation.
28 Richard Walsh, *The Rhetoric of Fictionality: Narrative Theory and the Idea of Fiction* (Columbus: Ohio State University Press, 2007), 68.
29 Brian Richardson, "Beyond Story and Discourse," 52–53.
30 Wittenberg, *Time Travel*, 124.
31 Shlomith Rimmon-Kenan, *Narrative Fiction: Contemporary Poetics* (London: Routledge, 2003).
32 Culler, *Pursuit of Signs*, 207–208.
33 Culler, *Pursuit of Signs*, 208.
34 Monika Fludernik, *Towards a "Natural" Narratology* (London: Routledge, 1996), 336.
35 David Herman: *Problems and Possibilities of Narrative* (Lincoln: University of Nebraska Press, 2002), 211.
36 Georg Lukács, *History and Class Consciousness*, trans. Rodney Livingstone (Cambridge: MIT Press, 1971), 110–149.
37 Aristotle, *Poetics*, in *The Complete Works of Aristotle: The Revised Oxford Translation*, ed. Jonathan Barnes, 2 vols. (Princeton, NJ: Princeton University Press, 1984), II:2316 (1447a).
38 Heta Pyrhönen, "Genre," in Herman, *Cambridge Companion*.
39 *Stranded in the Present: Modern Time and the Melancholy of History* (Cambridge, MA: Harvard University Press, 2004), 16–17.
40 Terry Eagleton, *Ideology: An Introduction* (London: Verso Books, 1991), 106.
41 Ian Duncan, *Scott's Shadow: The Novel in Romantic Edinburgh* (Princeton, NJ: Princeton University Press, 2007), 136.
42 Margaret Cohen, *The Sentimental Education of the Novel* (Princeton, NJ: Princeton University Press, 1999), 76; see 70–76.
43 Leo Strauss, "On a Forgotten Kind of Writing," *Chicago Review* 8.1 (Winter–Spring 1954), 64–75; at 64.

44 *Philosophy between the Lines: The Lost History of Esoteric Writing* (Chicago: University of Chicago Press, 2014), 187.

45 *Knight's Move*, trans. Richard Sheldon (Normal, IL: Dalkey Archive Press, 2005), 3.

46 *Theory of Prose*, trans. Benjamin Sher (Elmwood Park, IL: Dalkey Archive Press, 1990), 15.

47 Svetlana Boym, "Poetics and Politics of Estrangement: Victor Shklovsky and Hannah Arendt," *Poetics Today* 26:4 (Winter 2005), 581–611, at 586.

48 *Third Factory*, trans. and ed. Richard Sheldon (Ann Arbor, MI: Ardis, 1977), 36.

49 Joan Didion, *The White Album: Essays* (New York: Noonday, 1979, 1990), 11.

50 Didion, *White Album*, 11.

51 Ibid.

52 Abbott, *Introduction to Narrative* 3.

53 Brian Boyd, *On the Origin of Stories: Evolution, Cognition, and Fiction* (Cambridge, MA: Belknap Press of the Harvard University Press, 2009), 176. For other recent work on the relation between narrative and evolutionary models, see Blakey Vermeule, *Why Do We Care about Literary Characters?* (Baltimore: Johns Hopkins University Press, 2010); and William Flesch, *Comeuppance: Costly Signaling, Altruistic Punishment, and Other Biological Components of Fiction* (Cambridge, MA: Harvard University Press, 2009).

54 Didion, *White Album*, 11.

55 Thomas Carlyle, "Characteristics," in *A Carlyle Reader*, ed. G. B. Tennyson (Cambridge: Cambridge University Press, 1984), 67.

Chapter 2

1 Aristotle, *Poetics*, in Barnes, ed., *Complete Works*, II:2321 (1450b).

2 Cynthia A. Freeland, "Plot Imitates Action: Aesthetic Evaluation and Moral Realism in Aristotle's *Poetics*," in *Essays on Aristotle's* Poetics, ed. Amélie Oksenberg Rorty (Princeton, NJ: Princeton University Press, 1992), 112.

3 *Complete Works* II:2320.

4 Ibid., II:2321–2322.

5 Ibid.

6 Seymour Chatman, *Story and Discourse* 19.

7 For more on the complex relation between objects, representations, and intention in the whole of Aristotle's philosophy, see Victor Caston, "Aristotle and the Problem of Intentionality." *Philosophy and Phenomenological Research* 58 (1998), 249–298.

8 Aristotle, *Complete Works* II:2322.

9 E. M. Forster, *Aspects of the Novel* (New York: Harcourt, 1955), 53.

10 D. A. Miller, *Narrative and Its Discontents: Problems of Closure in the Traditional Novel* (Princeton, NJ: Princeton University Press, 1989).

11 Abbott, *Introduction to Narrative* 25.

12 David Herman, "Action Theory," in *Routledge Encyclopedia*, eds. David Herman, Manfred Jahn, and Marie-Laure Ryan (London: Routledge, 2005), 3.

13 Gerald Prince, "Narrativity," in Herman et al., *Routledge Encyclopedia of Narrative Theory*, 387.

14 Gerald Prince, "Revisiting Narrativity," in *Grenzüberschreitungen: Narratologie Im Kontext* (Gunter Narr Verlag, 1999), 45.

15 Ibid., 46.; Ryan, "Toward a Definition of Narrative," in *The Cambridge Companion to Narrative* (Cambridge: Cambridge University Press, 2007), 28.

16 Fludernik, *Towards a 'Natural' Narratology* 30.

17 Ibid.

18 Fludernik, *Towards a 'Natural' Narratology*, 27.

19 Franz Kafka, *The Blue Octavo Notebooks*, ed. Max Brod, trans. Ernst Kaiser and Eithne Wilkins (Cambridge: Exact Change, 1991), 20.

20 Aristotle, *Complete Works* II:2320.

21 *Ibid.*, II:2321.

22 Alfred Lord Tennyson, "Ulysses," ll. 33–34; for more on the "spatial" patterning of the *Odyssey*, see Meir Sternberg, *Expositional Modes and Temporal Ordering in Fiction* (Bloomington: Indiana University Press, 1978), 56–90.

23 Aristotle, *Complete Works* II:2322.

24 Plato, *Phaedrus*, in John M. Cooper, ed., *Complete Works* (Indianapolis: Hackett, 1997), 541 (264c).

25 Aristotle, *Complete Works* II:2322.

26 For more on the historical association of whole aesthetic forms and organic life, see Murray Krieger, *A Reopening of Closure* (New York: Columbia University Press, 1989) and Denise Gigante, *Life: Organic Form and Romanticism* (Stanford, CA: Stanford University Press, 2009).

27 Wayne Booth, "The *Poetics* for a Practical Critic," in Rorty, *Essays on Aristotle's* Poetics, 395.

28 Paul Ricœur, *Time and Narrative*, vol. 2 (Chicago: University of Chicago Press, 1984), 8.

29 Although Stephen Halliwell and others insist on the relation between Plato and the *Poetics*, Paul Woodruff argues that such a reading is "entirely wrongheaded": "there is no good internal evidence that Aristotle was driven in the *Poetics* by the need to answer Plato." Halliwell, on the contrary, argues both that there is such evidence and that Aristotle may have made the stakes of his disagreement clearer in an earlier, more public draft of the *Poetics*, the lost *On*

Poets. Cf. Paul Woodruff, "Aristotle on Mimesis," in Rorty, *Essays on Aristotle's* Poetics, 73–74; Stephen Halliwell, *Aristotle's Poetics*, 2nd ed. (Chicago: University of Chicago Press, 1986, 1998).

30 *Virtues of Thought: Essays on Plato and Aristotle* (Cambridge, MA: Harvard University Press, 2014), 102.

31 Aristotle, *Complete Works* II:2326.

32 Plato, *Republic* X, in Cooper, *Complete Works*, 1200 (595b).

33 Halliwell, *Aristotle's Poetics* 117.

34 Aristotle, *On Poetry and Style*, ed. G. M. A. Grube (Indianapolis: Hackett, 1989), x.

35 Halliwell, *Aristotle's Poetics* 22.

36 Raymond Williams, *Modern Tragedy* (Toronto: Broadview Press, 2006), 39.

37 Deborah H. Roberts, "Outside the Drama: The Limits of Tragedy in Aristotle's *Poetics*," in Rorty, *Essays on Aristotle's* Poetics, 133.

38 Peter Burian, "Myth into *Muthos*: The Shaping of Tragic Plot," in *The Cambridge Companion to Greek Tragedy*, ed. P. E. Easterling (Cambridge: Cambridge University Press, 1997), 184.

39 Jean-Pierre Vernant, "Myth and Tragedy," in Rorty, *Essays on Aristotle's* Poetics, 33.

40 Hannah Arendt, *Between Past and Future* (London: Penguin Classics, 2006), 45–46.

41 Barbara Goward, *Telling Tragedy: Narrative Technique in Aeschylus, Sophocles, and Euripides* (London: Duckworth, 1999), 21.

42 Vernant, "Myth and Tragedy," 36.

43 Jean-Pierre Vernant and Pierre Vidal-Naquet, *Myth and Tragedy in Ancient Greece*, trans. Janet Lloyd (New York: Zone, 1988), 24.

44 Rebecca Bushnell, *Tragedy: A Short Introduction* (London: John Wiley & Sons, 2008), 106–107.

45 For more on the legal tensions within fifth and fourth century Athens, see Claude Mosse, "How a Political Myth Takes Shape: Solon, 'Founding Father' of the Athenian Democracy," in Athenian Democracy, ed. P. J. Rhodes (Oxford: Oxford University Press, 2004), 242–259.

46 Melissa Schwartzberg, "Athenian Democracy and Legal Change," *The American Political Science Review* 98.2 (May 2004), 311–325; at 312.

47 *The Landmark Thucydides*, ed. Robert B. Strassler, trans. Richard Crawley (New York: Free Press, 1996), I.71.3.

48 Emma Kafalenos, "Not (Yet) Knowing: Epistemological Effects of Deferred and Suppressed Information in Narrative," in Herman, *Narratologies*, ed., 39.

49 Abbott, *Introduction to Narrative*, 195.

50 Aristotle, *Complete Works* II:2326.

51 Vernant and Vidal-Naquet, *Myth and Tragedy* 120.

52 Thomas De Quincey, *Essays in Ancient History and Antiquities* (New York: Hurd and Houghton, 1878), 570.

53 Almut-Barbara Renger, *Oedipus and the Sphinx: The Threshold Myth from Sophocles through Freud to Cocteau* (Chicago: University of Chicago Press, 2013), 16.

54 Renger, *Oedipus and the Sphinx*, 11.

55 Thomas De Quincey, *Essays in Ancient History and Antiquities* (New York: Hurd and Houghton, 1878), 573.

56 De Quincey, *Essays*, 578.

57 Woloch, *The One vs. the Many*, 325.

58 For a comparison of *Oedipus* and Tzvetan Todorov's famous account of the detective story as a distinct form of the story-discourse relation, see Woloch, *The One vs. the Many*, 326.

59 Vernant and Vidal-Naquet, *Myth and Tragedy*, 138.

60 Marc Shell, *The End of Kinship: "Measure for Measure," Incest, and the Idea of Universal Siblinghood* (Stanford, CA: Stanford University Press, 1988), 40.

61 Roberts, "Outside the Drama," 148.

62 John Milton, *Paradise Lost* XII:553–556.

63 Milton, *Paradise Lost* I:263.

64 Aristotle, *Topics*, in Barnes, *Complete Works* I:174 (104b).

65 Pierre Corneille, *Discourses*, quoted in Monroe C. Beardsley, *Aesthetics from Classical Greece to the Present* (Birmingham: University of Alabama Press, 1975), 145.

66 Dennis J. Schmidt, *On Germans and Other Greeks: Tragedy and Ethical Life* (Bloomington: Indiana University Press, 2001), 83.

67 Saint Augustine, *The Confessions*, trans. Henry Chadwick (Oxford: Oxford University Press, 1998), 234.

68 Geoffrey Chaucer, *Canterbury Tales*: "The Monk's Prologue," 85–89.

69 *Oxford Lectures on Poetry* (London: Macmillan, 1909), 69.

70 *The Philosophy of Tragedy: From Plato to Žižek* (Cambridge: Cambridge University Press, 2013), 110.

71 Burian, "Myth into *Muthos*," 181.

72 Georg Lukács, *The Historical Novel*, trans. Hannah and Stanley Mitchell (Lincoln: University of Nebraska Press, 1983), 97.

73 David Herman, "Glossary," in Herman, *Cambridge Companion*.

74 J. G. Finlayson, "Conflict and Reconciliation in Hegel's Theory of the Tragic," *Journal of the History of Philosophy* 37:3 (1999), 494.

75 *Metahistory: The Historical Imagination in Nineteenth-Century Europe*, new ed. (Baltimore: Johns Hopkins University Press, 1973, 2014), 90.

76 For more on the conflict of *Antigone*, see Jacques Lacan, *The Ethics of Psychoanalysis: 1959–1960* (New York: W. W. Norton, 1992), 243–291; Judith Butler, *Antigone's Claim: Kinship Between Life and Death* (New York: Columbia University Press, 2002); Bonnie Honig, "Antigone's Laments, Creon's Grief: Mourning, Membership, and the Politics of Exception." *Political Theory*, 37.1 (February 2009), 5–43.

77 Margaret Cohen, *The Sentimental Education of the Novel* (Princeton, NJ: Princeton University Press, 1999), 33.

78 Peter J. Rabinowitz, "Path and Counterpoint in *The Long Goodbye*," in Phelan and Rabinowitz, *A Companion*, 183–184.

79 Karl Marx, "Economic and Philosophic Manuscripts of 1844," in *Early Writings*, trans. Rodney Livingstone and Gregor Benton (London: Penguin/New Left Review, 1992), 383.

80 Paul Ricoeur, *Time and Narrative, Volume 3*, trans. Kathleen Blamey and David Pellauer (Chicago: The University of Chicago Press, 1988), 203.

81 Immanuel Kant, *Critique of Pure Reason*, trans. and ed. Paul Guyer and Allen W. Wood (Cambridge: Cambridge University Press, 1998), 185 (A42/B59–60).

82 Charles Taylor, *Hegel* (Cambridge: Cambridge University Press, 1975), 30–31.

83 Jonathan Rée, *Philosophical Tales* (London: Methuen, 1987), 57.

84 See Max Brod, *Franz Kafka: A Biography* (Da Capo, 1995), 75.

85 Lee Congdon, *The Young Lukács* (Chapel Hill: University of North Carolina Press, 1983), 184.

86 Ibid., 403.

87 Tom Rockmore, *Marx after Marxism: The Philosophy of Karl Marx* (Oxford: Blackwell, 2002), 167.

88 Susan Buck-Morss, *Hegel, Haiti, and Universal History* (University of Pittsburgh Press, 2009), 59.

89 "French Revolution," ll. 4–5.

90 Qtd. in Taylor, *Hegel*, 424.

91 Benedict Anderson, *Imagined Communities: Reflections on the Origin and Spread of Nationalism* (London: Verso Books, 2006), 35.

92 Mary Favret, *War at a Distance: Romanticism and the Making of Modern Wartime* (Princeton, NJ: Princeton University Press, 2009), 10.

93 Rebecca Comay, *Mourning Sickness: Hegel and the French Revolution* (Stanford, CA: Stanford University Press, 2011), 4.

94 Andrew Cole, *The Birth of Theory* (Chicago: The University of Chicago Press, 2014), xvii.

95 Rebecca Comay, *Mourning Sickness: Hegel and the French Revolution* (Stanford, CA: Stanford University Press, 2011), 50.

96 G. W. F. Hegel, *Phenomenology of Spirit*, trans. A. V. Miller (Oxford: Oxford University Press, 1977), 360 (§590).

97 James Schmidt, "Cabbage Heads and Gulps of Water: Hegel on the Terror." *Political Theory* 26:1 (Feb. 1998), 19.

98 Walter Benjamin, "The Storyteller," in *Selected Writings*. Vol. 3. *1935–1938*, ed. Howard Eiland and Michael W. Jennings (Cambridge, MA: Harvard University Press, 2006), 151.

99 Garrett Stewart, *Death Sentences: Styles of Dying in British Fiction* (Cambridge, MA: Harvard University Press, 1984), 194–195.

100 See Brian Richardson's entry on "Anti-Narrative," in Herman et al., *Routledge Encyclopedia*.

101 Abdul JanMohamed, *The Subject: Richard Write's Archaeology of Death* (Durham, NC: Duke University Press, 2005), 5.

102 Wright, "Bright Morning Star," quoted in JanMohamed, *Death-Bound*, 45.

103 JanMohamed, *Death-Bound*, 46.

104 Georg Lukács, *The Historical Novel*, trans. Hannah and Stanley Mitchell (Lincoln: University of Nebraska Press, 1983), 28.

105 Karl Mannheim, *Collected Works of Karl Mannheim*. Vol. 1. *Ideology and Utopia* (New York: Routledge, 1936, 2002), 83.

106 Comay, *Mourning Sickness*, 5.

107 Fredric Jameson, "In Hyperspace." *London Review of Books* 37:17 (September 2015).

108 Ricoeur, *Time and Narrative*, Vol. 3 (Chicago: University of Chicago Press, 1988), 201.

109 Geoffrey Hartman, "Romanticism and Anti-Self Consciousness," in *Beyond Formalism: Literary Essays, 1958–1970* (New Haven, CT: Yale University Press, 1970).

110 Hegel, *Hegel on Tragedy*, eds. Anne Paolucci and Henry Paolucci (New York: Doubleday, 1962), 113.

111 Cole, *The Birth of Theory*.

112 Vincent Descombes, *Modern French Philosophy*, trans. L. Scott-Fox and J. M. Harding (Cambridge: Cambridge University Press, 1980), 27.

113 Alexandre Kojève, *Introduction to the Reading of Hegel: Lectures on the Phenomenology of Spirit*, ed. Allan Bloom (Ithaca, NY: Cornell University Press, 1980), 4.

114 Kojève, *Introduction to Hegel* 7.

115 Ibid.

116 Ibid.

117 Ibid., 23.

118 Ibid., 9.

119 James Phelan, "Rhetoric/Ethics," in Herman, *Cambridge Companion*, 210.

120 James Phelan, "Rhetoric/Ethics," 211.

121 Ryan, "Toward a Definition of Narrative," 33.

122 Ibid., 30.

123 It makes sense, in that case, that Kojève's student Raymond Queneau was responsible not only for putting together an edition of Kojève's lectures but also for the wonderful, *Exercises in Style*, a retelling of the same story in 99 different discursive forms, a mad and self-consciously minor endeavor that does much to remind us after Hegel of the degree to which the meaning of events depends on how they're made to fit together.

124 Kojève, *Introduction to Hegel*, 5.

125 Brooks, *Reading for the Plot*, 37.

126 Hegel, *Phenomenology of Spirit*, 6 (§11).

127 Eagleton, *The Ideology of the Aesthetic*, 141.

128 Jonathan Rée, *Philosophical Tales* (London: Methuen, 1987), 84.

129 M. H. Abrams, *Natural Supernaturalism: Tradition and Revolution in Romantic Culture* (New York: Norton, 1971), 237.

130 Walter Kaufmann, *Hegel: Reinterpretation, Texts, and Commentary* (London: Weidenfeld and Nicolson, 1965), 171.

131 *Subjects of Desire: Hegelian Reflections in Twentieth-Century France*, new ed. (New York: Columbia University Press, 1999), 21.

132 Robert C. Tucker, ed., *The Marx-Engels Reader*, 2nd ed. (New York: Norton, 1978), 11.

133 Rée, *Philosophical Tales*, 63–64.

134 Martin Jay, *Marxism and Totality: The Adventures of a Concept from Lukács to Habermas* (Berkeley: University of California Press, 1984), 55.

135 Abrams, *Natural Supernaturalism* 229.

136 Terry Pinkard, *Hegel's Naturalism: Mind, Nature, and the Final Ends of Life* (Oxford: Oxford University Press, 2012), 177.

137 Georg Lukács, *Goethe and His Age*, trans. Robert Anchor (London: Merlin, 1968), 59.

138 Franco Moretti, *The Way of the World: The* Bildungsroman *in European Culture*, new ed. (London: Verso, 2000), 70.

139 Frederick Beiser, *Hegel* (London: Routledge, 2005), 168–169.

140 Rée, *Philosophical Tales*, 92.

Chapter 3

1 Dennis J. Schmidt, *On Germans and Other Greeks: Tragedy and Ethical Life* (Bloomington: Indiana University Press, 2001), 276.

2 Paul Ricoeur, *Time and Narrative*, Vol. 3, trans. Kathleen Blamey and David Pellauer (Chicago: University of Chicago Press, 1988), 203.

3 Qtd. in Valentine T. Bill, *Chekhov: The Silent Voice of Freedom* (New York: Philosophical Library, 1987), 79–80.

4 Just for instance, in a 2013 piece on political public-relations disasters, *USA Today* columnist Michael Wolff writes, "Among the most prevalent and up-to-date phrases in business, politics and savvy American life is 'controlling the narrative'" (Michael Wolff, "The importance of 'controlling the narrative,'" *USA Today*, December 29, 2013.) A Google search on "controlling the narrative" will produce many more examples.

5 Paul Ricoeur, *Freud and Philosophy: An Essay on Interpretation*, trans. Denis Savage (New Haven, CT: Yale University Press, 1970), 32.

6 Hegel, *Phenomenology of Spirit*, 493 (§808).

7 Mannheim, *Ideology and Utopia*, 64.

8 Karl Marx, *Later Political Writings*, trans. and ed. Terrell Carver (Cambridge: Cambridge University Press, 1996), 31.

9 Karl Marx and Frederick Engels, *Collected Works*. Vol. 6. *1845–1848* (London: Lawrence & Wishart, 1975), 519.

10 Brooks, *Reading for the Plot*, xiv.

11 Marx and Engels, *Collected Works*, Vol. 6, 487.

12 Ibid., 496.

13 Hayden White, "The Problem of Style in Realistic Representation: Marx and Flaubert," in *The Fiction of Narrative: Essays on History, Literature, and Theory, 1957–2007*, ed. Robert Doran (Baltimore: Johns Hopkins University Press, 2010), 180.

14 Fredric Jameson, *The Political Unconscious: Narrative as a Socially Symbolic Act* (Ithaca, NY: Cornell University Press, 1981), 281–282.

15 A. C. Bradley, *Shakespearean Tragedy* (London: Penguin Books, 1991), 28.

16 Comay, *Mourning Sickness*, 3–4.

17 Marx, *Later Political Writings*, 78.

18 Stephen Tifft, "Drôle de Guerre: Renoir, Farce, and the Fall of France," *Representations* 38 (Spring, 1992), 131–165, at 138.

19 "Preface to the Second Edition of *The Eighteenth Brumaire of Louis Bonaparte*," in *Collected Works*, vol. 21 (New York: International, 1976), 56.

20 White, *Metahistory*, 2.

21 Jameson, *Political Unconscious*, 19.

22 Marx, *Later Political Writings*, 1.

23 White, *Metahistory*, 310.

24 White, "Problem of Style in Realistic Representation," 184.

25 Marx, *Later Political Writings*, 32.

26 Frank Kermode, *The Sense of an Ending*, new ed. (Oxford: Oxford University Press, 2000), 7.

27 Margaret Cohen, *The Sentimental Education of the Novel* (Princeton, NJ: Princeton University Press, 1999), 17.

28 Karl Marx, "Preface to *A Contribution to the Critique of Political Economy*," in *Karl Marx: Selected Writings*, ed. Lawrence H. Simon (New York: Hackett, 1994), 211.

29 Ibid.

30 Louis Althusser, *Lenin and Philosophy and Other Essays* (New York: Monthly Review Press, 1971), 91.

31 Jameson, *Political Unconscious*, 102.

32 Claude Lévi-Strauss, *Tristes Tropiques* (Harmondsworth, UK: Penguin, 1976), 70.

33 Alexander Nehamas, *Nietzsche: Life as Literature* (Cambridge, MA: Harvard University Press, 1985), 27.

34 Michel Foucault, "Nietzsche, Genealogy, and History," *The Foucault Reader*, ed. Paul Rabinow (New York: Pantheon Books, 1984), 80.

35 Friedrich Nietzsche, *The Birth of Tragedy and Other Writings*, ed. Raymond Geuss and Ronald Speirs (Cambridge: Cambridge University Press, 1999), 22.

36 Ibid., 14.

37 Nietzsche, *Birth of Tragedy*, 27.

38 James Turner, *Philology: The Forgotten Origins of the Modern Humanities* (Princeton, NJ: Princeton University Press, 2014), x.

39 Edward Said, *Humanism and Democratic Criticism* (New York: Columbia University Press, 2004), 58.

40 Leo Spitzer, "Development of a Method," in *Leo Spitzer: Representative Essays*, eds. Alban K. Forcione, Herbert Lindenberger, and Madeline Sutherland (Stanford, CA: Stanford University Press, 1988), 435.

41 Qtd. in M. S. Silk and J. P. Stern, *Nietzsche on Tragedy* (Cambridge: Cambridge University Press, 1981), 31.

42 Silk and Stern, *Nietzsche on Tragedy*, 235.

43 Nietzsche, *Birth of Tragedy*, 23–24.

44 Ibid., 38.

45 Johan Huizinga, *Homo Ludens: A Study of the Play-Element in Culture* (Boston: Beacon Press, 1955), 10.

46 Ibid., 39.

47 James, *The Art of the Novel*, 5–6.

48 Ibid., 40.

49 Ibid., 40.

50 Gérard Genette, *Narrative Discourse: An Essay in Method*, trans. Jane Lewin (Ithaca, NY: Cornell University Press, 1980), 228.

51 Charlotte Brontë, *Jane Eyre* (London: Penguin Classics, 2006).

52 Genette, *Narrative Discourse*, 236.

53 Silk and Stern, *Nietzsche on Tragedy*, 198.

54 Ibid., 15

55 Qtd. in James I. Porter, *The Invention of Dionysus: An Essay on* The Birth of Tragedy (Stanford, CA: Stanford University Press, 2000), 13.

56 James I. Porter, "Nietzsche and Tragedy," in *A Companion to Tragedy*, ed. Rebecca Bushnell (Oxford: Blackwell, 2005), 73.

57 Sarah Kofman, *Nietzsche and Metaphor*, trans. Duncan Large (Stanford, CA: Stanford University Press, 1993), 6.

58 Algirdas Julien Greimas, *On Meaning: Selected Writings in Semiotic Theory*, trans. Paul J. Perron and Frank H. Collins (Minneapolis: University of Minnesota Press, 1976), 48.

59 Nietzsche, *Birth of Tragedy*, 40.

60 Kofman, *Nietzsche and Metaphor*, 18.

61 This idea is perhaps best expressed in the famous passage on "eternal recurrence" in *The Gay Science*: "What if some day or night a demon were to steal into your loneliest loneliness and say to you: 'This life as you now live it and have lived it you will have to live once again and innumerable times again; and

there will be nothing new in it, but every pain and every joy and every thought and sign and everything unspeakable small or great in your life must return to you . . .' Would you not throw yourself down and gnash your teeth and curse the demon who spoke thus? Or have you once experienced a tremendous moment when you would have answered him: 'You are a god, and never have I heard anything more divine.'" Nietzsche, *The Gay Science*, trans. Josefine Nauckhoff (Cambridge: Cambridge University Press, 2001), 194.

62 Friedrich Nietzsche, *The Complete Works of Friedrich Nietzsche*. Vol. 2. *Unfashionable Observations*, trans. Richard T. Gray (Stanford, CA: Stanford University Press, 1995), 106–107.

63 Ibid.

64 Rüdiger Safranski, *Nietzsche: A Philosophical Biography*, trans. Shelley Frisch (New York: Norton, 2002), 67–68.

65 See Sigmund Freud, *Three Essays on the Theory of Sexuality*, in *The Standard Edition of the Complete Psychological Works of Sigmund Freud*, 24 vols., trans. James Strachey (London: Hogarth Press, 1953–1974), 7: passim; *On Narcissism*, in *Standard Edition* 14:73–102.

66 Freud, *An Autobiographical Study*, in *Standard Edition*, 20:20.

67 *Standard Edition*, 7:195.

68 *Standard Edition*, 4:262.

69 "Tragedy and Psychoanalysis: Freud and Lacan," in Bushnell, ed., *Companion to Tragedy*, 96.

70 Freud, *On Narcissism*, in *Standard Edition*, 14:94.

71 "Repression," in *Standard Edition*, 14:147.

72 *Standard Edition*, 5:621.

73 *Civilization and Its Discontents*, in *Standard Edition*, 21:70.

74 *Interpretation of Dreams*, in *Standard Edition*, 5:506–507.

75 Henry Sussman, *The Hegelian Aftermath: Readings in Hegel, Kierkegaard, Freud, Proust and James* (Baltimore: Johns Hopkins University Press, 1982), 159.

76 Ibid.

77 Jacques Derrida, *Writing and Difference*, trans. Alan Bass (New York: Routledge, 1995), 292.

78 Brooks, *Reading for the Plot*, 103.

79 Ibid., 97.

80 Susan Winnett, "Coming Unstrung: Women, Men, Narrative, and Principles of Pleasure," in Richardson, *Narrative Dynamics*, 139.

81 Ibid., 146.

82 Lanser, "Toward a Feminist Narratology," *Style* 20:3 (1986), 342.

83 Robyn Warhol-Down, *Having a Good Cry: Effeminate Feelings and Pop-Culture Form* (Columbus: Ohio State University Press, 2003), 25.

84 Lee Edelman, *No Future: Queer Theory and the Death Drive* (Durham, NC: Duke University Press, 2004), 4.

85 Ibid., 9.

86 "Analysis Terminable and Interminable," in *Standard Edition*, 23: 219–220.

Chapter 4

1 Roman Jakobson, *Language in Literature*, ed. Krystyna Pomorska and Stephen Rudy (Cambridge, MA: Harvard University Press, 1987), 69.

2 Ryan, "Toward a Definition of Narrative," 22.

3 For some different examples of this kind of argument, see this very partial list: Karl Mannheim, *Collected Works of Karl Mannheim*. Vol. 1. *Ideology and Utopia* (New York: Routledge, 1936, 2002); Georg Lukács, *The Historical Novel*, trans. Hannah and Stanley Mitchell (Lincoln: University of Nebraska Press, 1983); Benedict Anderson, *Imagined Communities: Reflections on the Origin and Spread of Nationalism* (London: Verso Books, 2006); Tom Nairn, *The Break-Up of Britain* (London: Verso Books, 1981); Linda Colley, *Britons: Forging the Nation 1707–1837* (New Haven, CT: Yale University Press, 2009); *The Invention of Tradition*, eds. Eric Hobsbawm and Terence Ranger (Cambridge: Canto Classics, 2012).

4 Qtd. in Philip Horne, *Henry James: A Life in Letters* (New York: Viking, 1999), 463.

5 This distillation of the complex message of James's prefaces is often associated with Percy Lubbock's *The Craft of Fiction*, a book that did much to systematize and, for some, to oversimplify the terms of James's novel theory; most important and influential here is Wayne Booth's *The Rhetoric of Fiction*, which rigorously questions the wisdom of "show, don't tell" from a neo-Aristotelian standpoint. Part of his attack focused on Lubbock's apparent reduction of James: "Lubbock's account is clearer and more systematic than James's; he gives us a neat and helpful scheme of relationships among the terms *panorama, picture, drama,* and *scene.* It is a scheme that James can be made to support, but in James's account it is surrounded with important qualifications which in Lubbock are already beginning to be slighted." Wayne Booth, *The Rhetoric of Fiction* (Chicago: University of Chicago Press, 1961), 24–25. For a more generous reading of what's distinct and, indeed, odd about Percy Lubbock, see Dorothy J. Hale, *Social Formalism: The Novel in Theory from Henry James to the Present* (Stanford, CA: Stanford University Press, 1998), 21–64.

6 Chris Baldick, *The Oxford Dictionary of Literary Terms*, 3rd ed. (Oxford: Oxford University Press, 2008), 127.

7 Alex Woloch, *The One vs. the Many: Minor Characters and the Space of the Protagonist in Novel* (Princeton, NJ: Princeton University Press, 2003), 25.

8 Edgar Allan Poe, "The Philosophy of Composition" in *Literary Theory and Criticism*, ed. Lenoard Cassuto (Meneola, NY: Dover, 1999), 101.

9 James, *The Art of the Novel*, 323. For more on James's use of the ficelle as "expositional motivation," see Meir Sternberg, *Expositional Modes and Temporal Ordering in Fiction* (Bloomington: Indiana University Press, 1978), 284–290.

10 Ibid.

11 Ibid., 85.

12 Aristotle, *Complete Works*, II:2322.

13 Ibid., 5–6.

14 Robert Scholes, James Phelan, and Robert Kellogg, *The Nature of Narrative*, fortieth anniversary ed., rev. and expanded (Oxford: Oxford University Press, 2006), 265.

15 James, *Art of the Novel*, 66.

16 J. Hillis Miller, "Henry James and 'Focalization,' or Why James Loves Gyp," in *A Companion*, ed. Phelan and Rabinowitz, 125.

17 Abbott, *Introduction to Narrative*, 73.

18 Genette, *Narrative Discourse*, 162.

19 Thomas Hardy, *The Return of the Native* (New York: Oxford University Press, 2005), 9–10.

20 Prince, *A Dictionary of Narratology*, rev. ed. (Lincoln: University of Nebraska Press, 1987, 2003), 32.

21 Gerald Prince, "Narratology," in *The Cambridge History of Literary Criticism. Vol. VIII. From Formalism to Poststructuralism*, ed. Raman Selden (Cambridge: Cambridge University Press, 1995), 123.

22 Gérard Genette, *Narrative Discourse Revisited* (Ithaca, NY: Cornell University Press, 1988), 73.

23 Mieke Bal, *Narratology: Introduction to the Theory of Narrative* (Toronto: University of Toronto Press, 1997), 148.

24 Mieke Bal, "The Laughing Mice, or On Focalization." *Poetics Today* 2:2, *Narratology III: Narration and Perspective in Fiction* (Winter, 1981), 205.

25 Manfred Jahn, "The Mechanics of Focalization: Extending the Narratological Toolbox," *GRAAT* 21, 85–110.

26 Rimmon-Kenan, *Narrative Fiction*, 84.

27 For a synthetic take on the productive differences and relations between *narrative grammar, narrative poetics*, and *narrative rhetoric as they relate to* the development of narrative theory, see Herman, "Introduction: Narratologies," 4–14.

28 For a full account of the "narrative-communication situation," see Seymour Chatman, *Story and Discourse*, 147–158.

29 Harry E. Shaw, "Why Don't Our Terms Stay Put? The Narrative Communication Diagram Scrutinized and Historicized," in Phelan and Rabinowitz, eds., *A Companion*, 301.

30 Henry James, *The Princess Casamassima*, ed. Derek Brewer (New York: Penguin, 1987), 441.

31 Ibid.

32 *The Melodramatic Imagination: Balzac, Henry James, Melodrama, and the Mode of Excess* (New Haven, CT: Yale University press, 1995), 4.

33 *Social Formalism*, 32.

34 James, *The Art of the Novel*, 58.

35 Georg Lukács, *The Theory of the Novel: A Historico-Philosophical Essay on the Forms of Great Epic Literature*, trans. Anna Bostock (Cambridge, MA: MIT Press, 1971), 29.

36 Lukács, *Theory of the Novel*, 36.

37 Ibid., 29.

38 Ibid., 36.

39 Ibid., 56.

40 Ibid., 33–34.

41 Fredric Jameson, "In Hyperspace." *London Review of Books* 37:17 (September 2015).

42 Ibid., 56.

43 Georg Lukács, *The Historical Novel*, trans. Hannah and Stanley Mitchell (Lincoln: University of Nebraska Press, 1983), 91.

44 Frank M. Turner, *The Greek Heritage in Victorian Britain* (New Haven, CT: Yale University Press, 1981), 41.

45 Jay, *Marxism and Totality*, 76.

46 Ferdinand Tönnies, *Community and Civil Society*, ed. Jose Harris (Cambridge: Cambridge University Press, 2001), 247.

47 Gillian Rose, *The Melancholy Science: An Introduction to the Thought of Theodor W. Adorno* (London: Macmillan, 1978), 32.

48 Jay, *Marxism and Totality*, 77.

49 Georg Simmel, *Georg Simmel on Individuality and Social Forms*, ed. Donald N. Levine (Chicago: University of Chicago Press, 1971), 326.

50 György Márkus, "Life and Soul: the Young Lukács and the Problem of Culture," in *Lukács Reappraised*, ed. Agnes Heller (New York: Columbia University Press, 1983), 19.

51 Qtd. in Rose, *Hegel Contra Sociology*, 18.

52 Max Weber, "Science as a Profession and a Vocation," in *Max Weber: Collected Methodological Writings*, ed. Hans Henrik Bruun and Sam Whimster (London: Routledge, 2012), 342.

53 Márkus, "Life and Soul," 3.

54 Qtd. in Márkus, "Life and Soul," 4.

55 J. M. Bernstein, *The Philosophy of the Novel: Lukács, Marxism, and the Dialectics of Form* (Minneapolis: University of Minnesota Press, 1984), 50.

56 Lukács, *The Theory of the Novel*, 34.

57 Marx and Engels, *Collected Works*, Vol. 6, 489.

58 Lukács, *The Theory of the Novel*, 56.

59 Ibid., 38.

60 Ibid., 48.

61 Ibid., 56.

62 Ibid., 84.

63 Ibid., 77.

64 Homer, *Iliad*, trans. Richard Lattimore (Chicago: University of Chicago Press, 1961), 59.

65 Sophocles, *Oedipus Rex* ll.1–5, in *The Three Theban Plays*, trans. Robert Fagles (New York: Penguin, 1982).

66 Sophocles, *Oedipus Rex*, ll. 190–193.

67 Daniel Defoe, *Robinson Crusoe*, ed. John Richetti (New York: Penguin, 2001), 5.

68 Laurence Sterne, *The Life and Opinions of Tristram Shandy, Gentleman*, ed. Ian Campbell Ross (Oxford: Oxford World's Classics, 2009), 5.

69 Charles Dickens, *Great Expectations*, ed. Charlotte Mitchell (New York: Penguin, 1996), 3.

70 James Joyce, *A Portrait of the Artist as a Young Man*, ed. John Paul Riquelme (New York: Norton, 2007), 5.

71 James, *Art of the Novel*, 5.

72 Benjamin, "The Storyteller," 151.

73 Lukács, *Theory of the Novel*, 79–80.

74 Ibid., 125.

75 Ibid., 85.

76 Ibid., 126.

77 Ibid., 23.

78 Ibid., 11.

79 Ibid., 73.

80 Ibid., 152.

81 Qtd. in Gary Saul Morson and Caryl Emerson, *Mikhail Bakhtin: Creation of a Prosaics* (Stanford, CA: Stanford University Press, 1990), 5.

82 Katerina Clark and Michael Holquist, *Mikhail Bakhtin* (Cambridge, MA: Harvard University Press, 1984), 99.

83 Clark and Holquist, *Mikhail Bakhtin*, 275.

84 Gary Saul Morson and Caryl Emerson, *Mikhail Bakhtin: Creation of a Prosaics* (Stanford, CA: Stanford University Press, 1990), 281.

85 Clark and Holquist, *Mikhail Bakhtin*, 275.

86 Mikhail Bakhtin, *The Dialogic Imagination: Four Essays*, ed. Michael Holquist (Austin: University of Texas Press, 1981), 84–85.

87 Bakhtin, *The Dialogic Imagination*, 250.

88 Morson and Emerson, *Creation of a Prosaics*, 369.

89 Mikhail Bakhtin, *Art and Answerability: Early Philosophical Essays*, ed. Michael Holquist and Vadim Liapunov (Austin: University of Texas Press, 1990), xiv.

90 Qtd. in *The Palgrave Handbook of German Idealism*, ed. Matthew C. Altman (New York: Palgrave, 2014), 762.

91 Michael Holquist, *Dialogism: Bakhtin and His World*, 2nd ed. (New York: Routledge, 2002), 6.

92 Mikhail Bakhtin, *Problems of Dostoevsky's Poetics*, ed. Caryl Emerson (Minneapolis: University of Minnesota Press, 1984), 3.

93 Dorothy J. Hale, *Social Formalism: The Novel in Theory from Henry James to the Present* (Stanford, CA: Stanford University Press, 1998), 193.

94 Ibid.

95 Bakhtin, *The Dialogic Imagination*, 27.

96 Ibid., 16.

97 Michael Holquist, "Prologue," in Mikhail Bakhtin, *Rabelais and His World*, trans. Hélène Iswolsky (Indianapolis: Indiana University Press, 1984), xvii.

98 Holquist, "Prologue," xix.

99 Jean-Michel Rabaté, *The Future of Theory* (Hoboken, NJ: Wiley-Blackwell, 2002), 70.

100 Antonio Gramsci, "The Intellectuals," in *Selections from the Prison Notebooks of Antonio Gramsci*, eds. Quinton Hoare and Geoffrey Nowell Smith (London: Lawrence and Wishart, 1971), 5.

101 See Gramsci, 5–24.

102 Susan Lanser, *Fictions of Authority: Women Writers and Narrative Voice* (Ithaca, NY: Cornell University Press, 1992), 5.

103 Henry Louis Gates Jr., *The Signifying Monkey: A Theory of Afro-American Literary Criticism* (New York: Oxford University Press, 2014), 120.

104 Ibid., 122–123.

105 For an account that argues that Gates takes on some of Bakhtin's contradictory and overconfident assumptions about the literary form's capacity to affect social facts, see Hale, *Social Formalism*, 197–220.

106 Bakhtin, *Problems in Dostoevsky's Poetics*, 6 (emphasis in original).

107 Morson and Emerson, *Creation of A Prosaics*, 286.

108 Bakhtin, *Problems of Dostoevsky's Poetics*, 284.

109 Erich Auerbach, *Mimesis: The Representation of Reality in Western Literature*, 50th anniversary ed., trans. William R. Trask (Princeton, NJ: Princeton University Press, 2003), 557.

110 Edward Said, "Secular Criticism," in *The World, the Text, and the Critic* (Cambridge, MA: Harvard University Press, 1983), 6.

111 Auerbach, *Mimesis*, 3.

112 Ibid., 11–12.

113 Ibid., 23.

114 Ibid.

115 François Truffaut with Helen G. Scott, *Hitchcock* (New York: Simon & Schuster, 1983), 73.

116 Meir Sternberg, "Telling in Time (II): Chronology, Teleology, Narrativity," *Poetics Today* 13:3 (Autumn 1992), 529.

117 Auerbach, *Mimesis*, 4.

118 Ibid., 7.

119 Meir Sternberg, *Expositional Modes and Temporal Ordering in Fiction* (Bloomington: Indiana University Press, 1978), 69.

120 Sternberg, *Expositional Modes*, 84.

121 Auerbach, *Mimesis*, 11.

122 Ibid., 73–74.

123 Ibid., 17.

124 Ibid., 33.

125 Catherine Gallagher and Stephen Greenblatt, *Practicing New Historicism* (Chicago: University of Chicago Press, 2000), 40.

126 Auerbach, *Mimesis*, 21.

127 Ibid., 554.

128 Ibid., 19.

129 Ibid., 19–20.

130 Seth Lerer, *Error and the Academic Self* (New York: Columbia University Press, 2002), 222.

Chapter 5

1 David Herman, "Histories of Narrative Theory. (I). A Genealogy of Early Developments," in Phelan and Rabinowitz, *A Companion*, 31.

2 Ibid., 19.

3 Ibid., 23.

4 Peter J. Rabinowitz, *Before Reading: Narrative Conventions and the Politics of Interpretation* (Columbus: Ohio State University Press, 1987), 110.

5 Holquist, *Dialogism*, 42.

6 François Dosse, *History of Structuralism: The Rising Sign, 1945–1966*, trans. Deborah Glassman (Minneapolis: University of Minnesota Press, 1997), 53.

7 David Bordwell, "ApPropriations and ImPropprieties: Problems in the Morphology of Film Narrative," *Cinema Journal* 27:3 (Spring 1988), 5.

8 Vladimir Propp, *Morphology of the Folktale*, 2nd ed., ed. Louis A. Wagner (Austin: University of Texas Press, 2003), 19.

9 See Bordwell, "ApProppriations," 5.

10 Propp, *Morphology*, 7.

11 Ibid., xxv.

12 Vladimir Propp, "Fairy-Tale Transformations," in *Narrative Dynamics*, ed. Richardson, 73.

13 Herman, "Histories of Narrative Theory," 25.

14 Johann Wolfgang Goethe, *The Metamorphosis of Plants*, ed. Gordon Miller (Cambridge, MA: MIT Press, 2009), xvi.

15 In *Speech Genres and Other Late Essays*, eds. Caryl Emerson and Michael Holquist (Austin: University of Texas Press, 1986), 10–59.

16 Propp, *Morphology*, 21.

17 William Nelles, "Function (Propp)," in Herman et al., *Routledge Encyclopedia*, 191.

18 Propp, "Fairy-Tale Transformations," 74.

19 Bordwell, "ApProppriations," 9.

20 Shlomith Rimmon-Kenan, *Narrative Fiction: Contemporary Poetics* (London: Routledge, 2003), 23–24.

21 Algirdas Julien Greimas, *On Meaning: Selected Writings in Semiotic Theory*, trans. Paul J. Perron and Frank H. Collins (Minneapolis: University of Minnesota Press, 1976).

22 See Greimas, "Actants, Actors, and Figures" in *On Meaning*, 106–120.

23 Sharon Marcus, *Between Women: Friendship, Desire, and Marriage in Victorian England* (Princeton, NJ: Princeton University Press, 2007), 78.

24 Ibid., 75.

25 Ibid., 79.

26 Ibid., 75, 79.

27 Bordwell, "ApProppriations," 5.

28 Qtd. in Georges Polti, *The Thirty-Six Dramatic Situations*, trans. Lucille Ray (Franklin, OH: James Knapp Reeve, 1921), 9.

29 See www.matthewjockers.net/2015/02/02/syuzhet/.

30 Leon Trotsky, *Literature and Revolution*, trans. Rose Strunsky (Chicago: Haymarket Books, 2005).

31 Wellek and Warren, *Theory of Literature* (New York: Harcourt, Brace, 1949), 140; for more on the significance of Wellek and Warren to narrative theory, see David Herman, "Histories of Narrative Theory," 21–22.

32 Wellek and Warren, *Theory of Literature*, 226.

33 Dosse, *History of Structuralism*, 343.

34 Victor Erlich, *Russian Formalism: History-Doctrine* (The Hague: Mouton, 1955), 171–172.

35 Boris Eichenbaum, "The Theory of the 'Formal Method'," in *Russian Formalist Criticism: Four Essays*, eds. Lee T. Lemon and Marion J. Reis (Lincoln: University of Nebraska Press, 1965), 105.

36 Fredric Jameson, *The Prison-House of Language: A Critical Account of Structuralism and Russian Formalism* (Princeton, NJ: Princeton University Press, 1972), 48.

37 Eichenbaum, "'Formal Method,'" 102.

38 Qtd. in Shklovsky, *Theory of Prose*, 3.

39 Herbert Spencer, "The Philosophy of Style" *Westminster Review* (Oct. 1852), 235.

40 Eichenbaum, "'Formal Method,'" 112.

41 Ibid., 114.

42 Shklovsky, "Art as Technique," in Lemon and Reis, *Russian Formalist Criticism*, 12.

43 Ibid.

44 Shklovsky, *Theory of Prose*, 15.

45 Jakobson, *Language in Literature*, 69–70.

46 Shklovsky, "Sterne's *Tristram Shandy*: Stylistic Commentary," in Lemon and Reis. *Russian Formalist Criticism*, 57.

47 Brian Richardson, "Beyond the Poetics of Plot," in Phelan and Rabinowitz, *Companion*, 170.

48 Erlich, *Russian Formalism*, 240.

49 Boris Tomashevsky, "Thematics," in *The Narrative Reader*, ed. Martin McQuillan (New York: Routledge, 2000), 68.

50 Ibid.

51 Tomashevsky, "Thematics," in Lemon and Reis, *Russian Formalism*, 78. Also see Shklovsky, *Bowstring*, 59: "In Aristotle's definition the whole here is, first of all, a myth or fabula – a story. But the fable that unfolds, for example, in a tragedy or an epic, naturally being a whole, is not the only whole and it itself is divided into its own integral parts, which can be not only arranged in a new whole but also isolated and evaluated on their own."

52 Tomashevsky, "Thematics," 79.

53 Ibid.

54 James, *Art of the Novel*, 5.

55 Tomashevsky, "Thematics," 80.

56 Tzvetan Todorov, *Poetics of Prose*, trans. Richard Howard (Ithaca, NY: Cornell University Press, 1977), 83.

57 Gérard Genette, "*Vraisemblance* and Motivation" (1968), trans. David Gorman, *Narrative* 9:3 (October 2001), 242.

58 Marie-Laure Ryan, *Narrative as Virtual Reality. 2. Revisiting Immersion and Interactivity in Literature and Electronic Media* (Baltimore: Johns Hopkins University Press, 2015), 99.

59 Ibid., 99.
60 Ibid., 102.
61 Ibid., 103.
62 Lubomir Dolezel, "Fictional and Historical Narrative: Meeting the Postmodernist Challenge," in Herman, *Narratologies*, 256.
63 Herman, *Story Logic*, 14.
64 Tomashevsky, "Story, Plot, and Motivation," in Richardson, *Narrative Dynamics*, 174–175.
65 Ibid., 67
66 Jameson, *Prison-House of Language*, 52.
67 Jane Austen, *Pride and Prejudice* (New York: Modern Library, 2005), 35.
68 Ibid., 152.
69 Susan Lanser, "Sapphic Dialogics: Historical Narratology and the Sexuality of Form," in *Postclassical Narratology*, 200.
70 Lanser, "Sapphic Dialogics," 188.
71 Jameson, *Prison-House*, 58.
72 Ibid., 51.
73 Ferdinand de Saussure, *Course in General Linguistics*, trans. Wade Baskin, eds. Perry Meisel and Haun Saussy (New York: Columbia University Press, 2011), liii.
74 See George Steiner, *After Babel: Aspects of Language and Translation* (Oxford: Oxford University Press, 1998).
75 Qtd. in Jonathan Culler, *Ferdinand de Saussure*, rev. ed. (Ithaca, NY: Cornell University Press, 1986), 24.
76 Saussure, *General Linguistics*, 11.
77 Ibid., 13.
78 Ibid., 13–14.
79 John Joseph, *Saussure* (Oxford: Oxford University Press, 2012), 515.
80 Culler, *Ferdinand de Saussure*, 47.
81 Claudine Normand, "System, Arbitrariness, Value," in *Cambridge Companion to Saussure*, ed. Carol Sanders (Cambridge: Cambridge University Press, 2004), 93.
82 Roland Barthes, *Elements of Semiology*, trans. Annette Laves and Colin Smith (New York: Hill & Wang, 1973), 14–15.
83 Noam Chomsky, *Aspects of the Theory of Syntax* (Cambridge, MA: MIT Press, 1965), 3.
84 Barthes, *Elements*, 15.
85 Saussure, *General Linguistics*, 66.
86 Barthes, *Elements*, 39.
87 Fredric Jameson, "In Hyperspace." *London Review of Books* 37:17 (September 2015).
88 Culler, *Saussure*, 29.
89 Saussure, *General Linguistics*, 33.

90 Joseph, *Saussure*, 536.

91 Saussure, *General Linguistics*, 120.

92 Dosse, *History of Structuralism*, 45.

93 Fredric Jameson, "In Hyperspace." *London Review of Books* 37:17 (September 2015).

94 Saussure, *General Linguistics*, 16.

95 Patrick Wilcken, *Claude Lévi-Strauss: The Poet in the Laboratory* (New York: Penguin, 2010), 145.

96 Dosse, *History of Structuralism*, 12.

97 Wilcken, *Lévi-Strauss*, 165.

98 Ibid., 229.

99 Claude Lévi-Strauss, *The Elementary Structures of Kinship*, ed. Rodney Needham (Boston: Beacon Press, 1969), 490.

100 Descombes, *Modern French Philosophy*, 3.

101 Wilcken, *Lévi-Strauss*, 147.

102 Dosse, *History of Structuralism*, 19.

103 Claude Lévi-Strauss, *Structural Anthropology*, trans. Claire Jacobson and Brooke Grundfest Schoepf (New York: Basic, 1963), 107.

104 Ibid., 208.

105 Ibid., 209.

106 Genette, *Narrative Discourse*, 23.

107 Herman, "Structuralist Narratology," in Herman, et al., *Routledge Encyclopedia*, 573.

108 Lévi-Strauss, *Tristes Tropiques*, 70.

109 Lévi-Strauss, *Structural Anthropology*, 216.

Chapter 6

1 Qtd. in Richard Wolin, *The Wind from the East: French Intellectuals, the Cultural Revolution, and the Legacy of the 1960s* (Princeton, NJ: Princeton University Press, 2010), 234 (emphasis added).

2 Ibid., 237.

3 Danielle Marx-Scouras, *The Cultural Politics of Tel Quel: Literature and the Left in the Wake of Engagement* (University Park: Pennsylvania State University Press, 1996), 116.

4 Ibid., 118.

5 Jean-Michel Rabaté, *Future of Theory*, 82.

6 Dosse, *Sign Sets*, 91.

7 "Introduction to Special Issue on France May 1968," *New Left Review* I:52, (November–December 1968), 4.

8 Leon S. Roudiez, "Introduction," Julia Kristeva, *Desire in Language: A Semiotic Approach to Literature and Art* (New York: Columbia University Press, 1980), 8.

9 Wolin, *Wind from the East*, 245.

10 Dosse, *History of Structuralism*, 343.

11 Julia Kristeva, "Toward a Semiology of Paragrams," in *The Tel Quel Reader*, ed. Patrick ffrench and Roland-François Lack (New York: Routledge, 1998), 28.

12 Susan Stanford Friedman, "Spatialization: A Strategy for Reading Narrative," in Richardson, *Narrative Dynamics*, 218.

13 Kristeva, "Paragrams" 29.

14 Julia Kristeva, *Revolution in Poetic Language*, trans. Margaret Waller (New York: Columbia University Press, 1984), 87.

15 Kristeva, *Desire in Language: A Semiotic Approach to Literature and Art* (New York: Columbia University Press, 1980), 55.

16 Ibid., 56.

17 Ibid.

18 Ibid., 37.

19 Ibid., 93.

20 Ibid., 99.

21 Roland Barthes, "Introduction to the Structural Analysis of Narratives," in *Image-Music-Text*, trans. Stephen Heath (New York: Hill & Wang, 1977), 79.

22 Ibid.

23 The term first appears in Todorov's *Grammaire du Décaméron* (The Hague: Mouton, 1969).

24 Ibid., 87–88.

25 Barthes, *Elements*, 12.

26 Dosse, 225–226.

27 Barthes, "Structural Analysis," 85.

28 See Jakobson, "Two Aspects of Language and Two Types of Aphasic Disturbances," in *Language in Literature*.

29 Herman and Vervaeck, *Handbook*, 49.

30 Barthes, "Structural Analysis" 89.

31 Ibid.

32 See Roland Barthes, "The Reality Effect" (1968), in *The Rustle of Language*, trans. Richard Howard (Berkeley: University of California Press, 1989), 141–148.

33 Barthes, "Structural Analysis," 94.

34 Émile Benveniste, *Problems in General Linguistics*, trans. Mary Elizabeth Meek (Coral Gables, FL: University of Miami Press, 1971), 218.

35 Barthes, "Structural Analysis," 119.

36 Ibid., 124.

37 Herman and Vervaeck, *Handbook*, 49.
38 Jeremey Black, *The Politics of James Bond: From Fleming's Novels to the Big Screen* (Lincoln: University of Nebraska Press, 2000), 4.
39 Ian Fleming, *Goldfinger* (Las Vegas, NV: Thomas & Mercer, 2012), 216.
40 Roland Barthes, *S/Z*, trans. Richard Miller (New York: Hill & Wang, 1974), 13.
41 Ibid., 5.
42 D. A. Miller, *Bringing Out Roland Barthes* (Berkeley: University of California Press, 1992).
43 Barthes, *S/Z*, 12–13.
44 Ibid., 20.
45 Ibid., 5.
46 Ibid., 20.
47 Ibid., 17.
48 Ibid., 19.
49 Ibid., 87.
50 Barthes, *S/Z*, 20.
51 Ibid., 8.
52 Ibid., 7.
53 Ibid., 9.
54 Ibid., 17.
55 D. A. Miller, *Bringing Out Roland Barthes* (Berkeley: University of California Press, 1992).
56 Barthes, *S/Z*, 40.
57 Barthes, *Mythologies*, 142.
58 Barthes, *S/Z*, 15–16.
59 Lee Congdon, *Exile and Social Thought: Hungarian Intellectuals in Germany and Austria, 1919–1933* (Princeton, NJ: Princeton University Press, 1991), 75.
60 Barthes, "The Return of the Poetician," in *Rustle*, 175.
61 Barthes, *S/Z*, 26–27.
62 Ibid., 56.
63 Julia Kristeva, "How Does One Speak to Literature?" 99.
64 Barthes, "Utopia," in *"The 'Scandal' of Marxism" and Other Writings on Politics*, trans. Chris Turner (London: Seagull Books, 2015), 107.
65 Roland Barthes, *The Preparation of the Novel*, trans. Kate Briggs (New York: Columbia University Press, 2011), 286.
66 Monika Fludernik, "Structuralist Narratology: The Rage for Binary Opposition, Categorization, and Typology," in *A Companion*, 39. Fludernik refers to Mieke Bal, *Narratology: Introduction to the Theory of Narrative*, 2nd ed. (Toronto: University of Toronto Press, 1997); Gerald Prince, *Narratology: The Form and Functioning of Narrative* (Berlin: Mouton, 1982); Prince, *A Dictionary of Narratology*; Shlomith Rimmon-Kennan, *Narrative Fiction: Contemporary Poetics* (London: Routledge, 2002).

67 Genette, *Narrative Discourse*, 263.

68 Fludernik, "Structuralist Narratology" 39.

69 *Narrative Discourse*, 158.

70 Jonathan Culler, "Foreword," in Genette, *Narrative Discourse*, 10.

71 Barthes, *Rustle*, 174.

72 Malcolm Bowie, *Proust Among the Stars* (New York: Columbia University Press, 1998), 64.

73 Genette, *Narrative Discourse*, 23.

74 Ibid.

75 Ibid., 94.

76 Monika Fludernik, *Towards a "Natural" Narratology* (London: Routledge, 1996), 331.

77 Genette, *Narrative Discourse*, 268.

78 Theodor Adorno, *Notes to Literature*, Vol. 1, trans. Shierry Weber Nicholsen (New York: Columbia University Press, 1991), 174.

79 "Foreword," in Genette, *Narrative Discourse*, 13.

80 *Narrative Discourse*, 26–27.

81 Ibid., 27.

82 Todorov, *Poetics of Prose*, 119.

83 Genette, *Narrative Discourse*, 31.

84 Ibid., 35.

85 Culler, *Pursuit of Signs*, 174–175.

86 Herman, *Story Logic*, 217.

87 Dr. Seuss, *The Lorax* (New York: Random House, 2013), 3.

88 Genette, *Narrative Discourse*, 36.

89 Ibid., 40.

90 See Fludernik, 38 for the rage for binaries.

91 George Eliot, *Middlemarch*, ed. Bert G. Hornback (New York: Norton, 2000), 91.

92 Narrative Discourse, 54.

93 See *Narrative Discourse*, 67–79.

94 Ibid., 78.

95 Genette, *Narrative Discourse*, 189.

96 Michel Foucault, "Of Other Spaces," trans. Jay Miskowiec, *Diacritics* 16:1 (Spring 1986): 24.

97 *Narrative Discourse*, 49.

98 Ibid., 222.

99 Joseph Conrad, *Lord Jim*, ed. Thomas C. Moser (New York: Norton, 1996), 5.

100 Ibid., 228.

101 The question of cinematic narration is a controversial one; see Jan Alber for an account of what he sees as the three available positions: that film "has narration but no narrator"; that "films are narrated by a *cinematic narrator*";

and that films are narrated by *"the implied filmmaker."* "Hypothetical Intentionalism: Cinematic Narration Reconsidered," in *Postclassical Narratology*, 163–164.

102 Ibid., 234.

103 For more on the nature and complexities of voice-over narration, see Seymour Chatman, "New Directions in Voice-Narrated Cinema," in Herman, *Narratologies*, 315–339.

104 Genette, *Narrative Discourse*, 265–266.

105 Barthes, *Rustle*, 174.

106 Genette, *Narrative Discourse*, 52–53.

107 See Brian Richardson's entry "Anti-Narrative" in Herman, et al., *Routledge Encyclopedia*.

108 Roland Barthes, *The Pleasure of the Text*, trans. Richard Miller (New York: Hill & Wang, 1975), 14.

109 Wolin, *Wind from the East*, 239.

110 Ibid.,

111 Barthes, *S/Z*, 16.

112 Ibid., 15.

113 Genette, *Narrative Discourse Revisited*, trans. Jane E. Lewin (Ithaca, NY: Cornell University Press, 1988), 156.

114 Ibid., 157.

115 In *Figures of Literary Discourse*, 143.

116 Jean-Michel Rabaté, *Future of Theory*, 83.

117 See Jacques Derrida, *Negotiations: Interventions and Interviews, 1971–2001*, ed. Elizabeth Rottenberg (Stanford, CA: Stanford University Press, 2002), 164: "Gérard Genette, who was a Party member until 1956, told me that he went to see Althusser after the Hungarian revolt to impart his distress, anguish, reasons, and probably to ask his advice. Althusser supposedly told him: 'But if what you say were true, then the Party would be in the wrong!' This seemed to Althusser to be precluded and he proceeded to demonstrate *ad absurdum* that what Genette was saying needed to be corrected. Genette laughed when he told me: 'I drew my conclusions from that extraordinary formulation and immediately left the Party.'"

118 Marx-Scouras, *Cultural Politics*, 120.

119 Ibid., 126.

120 Barthes, *Rustle*, 175.

121 See, for instance, Brian Richardson, *Unnatural Narrative: Theory, History, and Practice* (Columbus: Ohio State University Press, 2015).

122 Genette, *Narrative Discourse*, 64.

123 Ibid., 65.

124 Ibid., 66.

125 Ibid., 108.

126 Bowie, *Proust among the Stars*, 273.

127 Freud, "Mourning and Melancholia, in *Standard Edition*, 14:244–245.

128 Georg Lukács, *The Historical Novel*, trans. Hannah and Stanley Mitchell (Boston: Beacon Press, 1963), 58.

129 Ibid., 61.

Suggested Further Reading

Introduction: Story/Discourse

Abbott, H. Porter. *The Cambridge Introduction to Narrative*. 2nd ed. New York: Cambridge University Press, 2008.

Alber, Jan, and Monika Fludernik, eds. *Postclassical Narratology: Approaches and Analyses*. Columbus: Ohio State University Press, 2010.

Bal, Mieke. *Narratology: Introduction to the Theory of Narrative*. 2nd ed. Toronto: University of Toronto Press, 1997.

Chatman, Seymour. *Story and Discourse: Narrative Structure in Fiction and Film*. Ithaca, NY: Cornell University Press, 1978.

Herman, David, Manfred Jahn, and Marie-Laure Ryan, eds. *Routledge Encyclopedia of Narrative Theory*. New York: Routledge, 2005.

Herman, David, ed. *Narratologies: New Perspectives on Narrative Analysis*. Columbus: Ohio State University Press, 1999.

Herman, Luc, and Bart Vervaeck. *Handbook of Narrative Analysis*. Lincoln: University of Nebraska Press, 2005.

Keen, Suzanne. *Narrative Form*. Revised and expanded 2nd ed. London: Palgrave, 2015.

Phelan, James, and Peter J. Rabinowitz, eds. *A Companion to Narrative Theory*. Malden, MA: Blackwell, 2005.

Prince, Gerald. *A Dictionary of Narratology*. Revised ed. Lincoln: University of Nebraska Press, 2003.

Richardson, Brian, ed. *Narrative Dynamics: Essays on Time, Plot, Closure, and Frames*. Columbus: Ohio State University Press, 2002.

Rimmon-Kenan, Shlomith. *Narrative Fiction: Contemporary Poetics*. London: Routledge, 2002.

Scholes, Robert, James Phelan, and Robert Kellogg. *The Nature of Narrative*. 40th Anniversary ed. New York: Oxford University Press, 2006.

Warhol, Robyn, and Susan S. Lanser, eds. *Narrative Theory Unbound: Queer and Feminist Interventions*. Columbus: Ohio State University Press, 2015.

Action, Event, Conflict: The Uses of Narrative in Aristotle and Hegel

Beiser, Frederick. *Hegel*. New York: Routledge, 2005.

Buck-Morss, Susan. *Hegel, Haiti, and Universal History*. Pittsburgh: University of Pittsburgh Press, 2009.

Bushnell, Rebecca W., ed. *A Companion to Tragedy*. Malden, MA: Blackwell, 2005.

Butler, Judith. *Subjects of Desire: Hegelian Reflections in Twentieth-Century France*. New ed. New York: Columbia University Press, 1999.

Cole, Andrew. *The Birth of Theory*. Chicago: The University of Chicago Press, 2014.

Comay, Rebecca. *Mourning Sickness: Hegel and the French Revolution*. Stanford, CA: Stanford University Press, 2011.

Easterling, P. E., ed. *The Cambridge Companion to Greek Tragedy*. New York: Cambridge University Press, 1997.

Goward, Barbara. *Telling Tragedy: Narrative Technique in Aeschylus, Sophocles and Euripides*. London: Duckworth, 1999.

Halliwell, Stephen. *Aristotle's Poetics*. 2nd ed. Chicago: University of Chicago Press, 1986, 1998.

Kojève, Alexandre. *Introduction to the Reading of Hegel*. Trans. James H. Nichols, Jr. Ithaca, NY: Cornell University Press, 1980.

Rockmore, Tom. *Before and After Hegel: A Historical Introduction to Hegel's Thought*. Berkeley: University of California Press, 1992.

Rorty, Amélie, ed. *Essays on Aristotle's Poetics*. Princeton, NJ: Princeton University Press, 1992.

Schmidt, Dennis J. *On Germans and Other Greeks: Tragedy and Ethical Life*. Bloomington: Indiana University Press, 2001.

Taylor, Charles. *Hegel*. New York: Cambridge University Press, 1975.

Vernant, Jean-Pierre, and Pierre Vidal-Naquet. *Myth and Tragedy in Ancient Greece*. Trans. Janet Lloyd. Cambridge, MA: Zone Books; Distributed by MIT Press, 1988.

Williams, Raymond. *Modern Tragedy*. Edited by Pamela McCollum. Peterborough, Canada: Broadview Press, 2006.

Young, Julian. *The Philosophy of Tragedy: From Plato to Žižek*. New York: Cambridge University Press, 2013.

Lost Illusions: Narrative in Marx, Nietzsche, and Freud

Brooks, Peter. *Reading for the Plot: Design and Intention in Narrative*. Cambridge, MA: Harvard University Press, 1992.

Eagleton, Terry. *Marxism and Literary Criticism*. Berkeley: University of California Press, 1976.

Felman, Shoshana. *Literature and Psychoanalysis: The Question of Reading: Otherwise.* Baltimore: Johns Hopkins University Press, 1982.

Kofman, Sarah. *Nietzsche and Metaphor.* Stanford, CA: Stanford University Press, 1993.

Miller, D. A. *Narrative and Its Discontents: Problems of Closure in the Traditional Novel.* Princeton, NJ: Princeton University Press, 1989.

Nehamas, Alexander. *Nietzsche: Life as Literature.* Cambridge, MA: Harvard University Press, 1987.

Porter, James I. *The Invention of Dionysus: An Essay on the Birth of Tragedy.* Stanford, CA: Stanford University Press, 2000.

Silk, M. S., and J. P. Stern. *Nietzsche on Tragedy.* New York: Cambridge University Press, 1981.

Sussman, Henry. *The Hegelian Aftermath: Readings in Hegel, Kierkegaard, Freud, Proust, and James.* Baltimore: Johns Hopkins University Press, 1982.

White, Hayden V. *Metahistory: The Historical Imagination in Nineteenth-Century Europe.* New ed. Baltimore: Johns Hopkins University Press, 2014.

Williams, Raymond. *Marxism and Literature.* Oxford: Oxford University Press, 1978.

Winnett, Susan. "Coming Unstrung: Women, Men, Narrative, and Principles of Pleasure," in *Narrative Dynamics: Essays on Time, Plot, Closure, and Frames,* ed. Brian Richardson. Columbus: Ohio State University Press, 2002.

Epic, Novel, Narrative Theory: Henry James, Georg Lukács, Mikhail Bakhtin, and Erich Auerbach

Bernstein, J. M. *The Philosophy of the Novel: Lukács, Marxism, and the Dialectics of Form.* Minneapolis: University of Minnesota Press, 1984.

Booth, Wayne. *The Rhetoric of Fiction.* Chicago: University of Chicago Press, 1983.

Clark, Katerina, and Michael Holquist, eds. *Mikhail Bakhtin.* Cambridge, MA: Belknap Press of Harvard University Press, 1984.

Congdon, Lee. *The Young Lukács.* Chapel Hill: University of North Carolina Press, 1983.

Forster, E. M. *Aspects of the Novel.* New York: Harcourt Brace & World, 1955.

Gallagher, Catherine, and Stephen Greenblatt. *Practicing New Historicism.* Chicago: University of Chicago Press, 2000.

Hale, Dorothy. *Social Formalism: The Novel in Theory from Henry James to the Present.* Stanford, CA: Stanford University Press, 1998.

Heller, Agnes, ed. *Lukács Reappraised.* New York: Columbia University Press, 1983.

Holquist, Michael. *Dialogism: Bakhtin and His World.* 2nd ed. New York: Routledge, 2002.

Jameson, Fredric. *Marxism and Form: Twentieth-Century Dialectical Theories of Literature.* Princeton, NJ: Princeton University Press, 1974.

Jay, Martin. *Marxism and Totality: The Adventures of a Concept from Lukács to Habermas*. Berkeley: University of California Press, 1984.

Lerer, Seth. *Error and the Academic Self: The Scholarly Imagination, Medieval to Modern*. New York: Columbia University Press, 2003.

Lubbock, Percy. *The Craft of Fiction*. New York: Charles Scribner's Sons, 1921.

Morson, Gary Saul, and Caryl Emerson. *Mikhail Bakhtin: Creation of a Prosaics*. Stanford, CA: Stanford University Press, 1990.

Rose, Gillian. *Hegel Contra Sociology*. London: Humanities Press, 1981.

Said, Edward. "Secular Criticism," in *The World, the Text, and the Critic*. Cambridge, MA: Harvard University Press, 1983.

Sternberg, Meir. *Expositional Modes and Temporal Ordering in Fiction*. Bloomington: Indiana University Press, 1978.

Form, Structure, Narrative: Propp, Shklovsky, Saussure, Lévi-Strauss

Bordwell, David. "ApProppriations and ImPropprieties: Problems in the Morphology of Film Narrative," *Cinema Journal* 27.3 (Spring 1988): 5–20.

Culler, Jonathan. *Ferdinand De Saussure*. Ithaca, NY: Cornell University Press, 1986.

Culler, Jonathan. *Structuralist Poetics: Structuralism, Linguistics, and the Study of Literature*. London: Routledge, 2002.

Descombes, Vincent. *Modern French Philosophy*. Cambridge: Cambridge University Press, 1980.

Dosse, François. *History of Structuralism: The Rising Sign, 1945–1966*. Trans. Deborah Glassman. Minneapolis: University of Minnesota Press, 1997.

Erlich, Victor. *Russian Formalism: History, Doctrine*. The Hague: Mouton, 1955.

Jameson, Fredric. *The Prison-House of Language: A Critical Account of Structuralism and Russian Formalism*. Princeton, NJ: Princeton University Press, 1972.

Joseph, John E. *Saussure*. New York: Oxford University Press, 2012.

Lemon, Lee. T., and Marion J. Reis, eds. and trans. *Russian Formalist Criticism: Four Essays*. Lincoln: University of Nebraska Press, 1965.

Wellek, René, and Austin Warren. *Theory of Literature*. New York: Harcourt, Brace & World, 1956.

Wilcken, Patrick. *Claude Lévi-Strauss: The Poet in the Laboratory*. New York: Penguin Press, 2010.

Narratology and Narrative Theory: Kristeva, Barthes, and Genette

Culler, Jonathan. *Barthes: A Very Short Introduction*. Revised ed. Oxford: Oxford University Press, 2002.

Dosse, François. *History of Structuralism: The Sign Sets, 1967-Present.* Trans. Deborah Glassman. Minneapolis: University of Minnesota Press, 1997.

Eagleton, Terry. *Literary Theory: An Introduction.* Anniversary ed. Minneapolis: University of Minnesota Press, 2008.

Johnson, Barbara. "The Critical Difference: BartheS/BalZac" in *The Critical Difference.* Baltimore: Johns Hopkins University Press, 1985.

Marx-Scouras, Danielle. *The Cultural Politics of Tel Quel: Literature and the Left in the Wake of Engagement.* University Park: Pennsylvania State University Press, 1996.

Miller, D. A. *Bringing Out Roland Barthes.* Berkeley: University of California Press, 1992.

Rabaté, Jean-Michel. *The Future of Theory.* Hoboken, NJ: Wiley-Blackwell, 2002.

Robbe-Grillet, Alain. *For a New Novel: Essays on Fiction.* Trans. Richard Howard. Evanston, IL: Northwestern University Press 1989.

Roudiez, Leon S. "Introduction," in *Desire in Language: A Semiotic Approach to Literature and Art,* ed. Julia Kristeva. New York: Columbia University Press, 1980.

Wolin, Richard. *The Wind from the East: French Intellectuals, the Cultural Revolution, and the Legacy of the 1960s.* Princeton, NJ: Princeton University Press, 2010.

Index